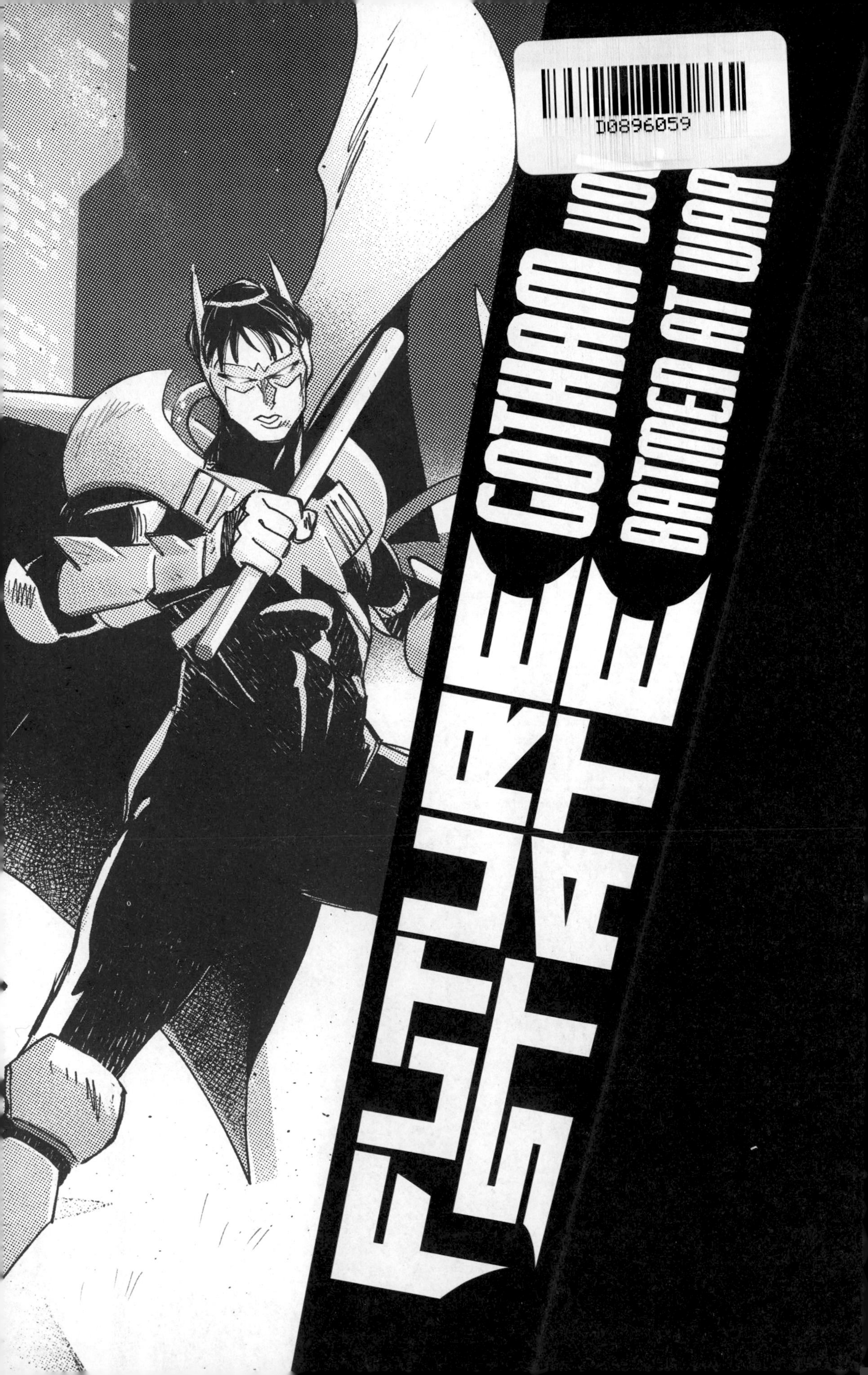
FUTURE STATE
GOTHAM VO
BATMEN AT WAR

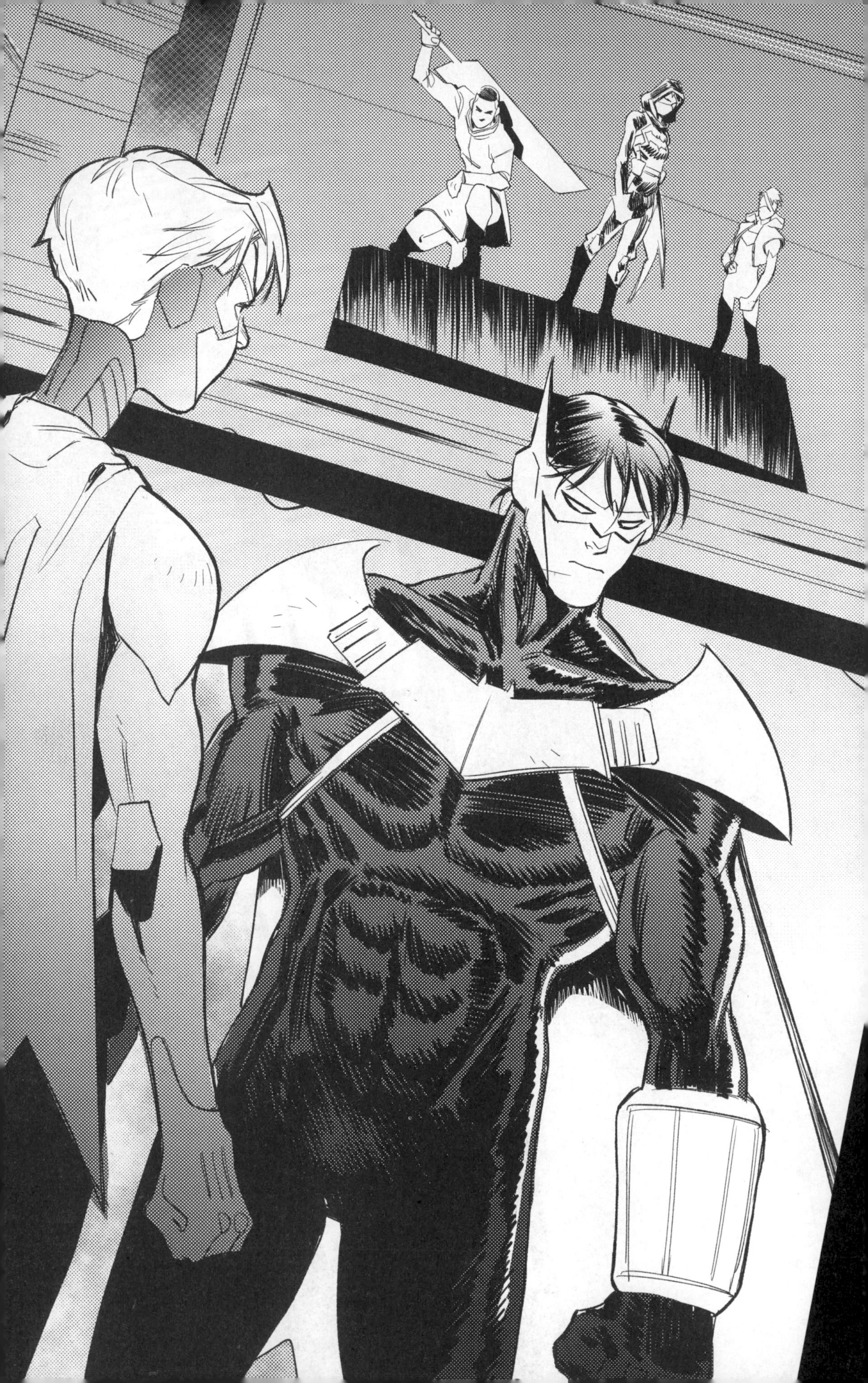

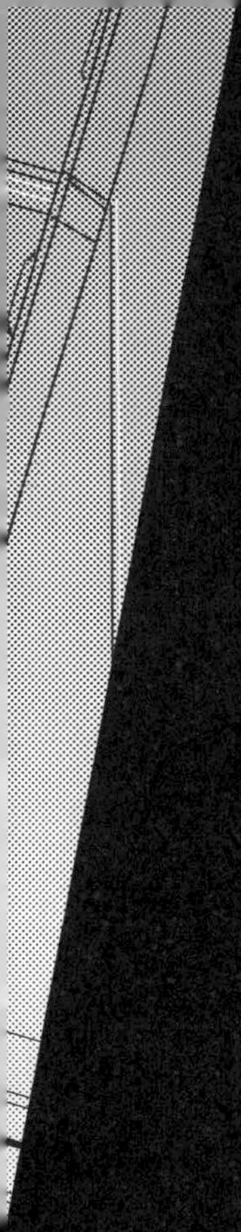

FUTURE STATE
GOTHAM VOL. 3
BATMEN AT WAR

WRITER
DENNIS CULVER

ARTISTS
GEOFFO
GIANNIS MILONOGIANNIS
JUSTIN GREENWOOD
BRAD SIMPSON
(COLORIST ON ISSUE №18)

LETTERER
TROY PETERI

COLLECTION COVER ARTIST
SIMONE DI MEO

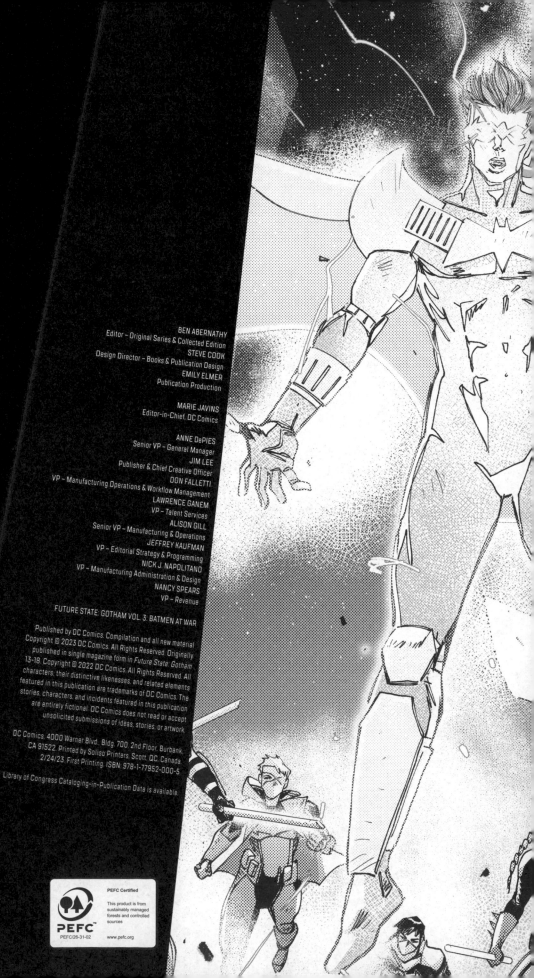

BEN ABERNATHY
Editor – Original Series & Collected Edition
STEVE COOK
Design Director – Books & Publication Design
EMILY ELMER
Publication Production

MARIE JAVINS
Editor-in-Chief, DC Comics

ANNE DePIES
Senior VP – General Manager
JIM LEE
Publisher & Chief Creative Officer
DON FALLETTI
VP – Manufacturing Operations & Workflow Management
LAWRENCE GANEM
VP – Talent Services
ALISON GILL
Senior VP – Manufacturing & Operations
JEFFREY KAUFMAN
VP – Editorial Strategy & Programming
NICK J. NAPOLITANO
VP – Manufacturing Administration & Design
NANCY SPEARS
VP – Revenue

FUTURE STATE: GOTHAM VOL. 3: BATMEN AT WAR

DC Comics, 4000 Warner Blvd., Bldg. 700, 2nd Floor, Burbank,
CA 91522. Printed by Solisco Printers, Scott, QC, Canada.
2/24/23. First Printing. ISBN: 978-1-77952-000-5.

Library of Congress Cataloging-in-Publication Data is available.

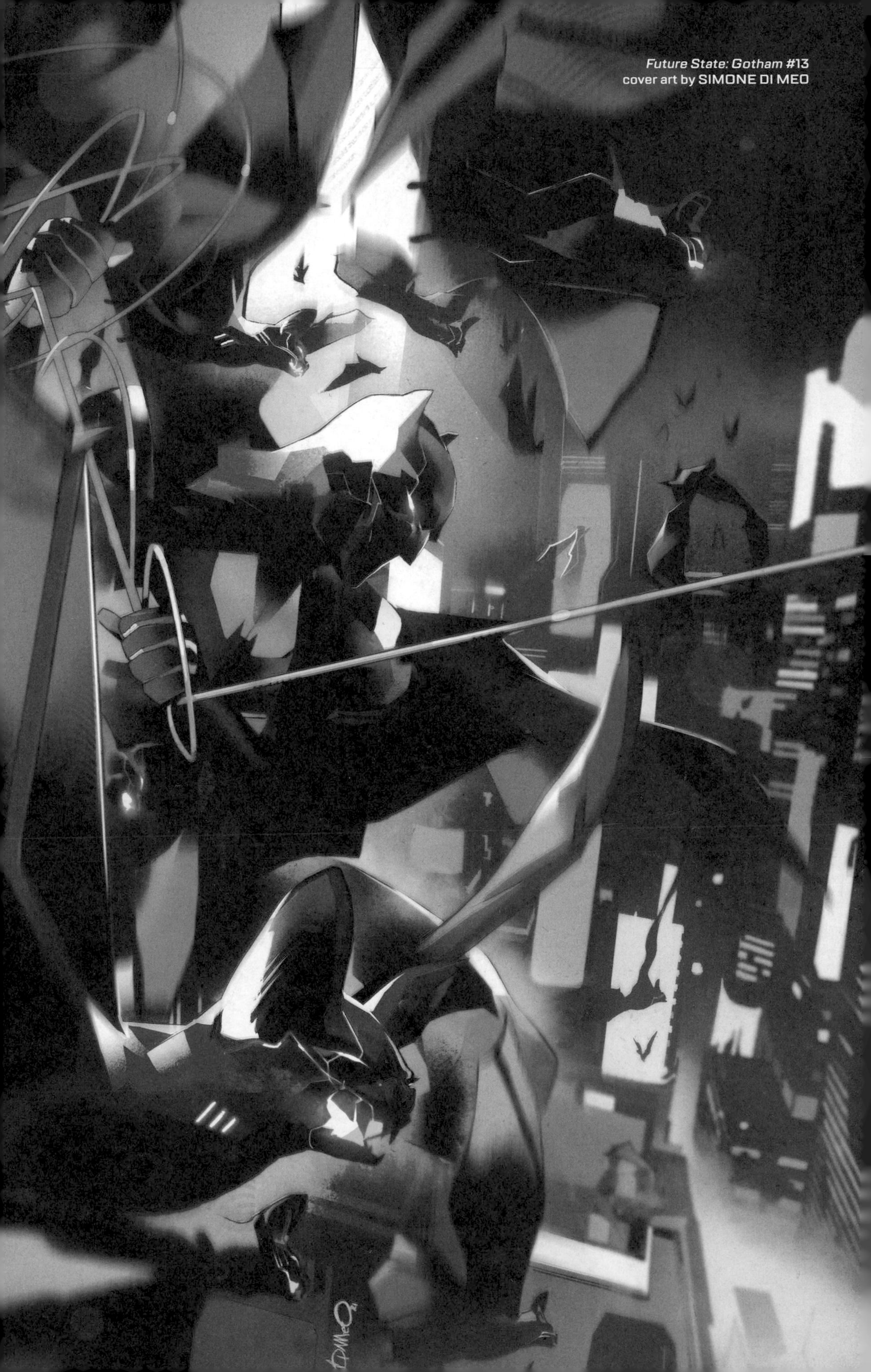

Future State: Gotham #13
cover art by SIMONE DI MEO

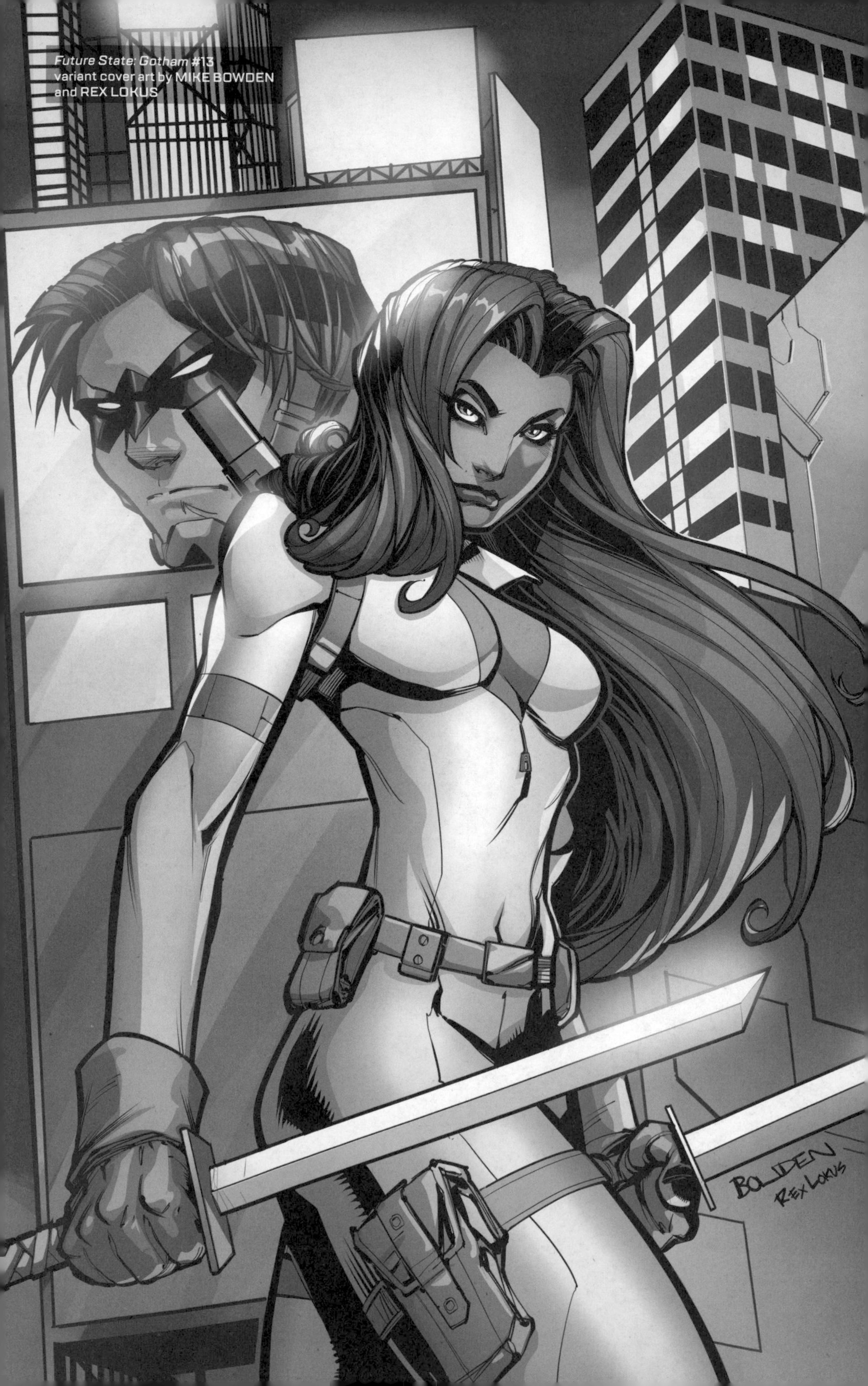
BOWDEN
REX LOKUS

Future State: Gotham #13
variant cover art by MIKE BOWDEN
and REX LOKUS

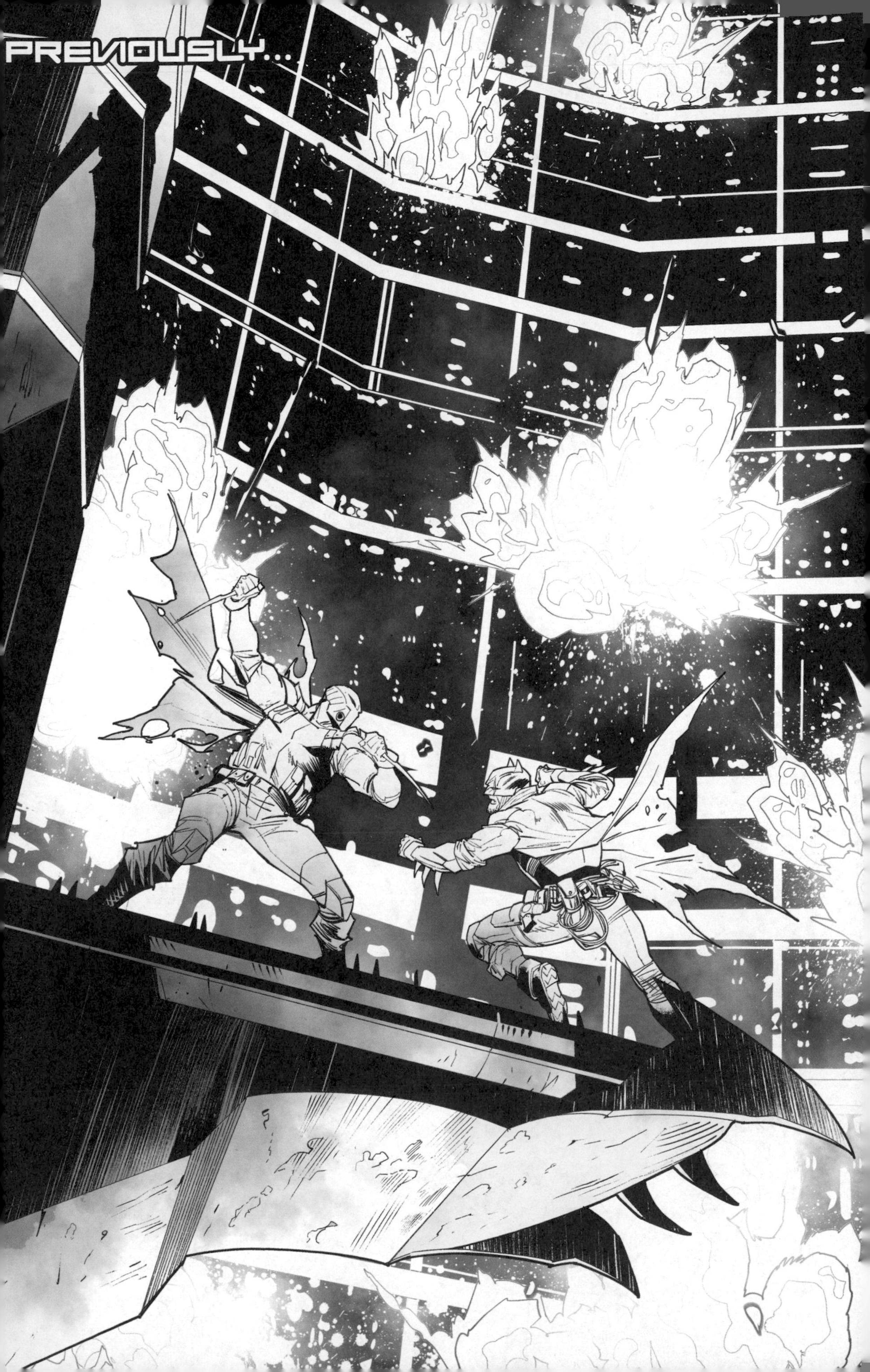
PREVIOUSLY...

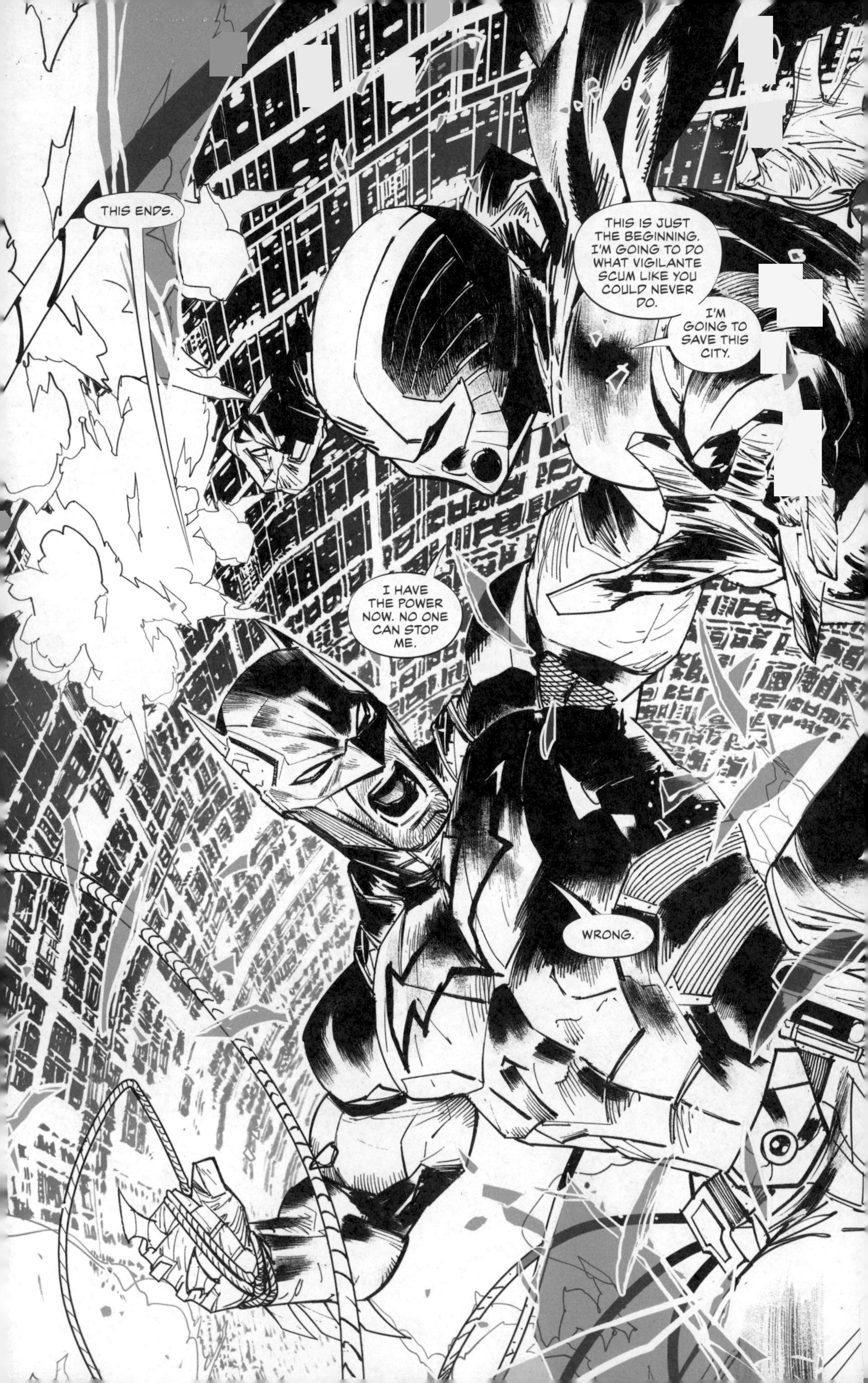
THIS ENDS.
THIS IS JUST THE BEGINNING. I'M GOING TO DO WHAT VIGILANTE SCUM LIKE YOU COULD NEVER DO.
I'M GOING TO SAVE THIS CITY.
I HAVE THE POWER NOW. NO ONE CAN STOP ME.
WRONG.

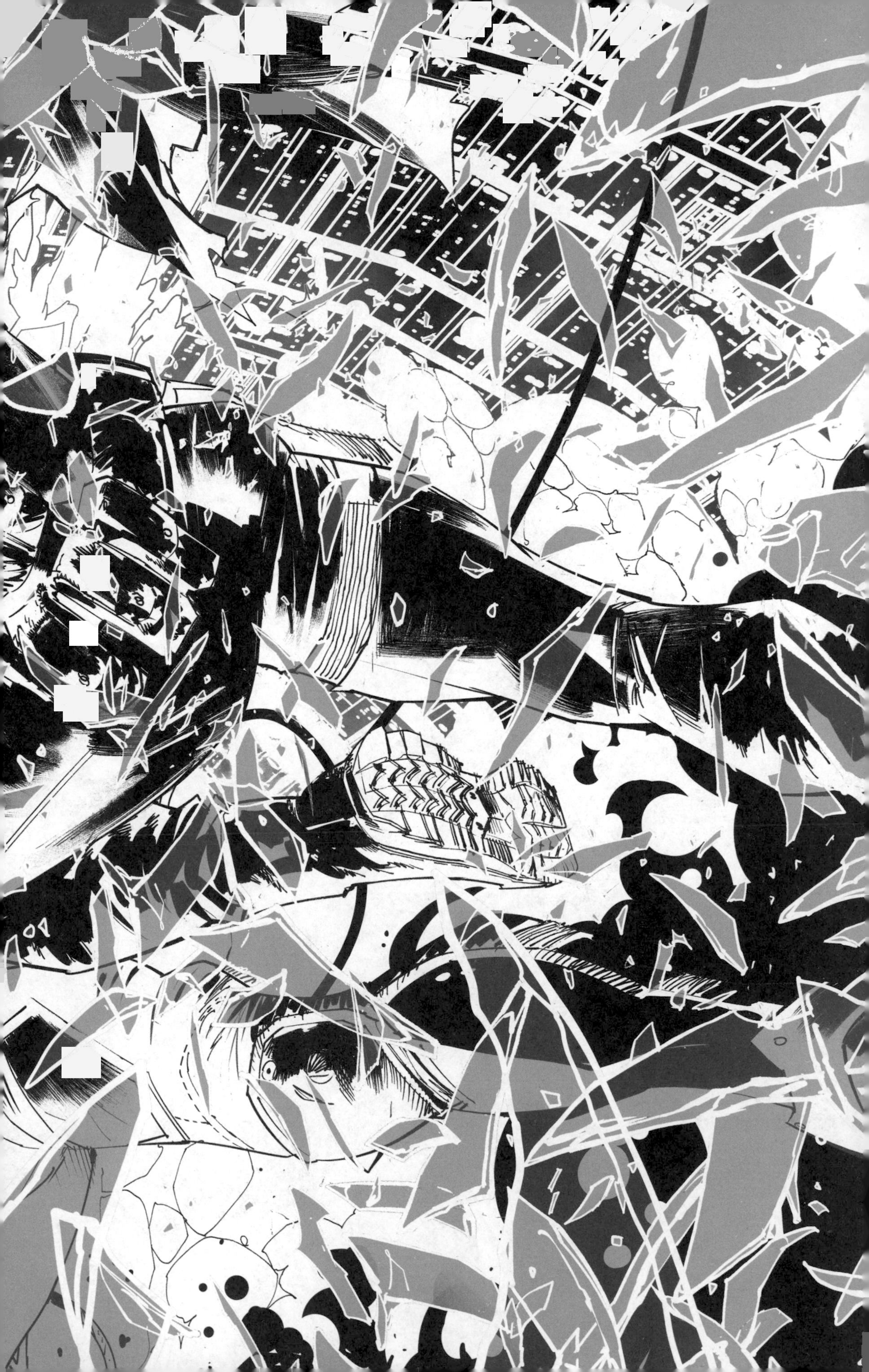

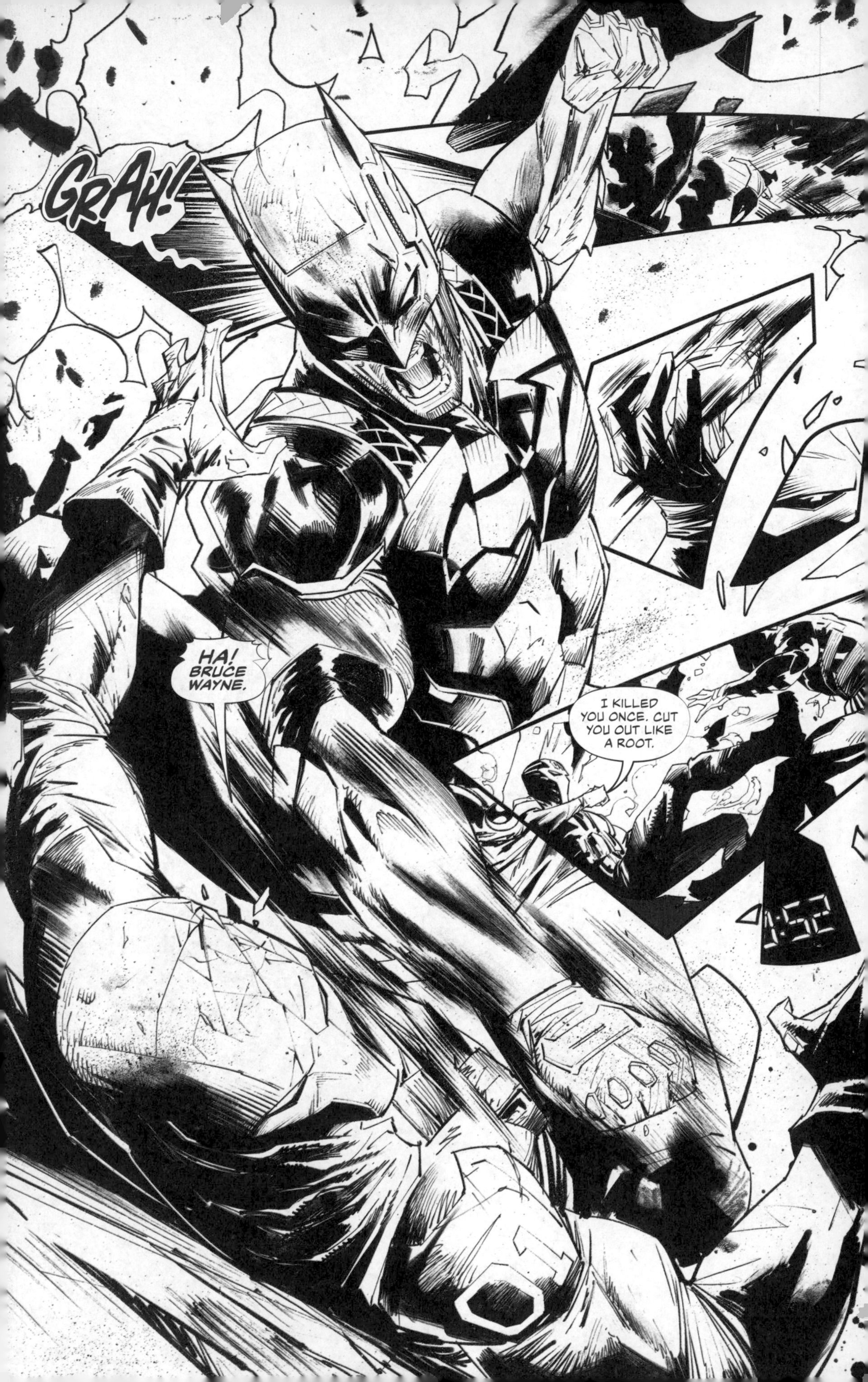
GRAH!!
HA! BRUCE WAYNE.
I KILLED YOU ONCE. CUT YOU OUT LIKE A ROOT.
1:52

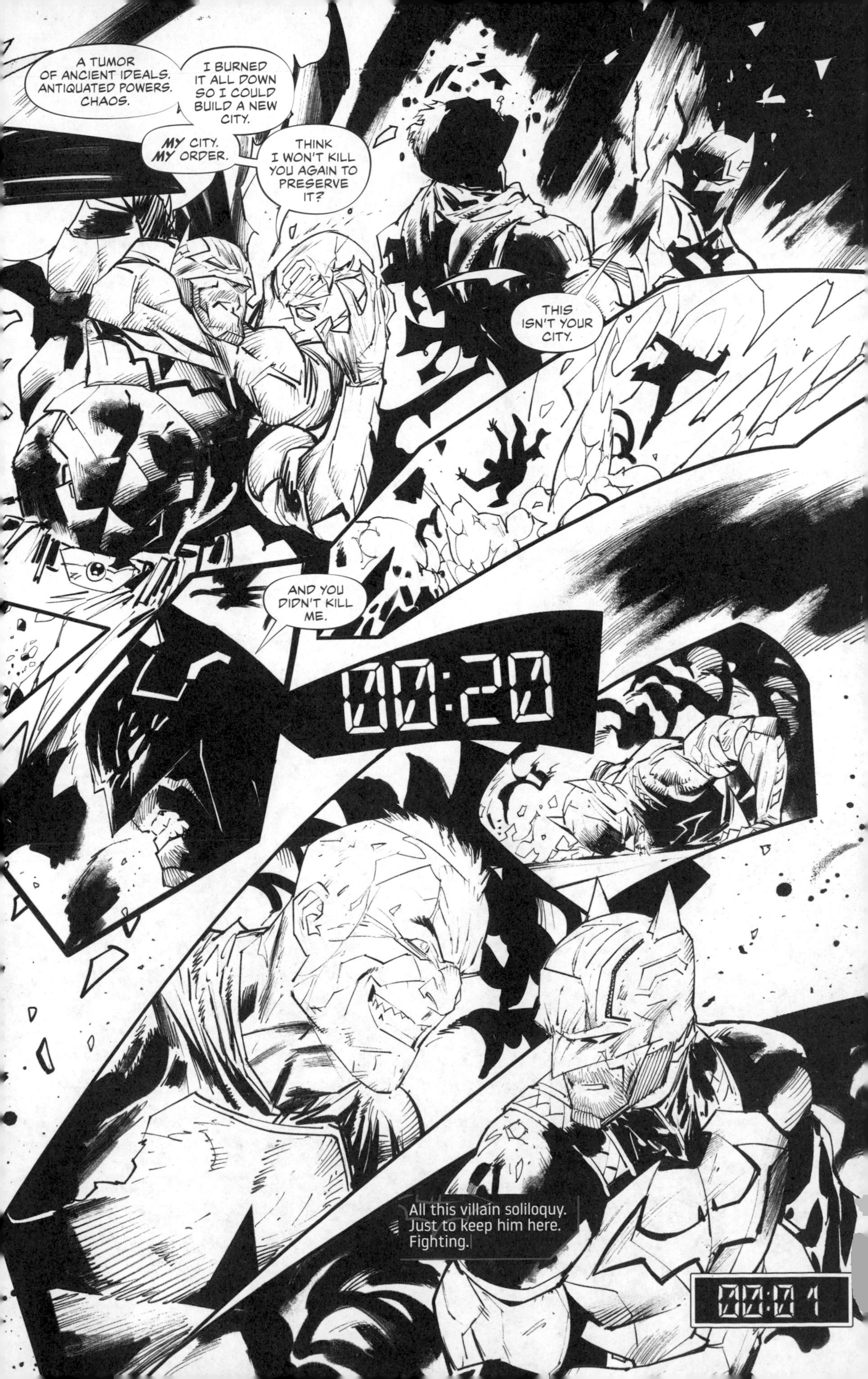
A TUMOR OF ANCIENT IDEALS. ANTIQUATED POWERS. CHAOS.
I BURNED IT ALL DOWN SO I COULD BUILD A NEW CITY.
MY CITY. MY ORDER.
THINK I WON'T KILL YOU AGAIN TO PRESERVE IT?
THIS ISN'T YOUR CITY.
AND YOU DIDN'T KILL ME.
00:20
All this villain soliloquy. Just to keep him here. Fighting.
00:01

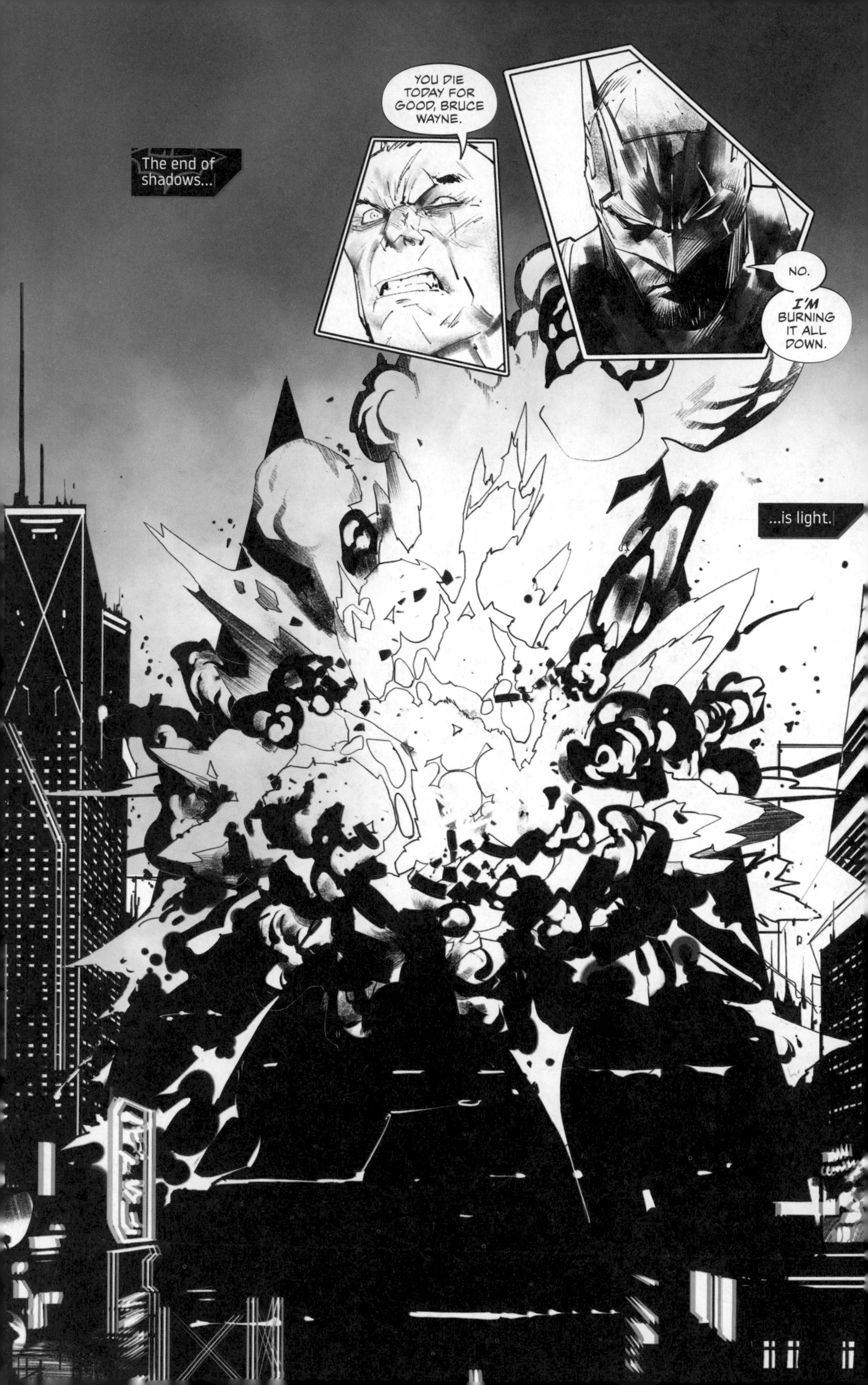

The end of shadows...
YOU DIE TODAY FOR GOOD, BRUCE WAYNE.
NO.
I'M BURNING IT ALL DOWN.
...is light.

BATMEN AT WAR

Part One: Whatever Happened to Bruce Wayne?

Written by Dennis Culver Art by Geoffo
Cover by Simone Di Meo Variant Cover by Mike Bowden & Rex Lokus
Lettered by Troy Peteri Edited by Ben Abernathy

Pages 1-6 originally presented in *Future State: Dark Detective* #4 by Mariko Tamaki, Dan Mora & Aditya Bidikar

Pages 10-13 originally presented in *Future State: Catwoman* #1 and #2 by Ram V, Otto Schmidt & Tom Napolitano

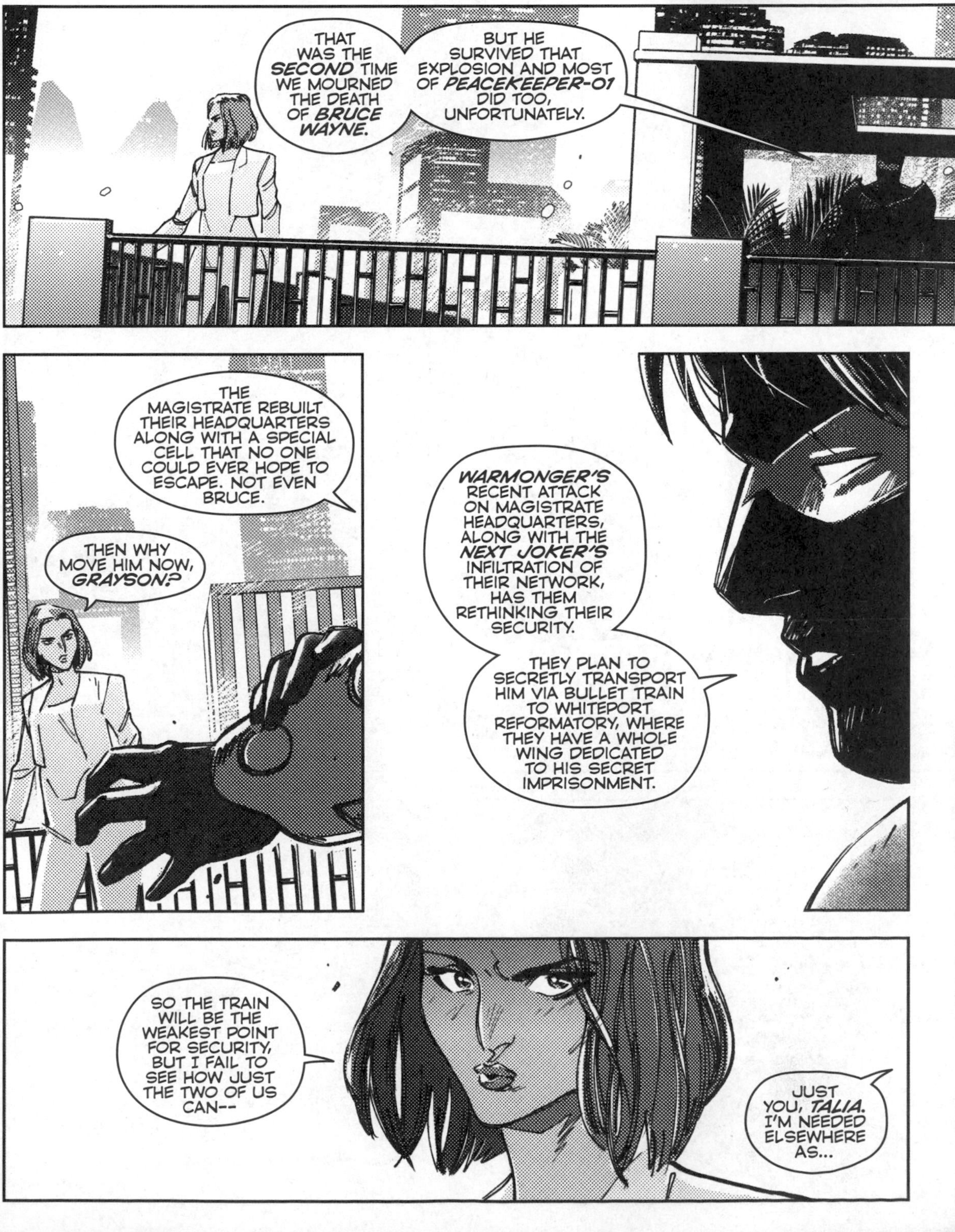
THAT WAS THE SECOND TIME WE MOURNED THE DEATH OF BRUCE WAYNE.
BUT HE SURVIVED THAT EXPLOSION AND MOST OF PEACEKEEPER-01 DID TOO, UNFORTUNATELY.
THE MAGISTRATE REBUILT THEIR HEADQUARTERS ALONG WITH A SPECIAL CELL THAT NO ONE COULD EVER HOPE TO ESCAPE. NOT EVEN BRUCE.
THEN WHY MOVE HIM NOW, GRAYSON?
WARMONGER'S RECENT ATTACK ON MAGISTRATE HEADQUARTERS, ALONG WITH THE NEXT JOKER'S INFILTRATION OF THEIR NETWORK, HAS THEM RETHINKING THEIR SECURITY.
THEY PLAN TO SECRETLY TRANSPORT HIM VIA BULLET TRAIN TO WHITEPORT REFORMATORY, WHERE THEY HAVE A WHOLE WING DEDICATED TO HIS SECRET IMPRISONMENT.
SO THE TRAIN WILL BE THE WEAKEST POINT FOR SECURITY, BUT I FAIL TO SEE HOW JUST THE TWO OF US CAN--
JUST YOU, TALIA. I'M NEEDED ELSEWHERE AS...

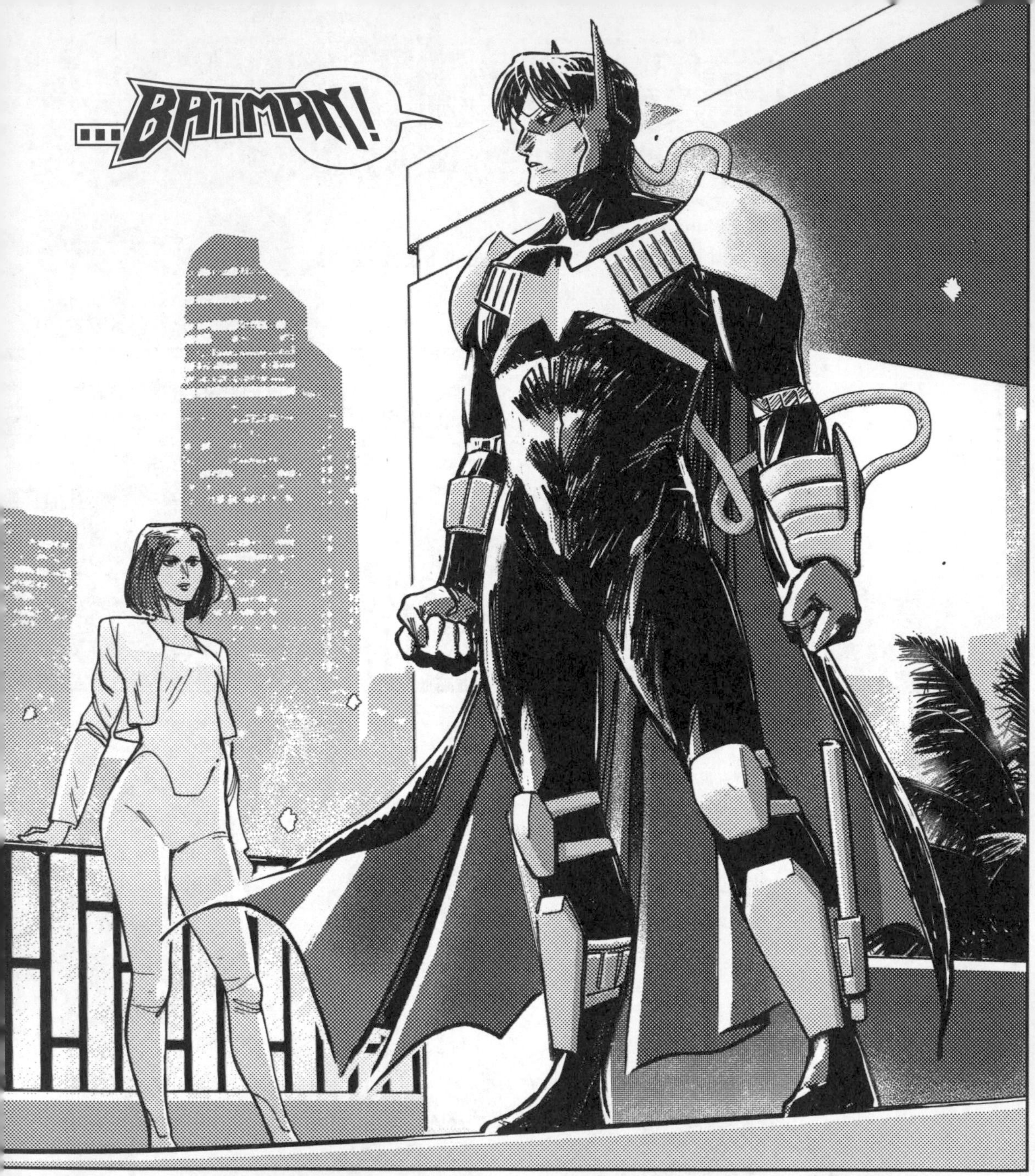
...BATMAN!

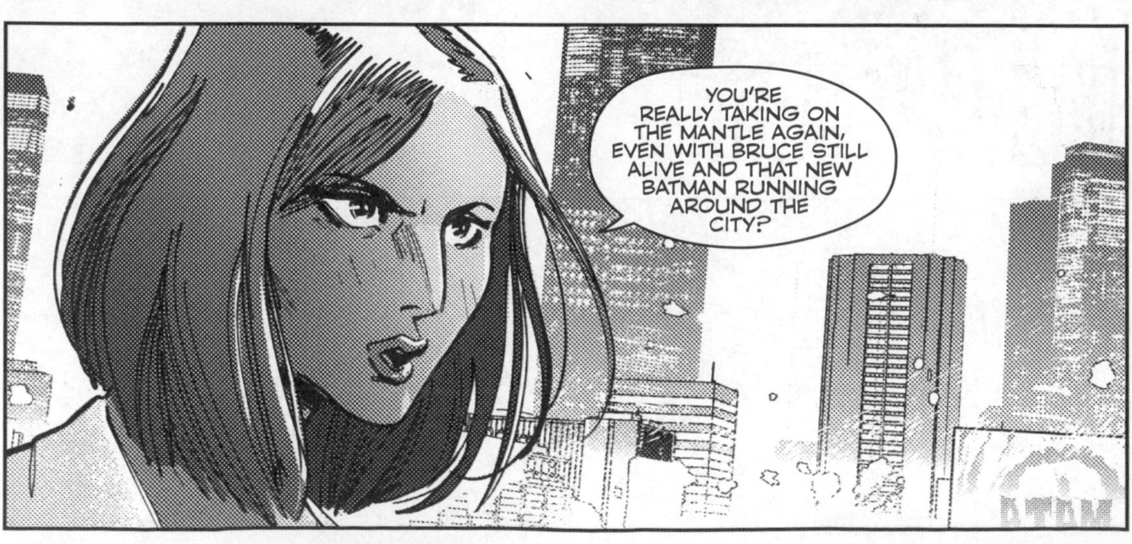
YOU'RE REALLY TAKING ON THE MANTLE AGAIN, EVEN WITH BRUCE STILL ALIVE AND THAT NEW BATMAN RUNNING AROUND THE CITY?

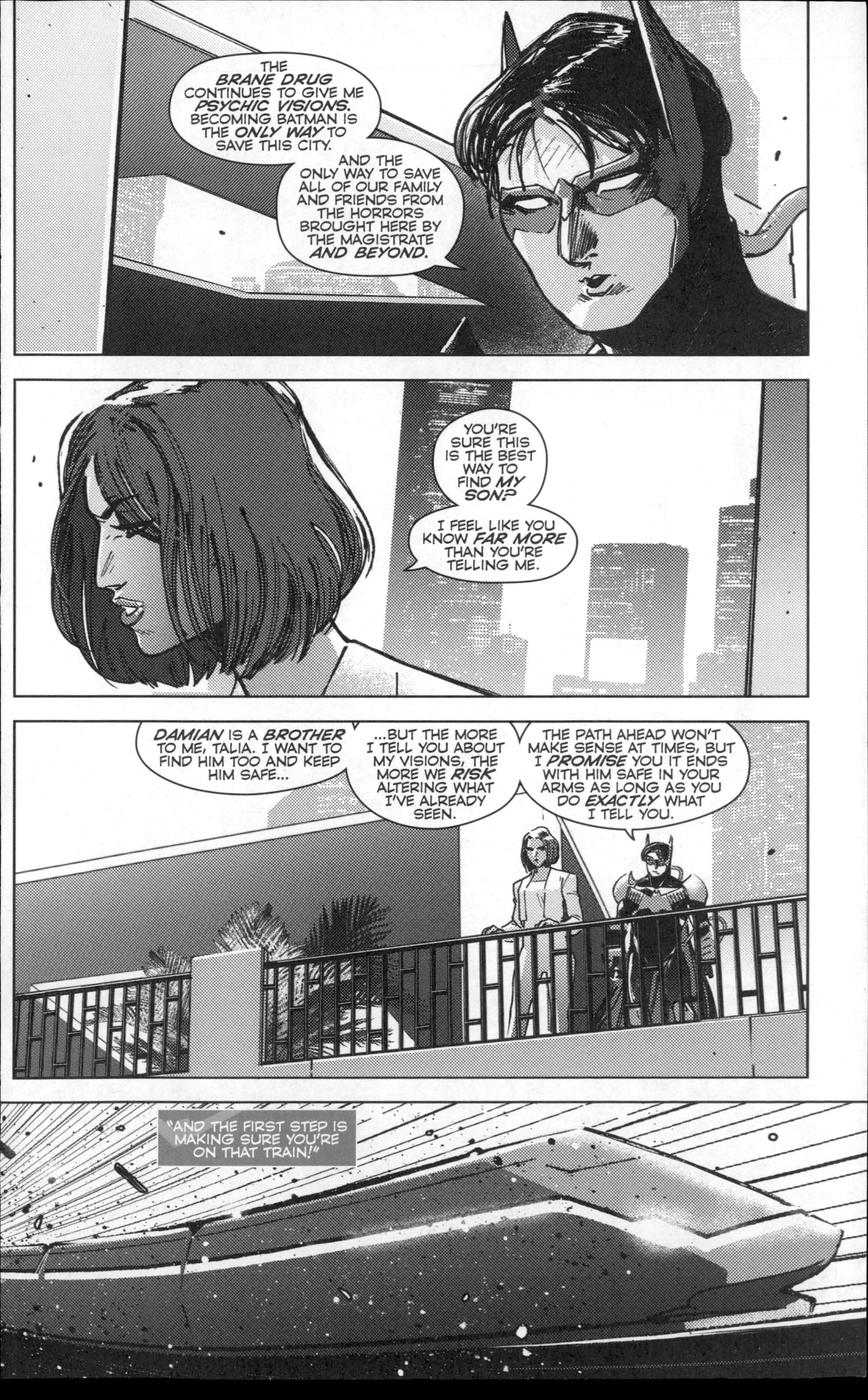
THE BRANE DRUG CONTINUES TO GIVE ME PSYCHIC VISIONS. BECOMING BATMAN IS THE ONLY WAY TO SAVE THIS CITY.
AND THE ONLY WAY TO SAVE ALL OF OUR FAMILY AND FRIENDS FROM THE HORRORS BROUGHT HERE BY THE MAGISTRATE AND BEYOND.
YOU'RE SURE THIS IS THE BEST WAY TO FIND MY SON?
I FEEL LIKE YOU KNOW FAR MORE THAN YOU'RE TELLING ME.
DAMIAN IS A BROTHER TO ME, TALIA. I WANT TO FIND HIM TOO AND KEEP HIM SAFE...
...BUT THE MORE I TELL YOU ABOUT MY VISIONS, THE MORE WE RISK ALTERING WHAT I'VE ALREADY SEEN.
THE PATH AHEAD WON'T MAKE SENSE AT TIMES, BUT I PROMISE YOU IT ENDS WITH HIM SAFE IN YOUR ARMS AS LONG AS YOU DO EXACTLY WHAT I TELL YOU.
"AND THE FIRST STEP IS MAKING SURE YOU'RE ON THAT TRAIN!"

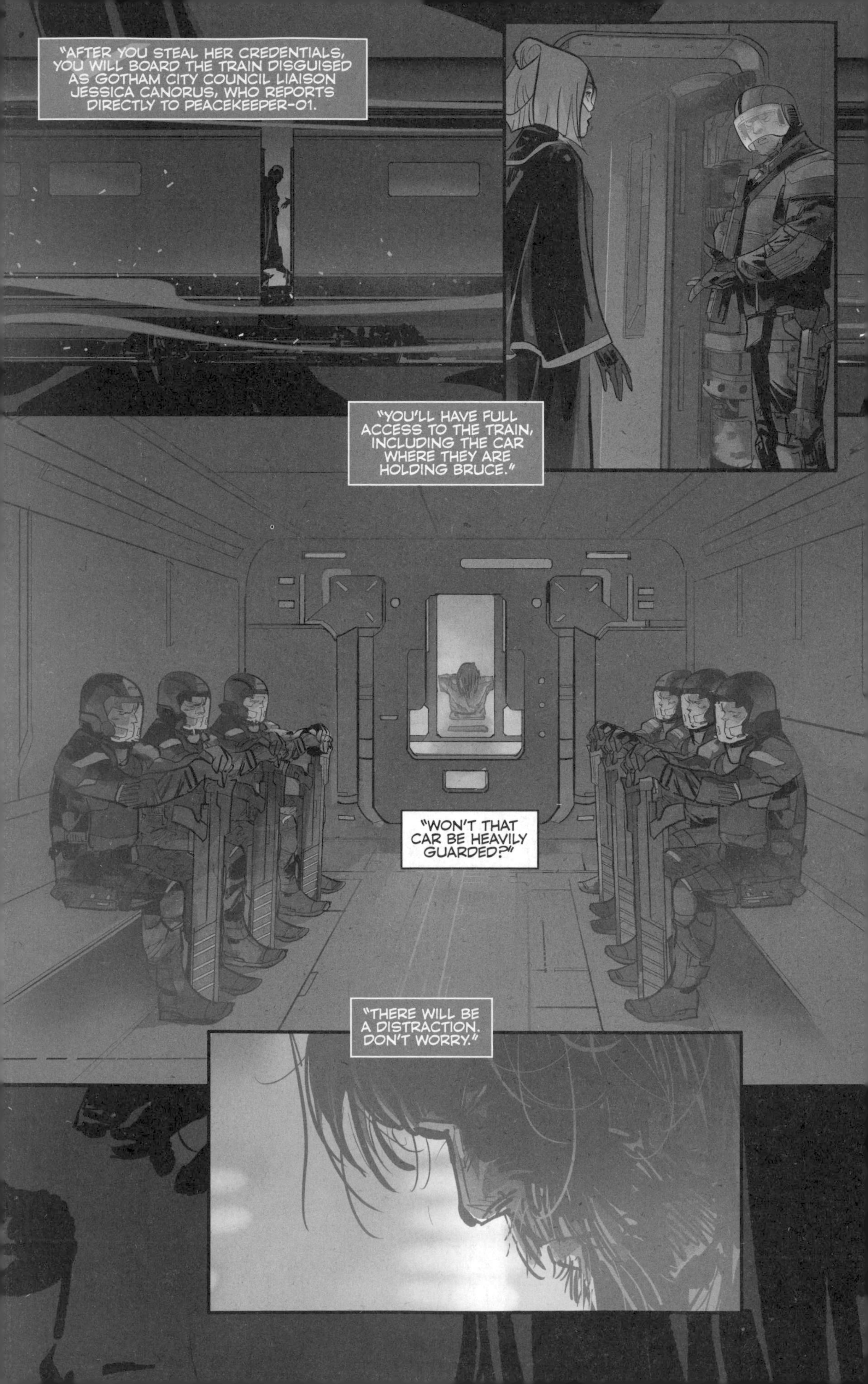
"AFTER YOU STEAL HER CREDENTIALS, YOU WILL BOARD THE TRAIN DISGUISED AS GOTHAM CITY COUNCIL LIAISON JESSICA CANORUS, WHO REPORTS DIRECTLY TO PEACEKEEPER-01.
"YOU'LL HAVE FULL ACCESS TO THE TRAIN, INCLUDING THE CAR WHERE THEY ARE HOLDING BRUCE."
"WON'T THAT CAR BE HEAVILY GUARDED?"
"THERE WILL BE A DISTRACTION. DON'T WORRY."

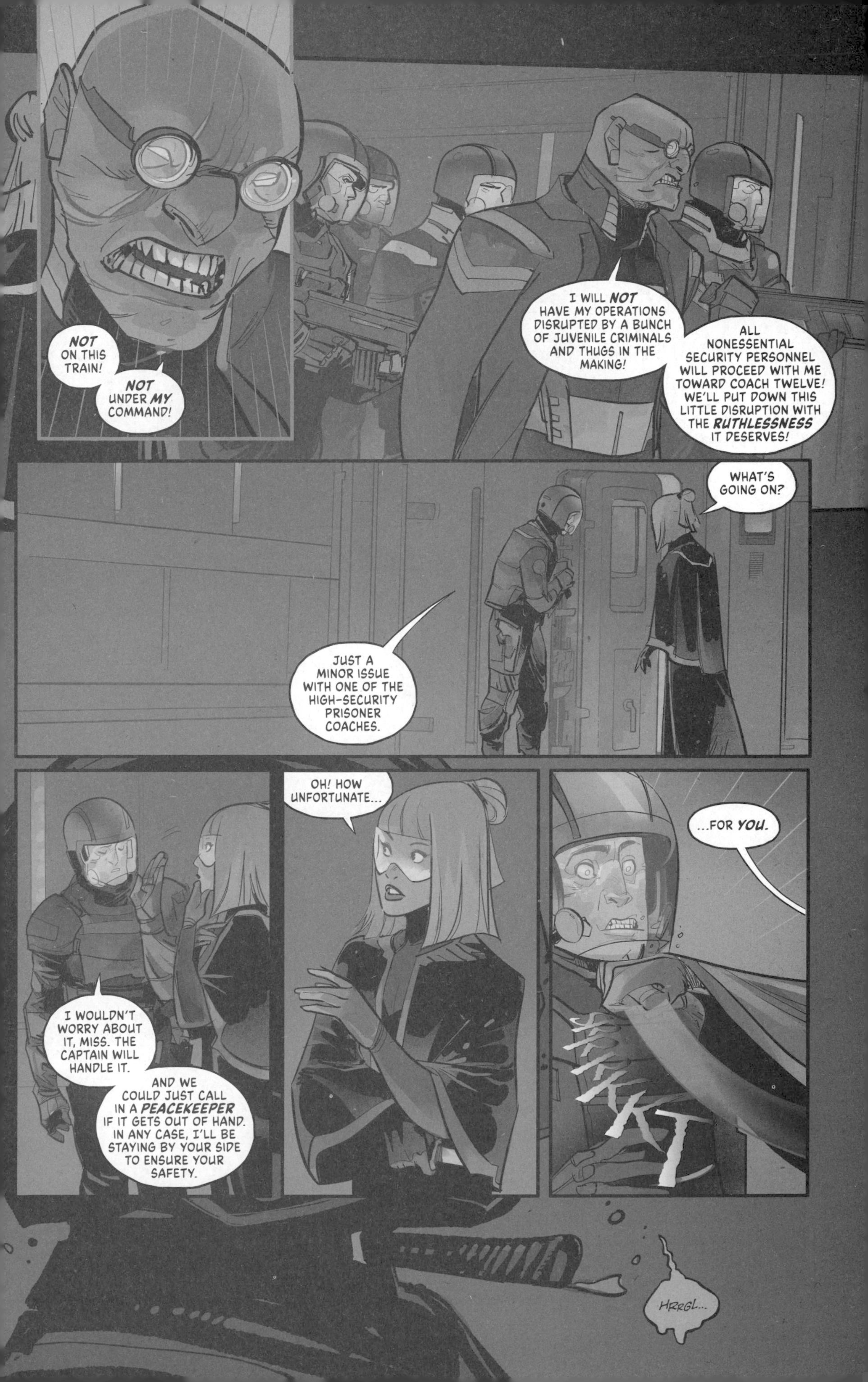
NOT ON THIS TRAIN!
NOT UNDER MY COMMAND!
I WILL NOT HAVE MY OPERATIONS DISRUPTED BY A BUNCH OF JUVENILE CRIMINALS AND THUGS IN THE MAKING!
ALL NONESSENTIAL SECURITY PERSONNEL WILL PROCEED WITH ME TOWARD COACH TWELVE! WE'LL PUT DOWN THIS LITTLE DISRUPTION WITH THE RUTHLESSNESS IT DESERVES!
WHAT'S GOING ON?
JUST A MINOR ISSUE WITH ONE OF THE HIGH-SECURITY PRISONER COACHES.
I WOULDN'T WORRY ABOUT IT, MISS. THE CAPTAIN WILL HANDLE IT.
AND WE COULD JUST CALL IN A PEACEKEEPER IF IT GETS OUT OF HAND. IN ANY CASE, I'LL BE STAYING BY YOUR SIDE TO ENSURE YOUR SAFETY.
OH! HOW UNFORTUNATE...
...FOR YOU.
SHKT
HRRGL...

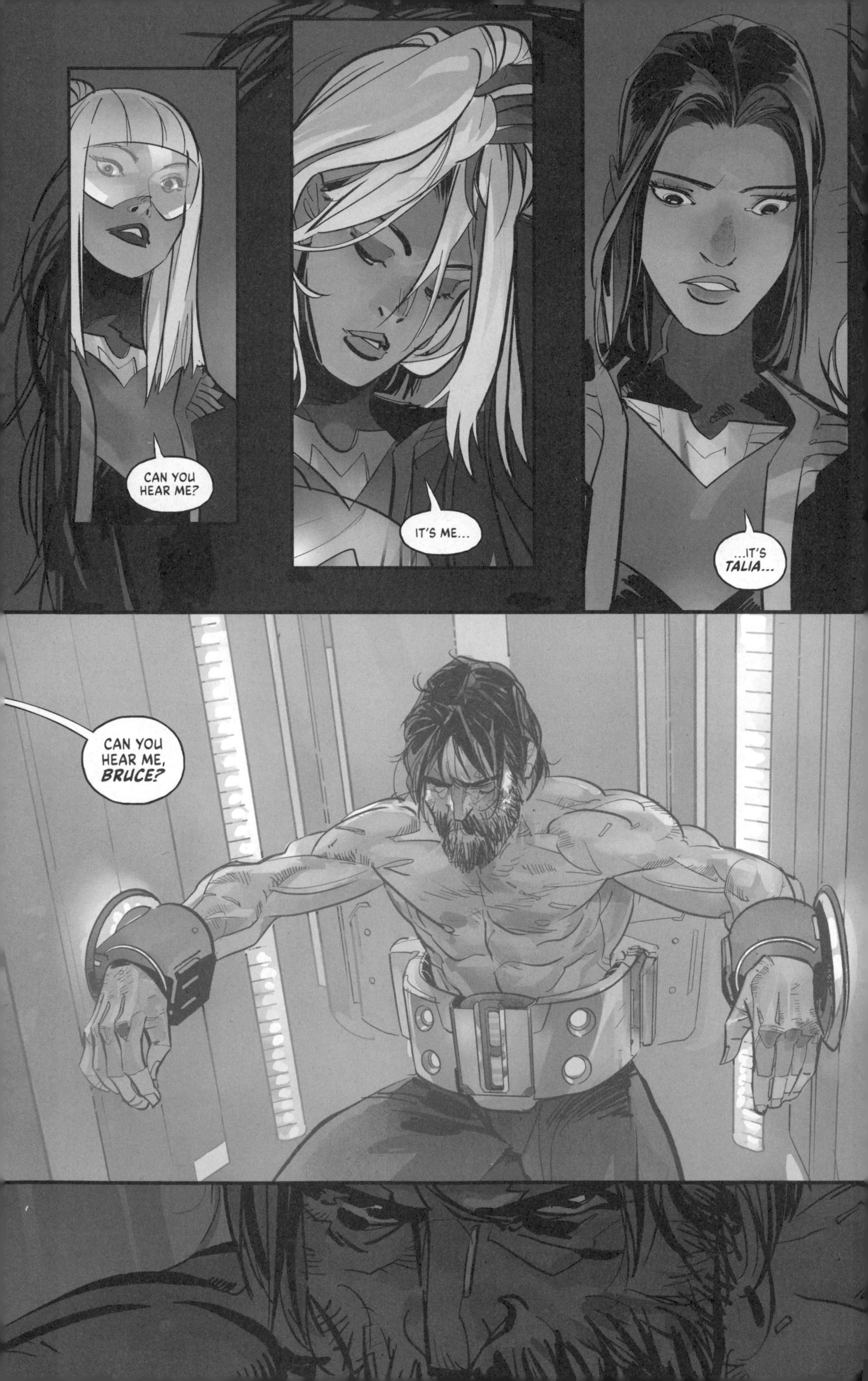
CAN YOU HEAR ME?
IT'S ME...
...IT'S TALIA...
CAN YOU HEAR ME, BRUCE?

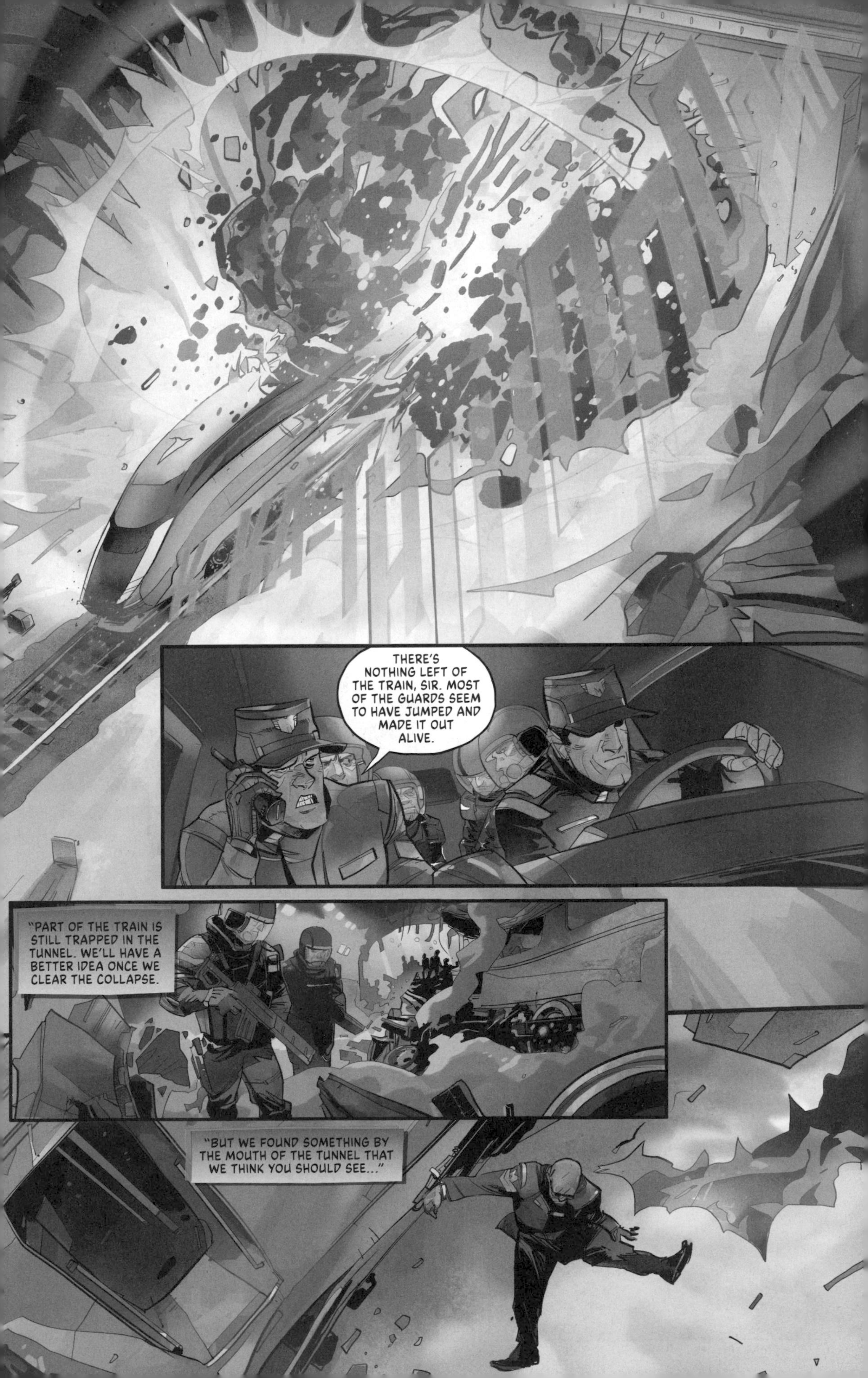
THERE'S NOTHING LEFT OF THE TRAIN, SIR. MOST OF THE GUARDS SEEM TO HAVE JUMPED AND MADE IT OUT ALIVE.
"PART OF THE TRAIN IS STILL TRAPPED IN THE TUNNEL. WE'LL HAVE A BETTER IDEA ONCE WE CLEAR THE COLLAPSE.
"BUT WE FOUND SOMETHING BY THE MOUTH OF THE TUNNEL THAT WE THINK YOU SHOULD SEE..."

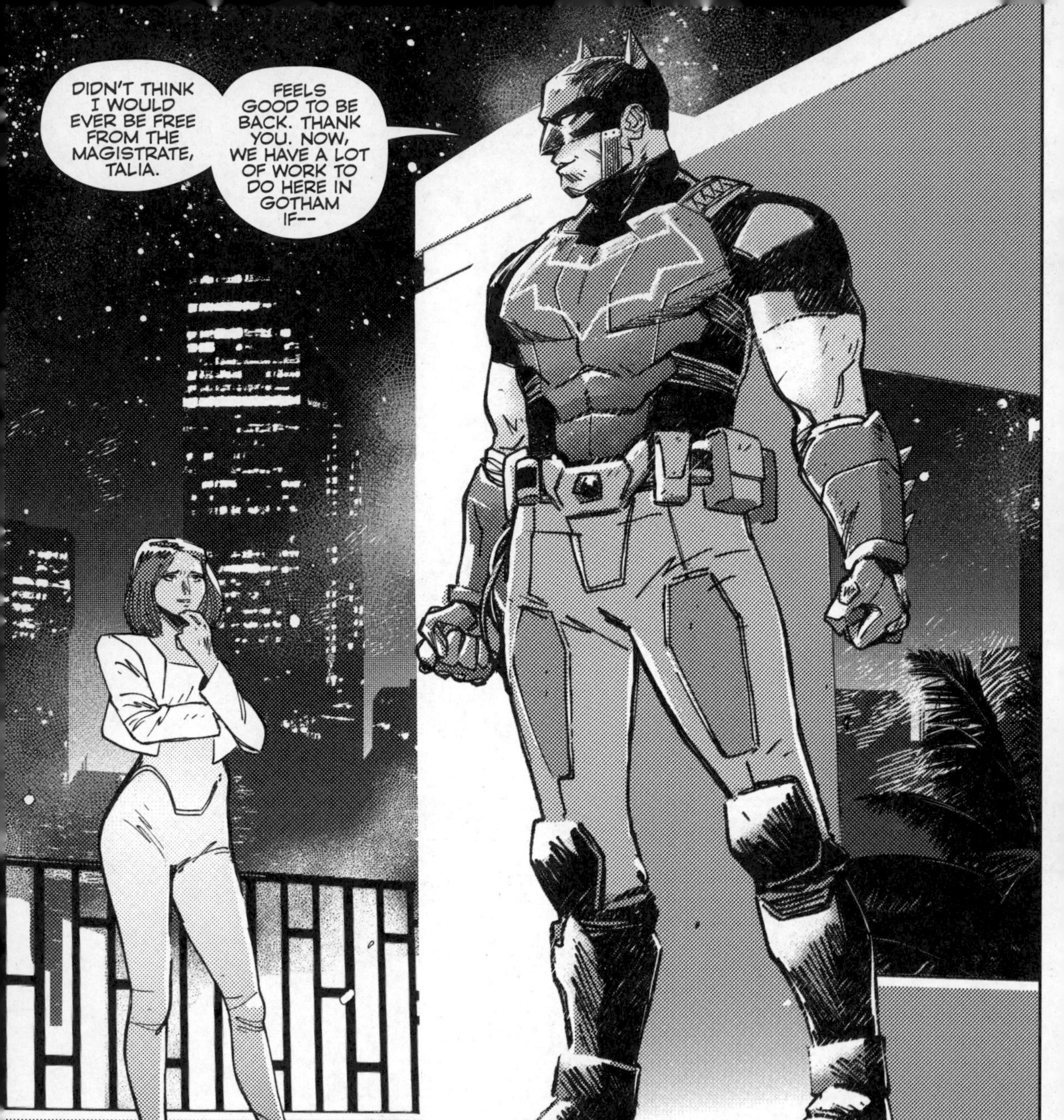
DIDN'T THINK I WOULD EVER BE FREE FROM THE MAGISTRATE, TALIA.
FEELS GOOD TO BE BACK. THANK YOU. NOW, WE HAVE A LOT OF WORK TO DO HERE IN GOTHAM IF--

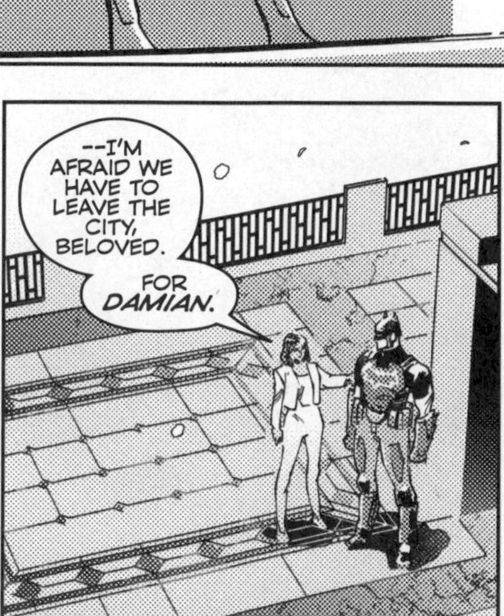
--I'M AFRAID WE HAVE TO LEAVE THE CITY, BELOVED.
FOR *DAMIAN*.

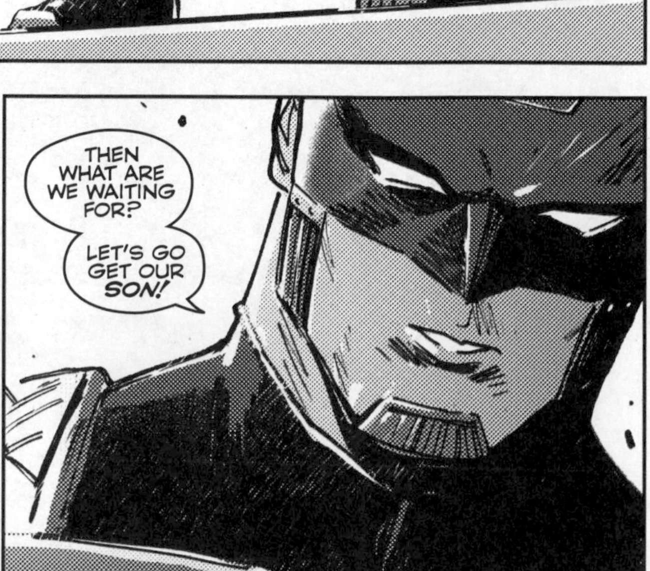
THEN WHAT ARE WE WAITING FOR?
LET'S GO GET OUR *SON!*

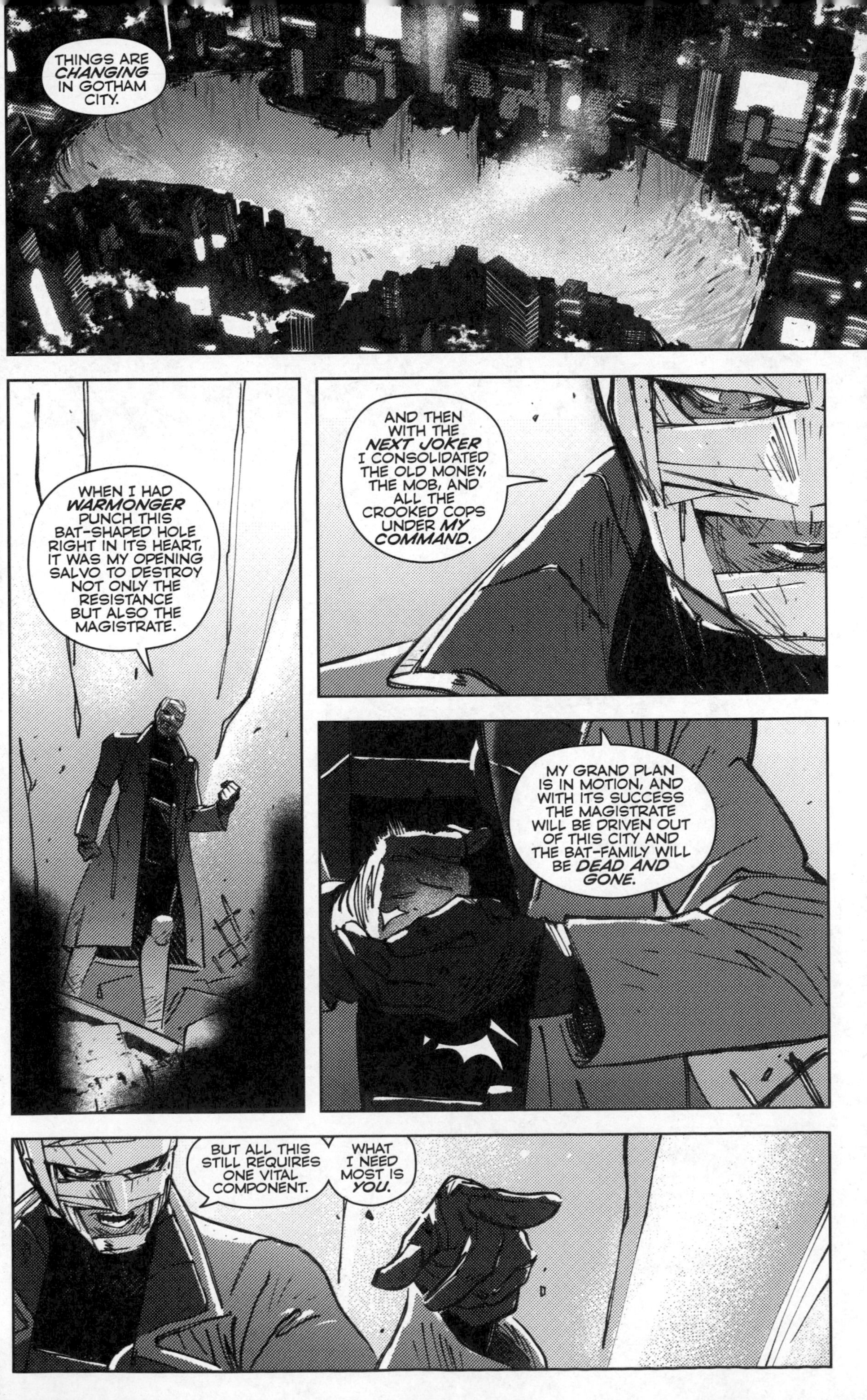
THINGS ARE CHANGING IN GOTHAM CITY.
WHEN I HAD WARMONGER PUNCH THIS BAT-SHAPED HOLE RIGHT IN ITS HEART, IT WAS MY OPENING SALVO TO DESTROY NOT ONLY THE RESISTANCE BUT ALSO THE MAGISTRATE.
AND THEN WITH THE NEXT JOKER I CONSOLIDATED THE OLD MONEY, THE MOB, AND ALL THE CROOKED COPS UNDER MY COMMAND.
MY GRAND PLAN IS IN MOTION, AND WITH ITS SUCCESS THE MAGISTRATE WILL BE DRIVEN OUT OF THIS CITY AND THE BAT-FAMILY WILL BE DEAD AND GONE.
BUT ALL THIS STILL REQUIRES ONE VITAL COMPONENT.
WHAT I NEED MOST IS YOU.

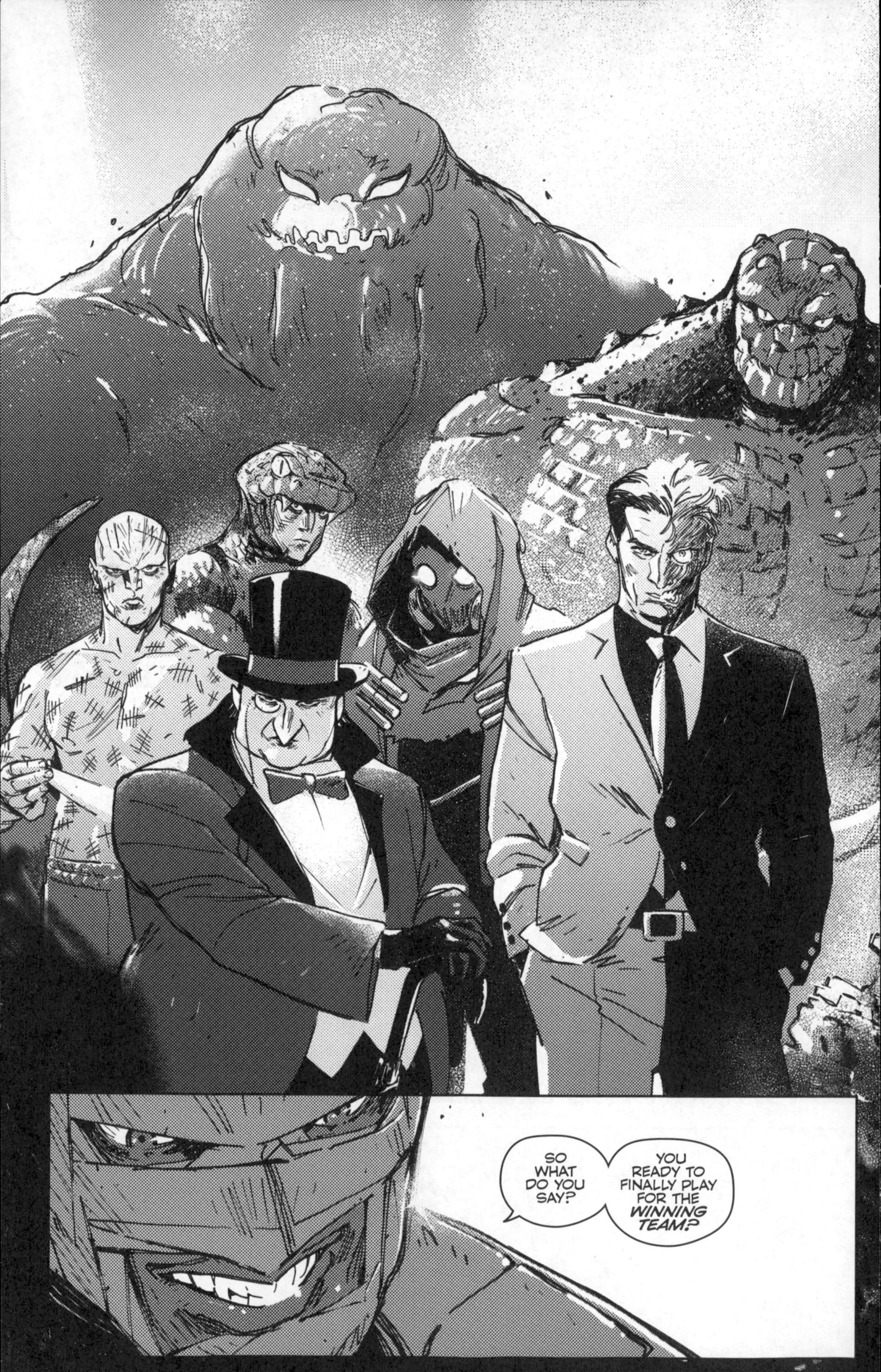
SO WHAT DO YOU SAY?
YOU READY TO FINALLY PLAY FOR THE *WINNING TEAM?*

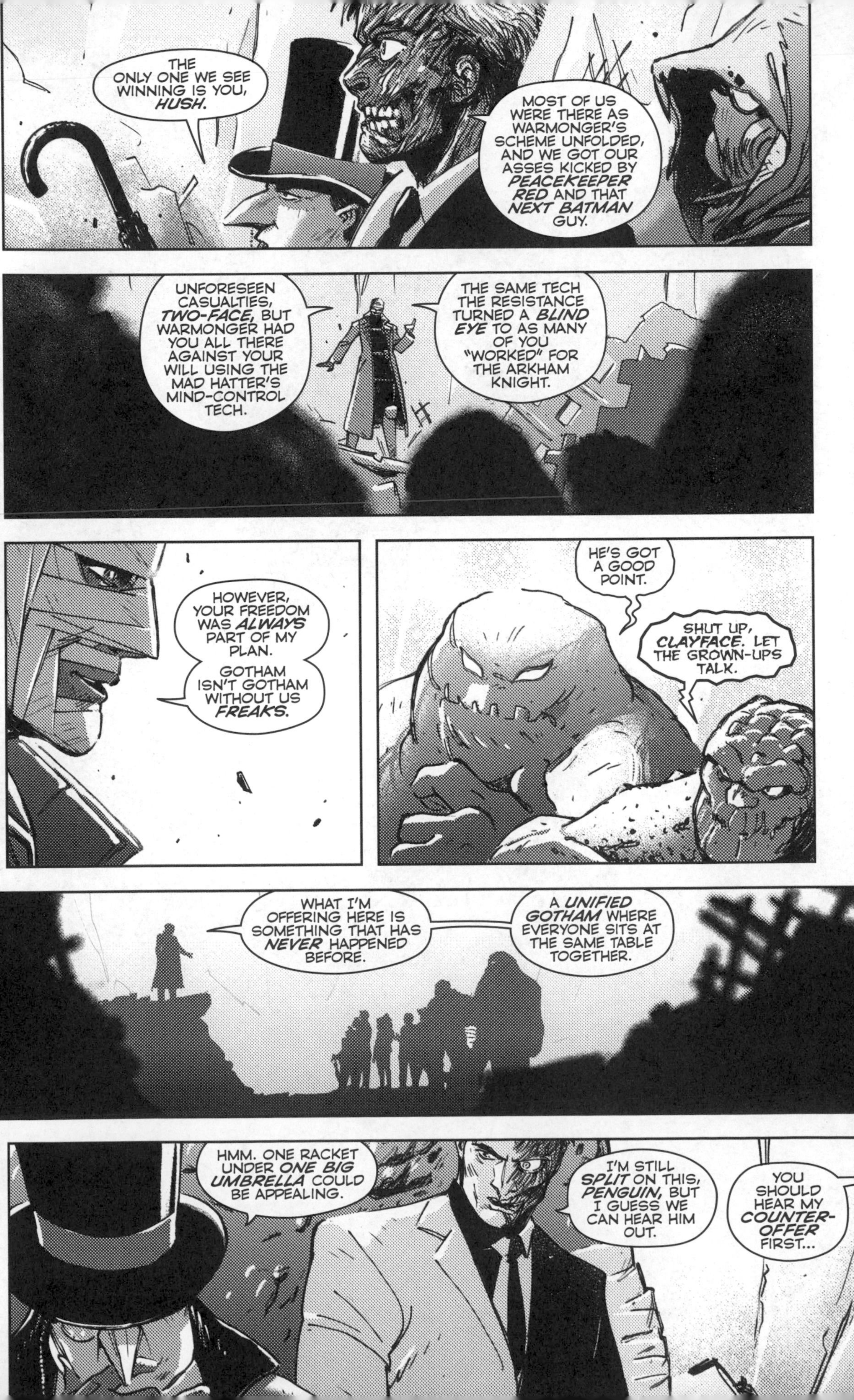
THE ONLY ONE WE SEE WINNING IS YOU, HUSH.
MOST OF US WERE THERE AS WARMONGER'S SCHEME UNFOLDED, AND WE GOT OUR ASSES KICKED BY PEACEKEEPER RED AND THAT NEXT BATMAN GUY.
UNFORESEEN CASUALTIES, TWO-FACE, BUT WARMONGER HAD YOU ALL THERE AGAINST YOUR WILL USING THE MAD HATTER'S MIND-CONTROL TECH.
THE SAME TECH THE RESISTANCE TURNED A BLIND EYE TO AS MANY OF YOU "WORKED" FOR THE ARKHAM KNIGHT.
HOWEVER, YOUR FREEDOM WAS ALWAYS PART OF MY PLAN.
GOTHAM ISN'T GOTHAM WITHOUT US FREAKS.
HE'S GOT A GOOD POINT.
SHUT UP, CLAYFACE. LET THE GROWN-UPS TALK.
WHAT I'M OFFERING HERE IS SOMETHING THAT HAS NEVER HAPPENED BEFORE.
A UNIFIED GOTHAM WHERE EVERYONE SITS AT THE SAME TABLE TOGETHER.
HMM. ONE RACKET UNDER ONE BIG UMBRELLA COULD BE APPEALING.
I'M STILL SPLIT ON THIS, PENGUIN, BUT I GUESS WE CAN HEAR HIM OUT.
YOU SHOULD HEAR MY COUNTER-OFFER FIRST...

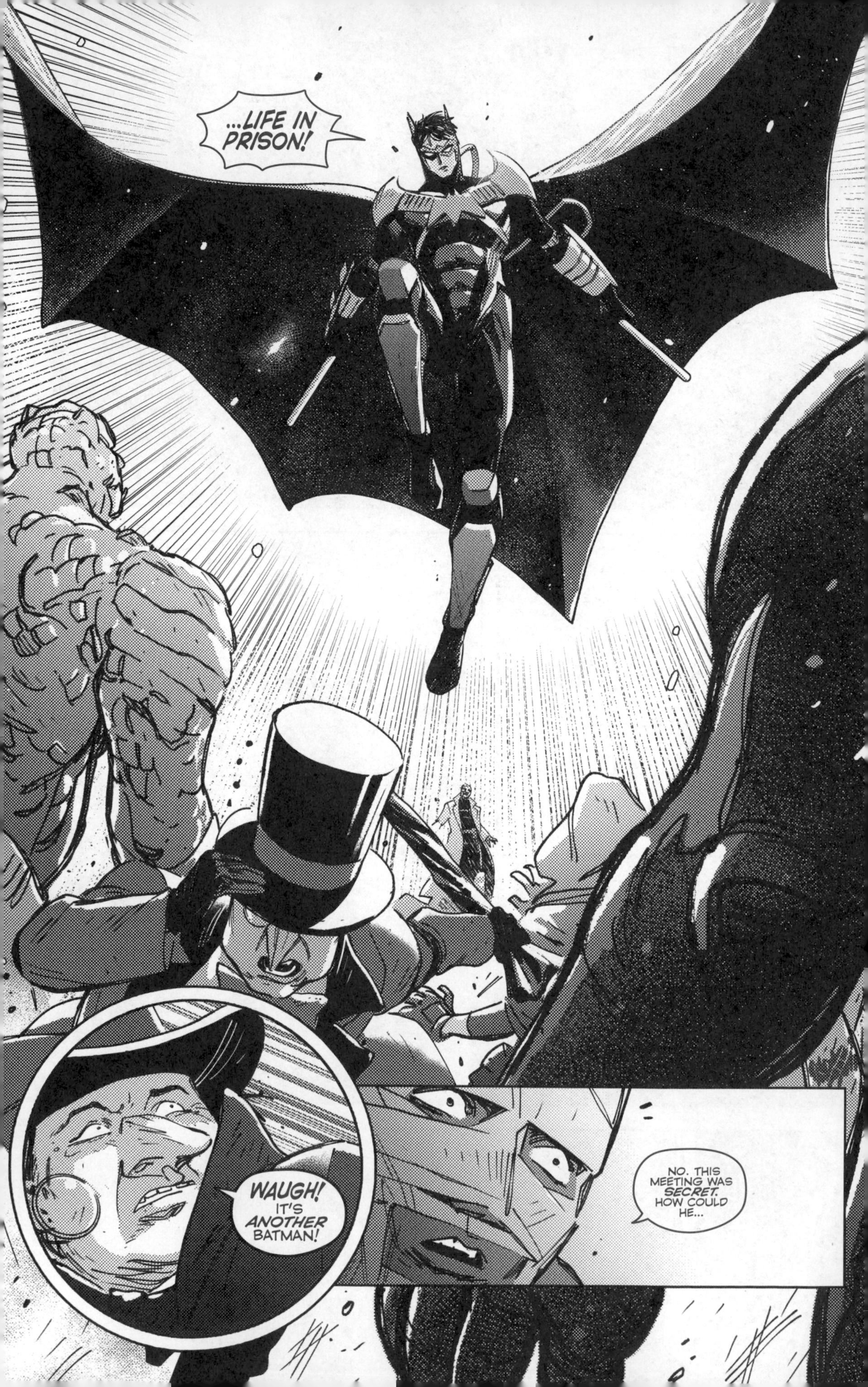
...LIFE IN PRISON!
WAUGH! IT'S ANOTHER BATMAN!
NO. THIS MEETING WAS SECRET. HOW COULD HE...

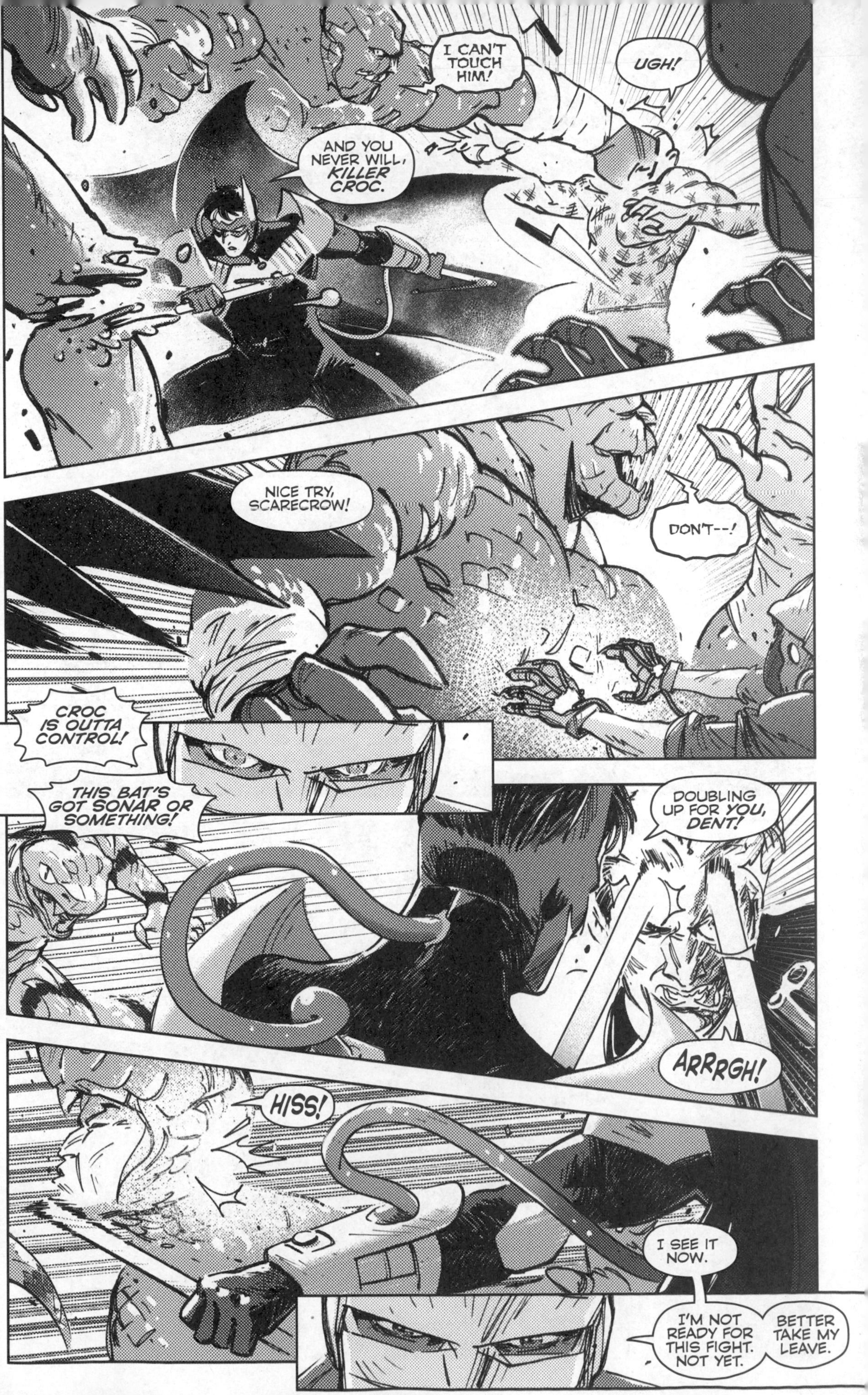
I CAN'T TOUCH HIM!
UGH!
AND YOU NEVER WILL, KILLER CROC.
NICE TRY, SCARECROW!
DON'T--!
CROC IS OUTTA CONTROL!
THIS BAT'S GOT SONAR OR SOMETHING!
DOUBLING UP FOR YOU, DENT!
ARRRGH!
HISS!
I SEE IT NOW.
I'M NOT READY FOR THIS FIGHT. NOT YET.
BETTER TAKE MY LEAVE.

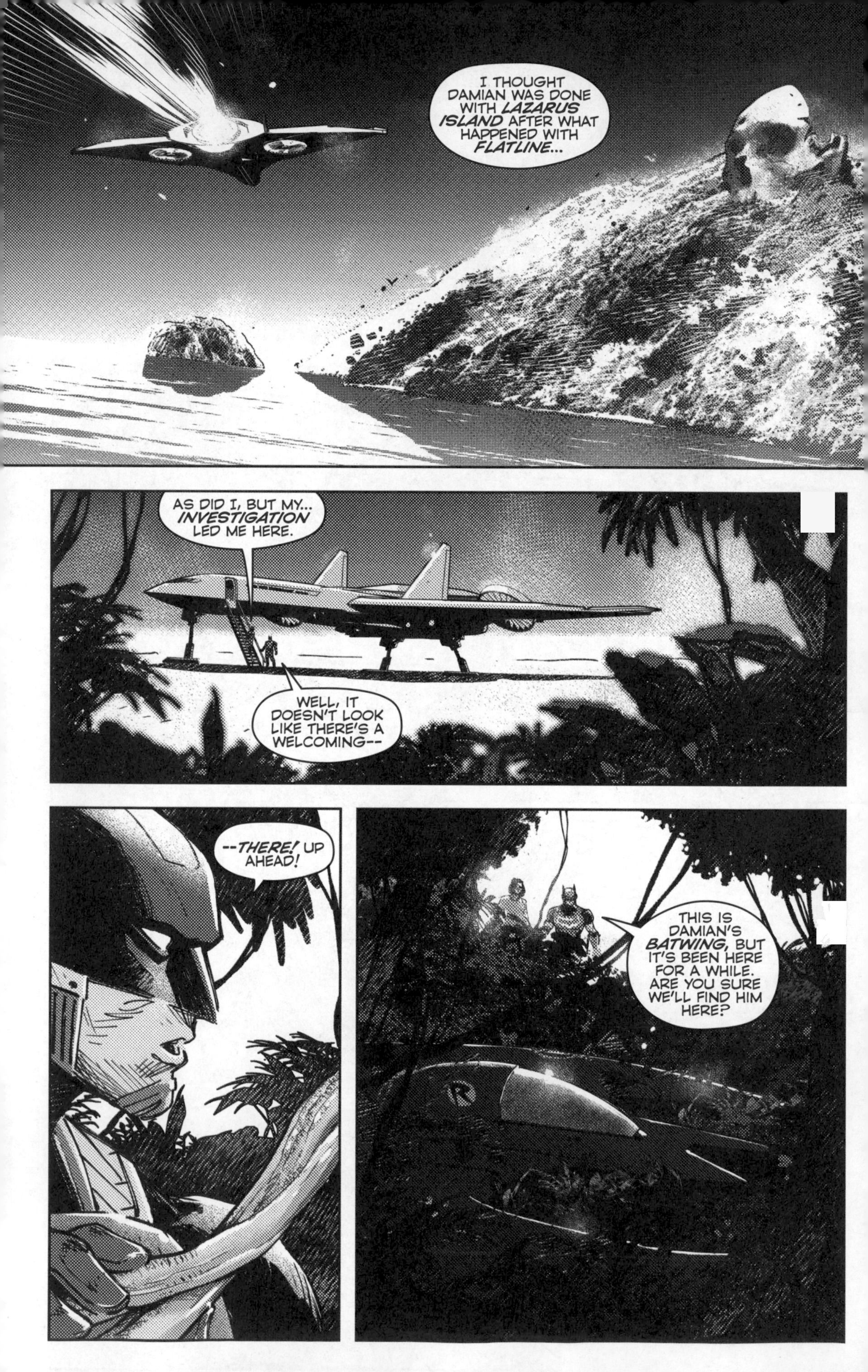
I THOUGHT DAMIAN WAS DONE WITH LAZARUS ISLAND AFTER WHAT HAPPENED WITH FLATLINE...
AS DID I, BUT MY... INVESTIGATION LED ME HERE.
WELL, IT DOESN'T LOOK LIKE THERE'S A WELCOMING--
--THERE! UP AHEAD!
THIS IS DAMIAN'S BATWING, BUT IT'S BEEN HERE FOR A WHILE. ARE YOU SURE WE'LL FIND HIM HERE?

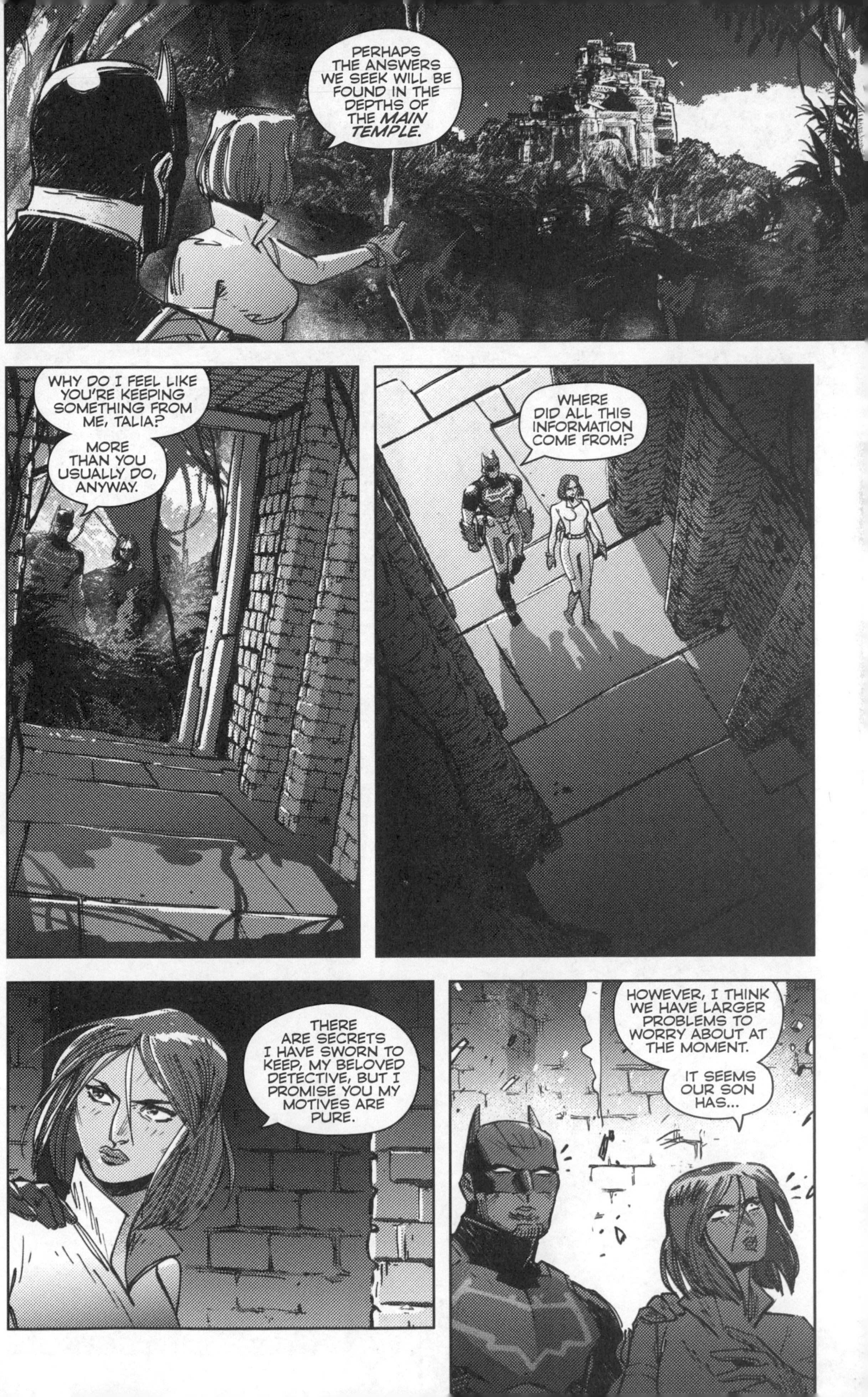
PERHAPS THE ANSWERS WE SEEK WILL BE FOUND IN THE DEPTHS OF THE *MAIN TEMPLE*.
WHY DO I FEEL LIKE YOU'RE KEEPING SOMETHING FROM ME, TALIA?
MORE THAN YOU USUALLY DO, ANYWAY.
WHERE DID ALL THIS INFORMATION COME FROM?
THERE ARE SECRETS I HAVE SWORN TO KEEP, MY BELOVED DETECTIVE, BUT I PROMISE YOU MY MOTIVES ARE PURE.
HOWEVER, I THINK WE HAVE LARGER PROBLEMS TO WORRY ABOUT AT THE MOMENT.
IT SEEMS OUR SON HAS...

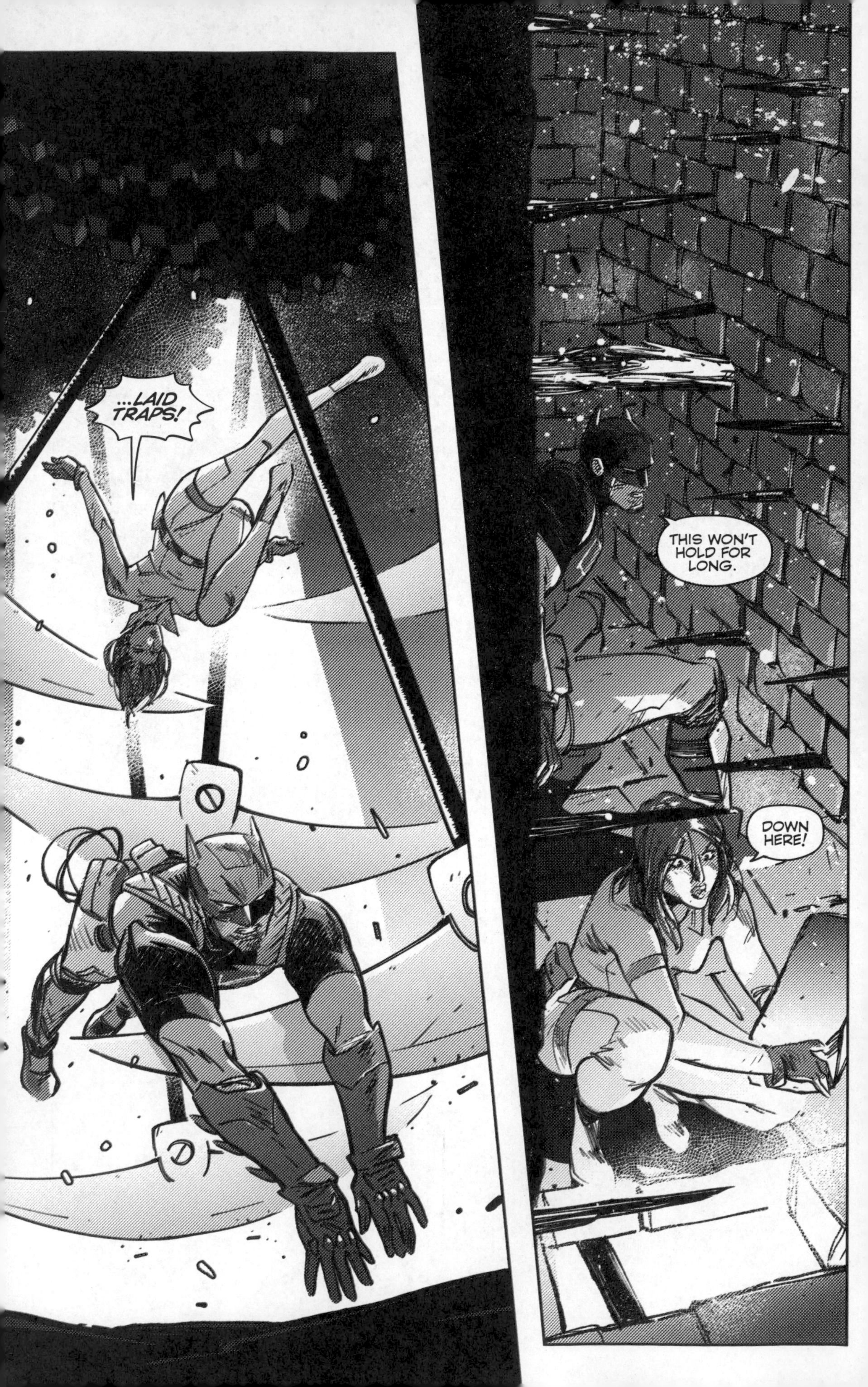
...LAID TRAPS!
THIS WON'T HOLD FOR LONG.
DOWN HERE!

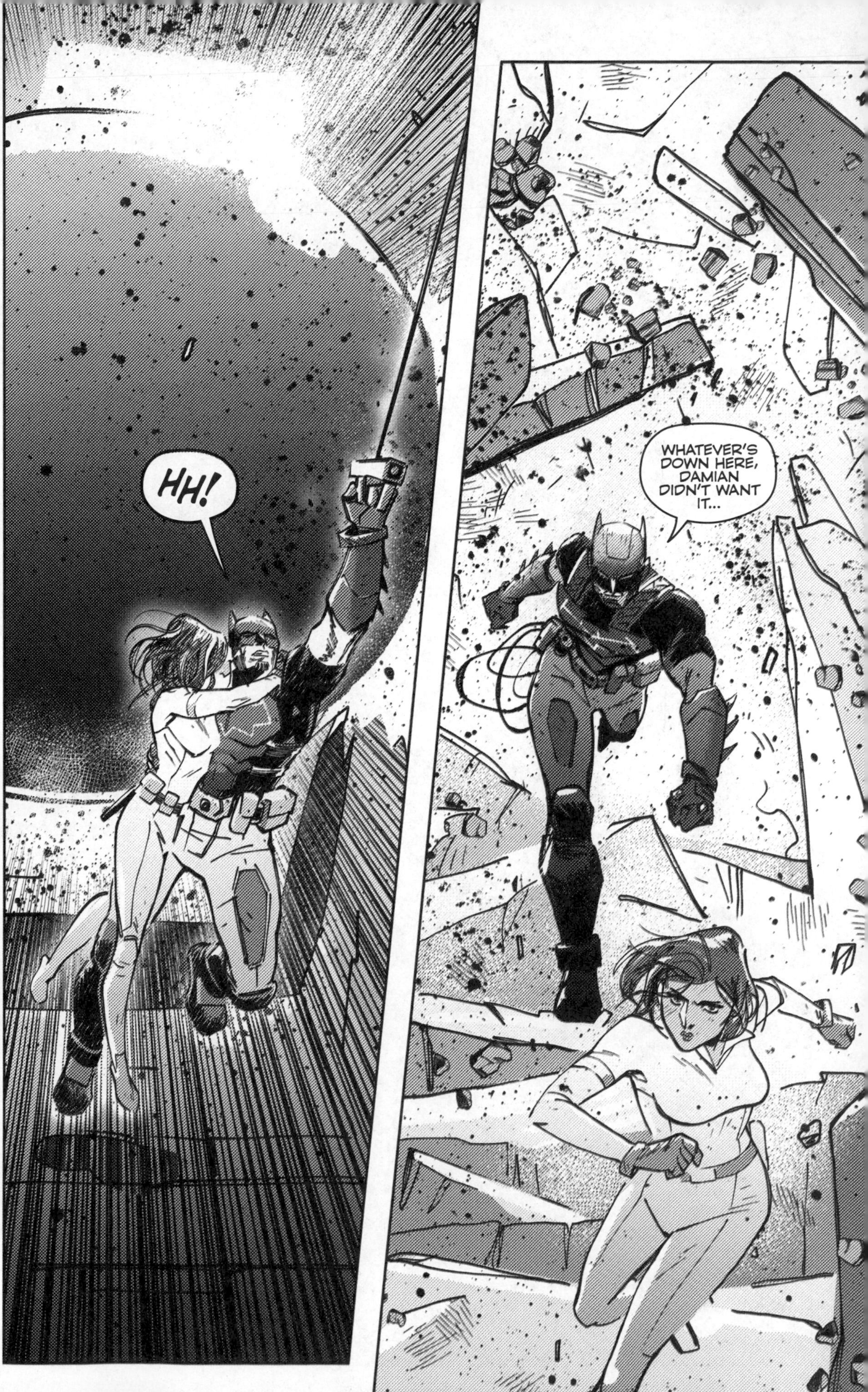
HH!
WHATEVER'S DOWN HERE, DAMIAN DIDN'T WANT IT...

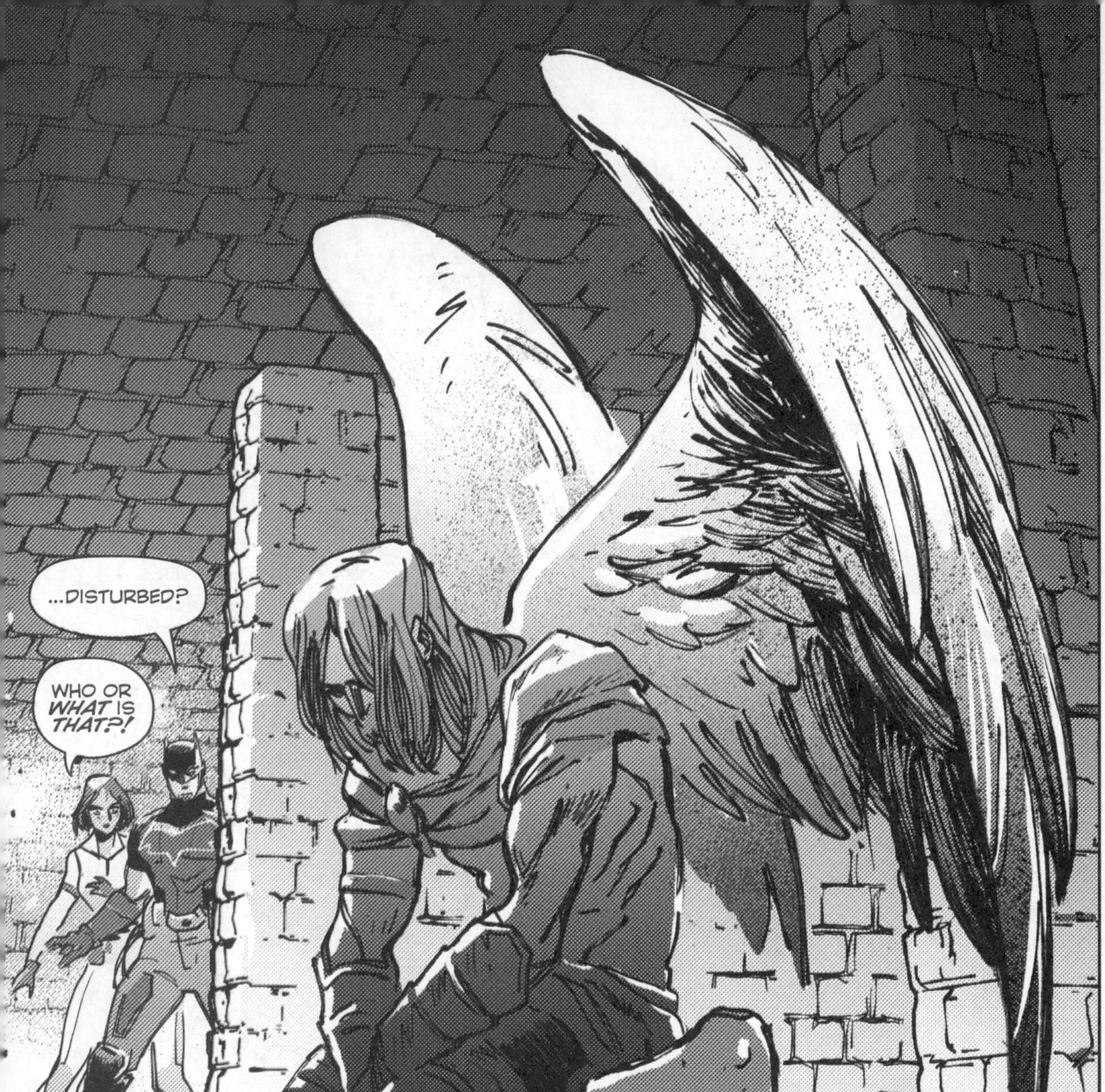
...DISTURBED?
WHO OR *WHAT* IS *THAT?!*

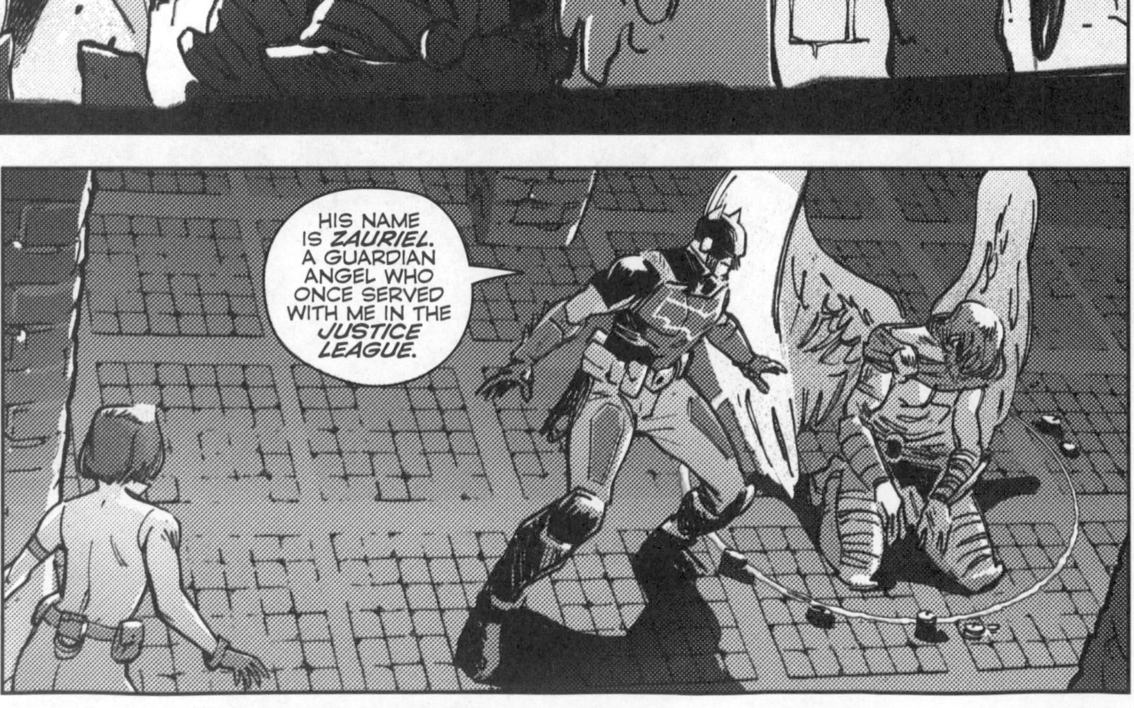
HIS NAME IS *ZAURIEL*. A GUARDIAN ANGEL WHO ONCE SERVED WITH ME IN THE *JUSTICE LEAGUE*.

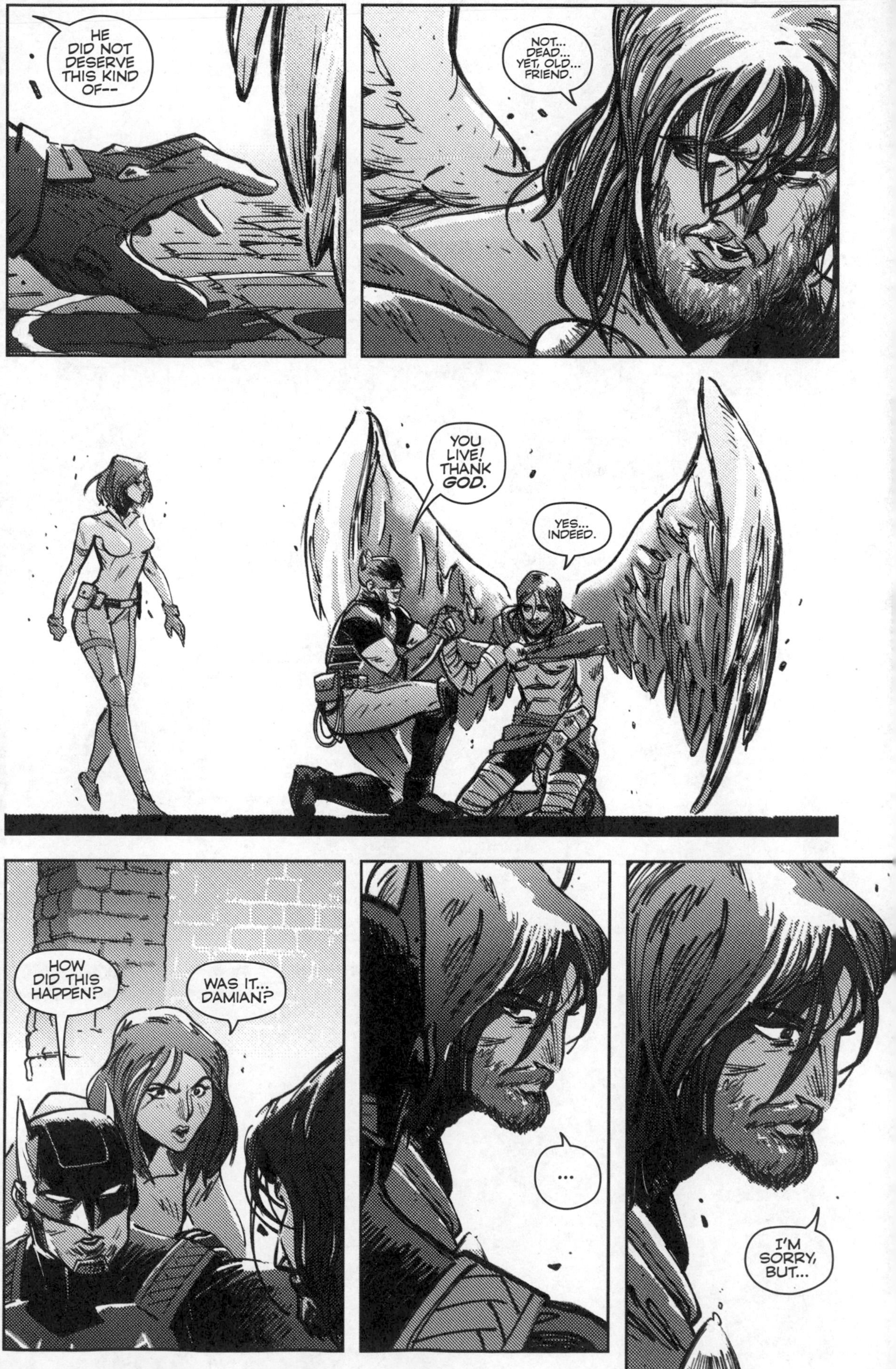
HE DID NOT DESERVE THIS KIND OF--
NOT... DEAD... YET, OLD... FRIEND.
YOU LIVE! THANK GOD.
YES... INDEED.
HOW DID THIS HAPPEN?
WAS IT... DAMIAN?
...
I'M SORRY, BUT...

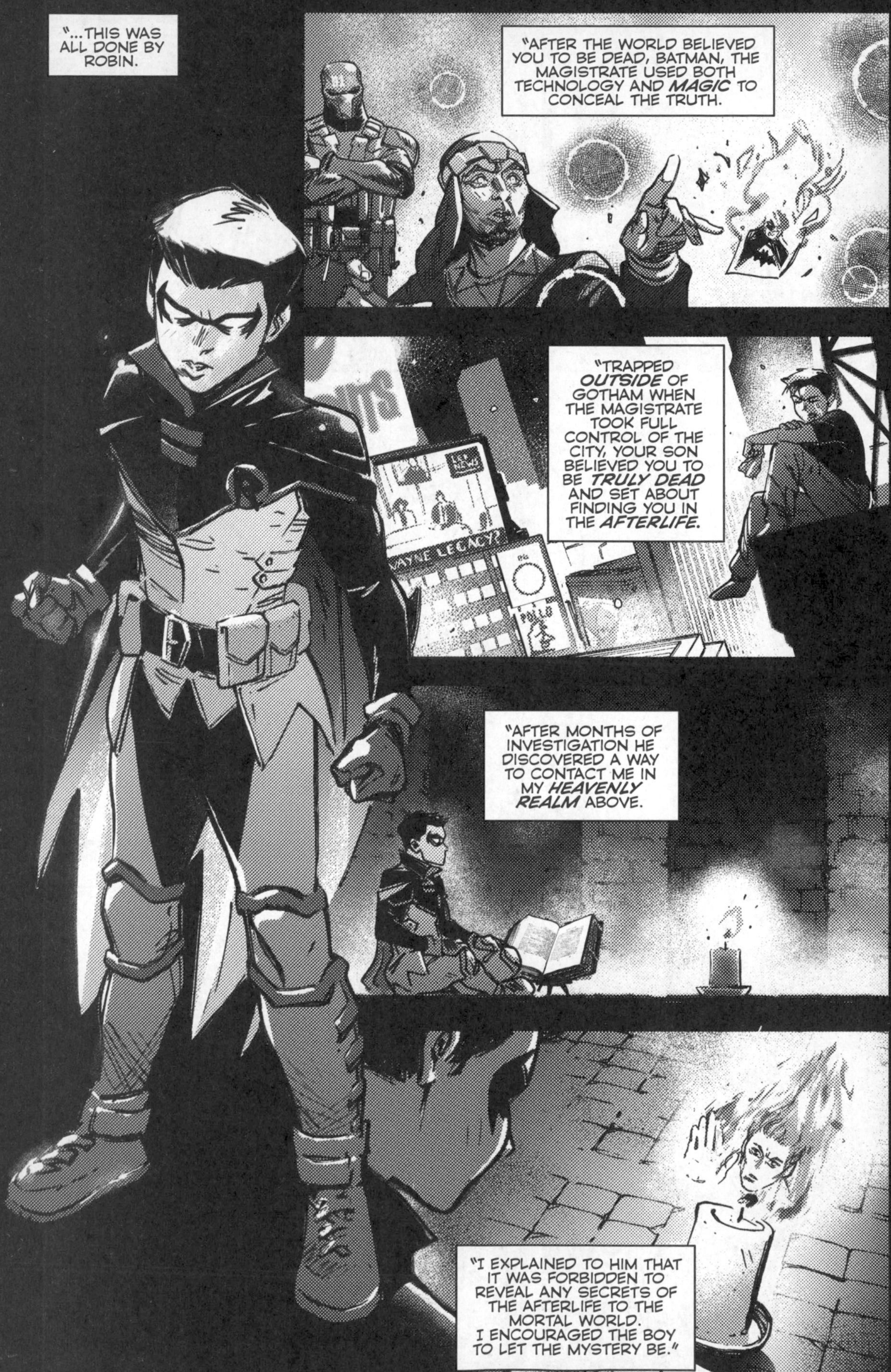
"...THIS WAS ALL DONE BY ROBIN.
"AFTER THE WORLD BELIEVED YOU TO BE DEAD, BATMAN, THE MAGISTRATE USED BOTH TECHNOLOGY AND *MAGIC* TO CONCEAL THE TRUTH.
"TRAPPED *OUTSIDE* OF GOTHAM WHEN THE MAGISTRATE TOOK FULL CONTROL OF THE CITY, YOUR SON BELIEVED YOU TO BE *TRULY DEAD* AND SET ABOUT FINDING YOU IN THE *AFTERLIFE.*
"AFTER MONTHS OF INVESTIGATION HE DISCOVERED A WAY TO CONTACT ME IN MY *HEAVENLY REALM* ABOVE.
"I EXPLAINED TO HIM THAT IT WAS FORBIDDEN TO REVEAL ANY SECRETS OF THE AFTERLIFE TO THE MORTAL WORLD.
I ENCOURAGED THE BOY TO LET THE MYSTERY BE."

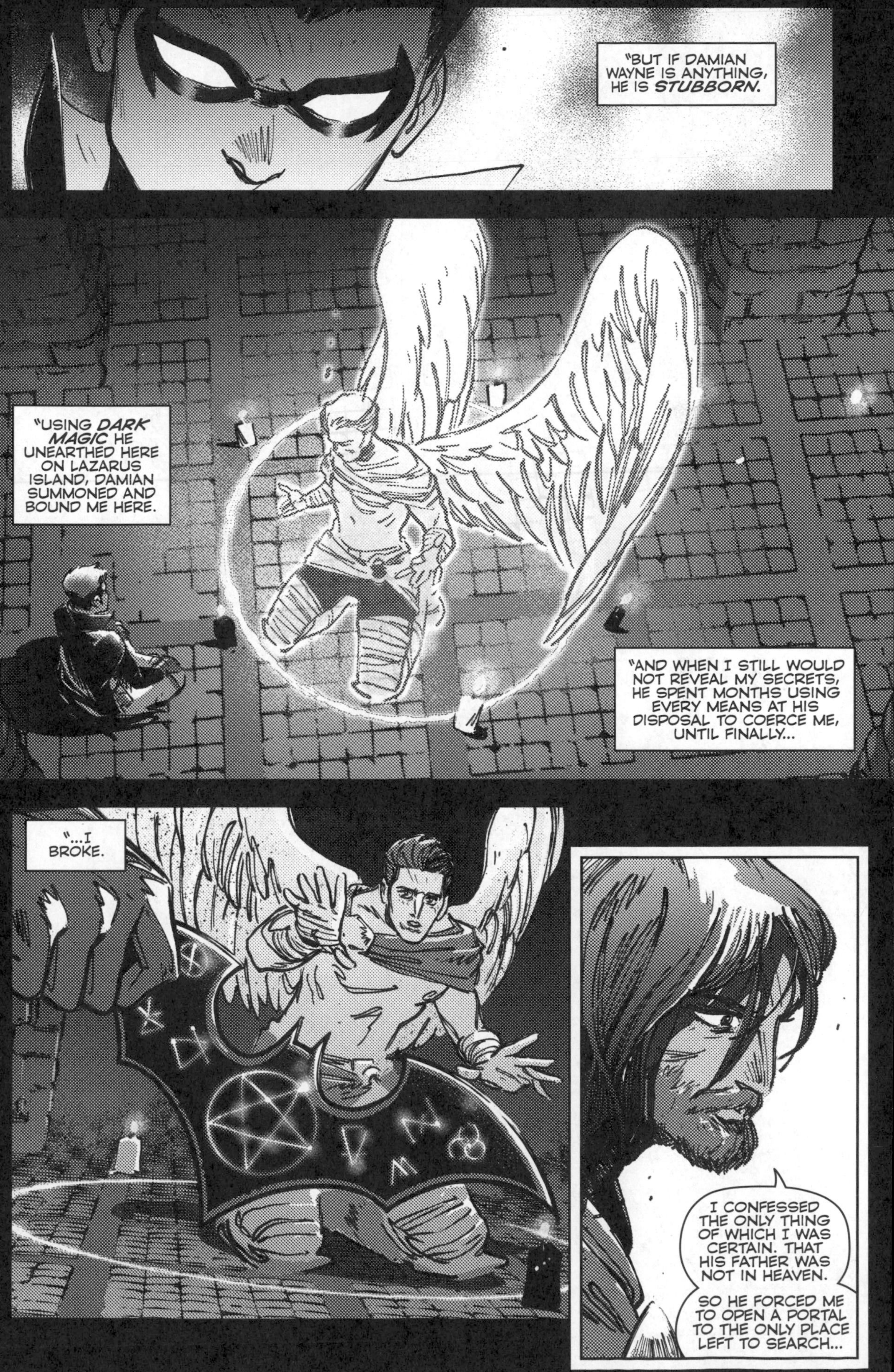
"BUT IF DAMIAN WAYNE IS ANYTHING, HE IS STUBBORN.
"USING DARK MAGIC HE UNEARTHED HERE ON LAZARUS ISLAND, DAMIAN SUMMONED AND BOUND ME HERE.
"AND WHEN I STILL WOULD NOT REVEAL MY SECRETS, HE SPENT MONTHS USING EVERY MEANS AT HIS DISPOSAL TO COERCE ME, UNTIL FINALLY...
"...I BROKE.
I CONFESSED THE ONLY THING OF WHICH I WAS CERTAIN. THAT HIS FATHER WAS NOT IN HEAVEN.
SO HE FORCED ME TO OPEN A PORTAL TO THE ONLY PLACE LEFT TO SEARCH...

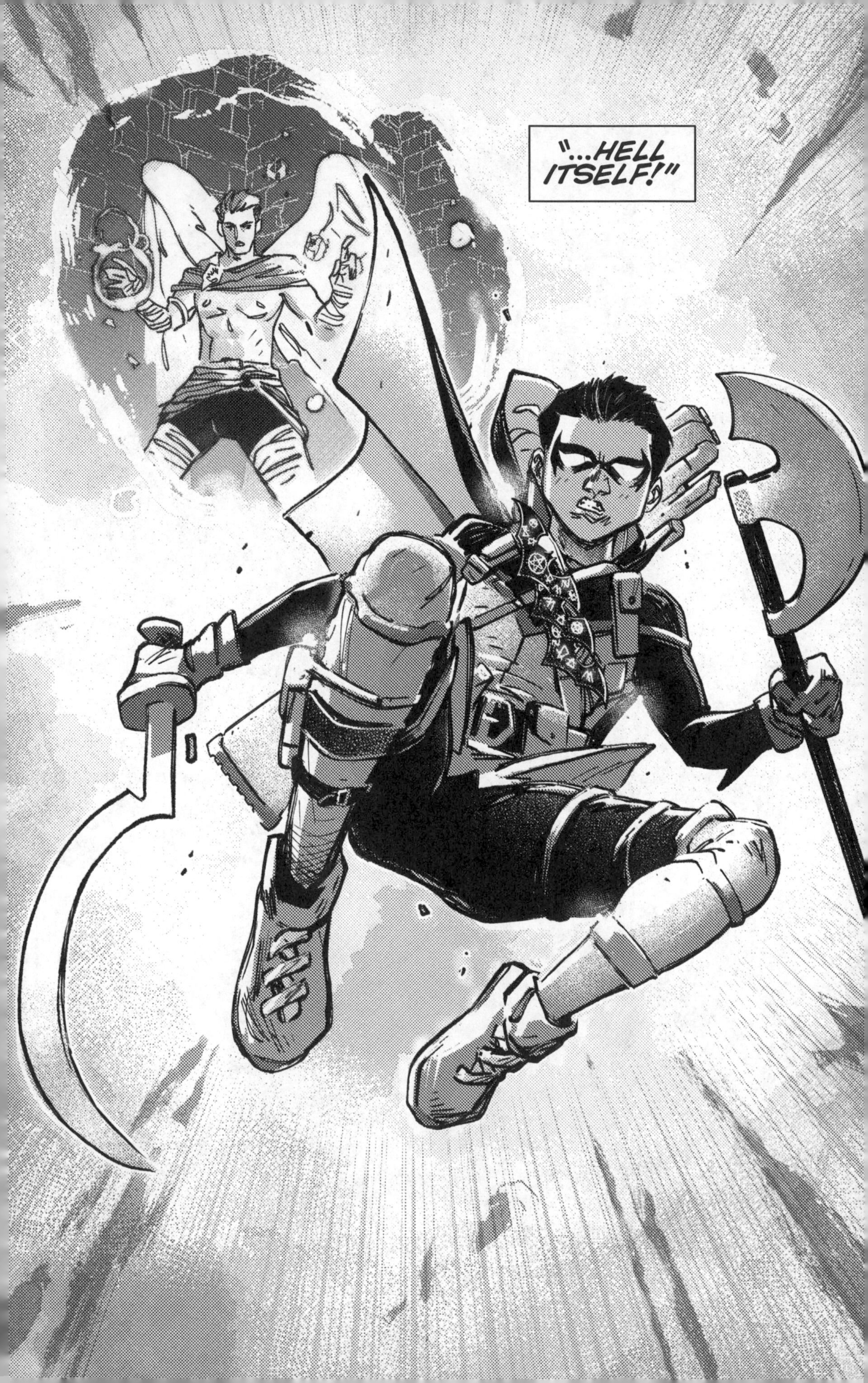
"...HELL ITSELF!"

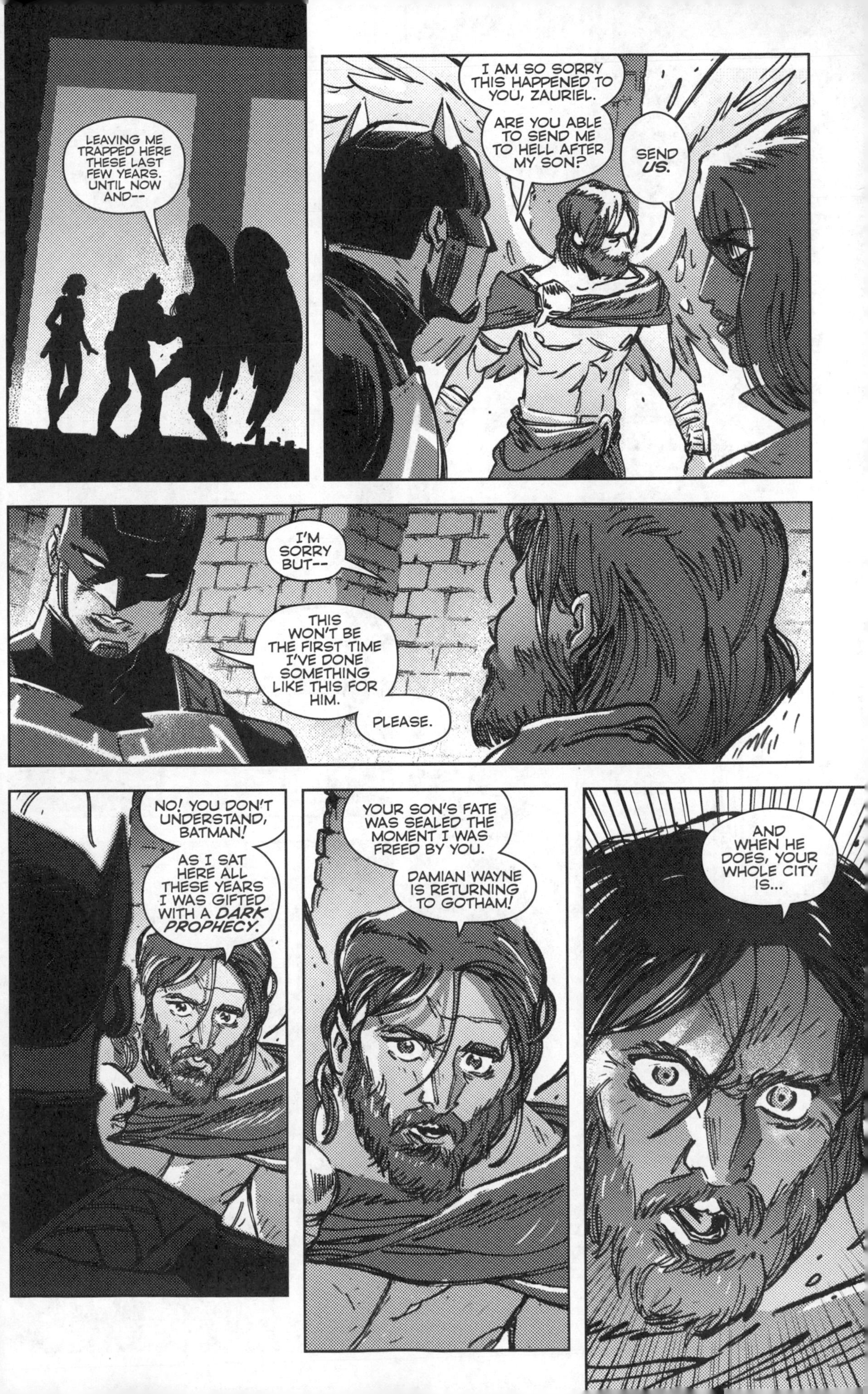

LEAVING ME TRAPPED HERE THESE LAST FEW YEARS. UNTIL NOW AND--
I AM SO SORRY THIS HAPPENED TO YOU, ZAURIEL.
ARE YOU ABLE TO SEND ME TO HELL AFTER MY SON?
SEND *US*.
I'M SORRY BUT--
THIS WON'T BE THE FIRST TIME I'VE DONE SOMETHING LIKE THIS FOR HIM.
PLEASE.
NO! YOU DON'T UNDERSTAND, BATMAN!
AS I SAT HERE ALL THESE YEARS I WAS GIFTED WITH A *DARK PROPHECY*.
YOUR SON'S FATE WAS SEALED THE MOMENT I WAS FREED BY YOU.
DAMIAN WAYNE IS RETURNING TO GOTHAM!
AND WHEN HE DOES, YOUR WHOLE CITY IS...

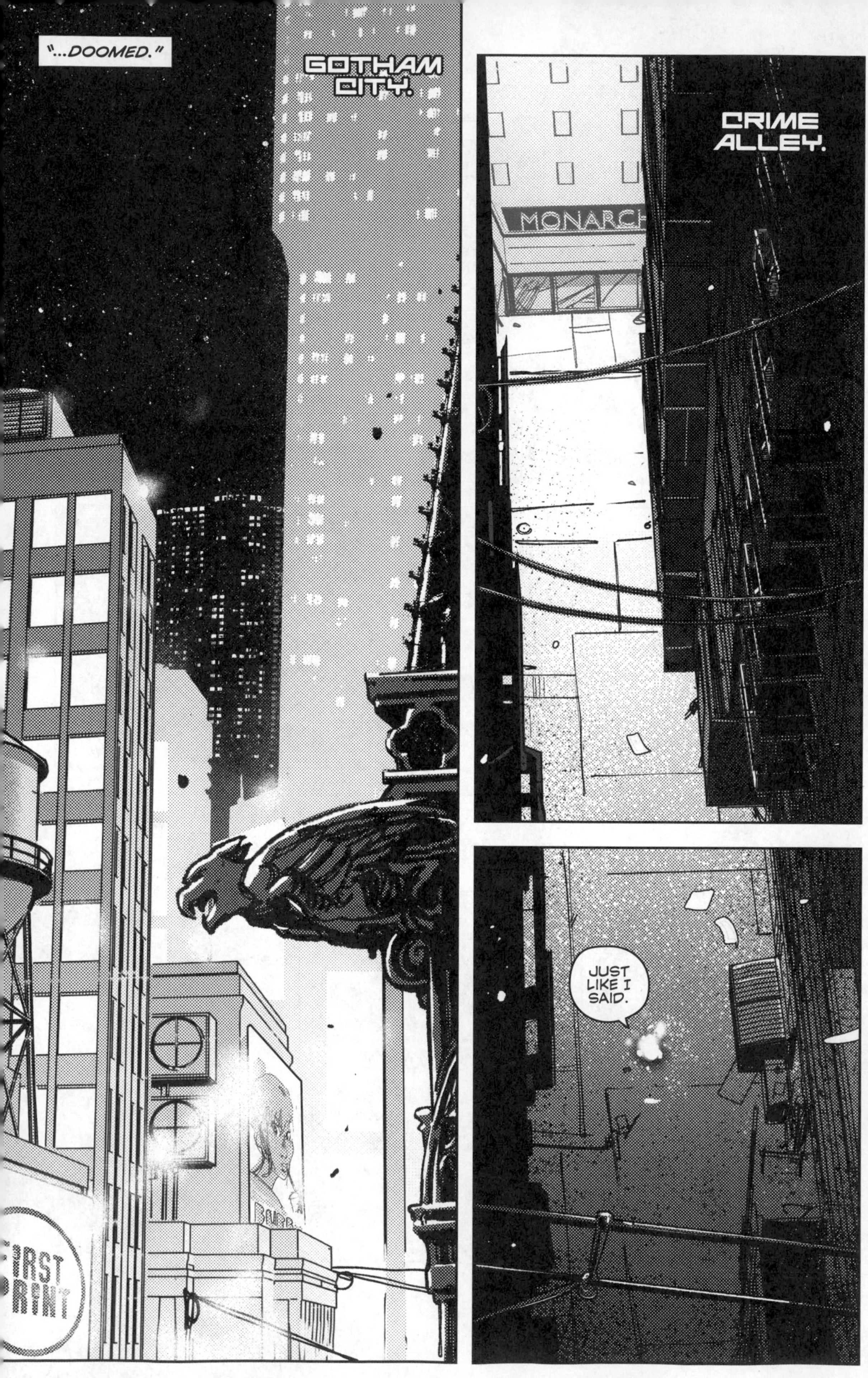
"...DOOMED."
GOTHAM CITY.
CRIME ALLEY.
JUST LIKE I SAID.

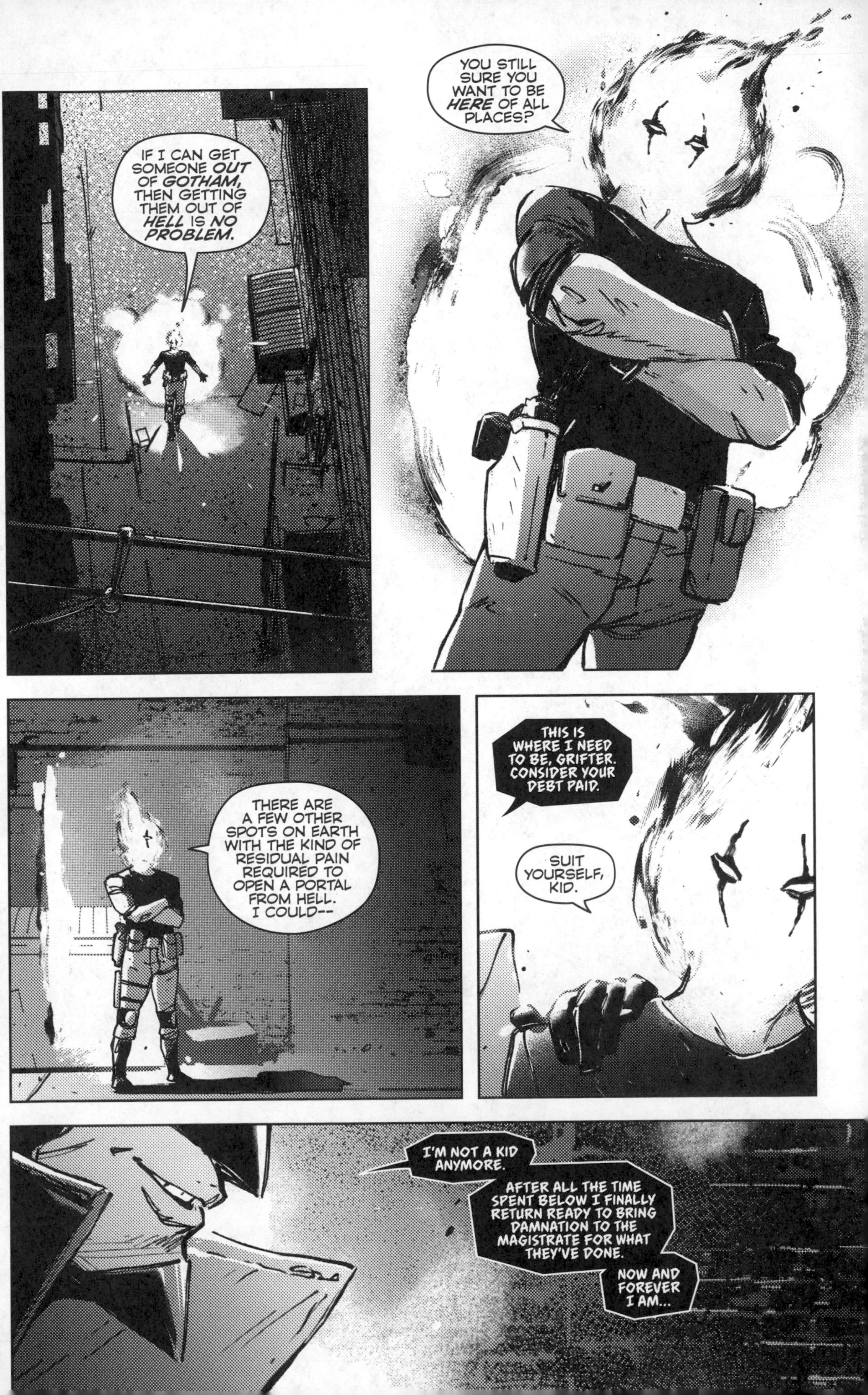
IF I CAN GET SOMEONE OUT OF GOTHAM, THEN GETTING THEM OUT OF HELL IS NO PROBLEM.
YOU STILL SURE YOU WANT TO BE HERE OF ALL PLACES?
THERE ARE A FEW OTHER SPOTS ON EARTH WITH THE KIND OF RESIDUAL PAIN REQUIRED TO OPEN A PORTAL FROM HELL. I COULD--
THIS IS WHERE I NEED TO BE, GRIFTER. CONSIDER YOUR DEBT PAID.
SUIT YOURSELF, KID.
I'M NOT A KID ANYMORE.
AFTER ALL THE TIME SPENT BELOW I FINALLY RETURN READY TO BRING DAMNATION TO THE MAGISTRATE FOR WHAT THEY'VE DONE.
NOW AND FOREVER I AM...

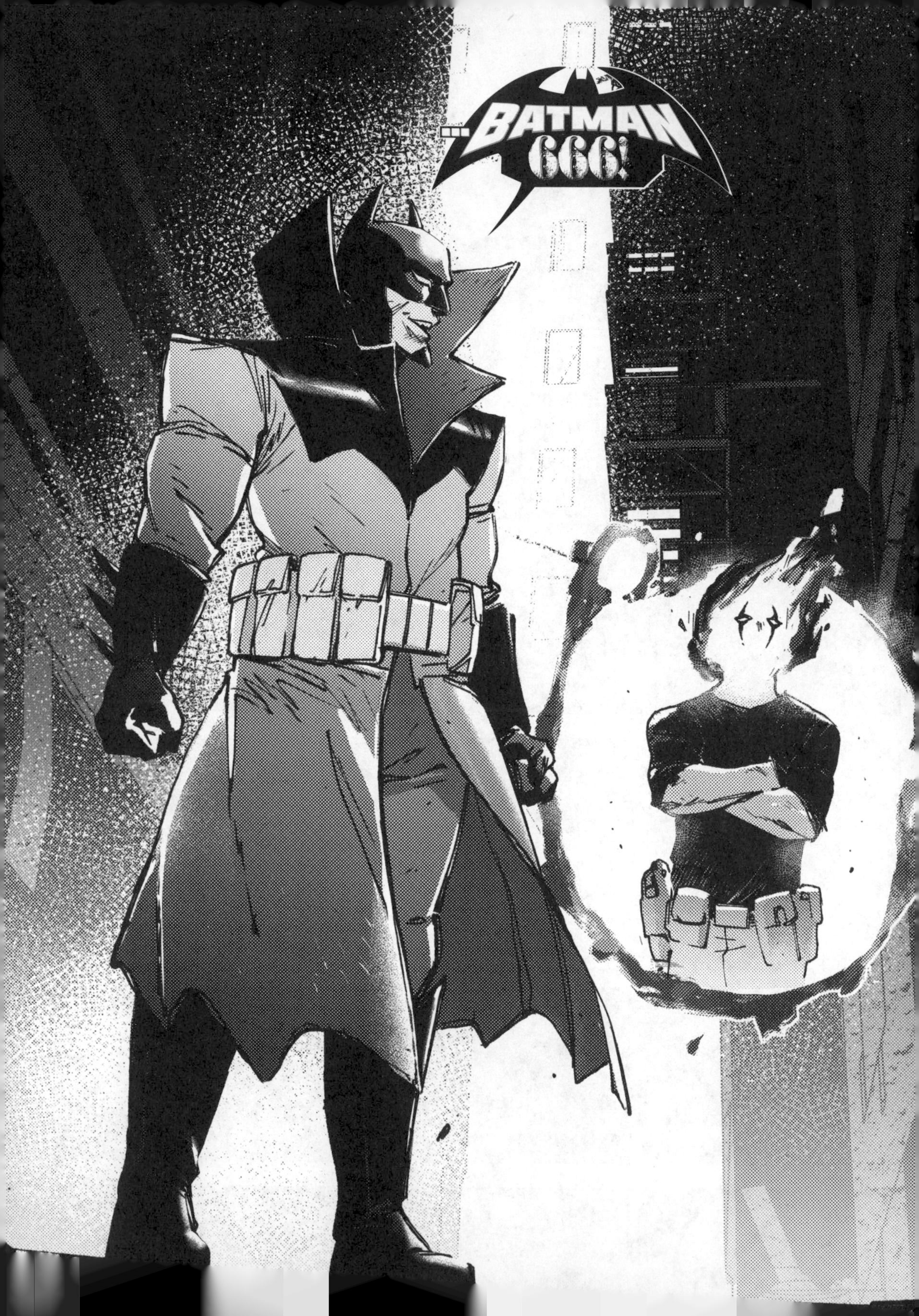
...BATMAN
666!

Future State: Gotham #14
cover art by SIMONE DI MEO

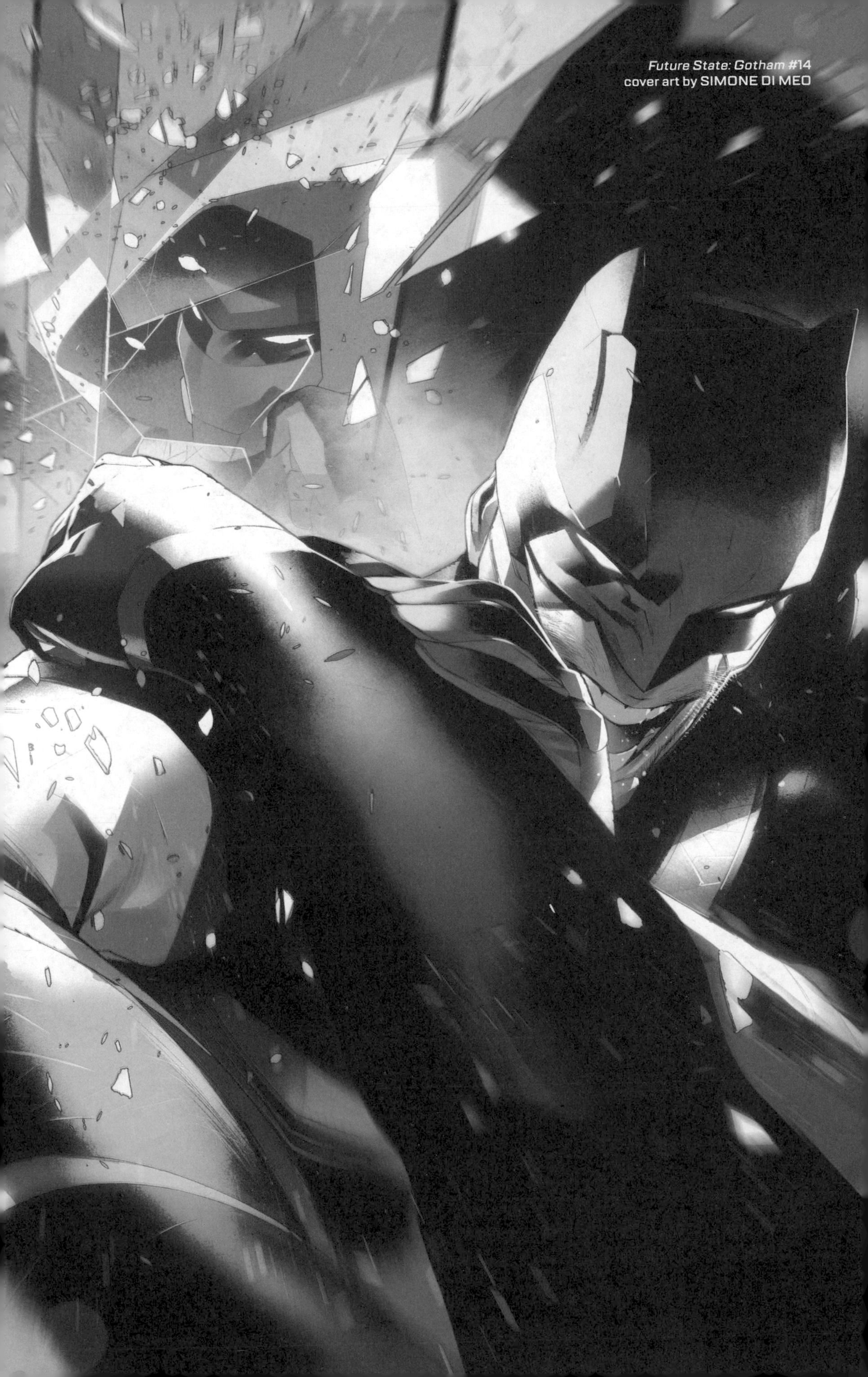

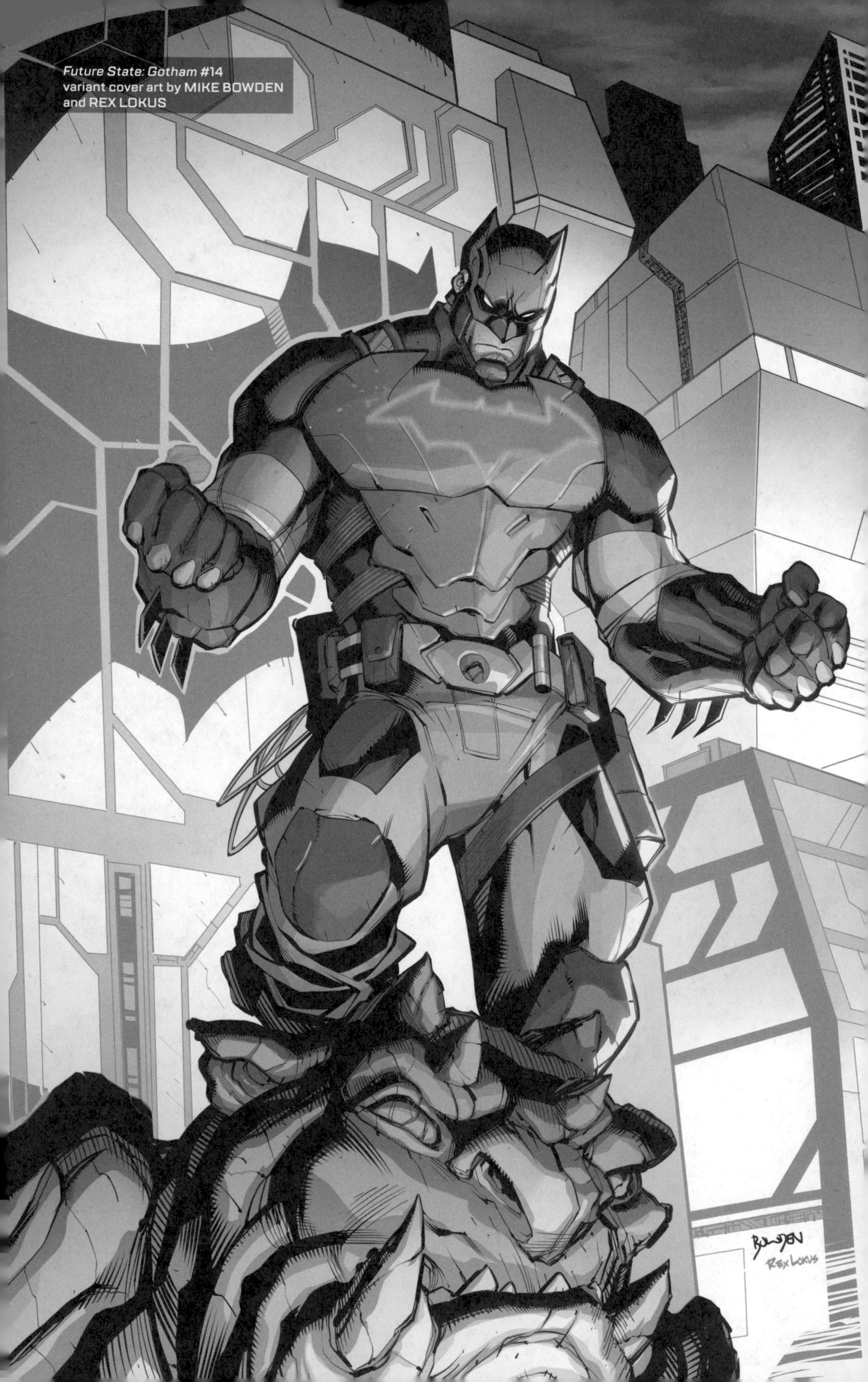
BOWDEN
REX LOKUS

Future State: Gotham #14
variant cover art by MIKE BOWDEN
and REX LOKUS

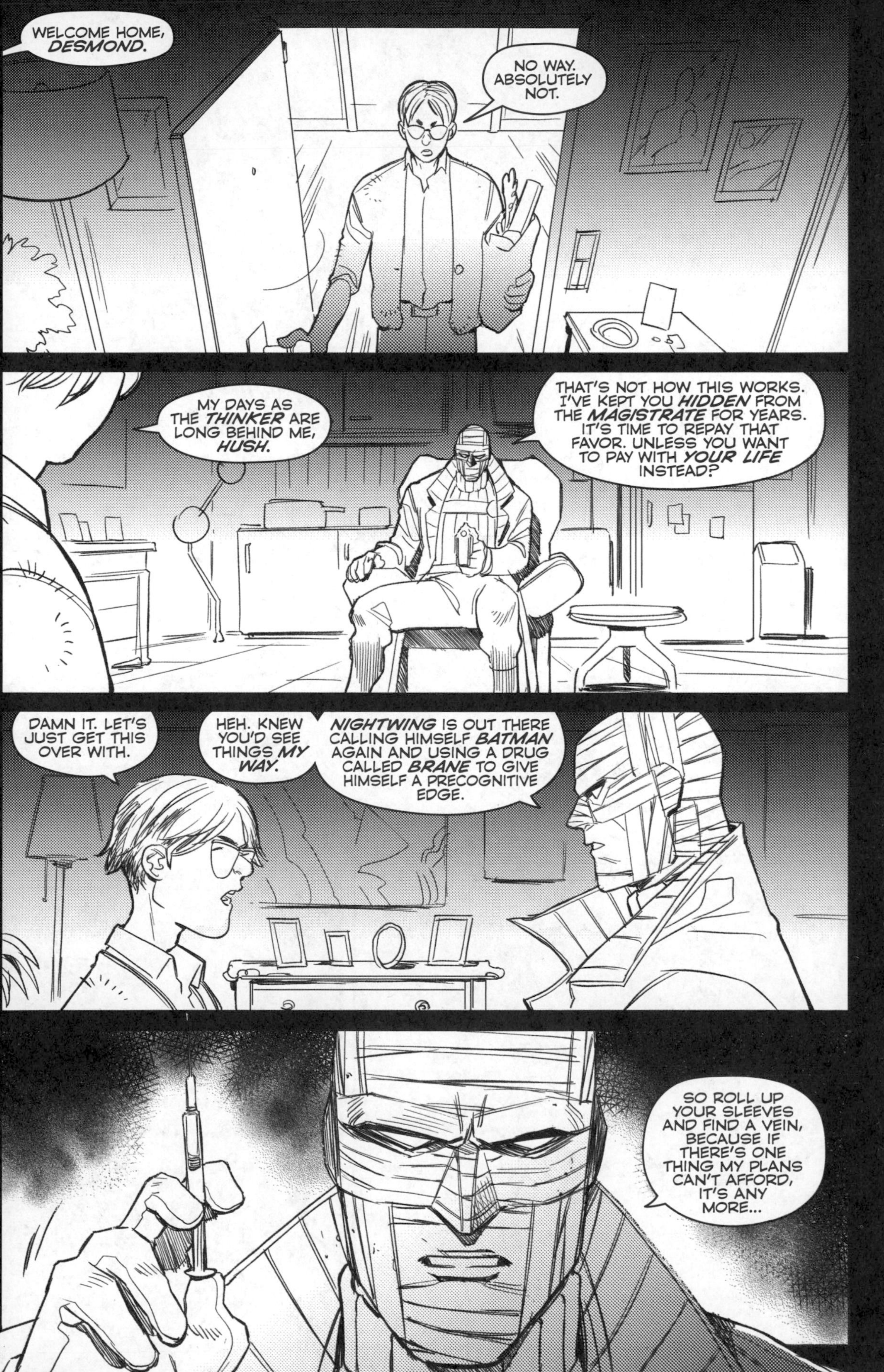
WELCOME HOME, DESMOND.
NO WAY. ABSOLUTELY NOT.
MY DAYS AS THE THINKER ARE LONG BEHIND ME, HUSH.
THAT'S NOT HOW THIS WORKS. I'VE KEPT YOU HIDDEN FROM THE MAGISTRATE FOR YEARS. IT'S TIME TO REPAY THAT FAVOR. UNLESS YOU WANT TO PAY WITH YOUR LIFE INSTEAD?
DAMN IT. LET'S JUST GET THIS OVER WITH.
HEH. KNEW YOU'D SEE THINGS MY WAY.
NIGHTWING IS OUT THERE CALLING HIMSELF BATMAN AGAIN AND USING A DRUG CALLED BRANE TO GIVE HIMSELF A PRECOGNITIVE EDGE.
SO ROLL UP YOUR SLEEVES AND FIND A VEIN, BECAUSE IF THERE'S ONE THING MY PLANS CAN'T AFFORD, IT'S ANY MORE...

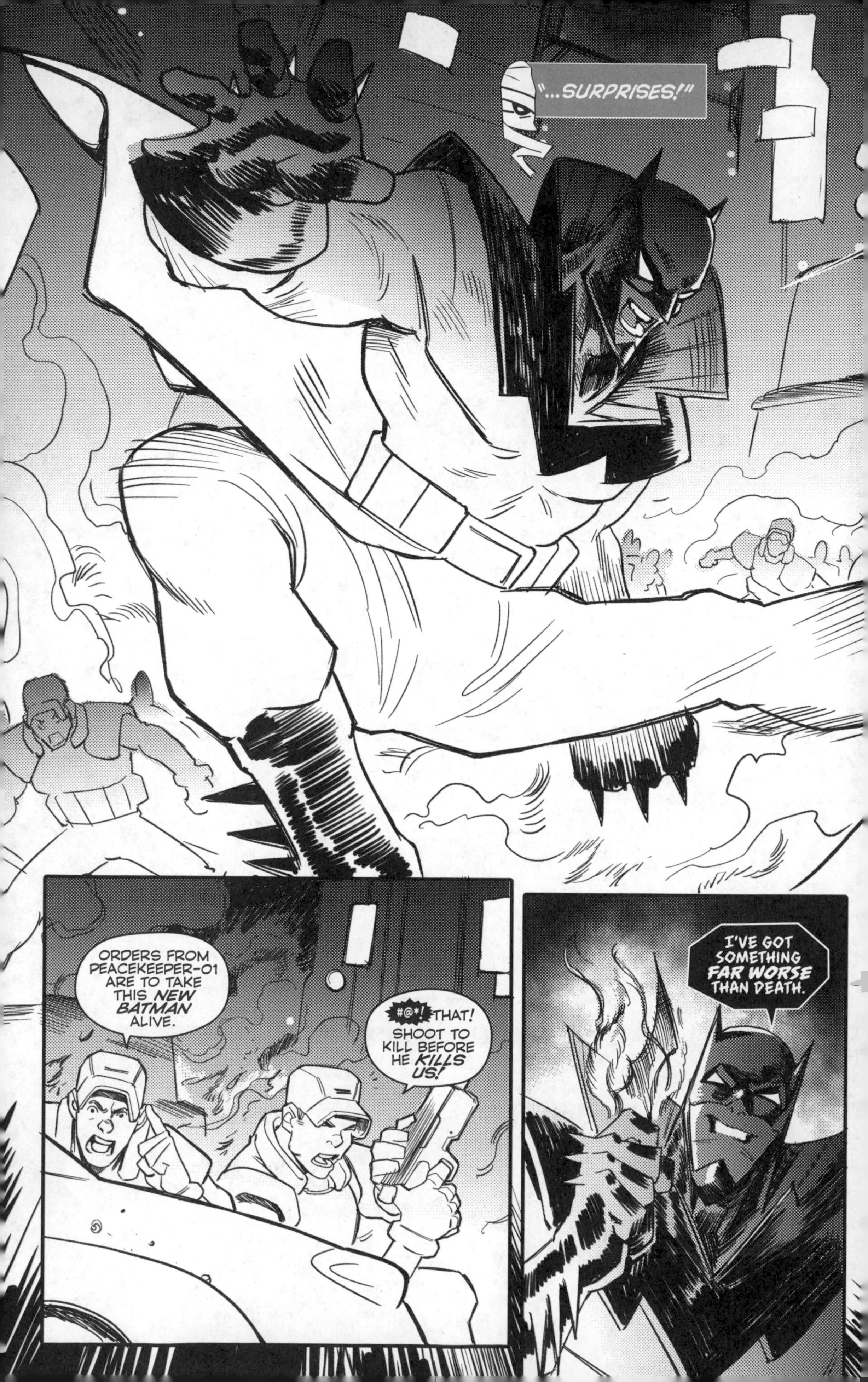
"...SURPRISES!"
ORDERS FROM PEACEKEEPER-01 ARE TO TAKE THIS NEW BATMAN ALIVE.
#@*! THAT! SHOOT TO KILL BEFORE HE KILLS US!
I'VE GOT SOMETHING FAR WORSE THAN DEATH.

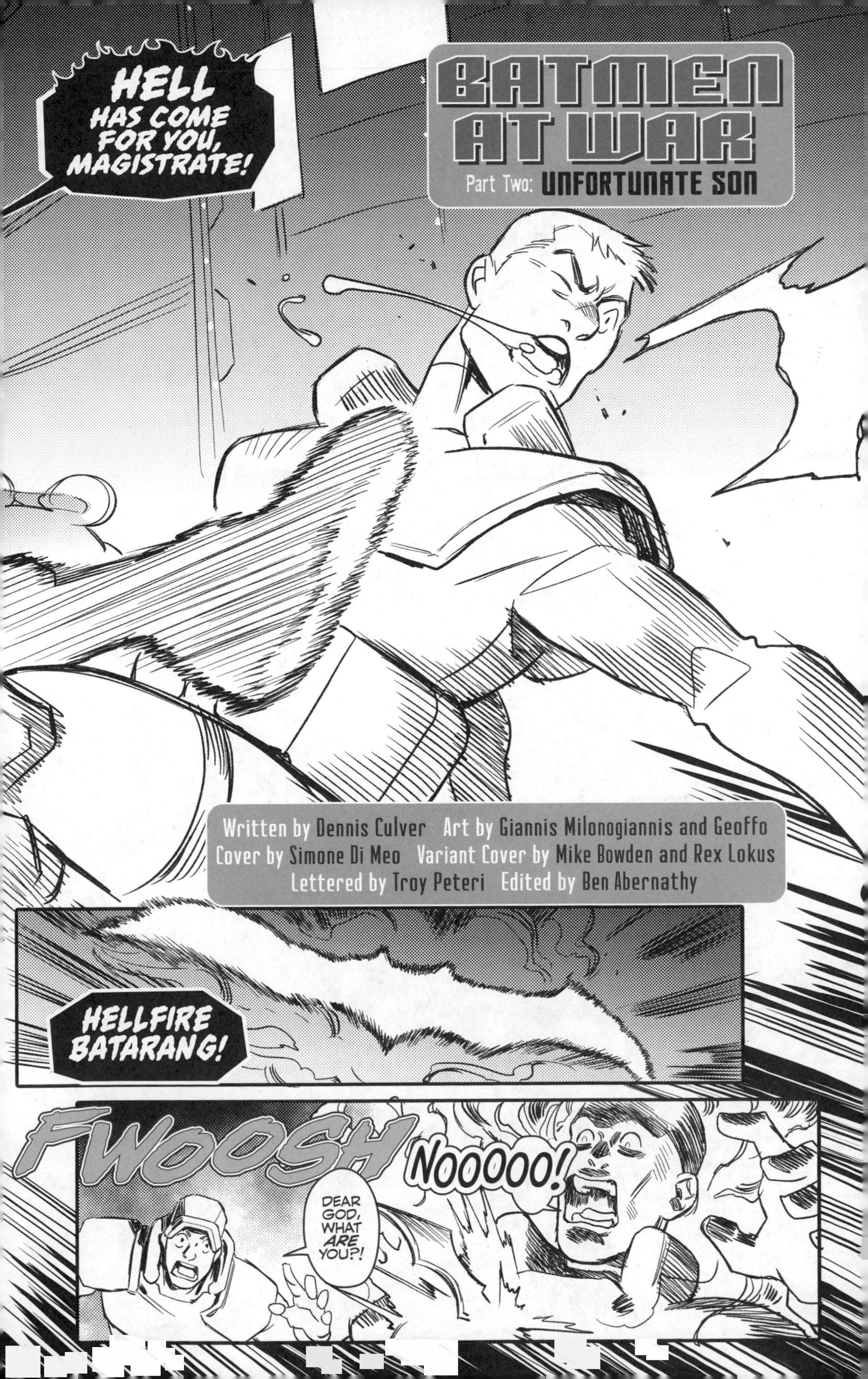
HELL HAS COME FOR YOU, MAGISTRATE!
BATMEN AT WAR
Part Two: UNFORTUNATE SON
Written by Dennis Culver Art by Giannis Milonogiannis and Geoffo
Cover by Simone Di Meo Variant Cover by Mike Bowden and Rex Lokus
Lettered by Troy Peteri Edited by Ben Abernathy
HELLFIRE BATARANG!
FWOOSH
NOOOOO!
DEAR GOD, WHAT ARE YOU?!

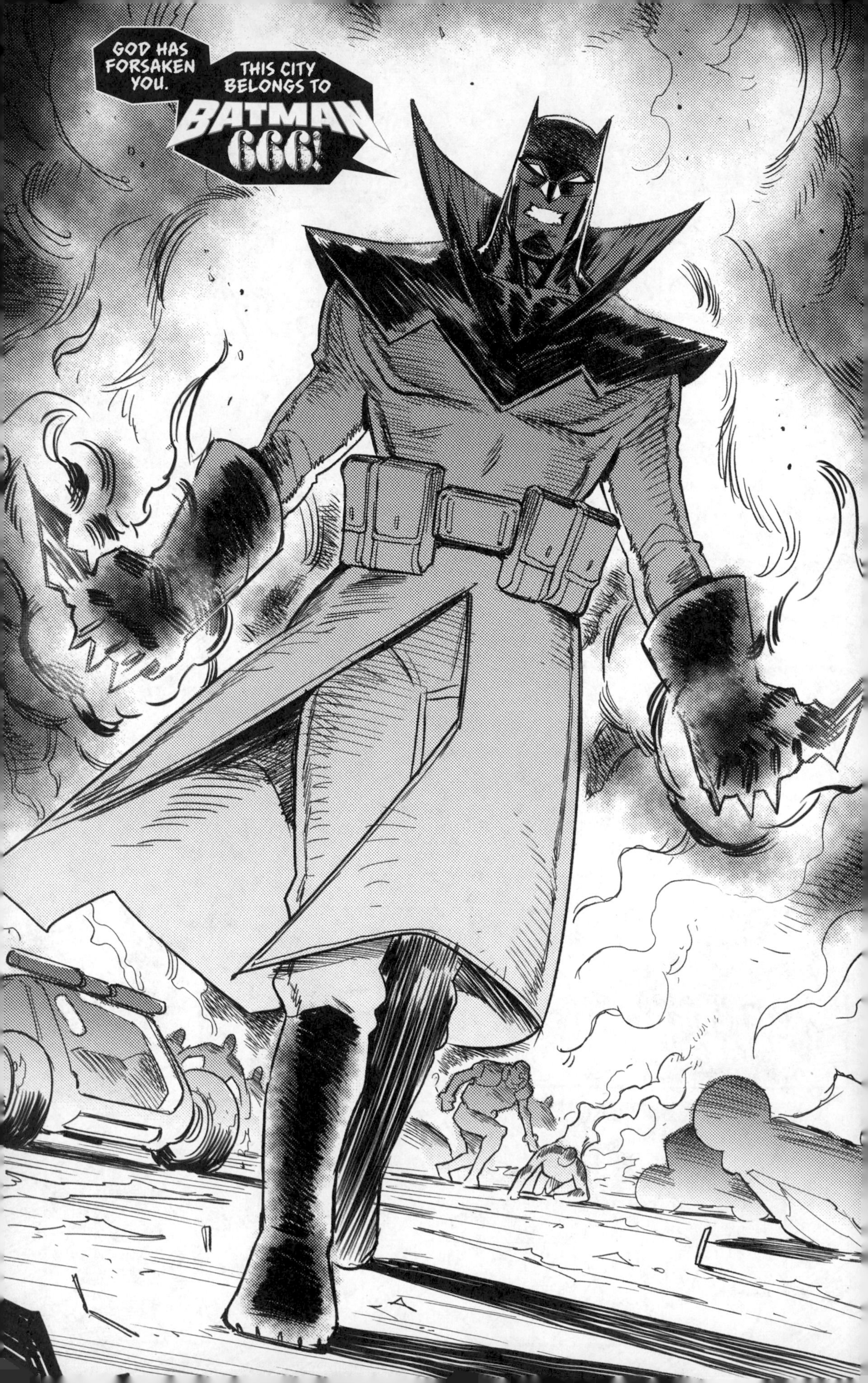
GOD HAS FORSAKEN YOU.
THIS CITY BELONGS TO BATMAN 666!

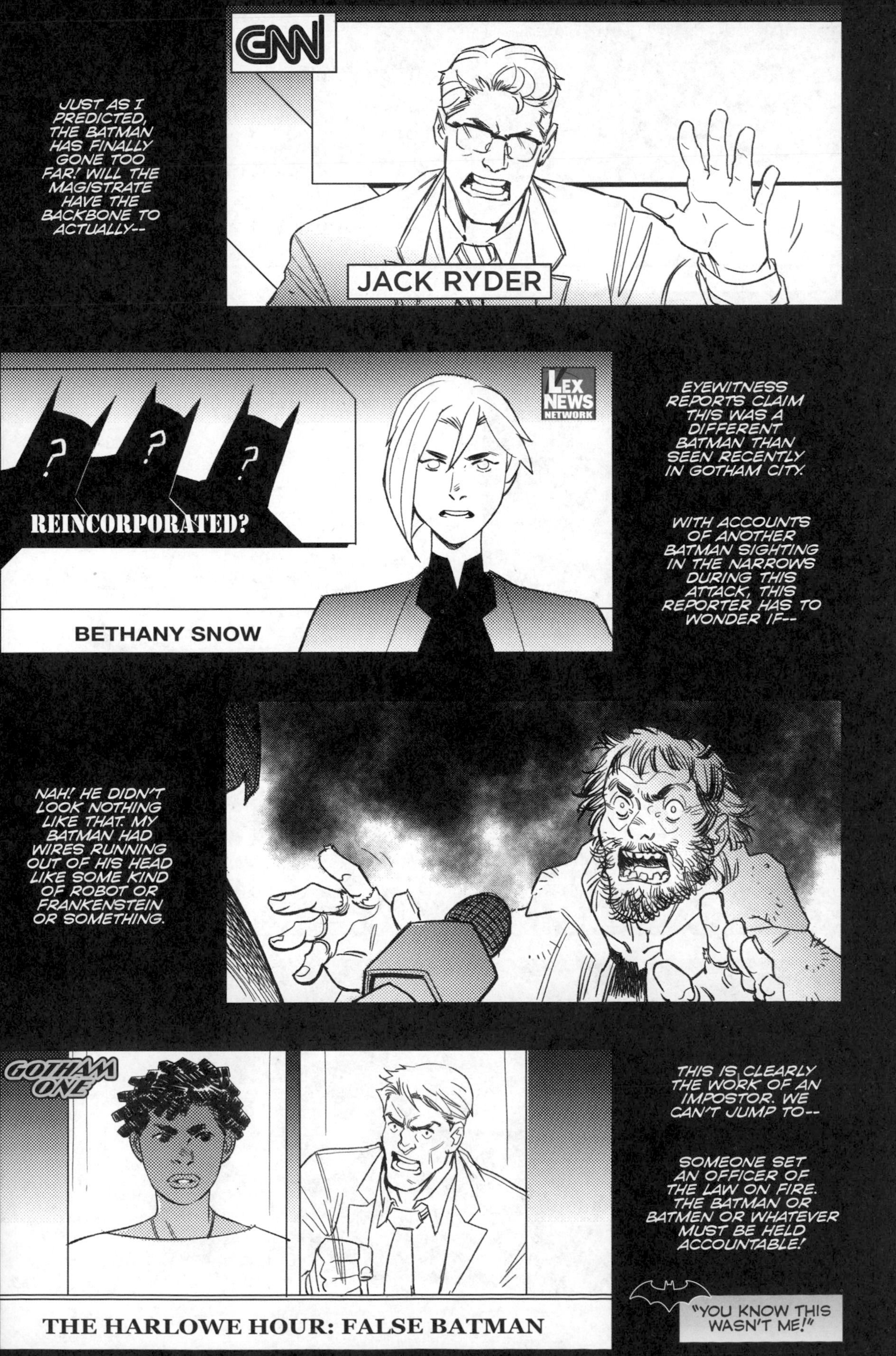
CNN
JUST AS I PREDICTED, THE BATMAN HAS FINALLY GONE TOO FAR! WILL THE MAGISTRATE HAVE THE BACKBONE TO ACTUALLY--
JACK RYDER
LEX NEWS NETWORK
REINCORPORATED?
BETHANY SNOW
EYEWITNESS REPORTS CLAIM THIS WAS A DIFFERENT BATMAN THAN SEEN RECENTLY IN GOTHAM CITY.
WITH ACCOUNTS OF ANOTHER BATMAN SIGHTING IN THE NARROWS DURING THIS ATTACK, THIS REPORTER HAS TO WONDER IF--
NAH! HE DIDN'T LOOK NOTHING LIKE THAT. MY BATMAN HAD WIRES RUNNING OUT OF HIS HEAD LIKE SOME KIND OF ROBOT OR FRANKENSTEIN OR SOMETHING.
GOTHAM ONE
THIS IS CLEARLY THE WORK OF AN IMPOSTOR. WE CAN'T JUMP TO--
SOMEONE SET AN OFFICER OF THE LAW ON FIRE. THE BATMAN OR BATMEN OR WHATEVER MUST BE HELD ACCOUNTABLE!
THE HARLOWE HOUR: FALSE BATMAN
"YOU KNOW THIS WASN'T ME!"

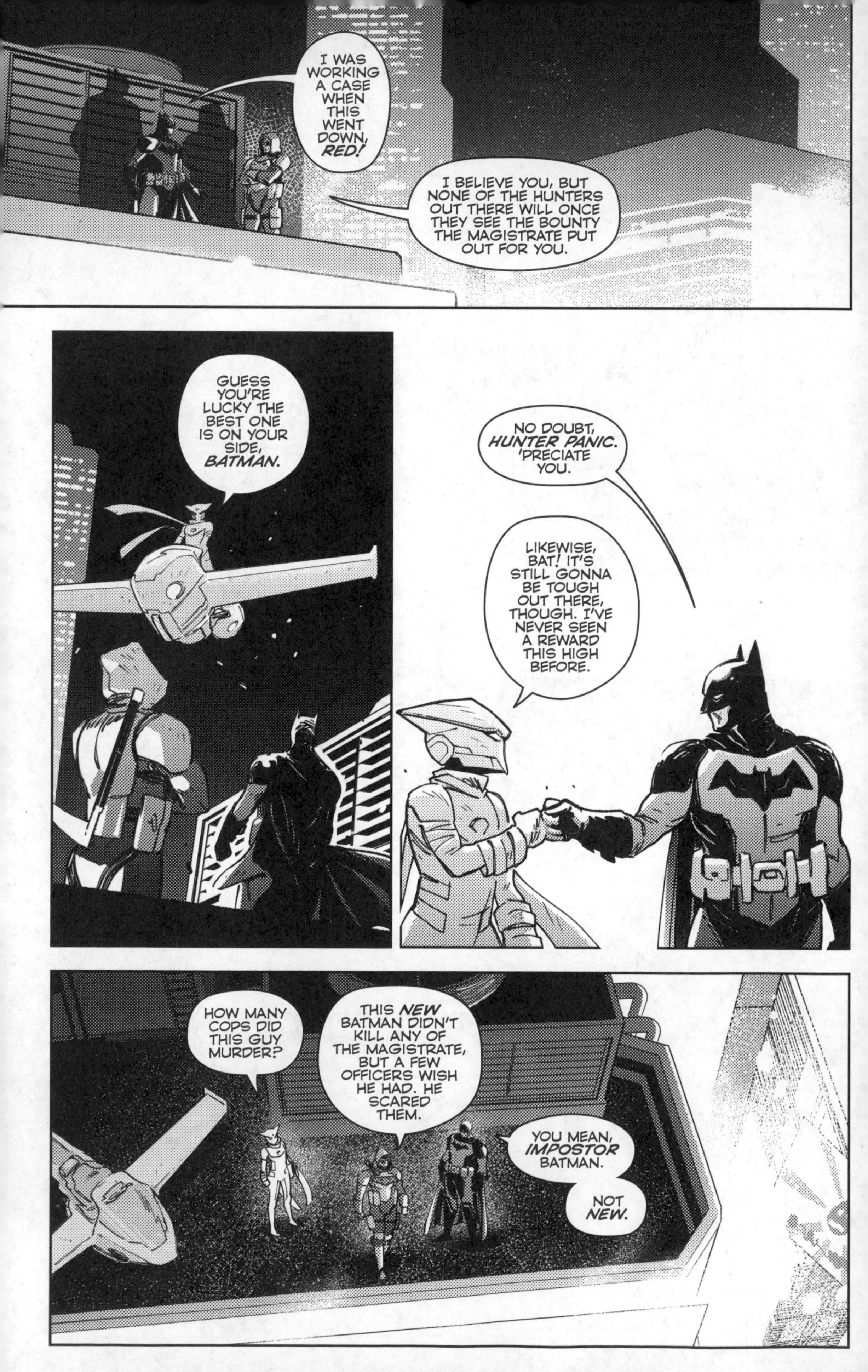
I WAS WORKING A CASE WHEN THIS WENT DOWN, *RED!*
I BELIEVE YOU, BUT NONE OF THE HUNTERS OUT THERE WILL ONCE THEY SEE THE BOUNTY THE MAGISTRATE PUT OUT FOR YOU.
GUESS YOU'RE LUCKY THE BEST ONE IS ON YOUR SIDE, *BATMAN.*
NO DOUBT, *HUNTER PANIC.* 'PRECIATE YOU.
LIKEWISE, BAT! IT'S STILL GONNA BE TOUGH OUT THERE, THOUGH. I'VE NEVER SEEN A REWARD THIS HIGH BEFORE.
HOW MANY COPS DID THIS GUY MURDER?
THIS *NEW* BATMAN DIDN'T KILL ANY OF THE MAGISTRATE, BUT A FEW OFFICERS WISH HE HAD. HE SCARED THEM.
YOU MEAN, *IMPOSTOR* BATMAN.
NOT *NEW.*

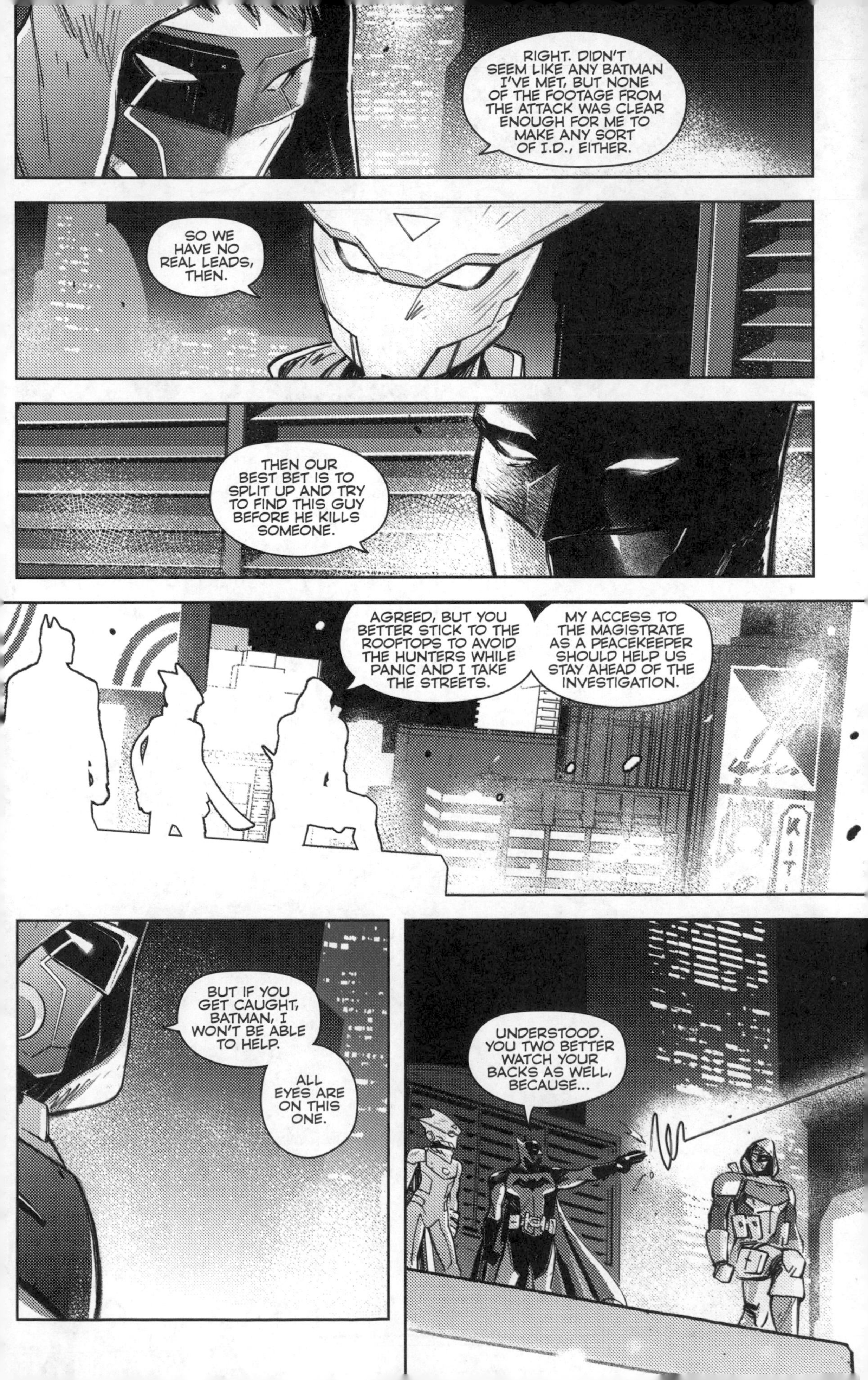
RIGHT. DIDN'T SEEM LIKE ANY BATMAN I'VE MET, BUT NONE OF THE FOOTAGE FROM THE ATTACK WAS CLEAR ENOUGH FOR ME TO MAKE ANY SORT OF I.D., EITHER.
SO WE HAVE NO REAL LEADS, THEN.
THEN OUR BEST BET IS TO SPLIT UP AND TRY TO FIND THIS GUY BEFORE HE KILLS SOMEONE.
AGREED, BUT YOU BETTER STICK TO THE ROOFTOPS TO AVOID THE HUNTERS WHILE PANIC AND I TAKE THE STREETS.
MY ACCESS TO THE MAGISTRATE AS A PEACEKEEPER SHOULD HELP US STAY AHEAD OF THE INVESTIGATION.
BUT IF YOU GET CAUGHT, BATMAN, I WON'T BE ABLE TO HELP.
ALL EYES ARE ON THIS ONE.
UNDERSTOOD. YOU TWO BETTER WATCH YOUR BACKS AS WELL, BECAUSE...

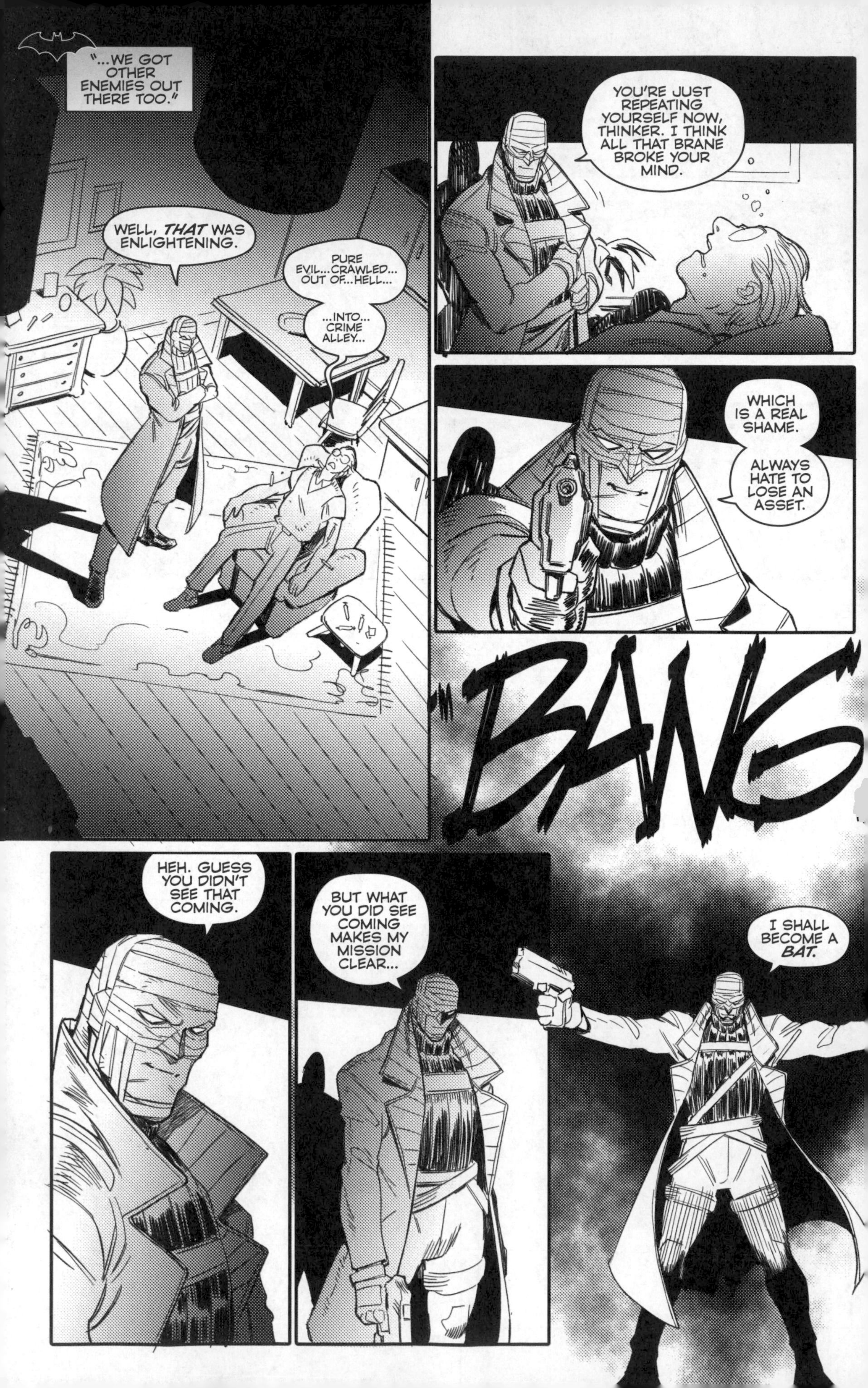
"...WE GOT OTHER ENEMIES OUT THERE TOO."
WELL, THAT WAS ENLIGHTENING.
PURE EVIL...CRAWLED... OUT OF...HELL...
...INTO... CRIME ALLEY...
YOU'RE JUST REPEATING YOURSELF NOW, THINKER. I THINK ALL THAT BRANE BROKE YOUR MIND.
WHICH IS A REAL SHAME.
ALWAYS HATE TO LOSE AN ASSET.
BANG
HEH. GUESS YOU DIDN'T SEE THAT COMING.
BUT WHAT YOU DID SEE COMING MAKES MY MISSION CLEAR...
I SHALL BECOME A BAT.

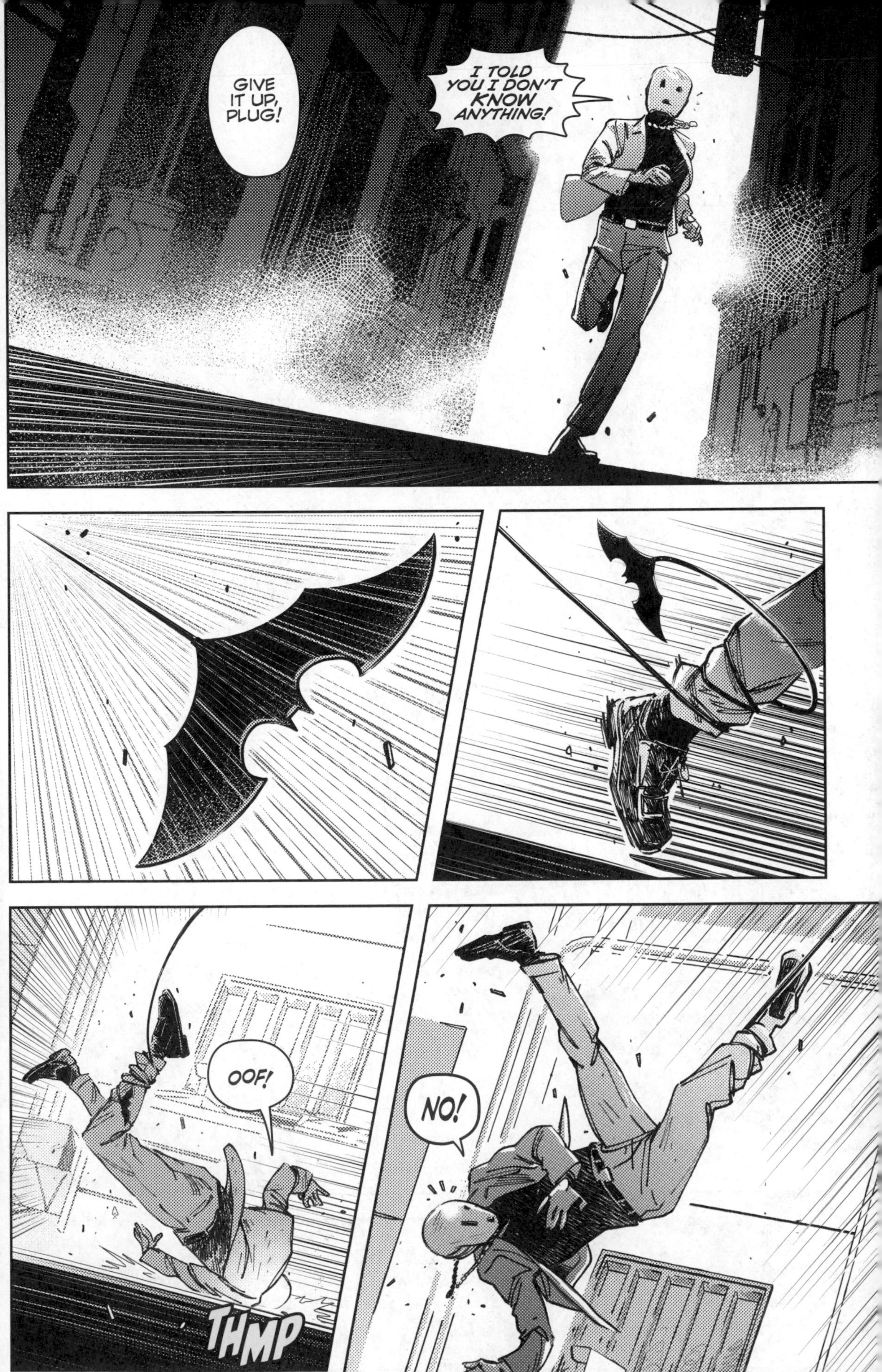
GIVE IT UP, PLUG!
I TOLD YOU I DON'T KNOW ANYTHING!
OOF!
THMP
NO!

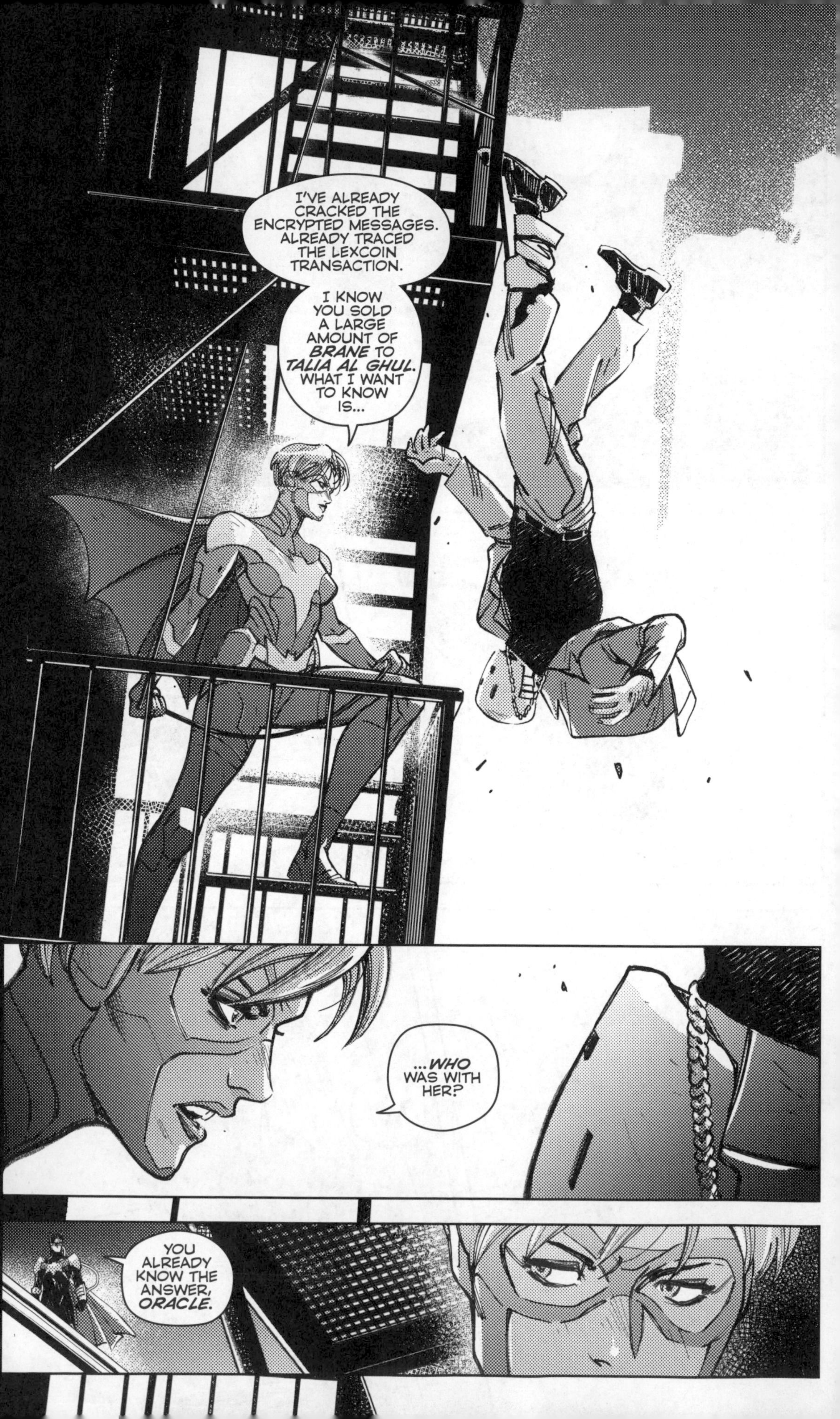
I'VE ALREADY CRACKED THE ENCRYPTED MESSAGES. ALREADY TRACED THE LEXCOIN TRANSACTION.
I KNOW YOU SOLD A LARGE AMOUNT OF BRANE TO TALIA AL GHUL. WHAT I WANT TO KNOW IS...
...WHO WAS WITH HER?
YOU ALREADY KNOW THE ANSWER, ORACLE.

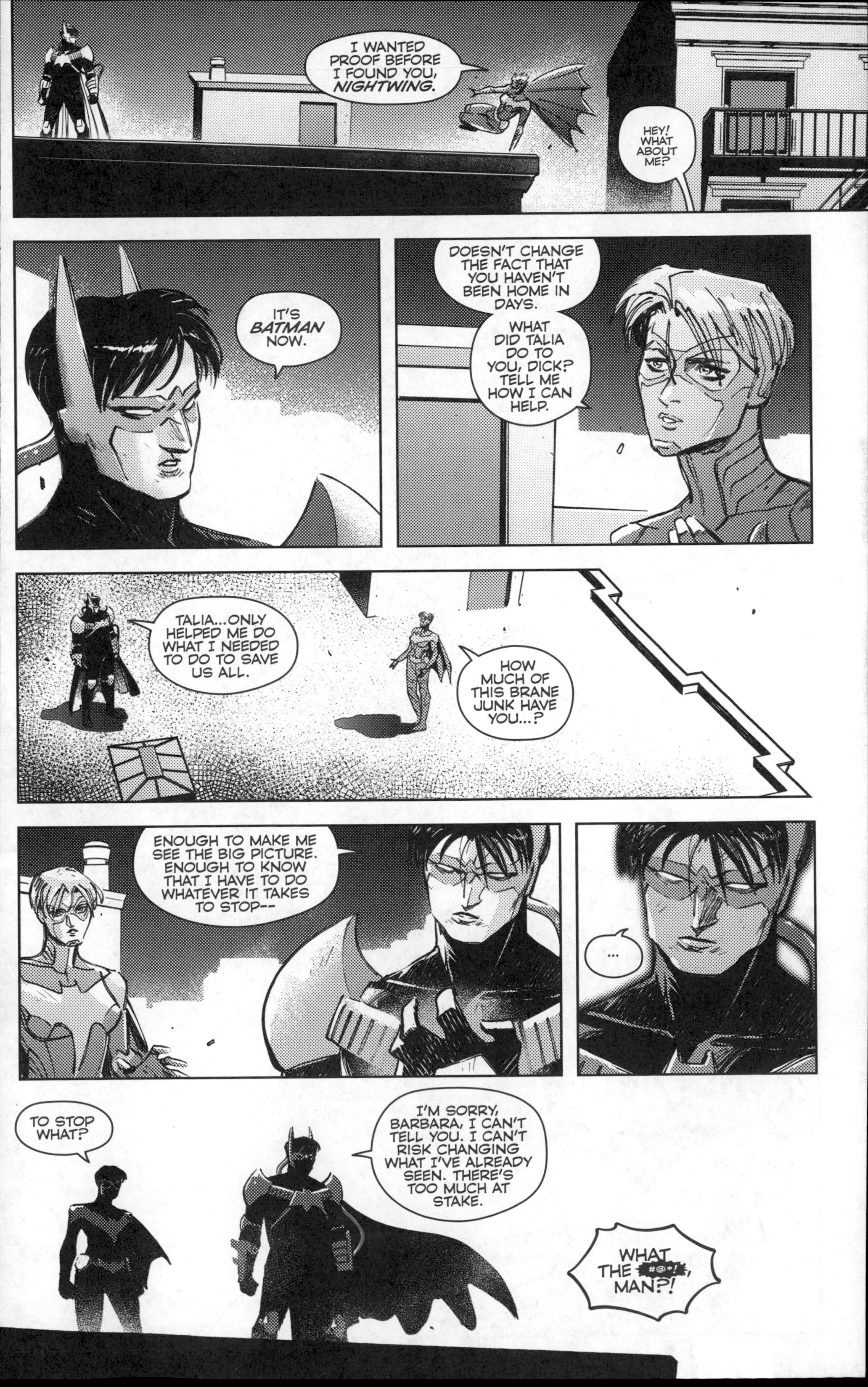

I WANTED PROOF BEFORE I FOUND YOU, NIGHTWING.
HEY! WHAT ABOUT ME?
IT'S BATMAN NOW.
DOESN'T CHANGE THE FACT THAT YOU HAVEN'T BEEN HOME IN DAYS.
WHAT DID TALIA DO TO YOU, DICK? TELL ME HOW I CAN HELP.
TALIA...ONLY HELPED ME DO WHAT I NEEDED TO DO TO SAVE US ALL.
HOW MUCH OF THIS BRANE JUNK HAVE YOU...?
ENOUGH TO MAKE ME SEE THE BIG PICTURE. ENOUGH TO KNOW THAT I HAVE TO DO WHATEVER IT TAKES TO STOP--
...
TO STOP WHAT?
I'M SORRY, BARBARA, I CAN'T TELL YOU. I CAN'T RISK CHANGING WHAT I'VE ALREADY SEEN. THERE'S TOO MUCH AT STAKE.
WHAT THE #@*!, MAN?!

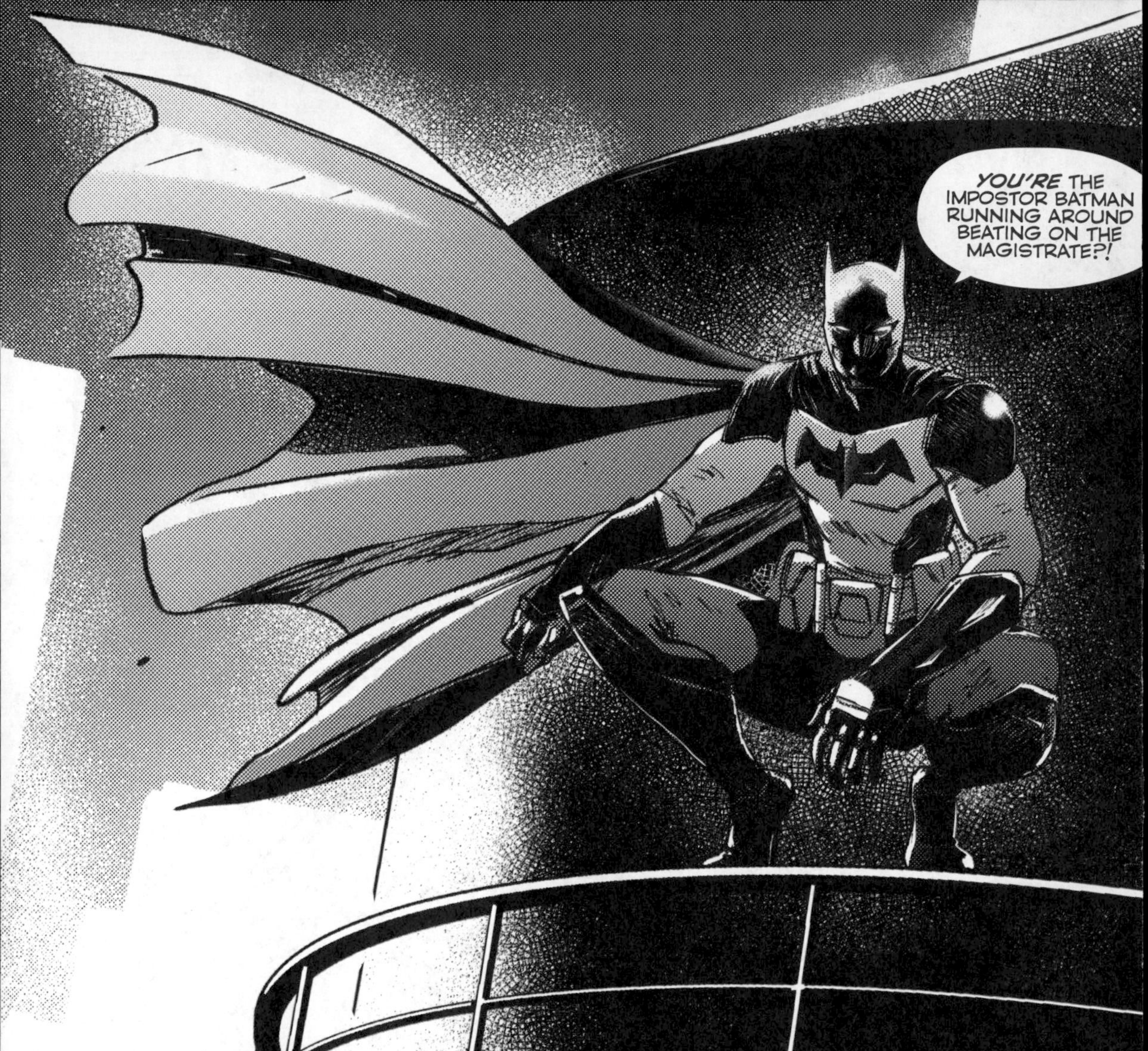
YOU'RE THE IMPOSTOR BATMAN RUNNING AROUND BEATING ON THE MAGISTRATE?!

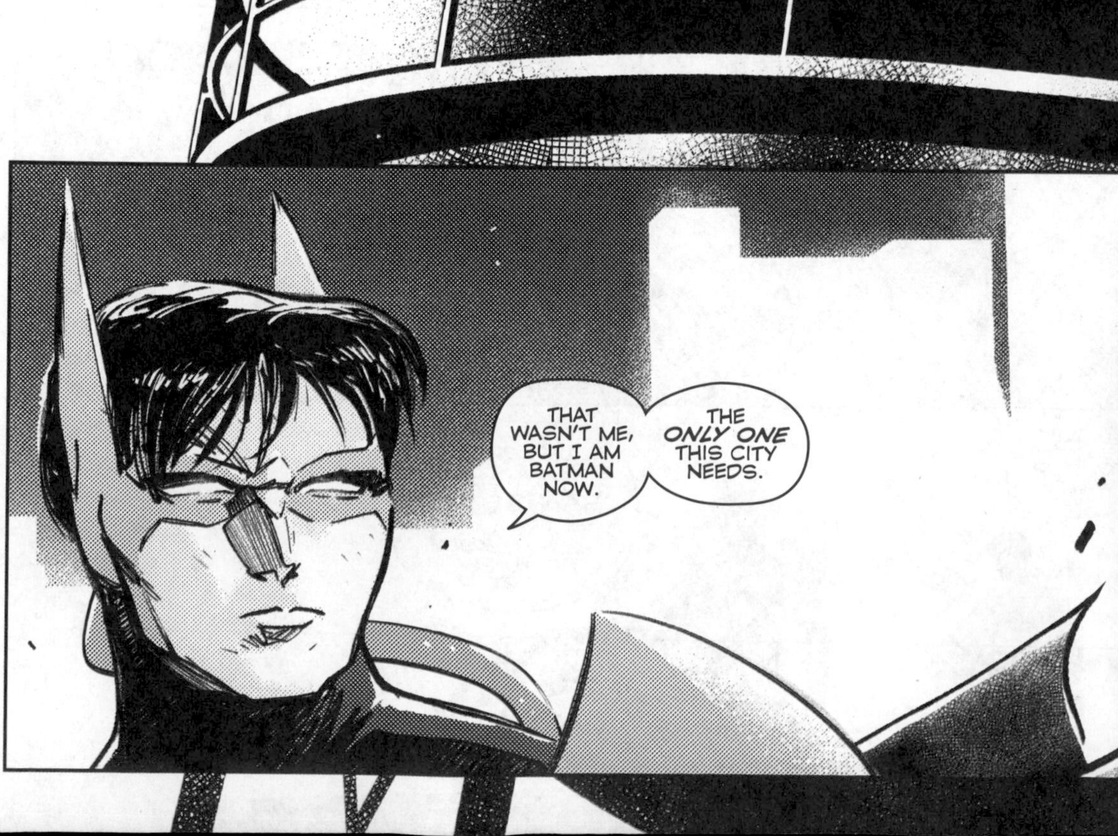
THAT WASN'T ME, BUT I AM BATMAN NOW.
THE *ONLY ONE* THIS CITY NEEDS.

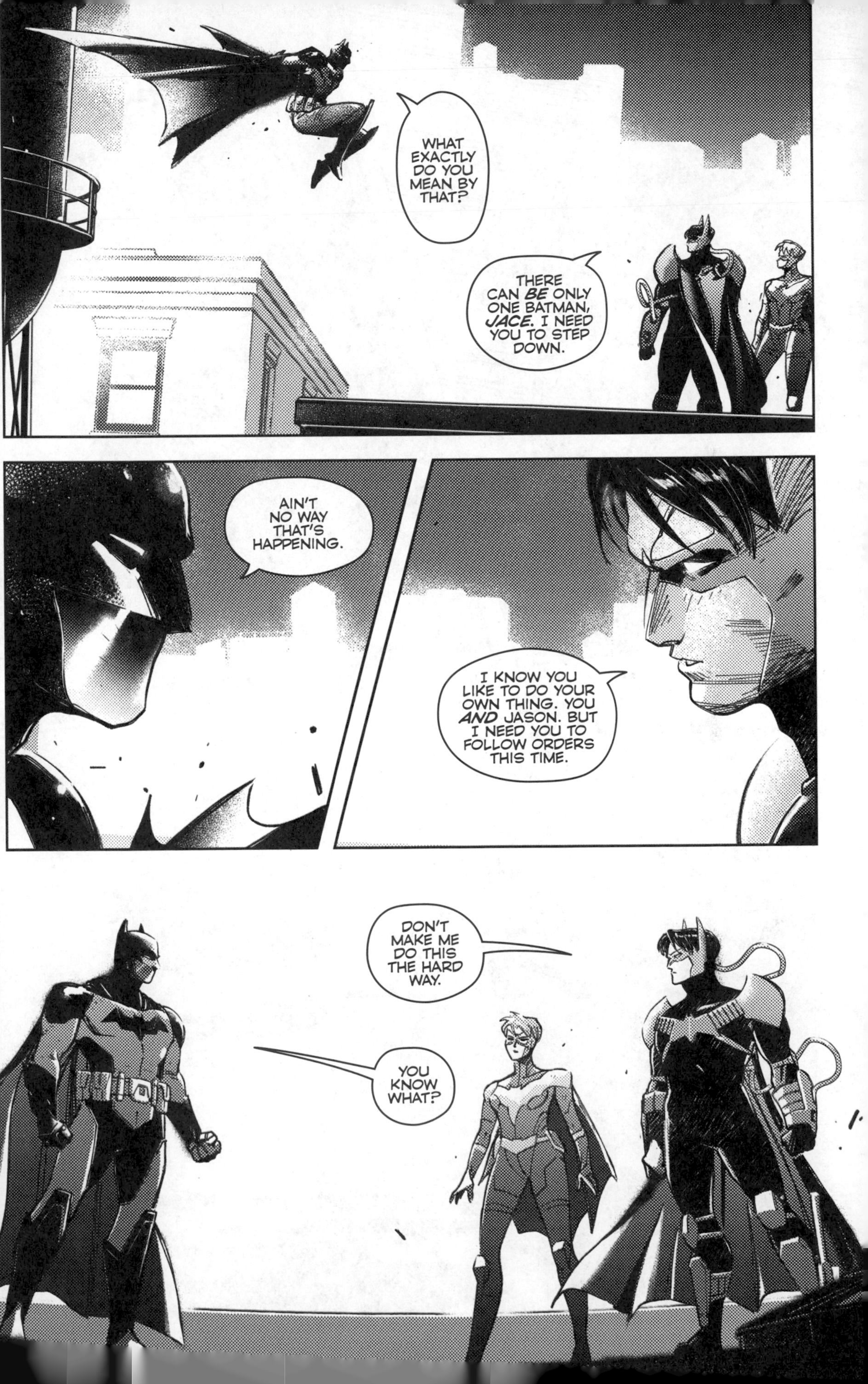

WHAT EXACTLY DO YOU MEAN BY THAT?
THERE CAN *BE* ONLY ONE BATMAN, *JACE*. I NEED YOU TO STEP DOWN.
AIN'T NO WAY THAT'S HAPPENING.
I KNOW YOU LIKE TO DO YOUR OWN THING. YOU *AND* JASON. BUT I NEED YOU TO FOLLOW ORDERS THIS TIME.
DON'T MAKE ME DO THIS THE HARD WAY.
YOU KNOW WHAT?

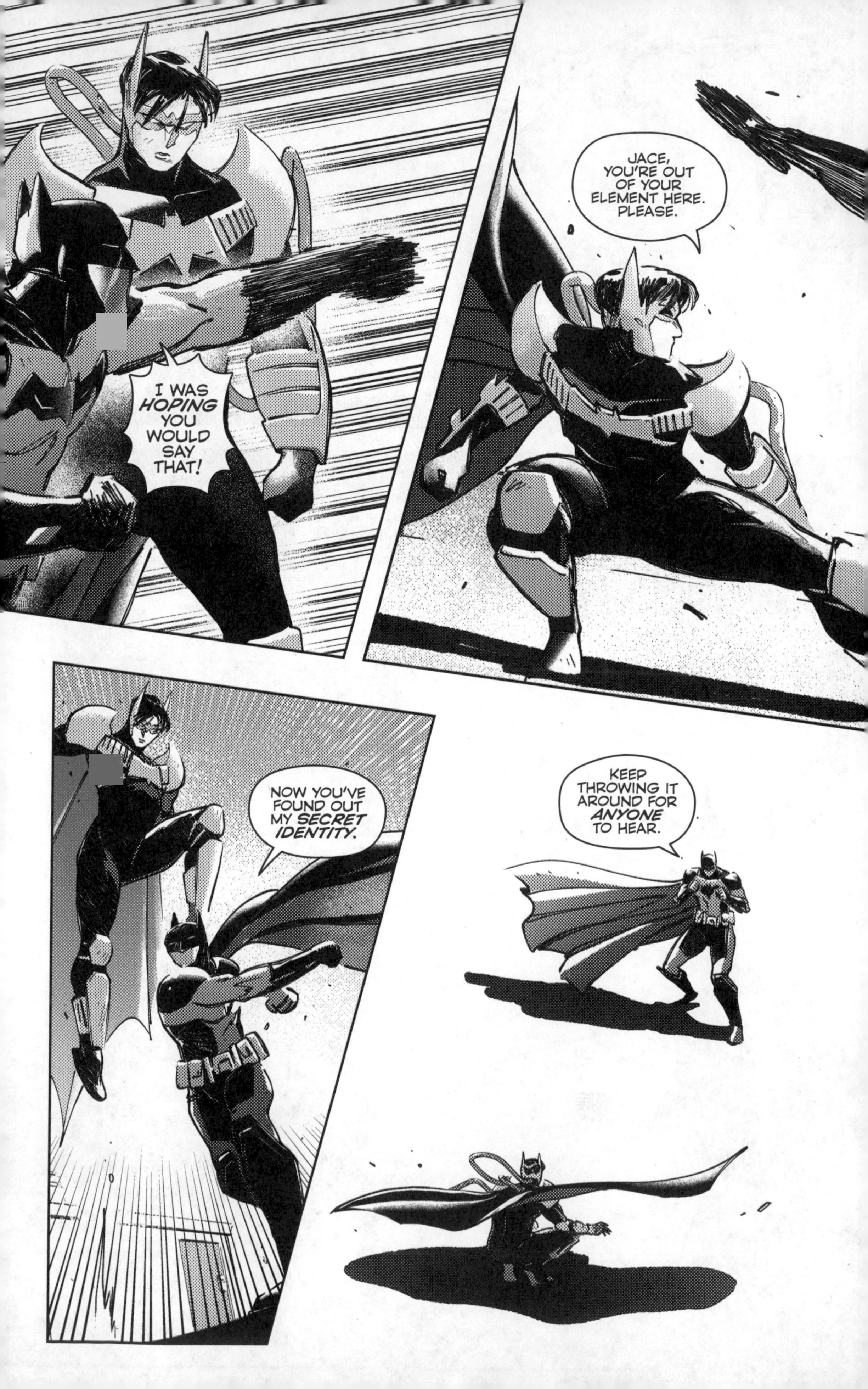
I WAS *HOPING* YOU WOULD SAY THAT!
JACE, YOU'RE OUT OF YOUR ELEMENT HERE. PLEASE.
NOW YOU'VE FOUND OUT MY *SECRET IDENTITY*.
KEEP THROWING IT AROUND FOR *ANYONE* TO HEAR.

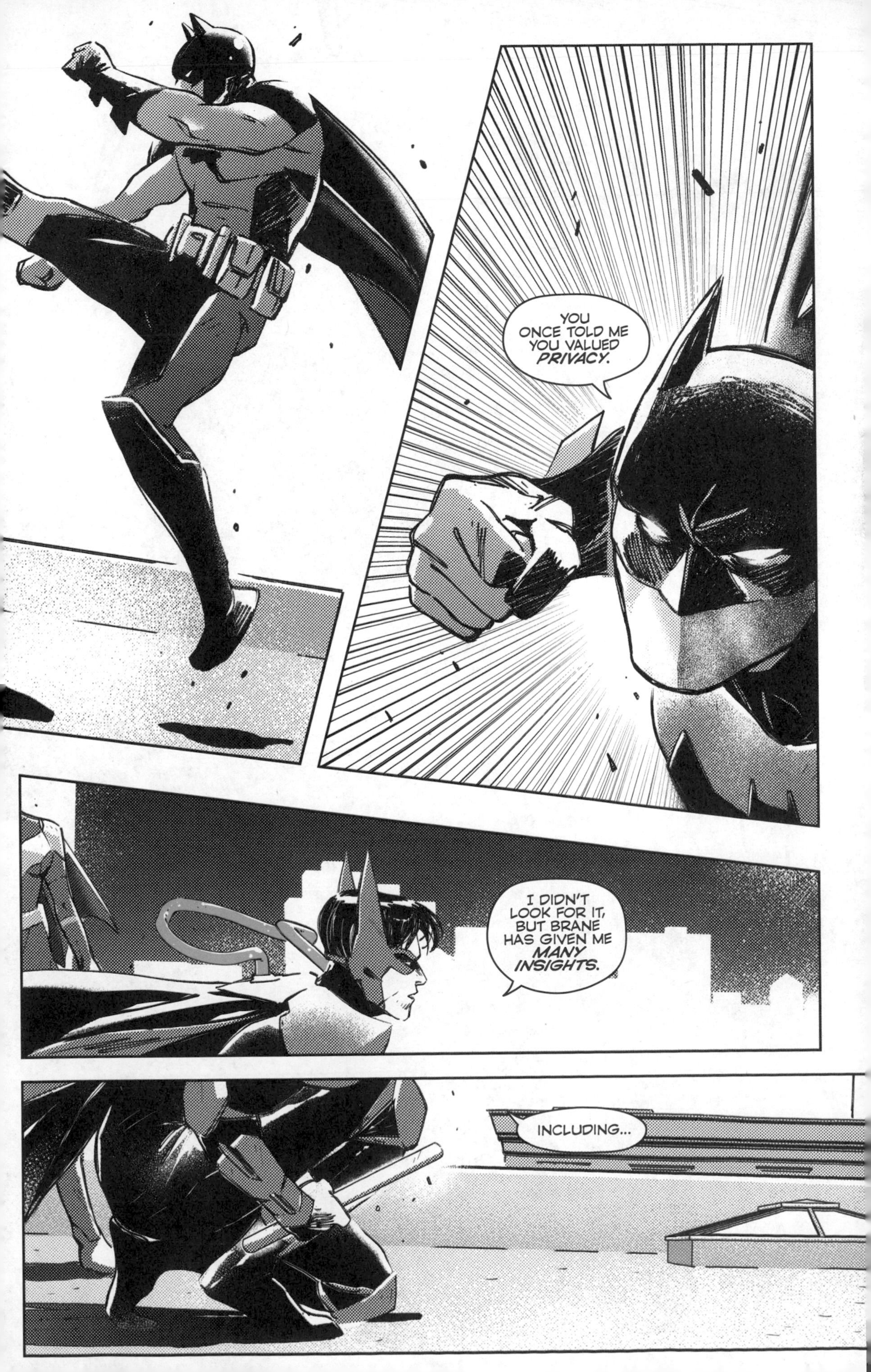
YOU ONCE TOLD ME YOU VALUED *PRIVACY*.
I DIDN'T LOOK FOR IT, BUT BRANE HAS GIVEN ME *MANY INSIGHTS*.
INCLUDING...

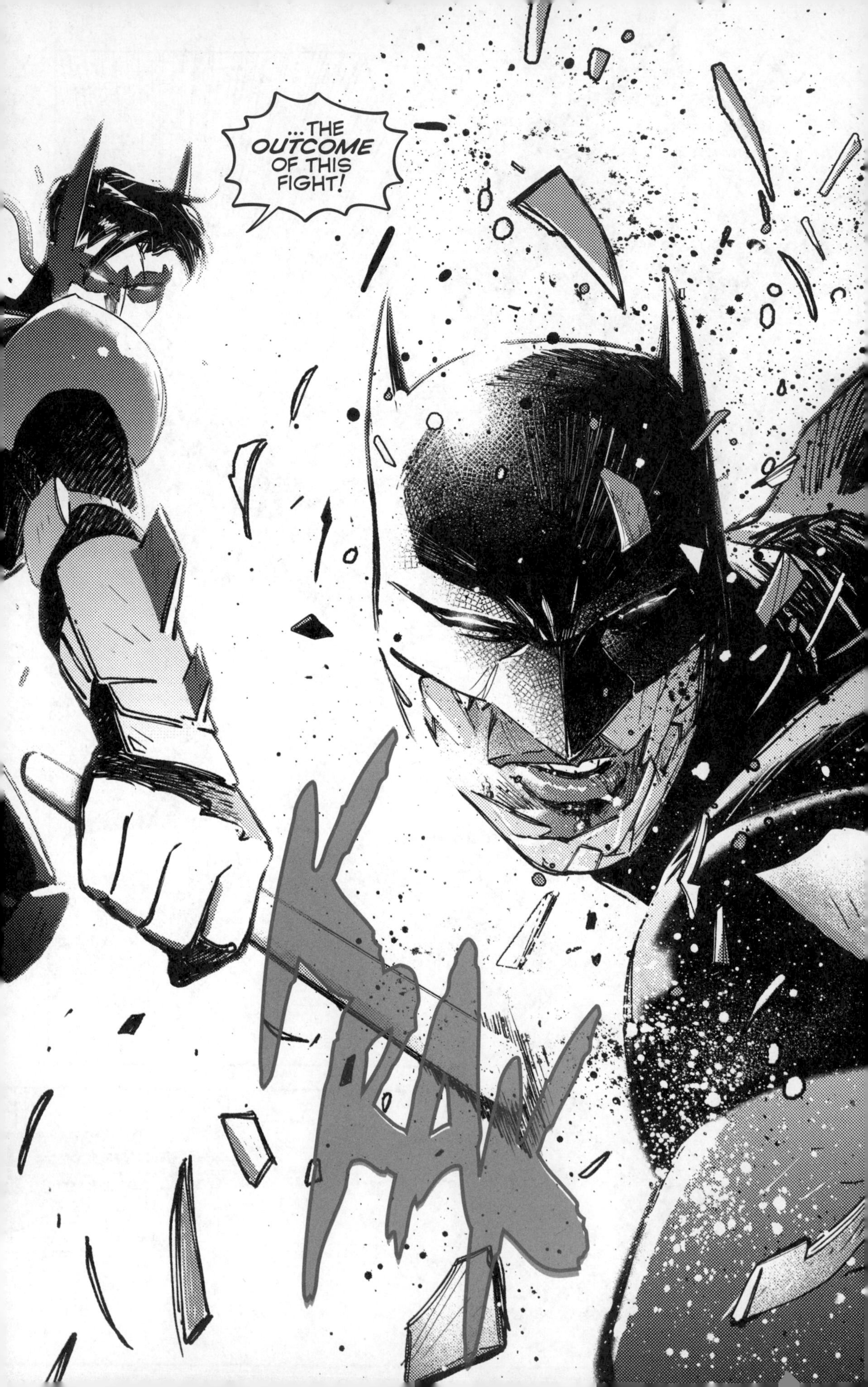
...THE *OUTCOME* OF THIS FIGHT!

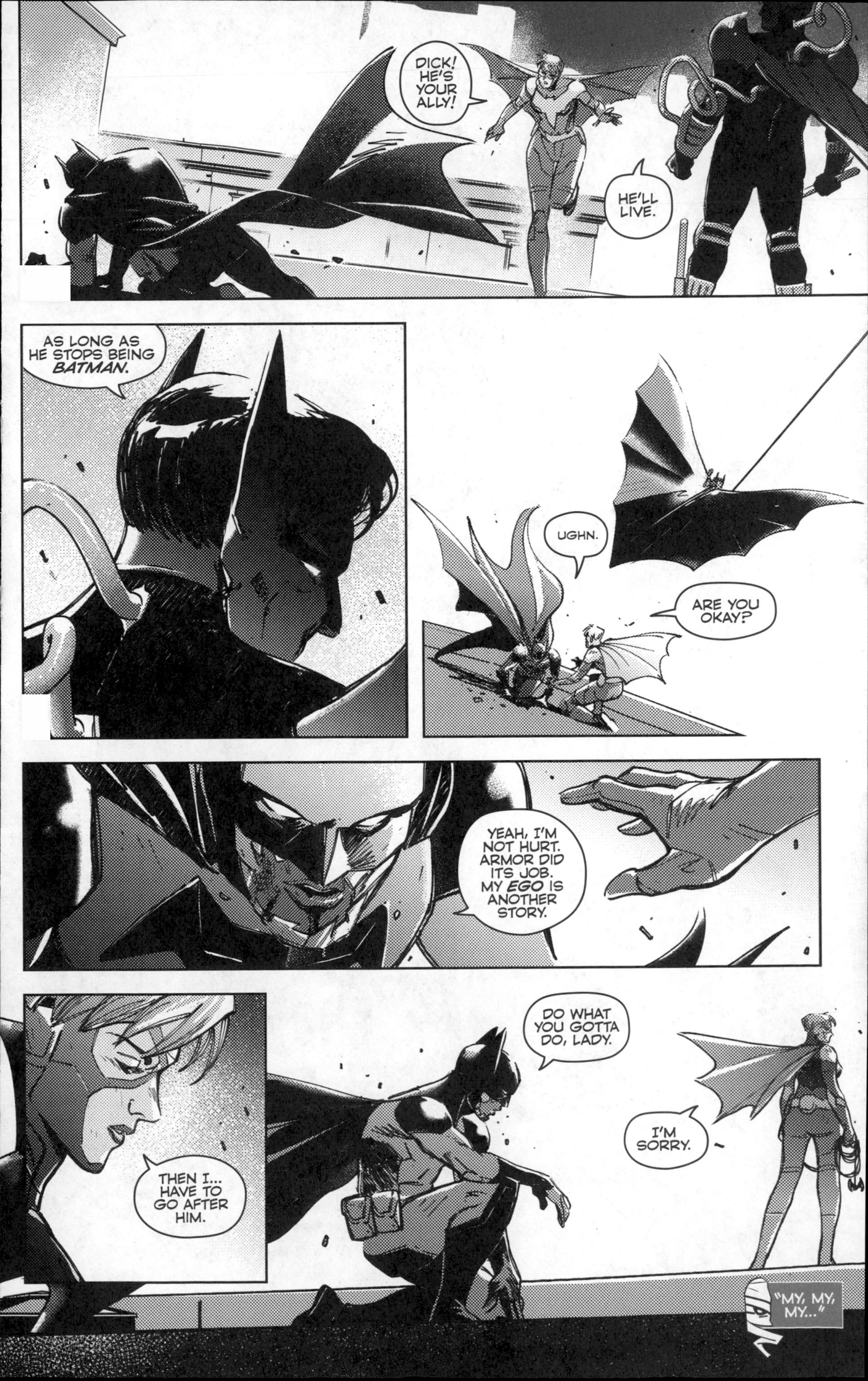
DICK! HE'S YOUR ALLY!
HE'LL LIVE.
AS LONG AS HE STOPS BEING BATMAN.
UGHN.
ARE YOU OKAY?
YEAH, I'M NOT HURT. ARMOR DID ITS JOB. MY EGO IS ANOTHER STORY.
DO WHAT YOU GOTTA DO, LADY.
I'M SORRY.
THEN I... HAVE TO GO AFTER HIM.
"MY, MY, MY..."

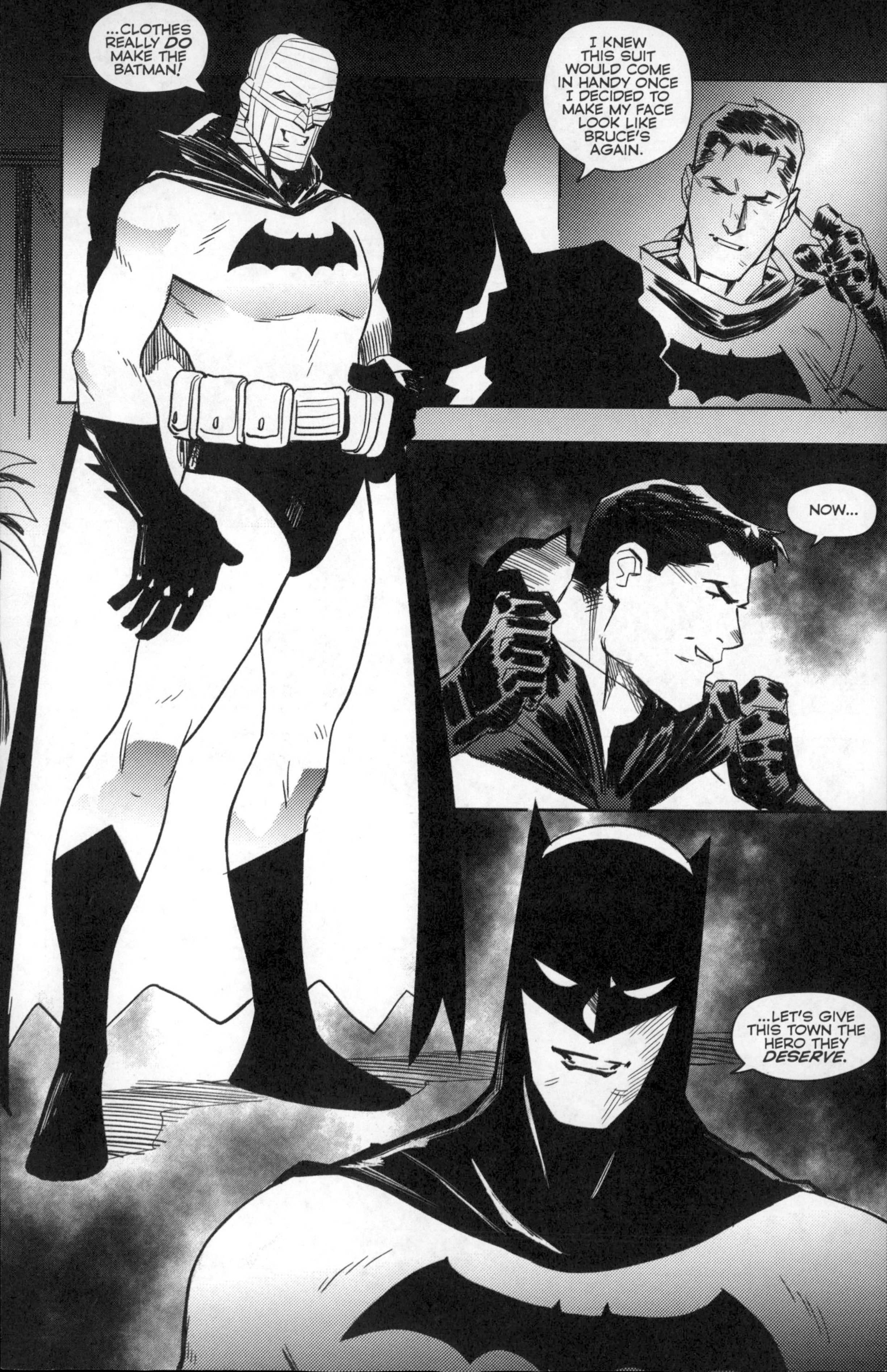
...CLOTHES REALLY *DO* MAKE THE BATMAN!
I KNEW THIS SUIT WOULD COME IN HANDY ONCE I DECIDED TO MAKE MY FACE LOOK LIKE BRUCE'S AGAIN.
NOW...
...LET'S GIVE THIS TOWN THE HERO THEY *DESERVE*.

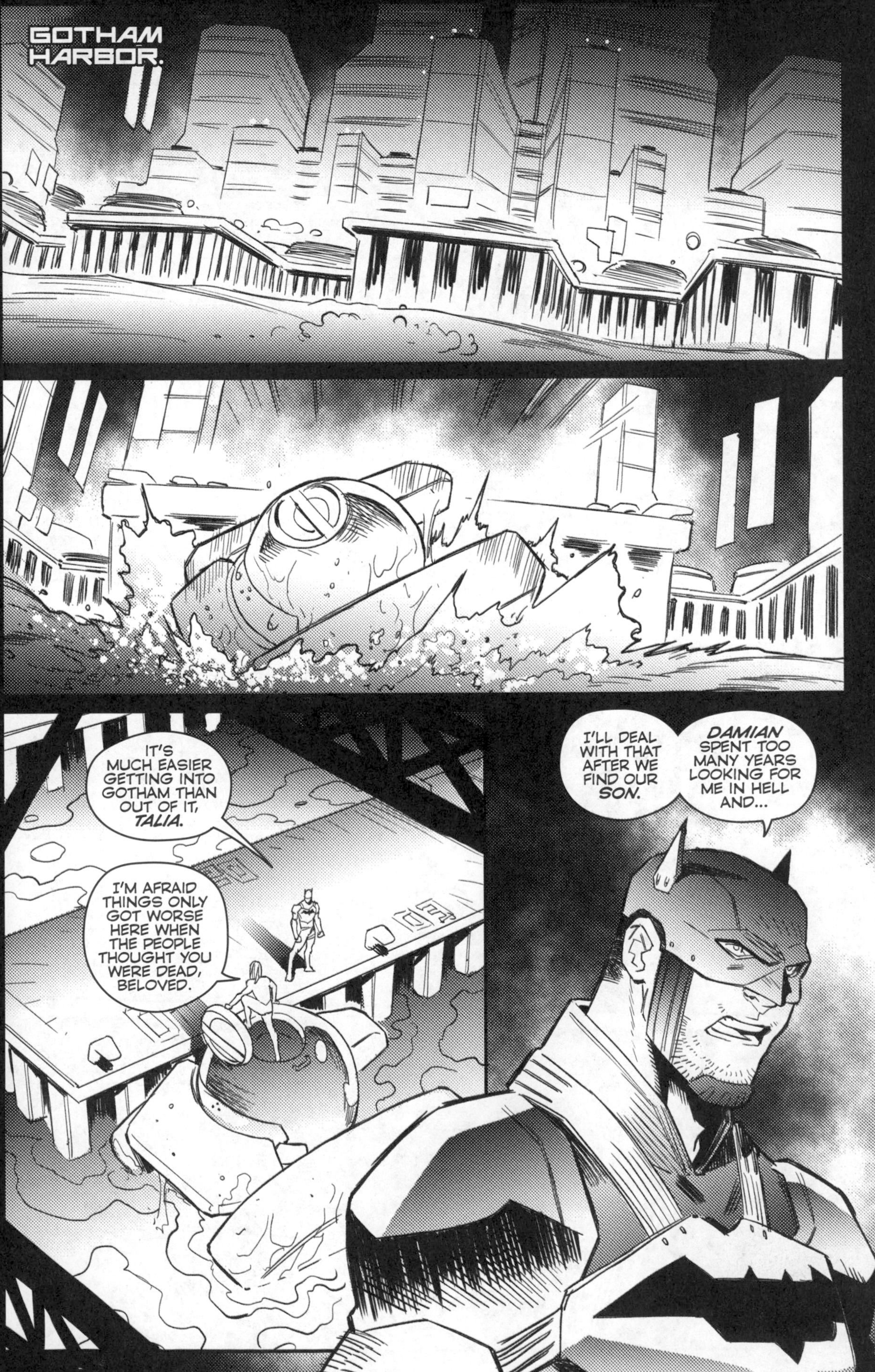
GOTHAM HARBOR.
IT'S MUCH EASIER GETTING INTO GOTHAM THAN OUT OF IT, TALIA.
I'M AFRAID THINGS ONLY GOT WORSE HERE WHEN THE PEOPLE THOUGHT YOU WERE DEAD, BELOVED.
I'LL DEAL WITH THAT AFTER WE FIND OUR SON.
DAMIAN SPENT TOO MANY YEARS LOOKING FOR ME IN HELL AND...

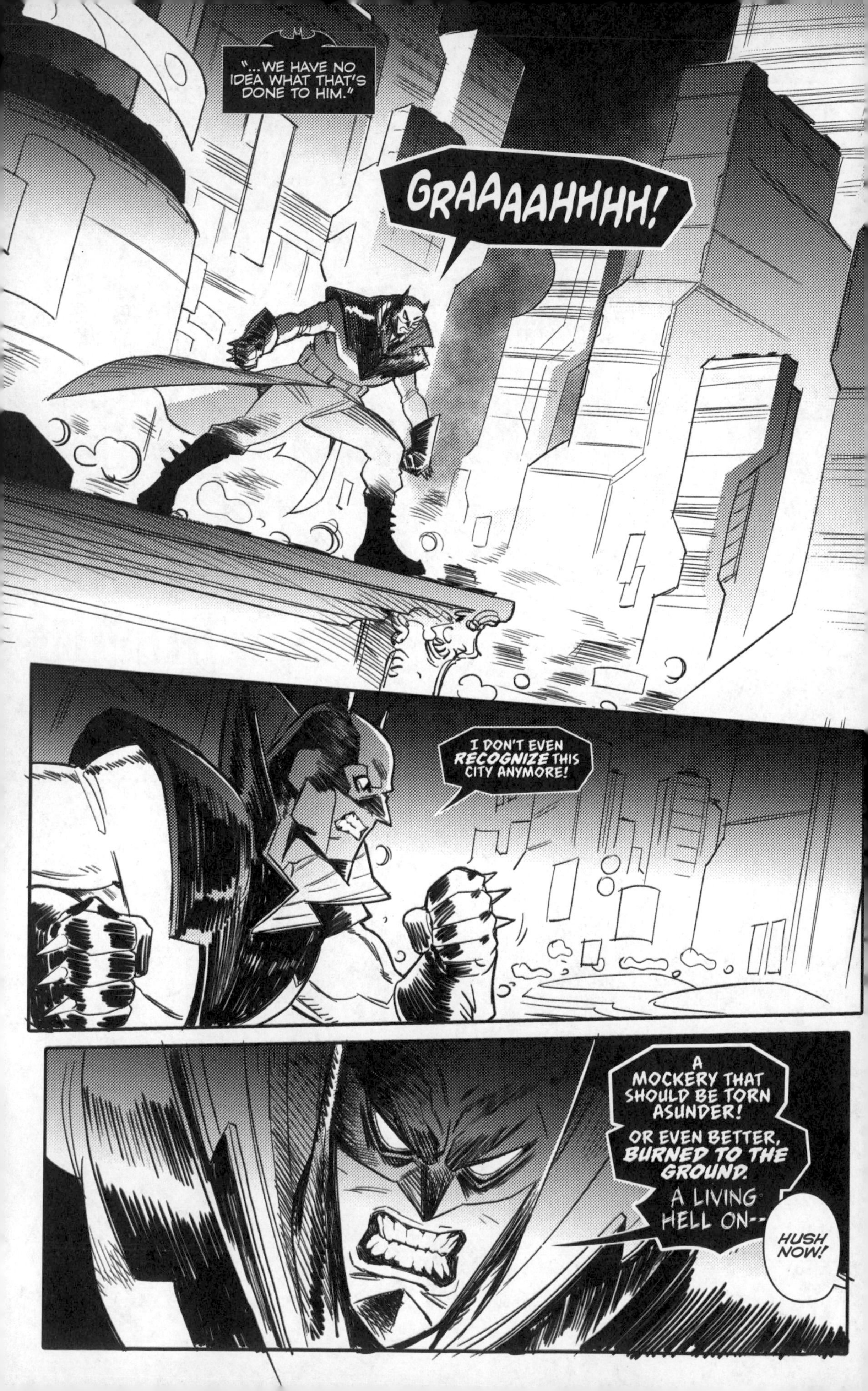
"...WE HAVE NO IDEA WHAT THAT'S DONE TO HIM."
GRAAAAHHHH!
I DON'T EVEN RECOGNIZE THIS CITY ANYMORE!
A MOCKERY THAT SHOULD BE TORN ASUNDER!
OR EVEN BETTER, BURNED TO THE GROUND.
A LIVING HELL ON--
HUSH NOW!

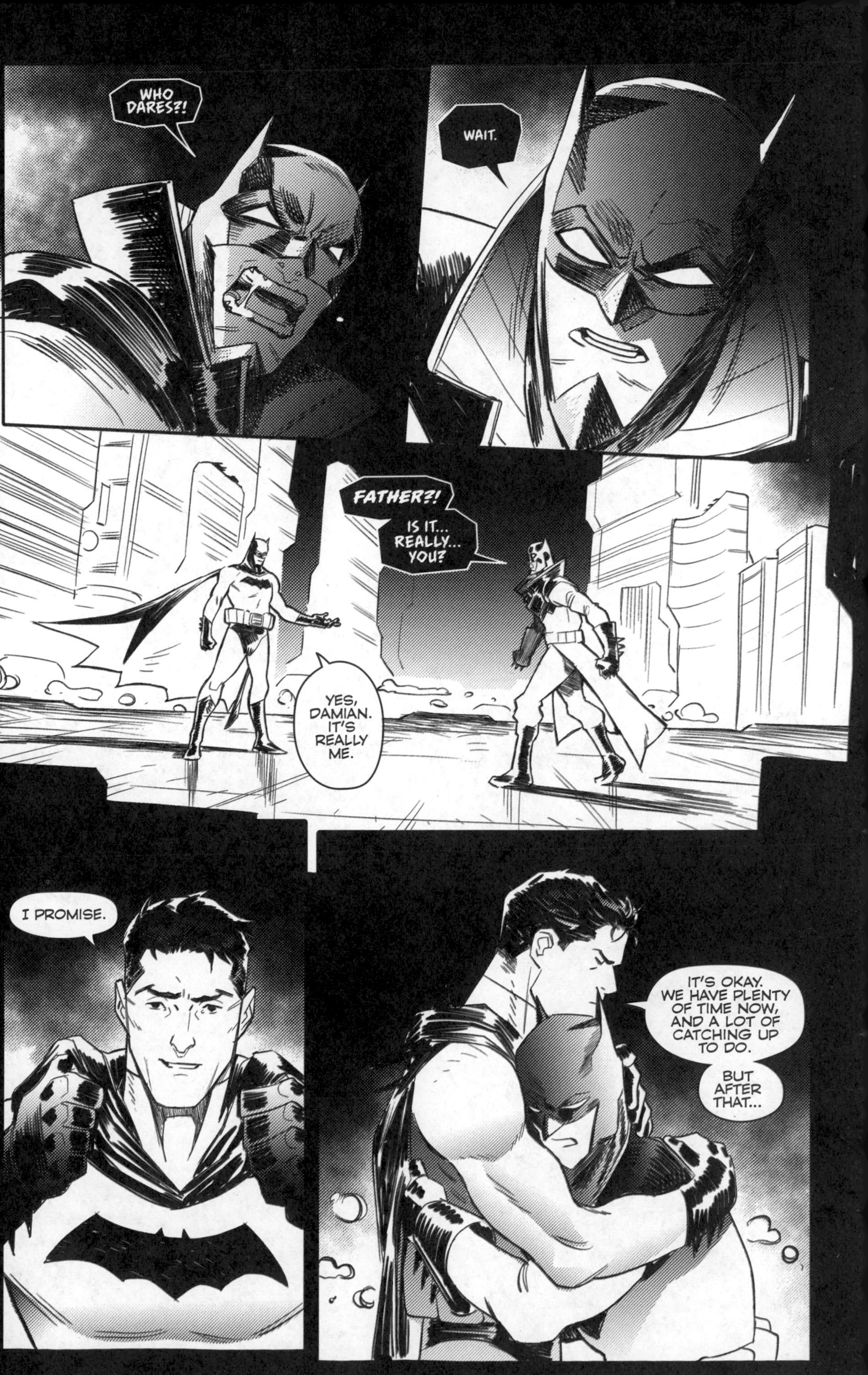
WHO DARES?!
WAIT.
FATHER?!
IS IT... REALLY... YOU?
YES, DAMIAN. IT'S REALLY ME.
I PROMISE.
IT'S OKAY. WE HAVE PLENTY OF TIME NOW, AND A LOT OF CATCHING UP TO DO.
BUT AFTER THAT...

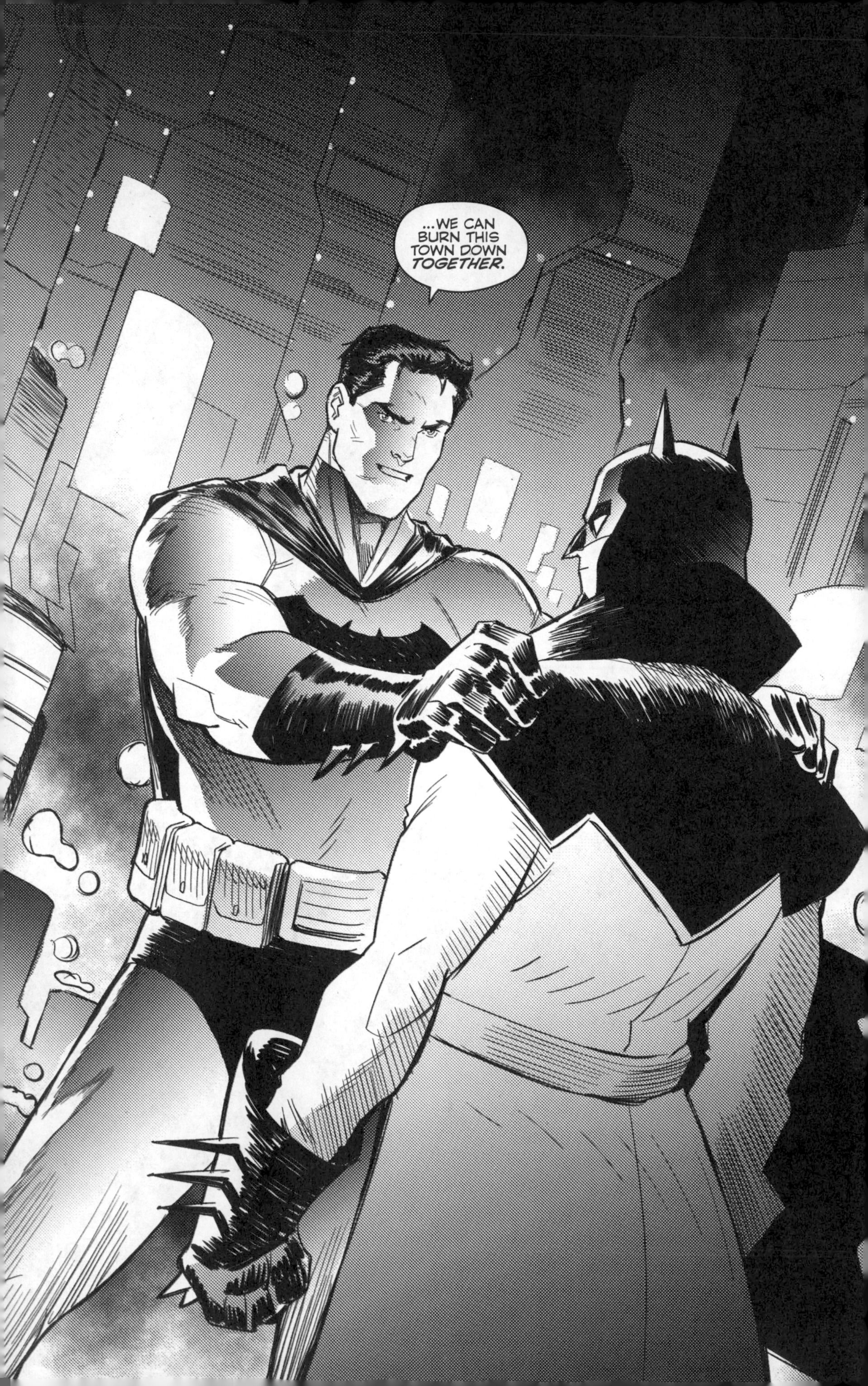
...WE CAN BURN THIS TOWN DOWN TOGETHER.

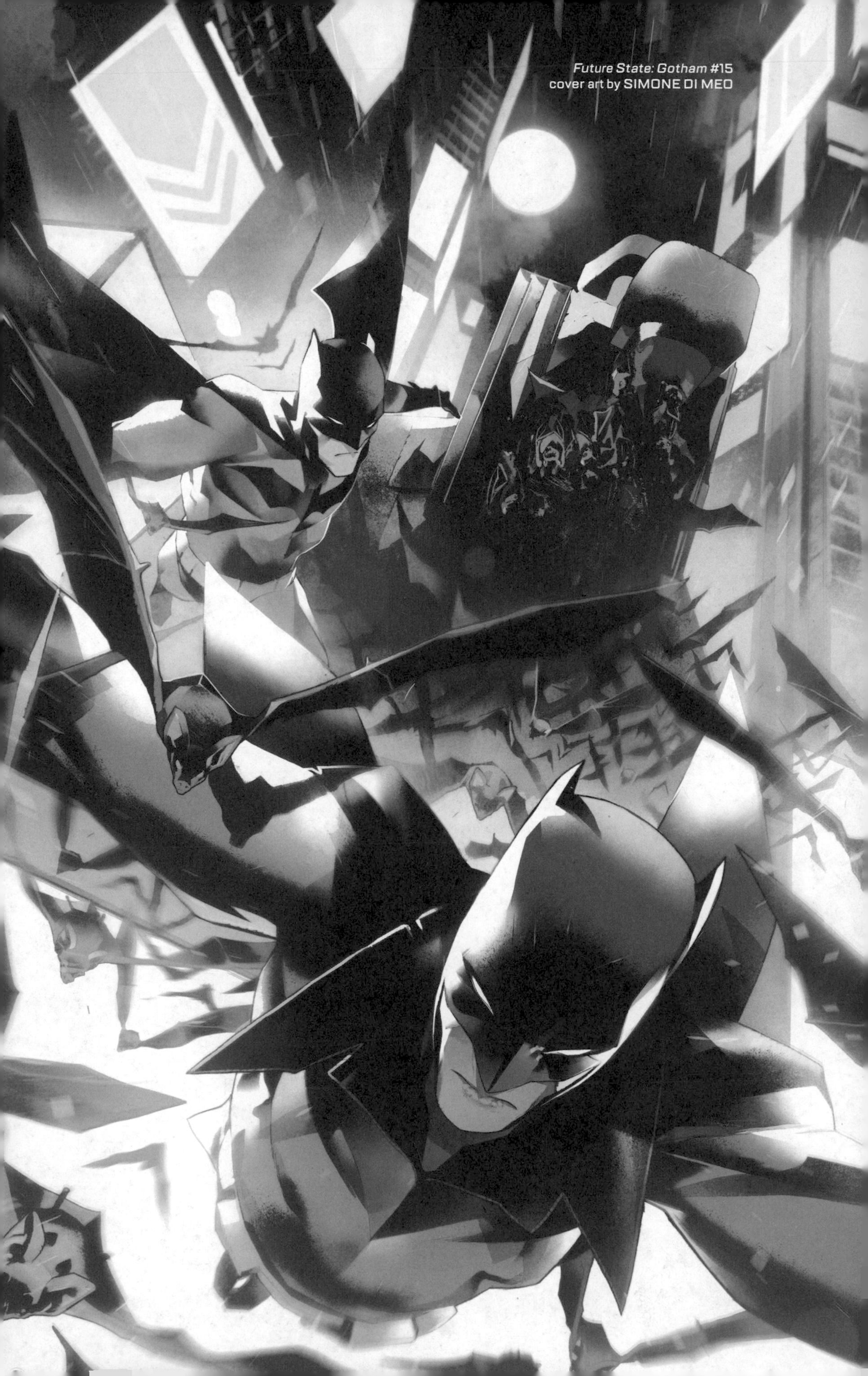

Future State: Gotham #15
cover art by SIMONE DI MEO

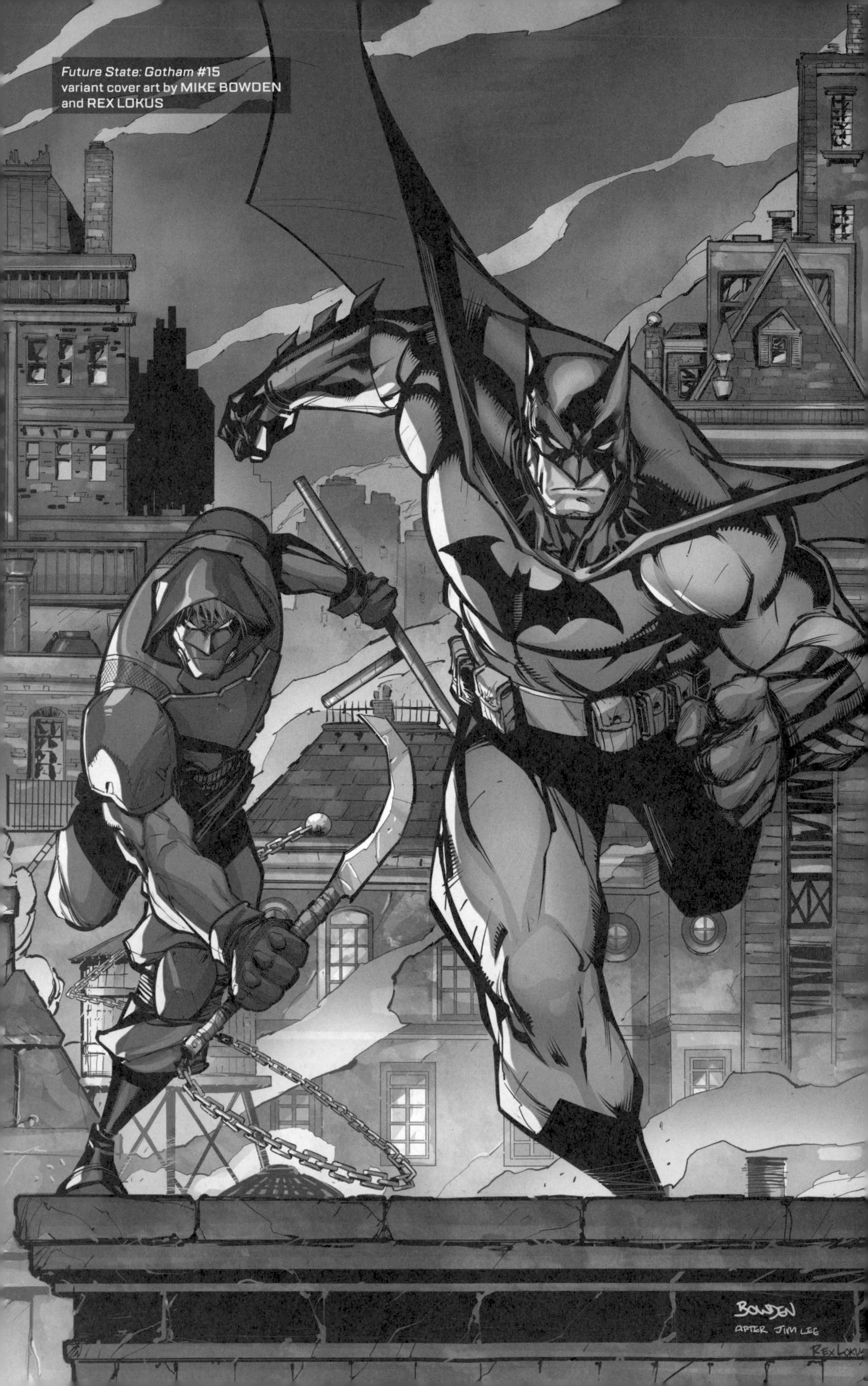
BOWDEN
AFTER JIM LEE
REX LOKUS

Future State: Gotham #15
variant cover art by MIKE BOWDEN
and REX LOKUS

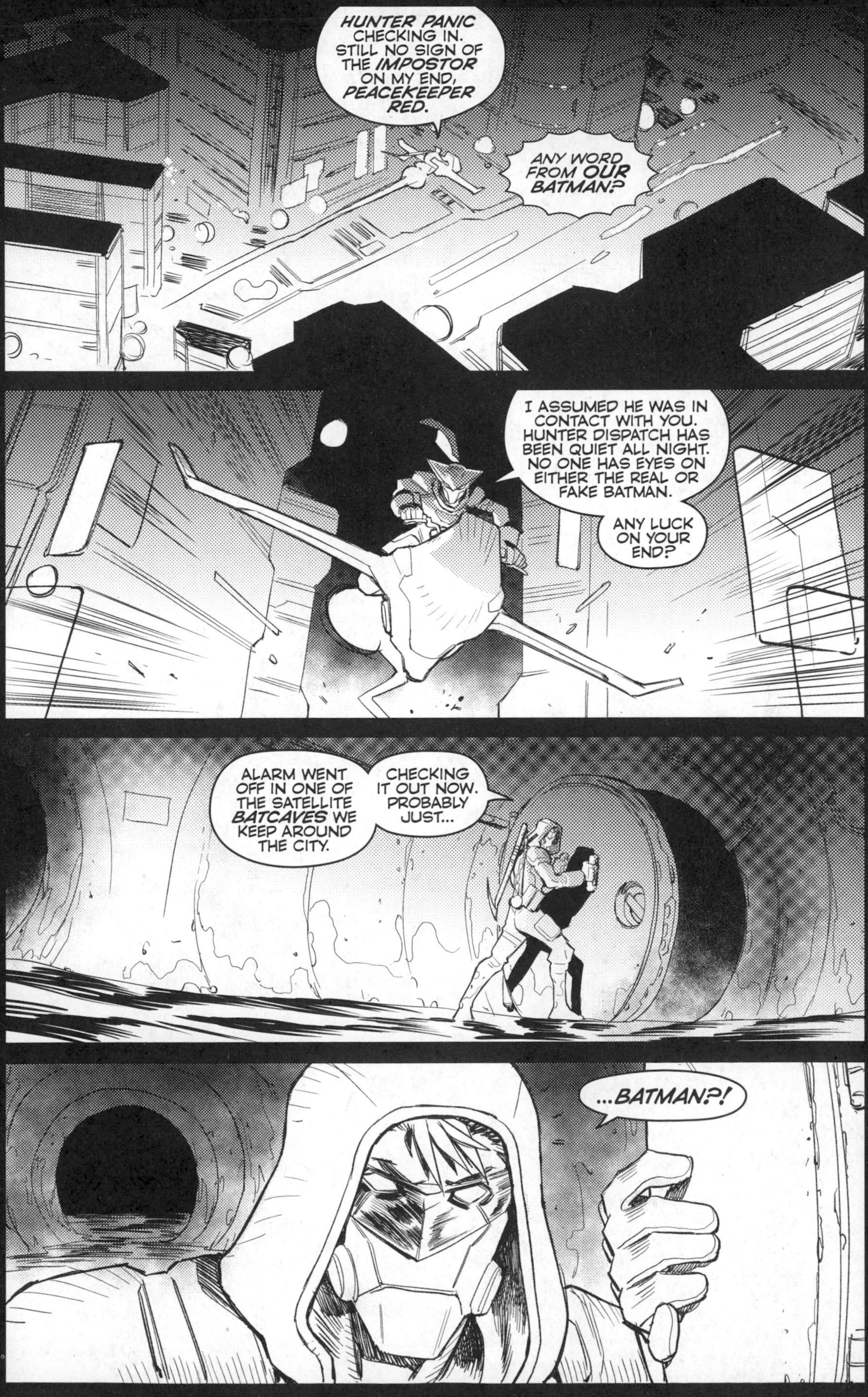
HUNTER PANIC CHECKING IN. STILL NO SIGN OF THE IMPOSTOR ON MY END, PEACEKEEPER RED.
ANY WORD FROM OUR BATMAN?
I ASSUMED HE WAS IN CONTACT WITH YOU. HUNTER DISPATCH HAS BEEN QUIET ALL NIGHT. NO ONE HAS EYES ON EITHER THE REAL OR FAKE BATMAN.
ANY LUCK ON YOUR END?
ALARM WENT OFF IN ONE OF THE SATELLITE BATCAVES WE KEEP AROUND THE CITY.
CHECKING IT OUT NOW. PROBABLY JUST...
...BATMAN?!

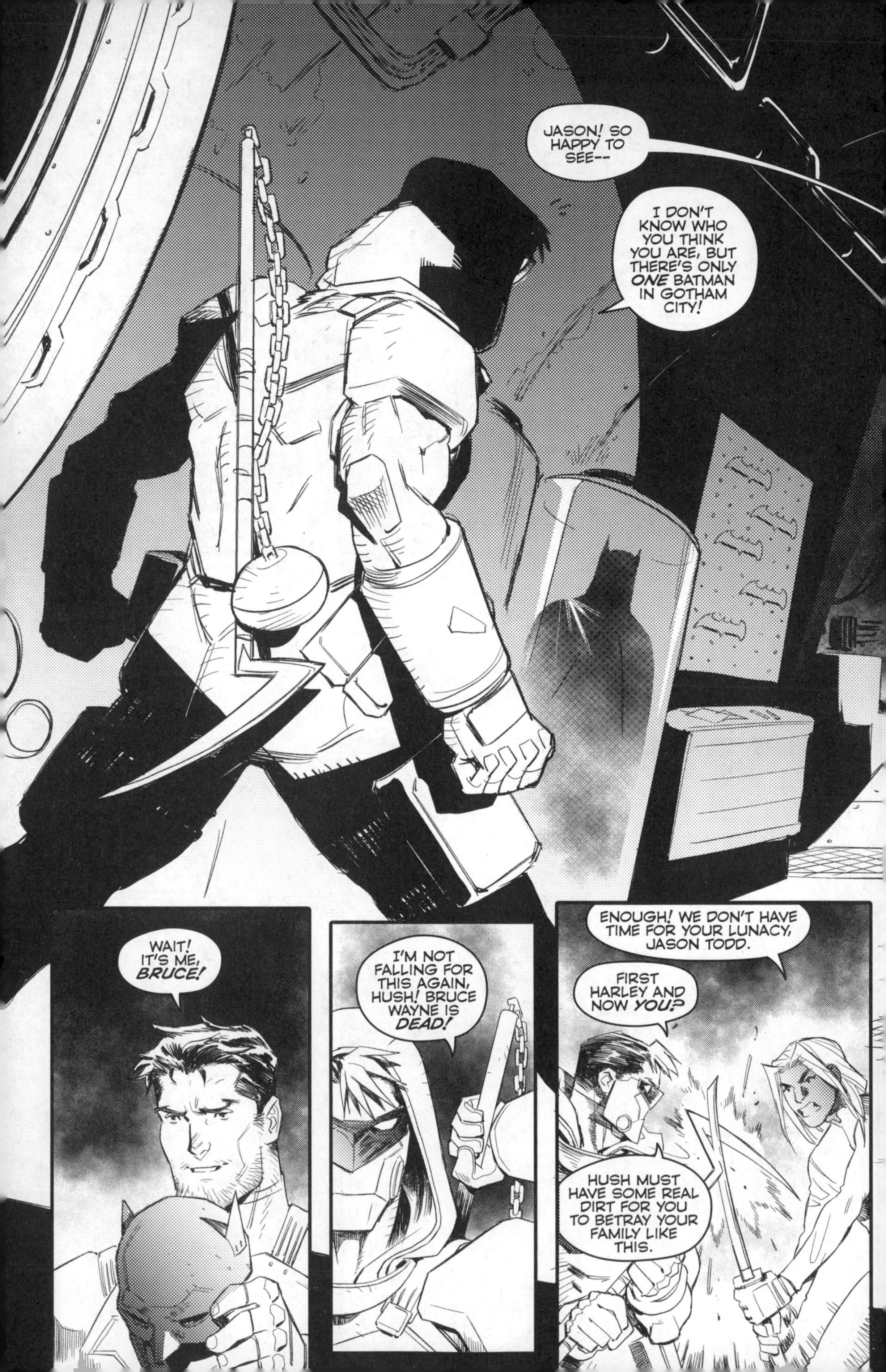
JASON! SO HAPPY TO SEE--
I DON'T KNOW WHO YOU THINK YOU ARE, BUT THERE'S ONLY *ONE* BATMAN IN GOTHAM CITY!
WAIT! IT'S ME, *BRUCE!*
I'M NOT FALLING FOR THIS AGAIN, HUSH! BRUCE WAYNE IS *DEAD!*
ENOUGH! WE DON'T HAVE TIME FOR YOUR LUNACY, JASON TODD.
FIRST HARLEY AND NOW *YOU?*
HUSH MUST HAVE SOME REAL DIRT FOR YOU TO BETRAY YOUR FAMILY LIKE THIS.

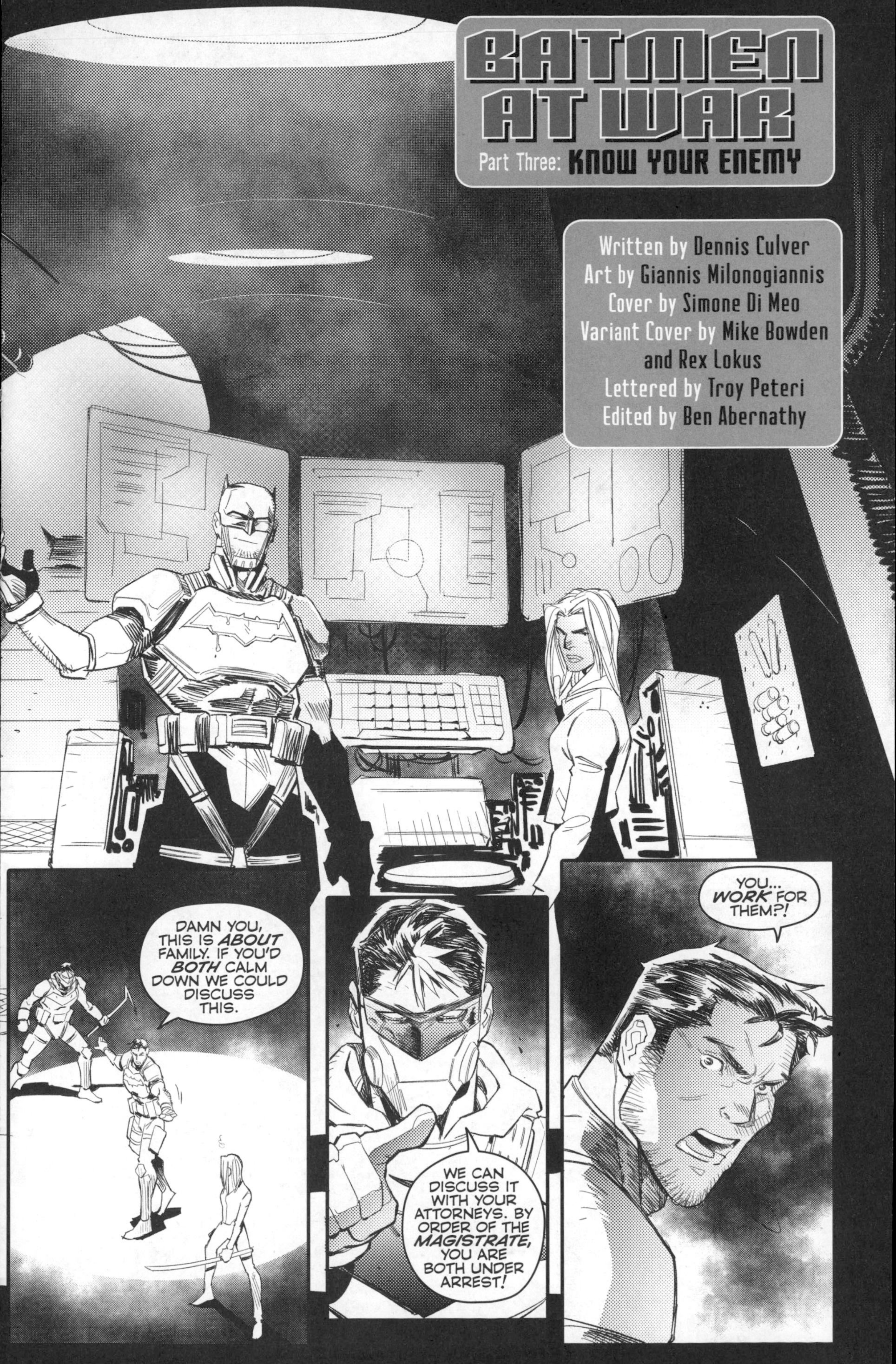
BATMEN
AT WAR
Part Three: KNOW YOUR ENEMY
Written by Dennis Culver
Art by Giannis Milonogiannis
Cover by Simone Di Meo
Variant Cover by Mike Bowden
and Rex Lokus
Lettered by Troy Peteri
Edited by Ben Abernathy
DAMN YOU, THIS IS ABOUT FAMILY. IF YOU'D BOTH CALM DOWN WE COULD DISCUSS THIS.
WE CAN DISCUSS IT WITH YOUR ATTORNEYS. BY ORDER OF THE MAGISTRATE, YOU ARE BOTH UNDER ARREST!
YOU... WORK FOR THEM?!

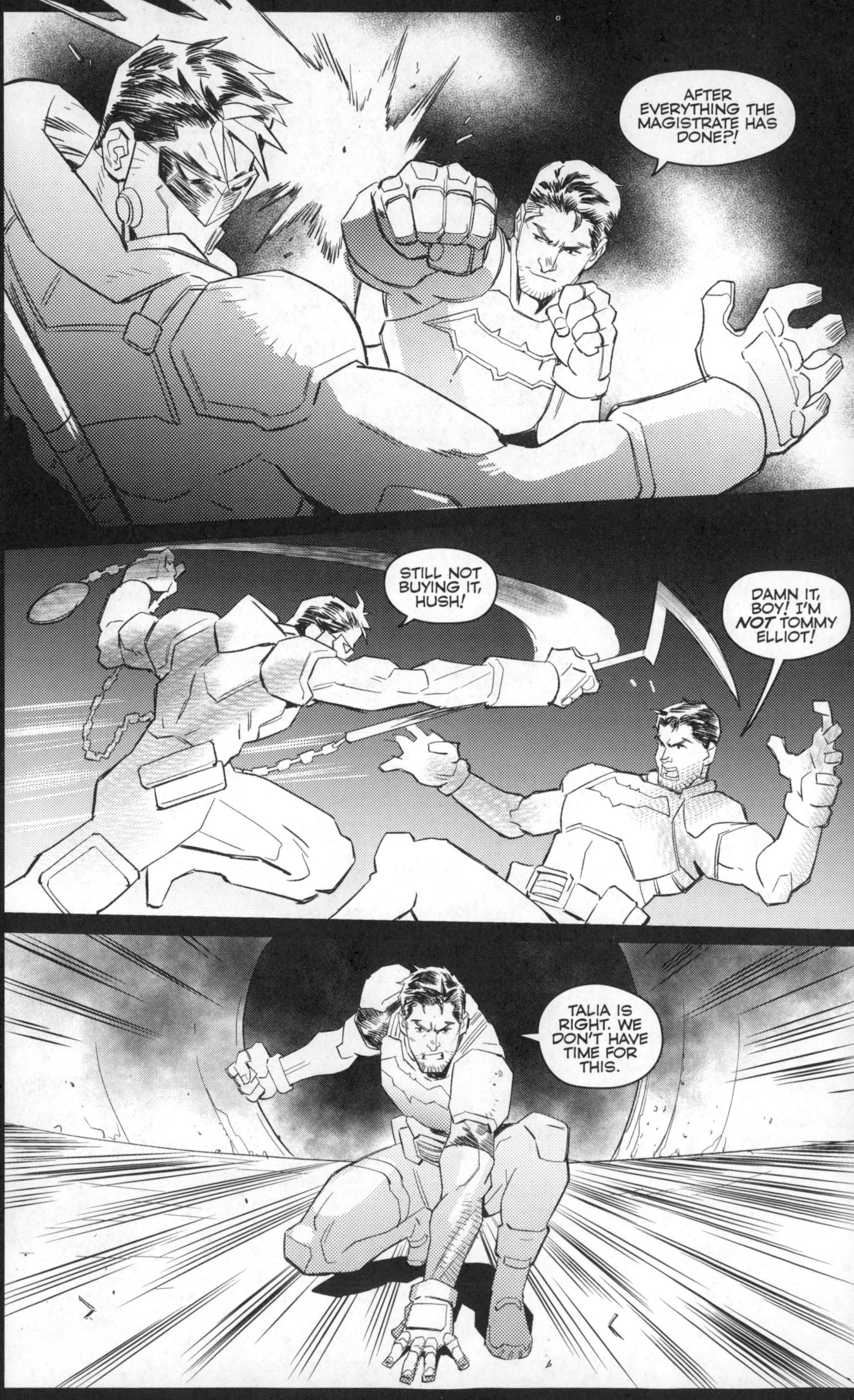
AFTER EVERYTHING THE MAGISTRATE HAS DONE?!
STILL NOT BUYING IT, HUSH!
DAMN IT, BOY! I'M NOT TOMMY ELLIOT!
TALIA IS RIGHT. WE DON'T HAVE TIME FOR THIS.

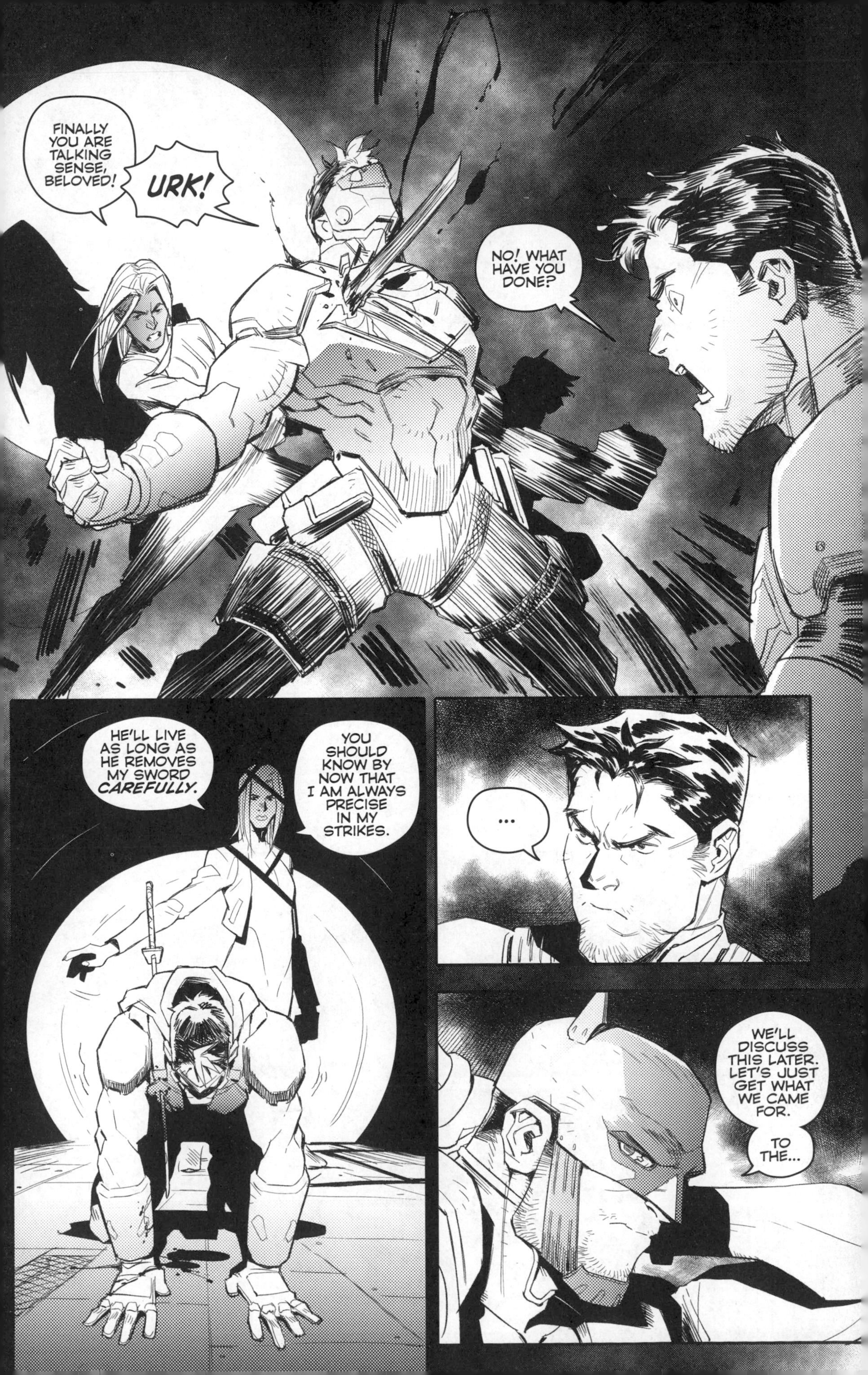
FINALLY YOU ARE TALKING SENSE, BELOVED!
URK!
NO! WHAT HAVE YOU DONE?
HE'LL LIVE AS LONG AS HE REMOVES MY SWORD *CAREFULLY*.
YOU SHOULD KNOW BY NOW THAT I AM ALWAYS PRECISE IN MY STRIKES.
...
WE'LL DISCUSS THIS LATER. LET'S JUST GET WHAT WE CAME FOR.
TO THE...

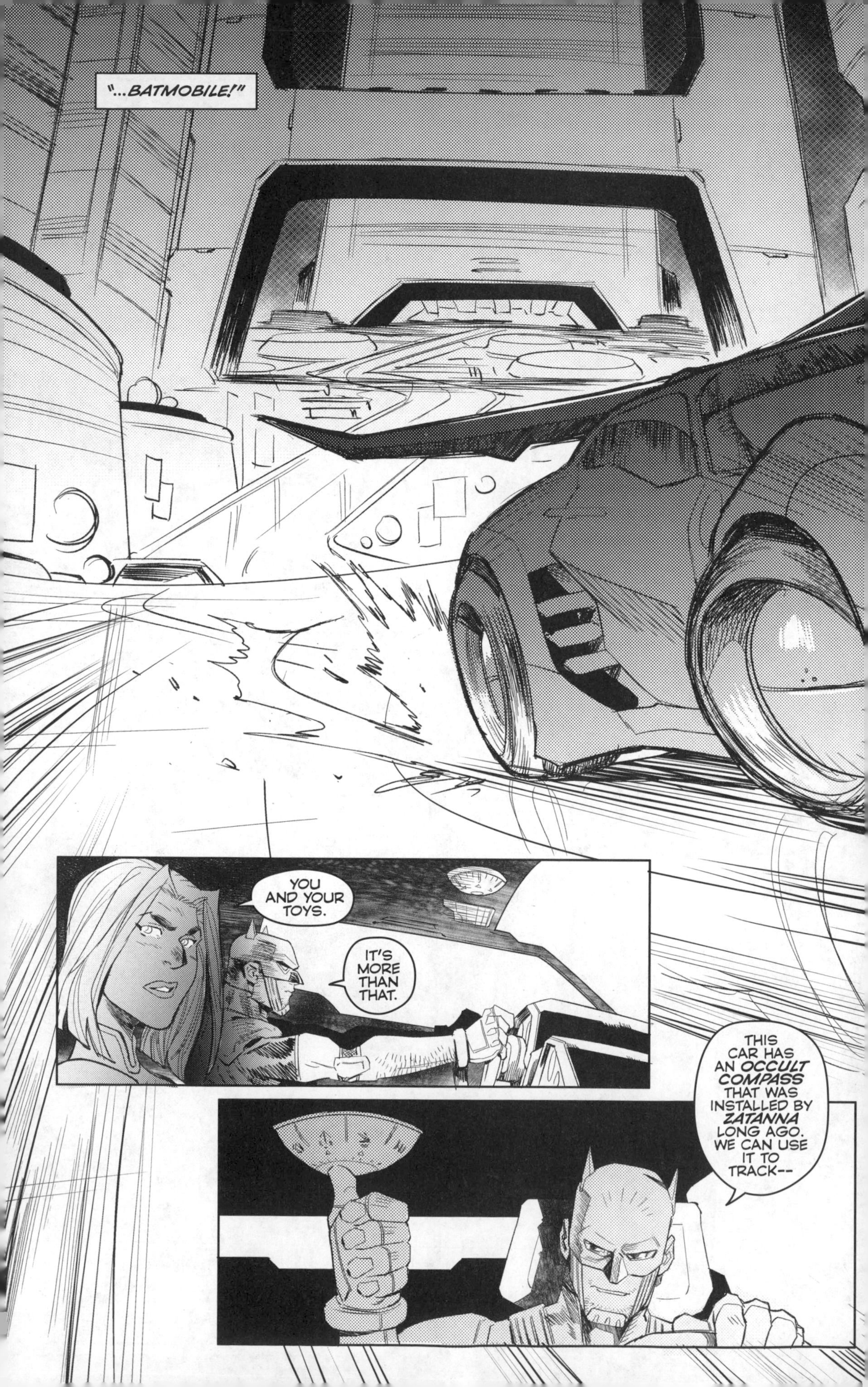
"...BATMOBILE!"
YOU AND YOUR TOYS.
IT'S MORE THAN THAT.
THIS CAR HAS AN OCCULT COMPASS THAT WAS INSTALLED BY ZATANNA LONG AGO. WE CAN USE IT TO TRACK--

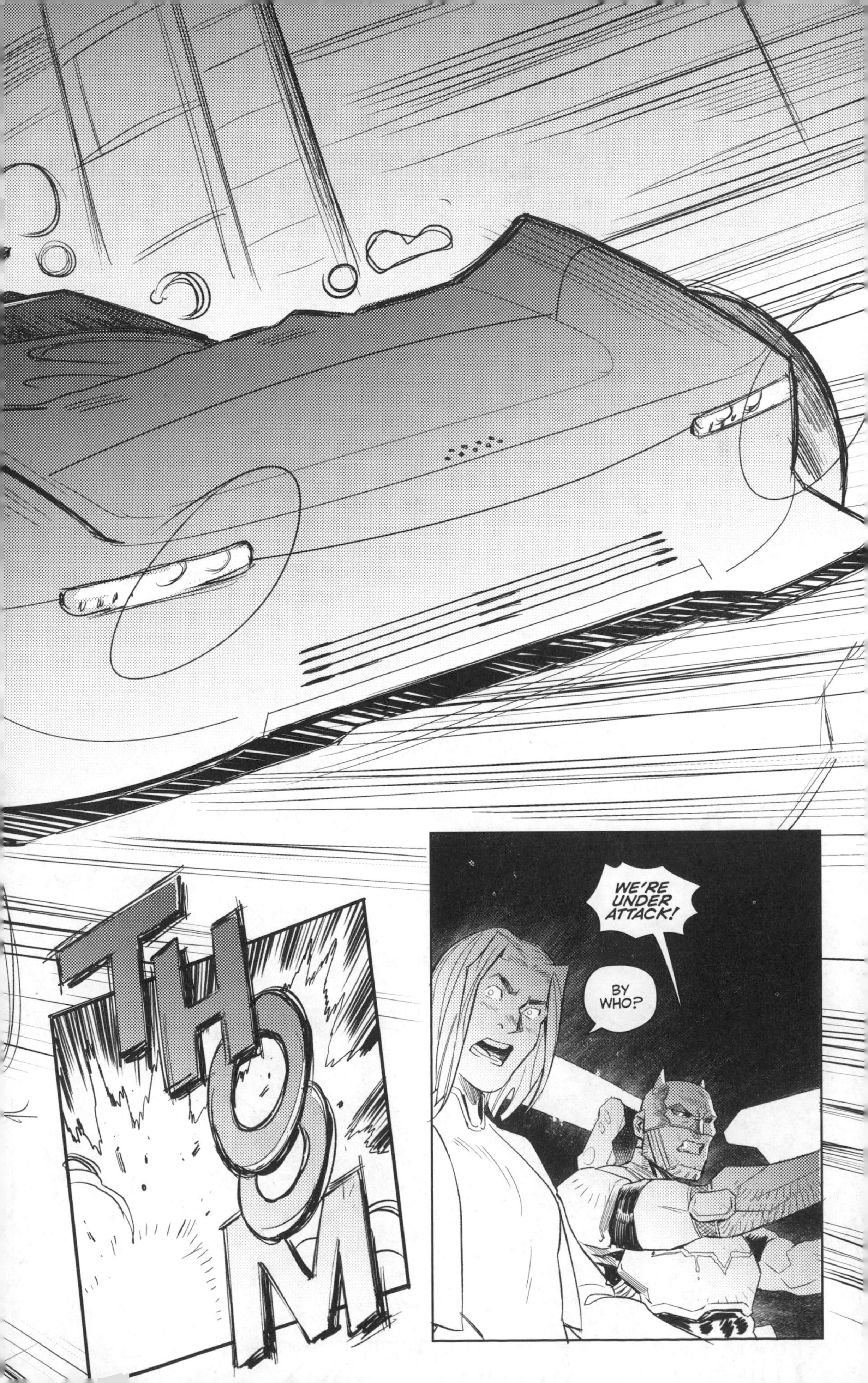
THOOM
WE'RE UNDER ATTACK!
BY WHO?

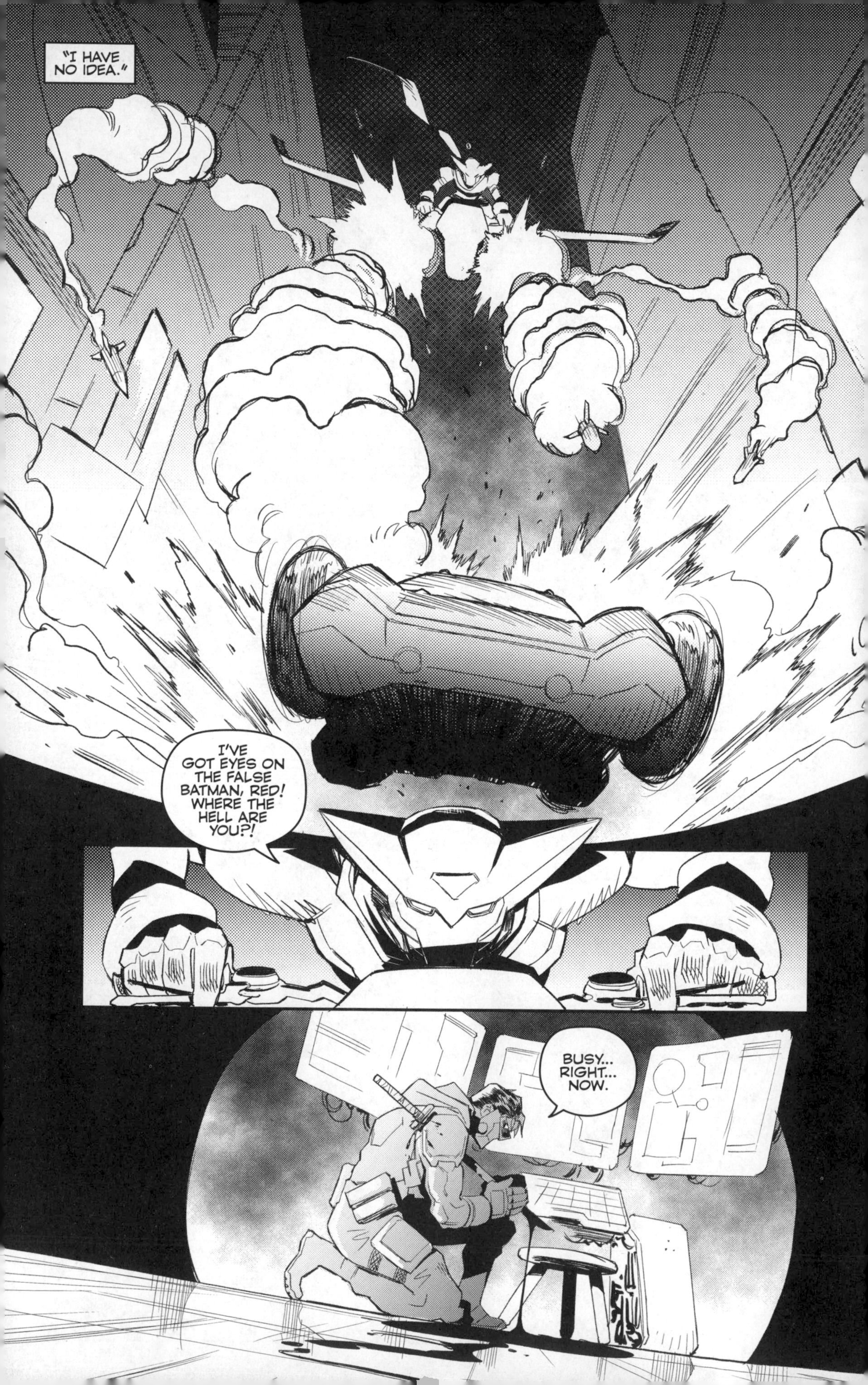
"I HAVE NO IDEA."
I'VE GOT EYES ON THE FALSE BATMAN, RED! WHERE THE HELL ARE YOU?!
BUSY... RIGHT... NOW.

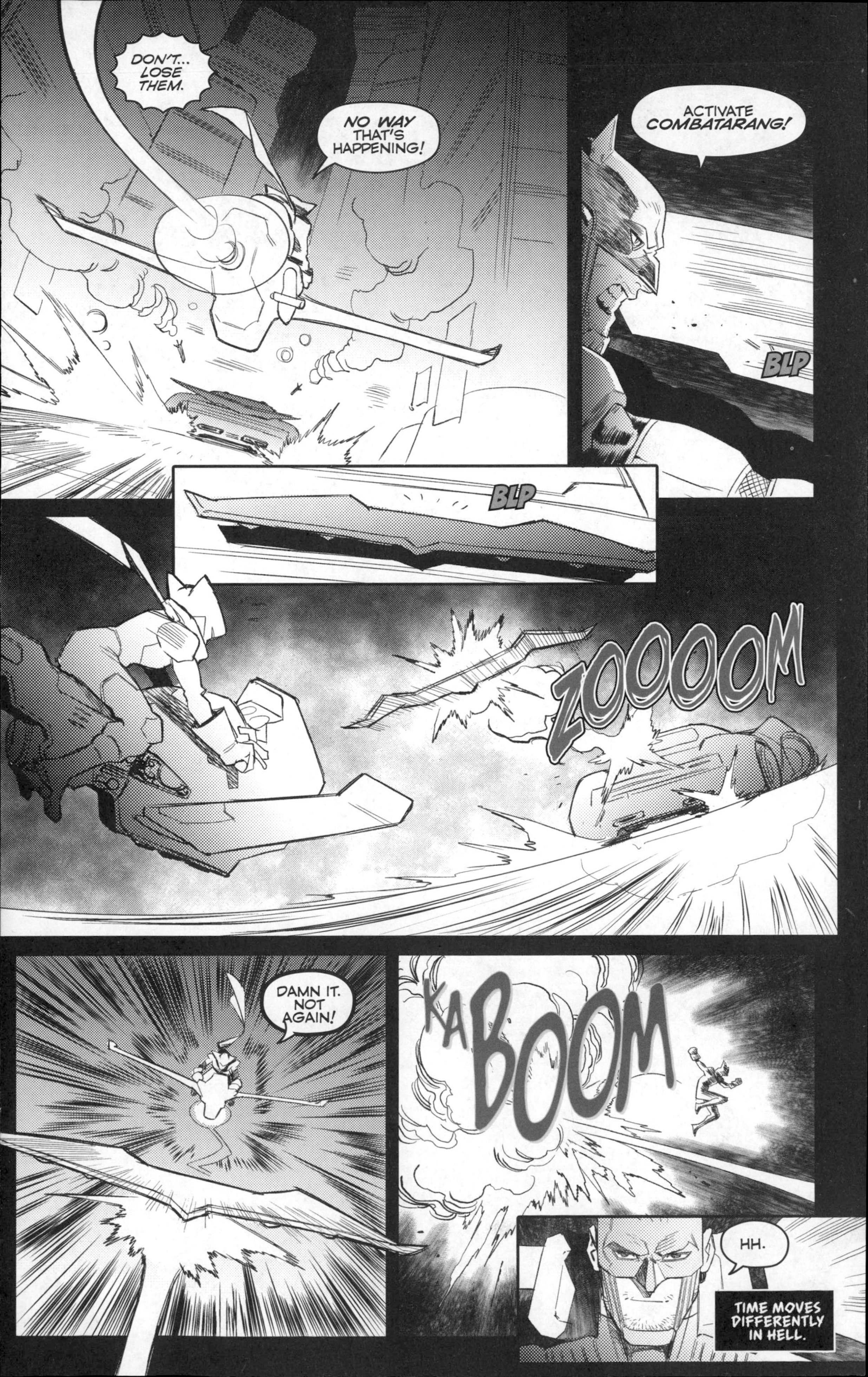
DON'T... LOSE THEM.
NO WAY THAT'S HAPPENING!
ACTIVATE COMBATARANG!
BLP
BLP
ZOOOOOM
DAMN IT. NOT AGAIN!
KABOOM
HH.
TIME MOVES DIFFERENTLY IN HELL.

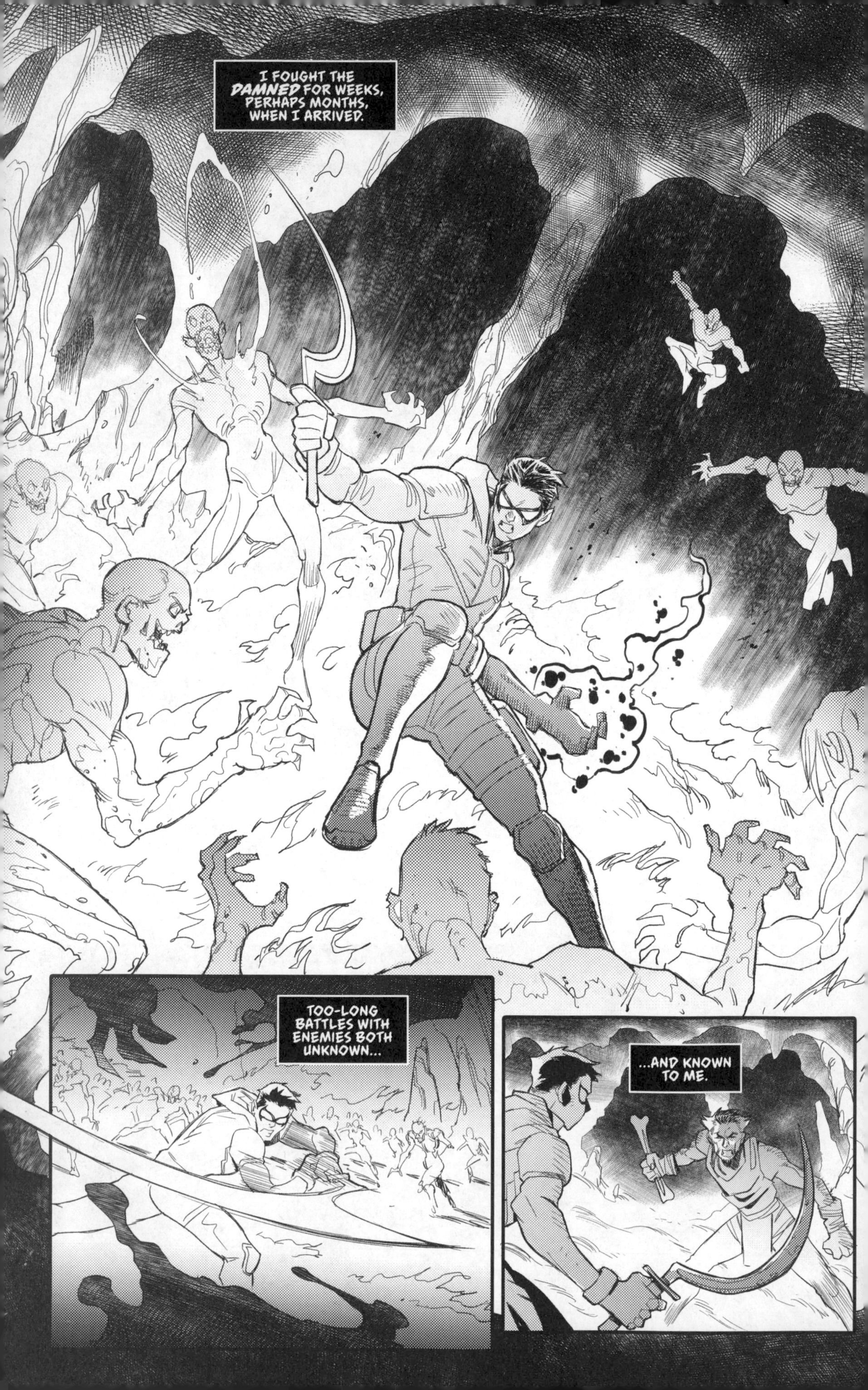
I FOUGHT THE DAMNED FOR WEEKS, PERHAPS MONTHS, WHEN I ARRIVED.
TOO-LONG BATTLES WITH ENEMIES BOTH UNKNOWN...
...AND KNOWN TO ME.

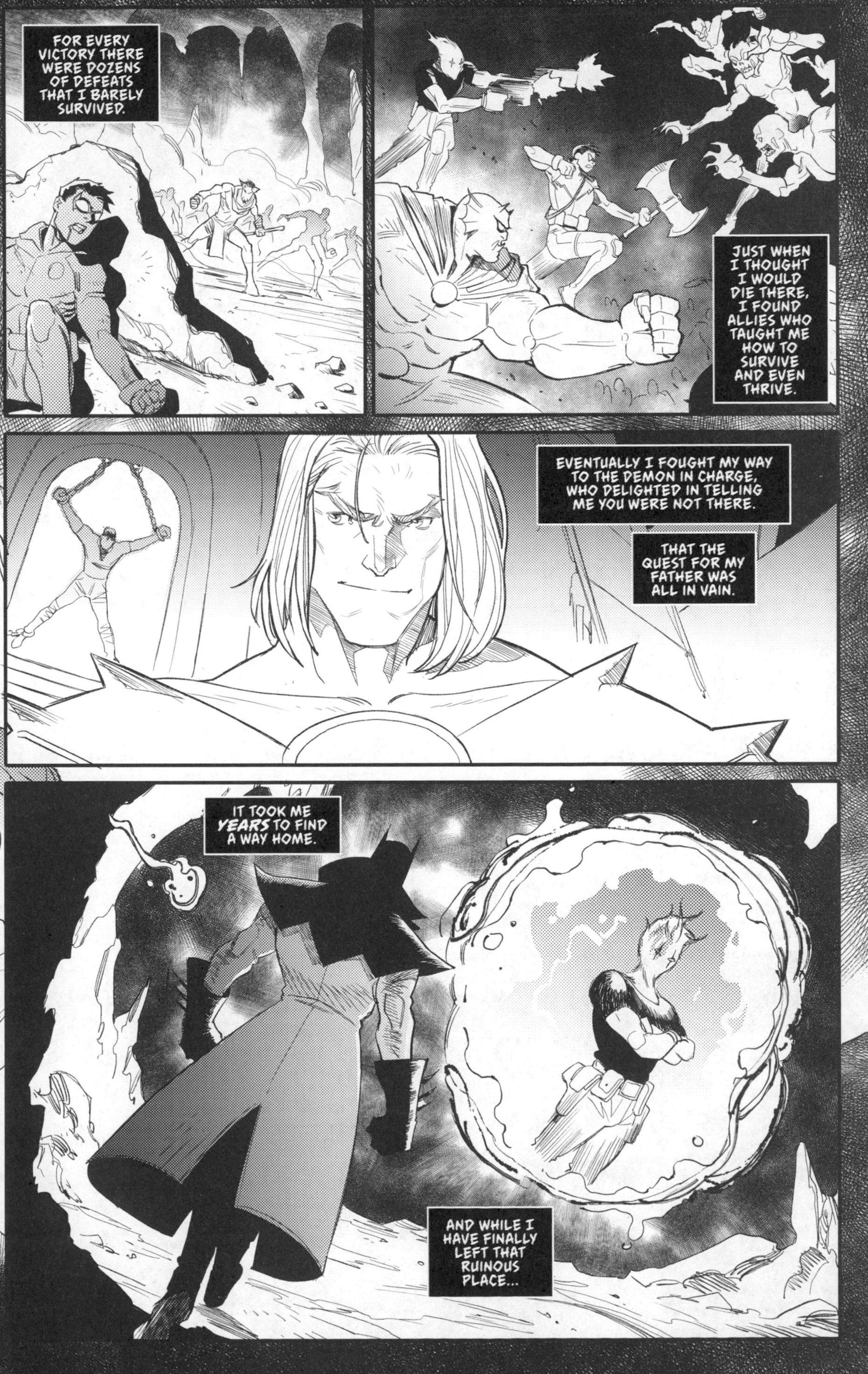

FOR EVERY VICTORY THERE WERE DOZENS OF DEFEATS THAT I BARELY SURVIVED.
JUST WHEN I THOUGHT I WOULD DIE THERE, I FOUND ALLIES WHO TAUGHT ME HOW TO SURVIVE AND EVEN THRIVE.
EVENTUALLY I FOUGHT MY WAY TO THE DEMON IN CHARGE, WHO DELIGHTED IN TELLING ME YOU WERE NOT THERE.
THAT THE QUEST FOR MY FATHER WAS ALL IN VAIN.
IT TOOK ME *YEARS* TO FIND A WAY HOME.
AND WHILE I HAVE FINALLY LEFT THAT RUINOUS PLACE...

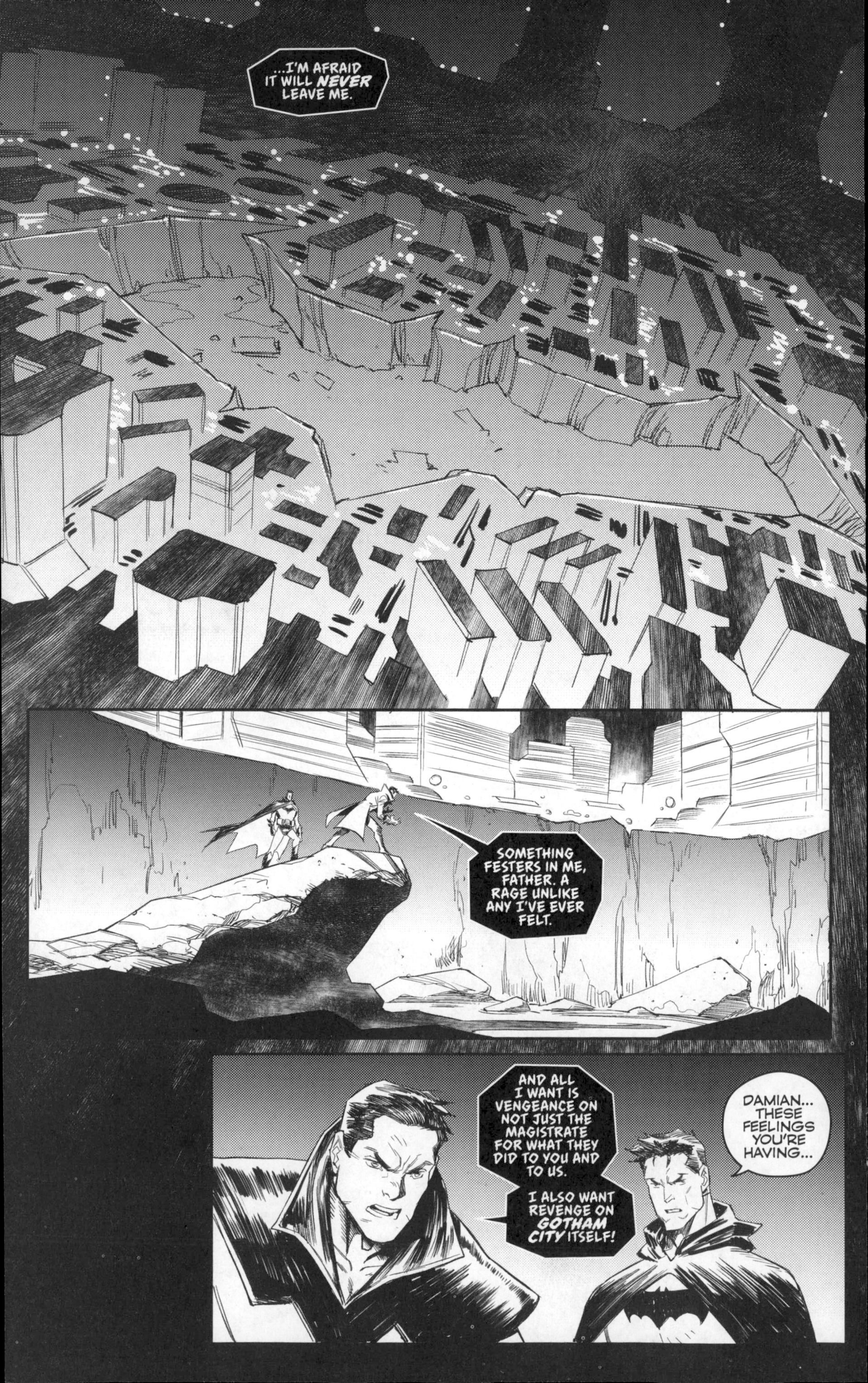
...I'M AFRAID IT WILL NEVER LEAVE ME.
SOMETHING FESTERS IN ME, FATHER. A RAGE UNLIKE ANY I'VE EVER FELT.
AND ALL I WANT IS VENGEANCE ON NOT JUST THE MAGISTRATE FOR WHAT THEY DID TO YOU AND TO US.
I ALSO WANT REVENGE ON GOTHAM CITY ITSELF!
DAMIAN... THESE FEELINGS YOU'RE HAVING...

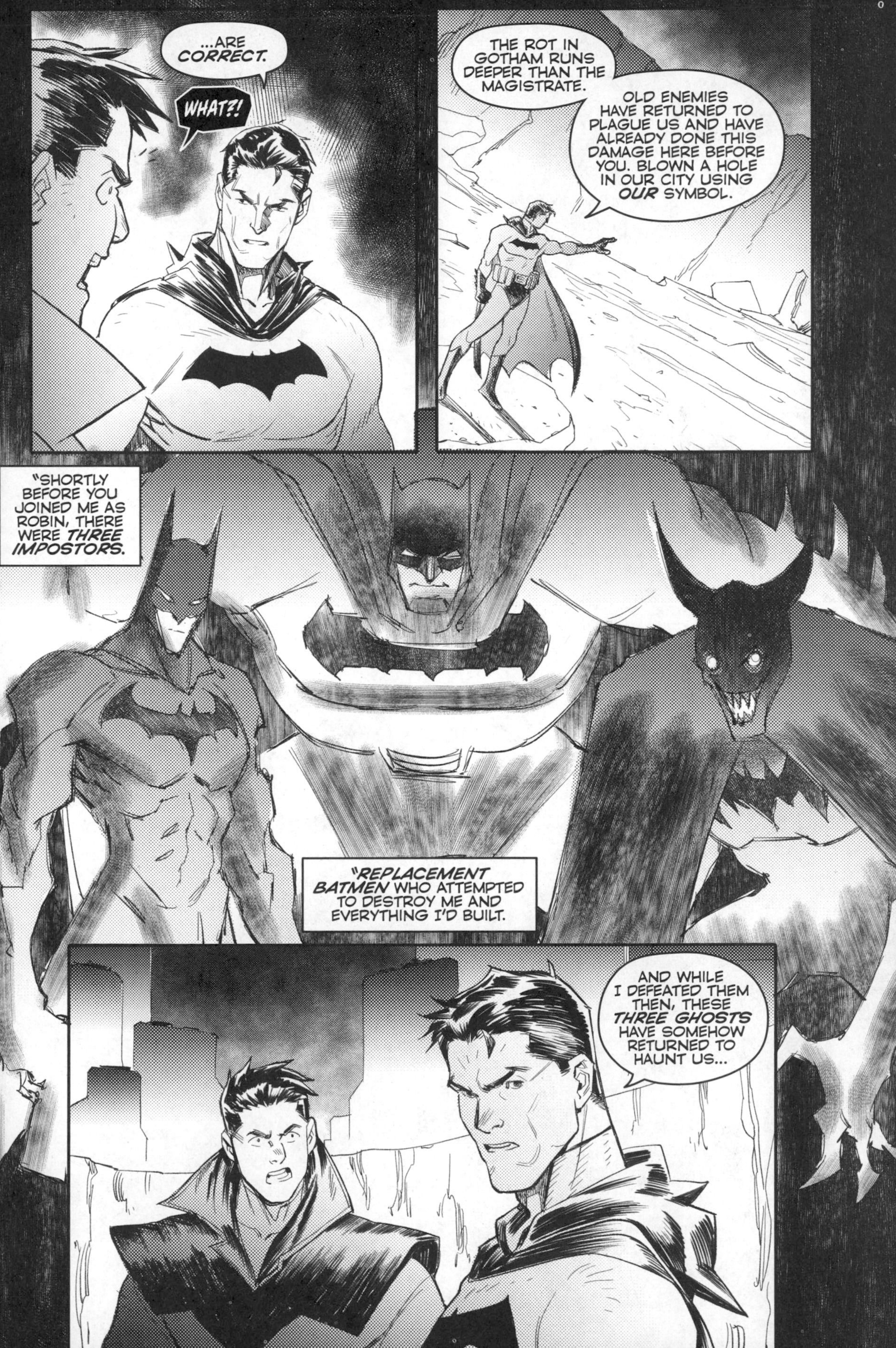

...ARE CORRECT.
WHAT?!
THE ROT IN GOTHAM RUNS DEEPER THAN THE MAGISTRATE.
OLD ENEMIES HAVE RETURNED TO PLAGUE US AND HAVE ALREADY DONE THIS DAMAGE HERE BEFORE YOU. BLOWN A HOLE IN OUR CITY USING OUR SYMBOL.
"SHORTLY BEFORE YOU JOINED ME AS ROBIN, THERE WERE THREE IMPOSTORS.
"REPLACEMENT BATMEN WHO ATTEMPTED TO DESTROY ME AND EVERYTHING I'D BUILT.
AND WHILE I DEFEATED THEM THEN, THESE THREE GHOSTS HAVE SOMEHOW RETURNED TO HAUNT US...

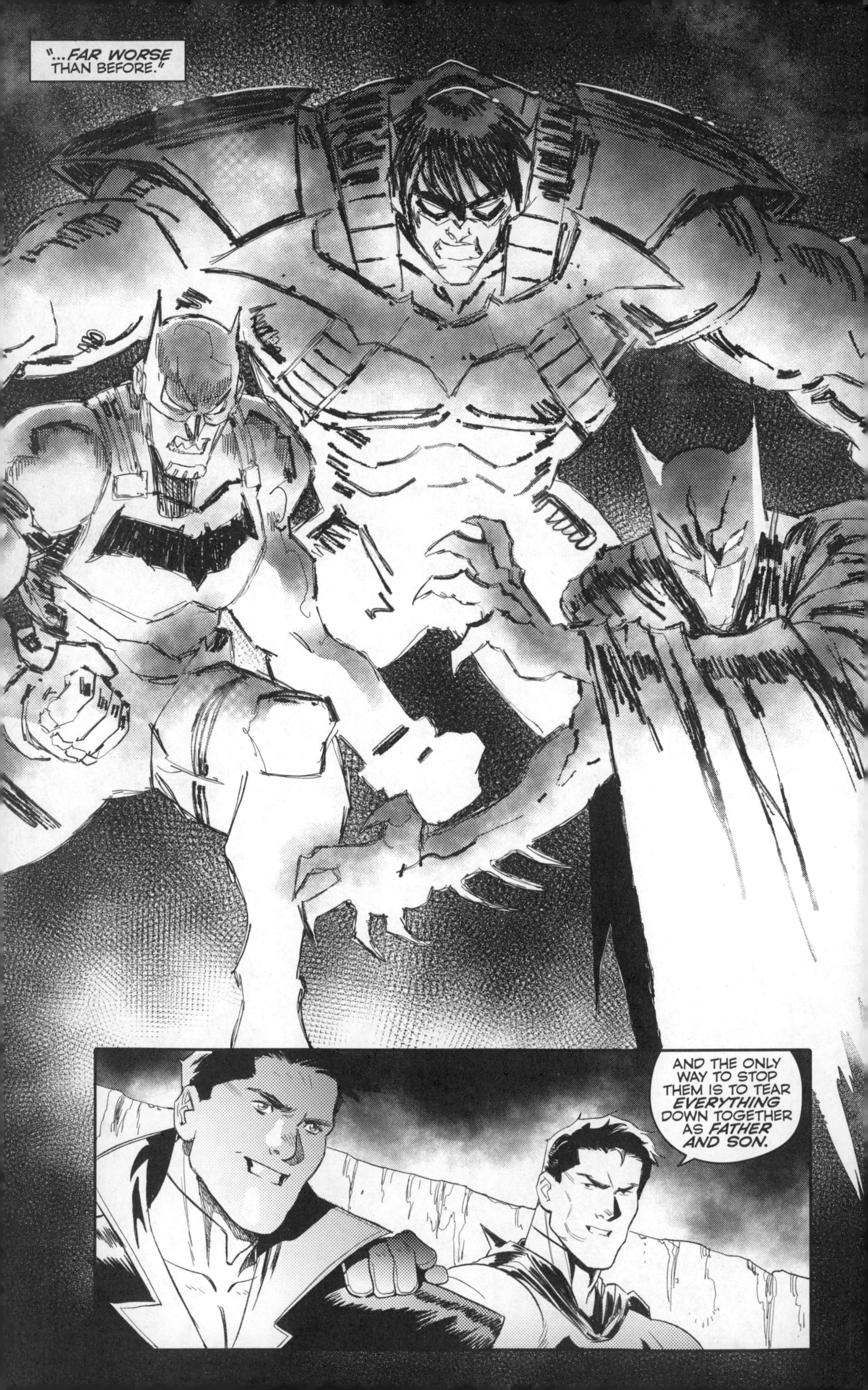
"...FAR WORSE THAN BEFORE."
AND THE ONLY WAY TO STOP THEM IS TO TEAR EVERYTHING DOWN TOGETHER AS FATHER AND SON.

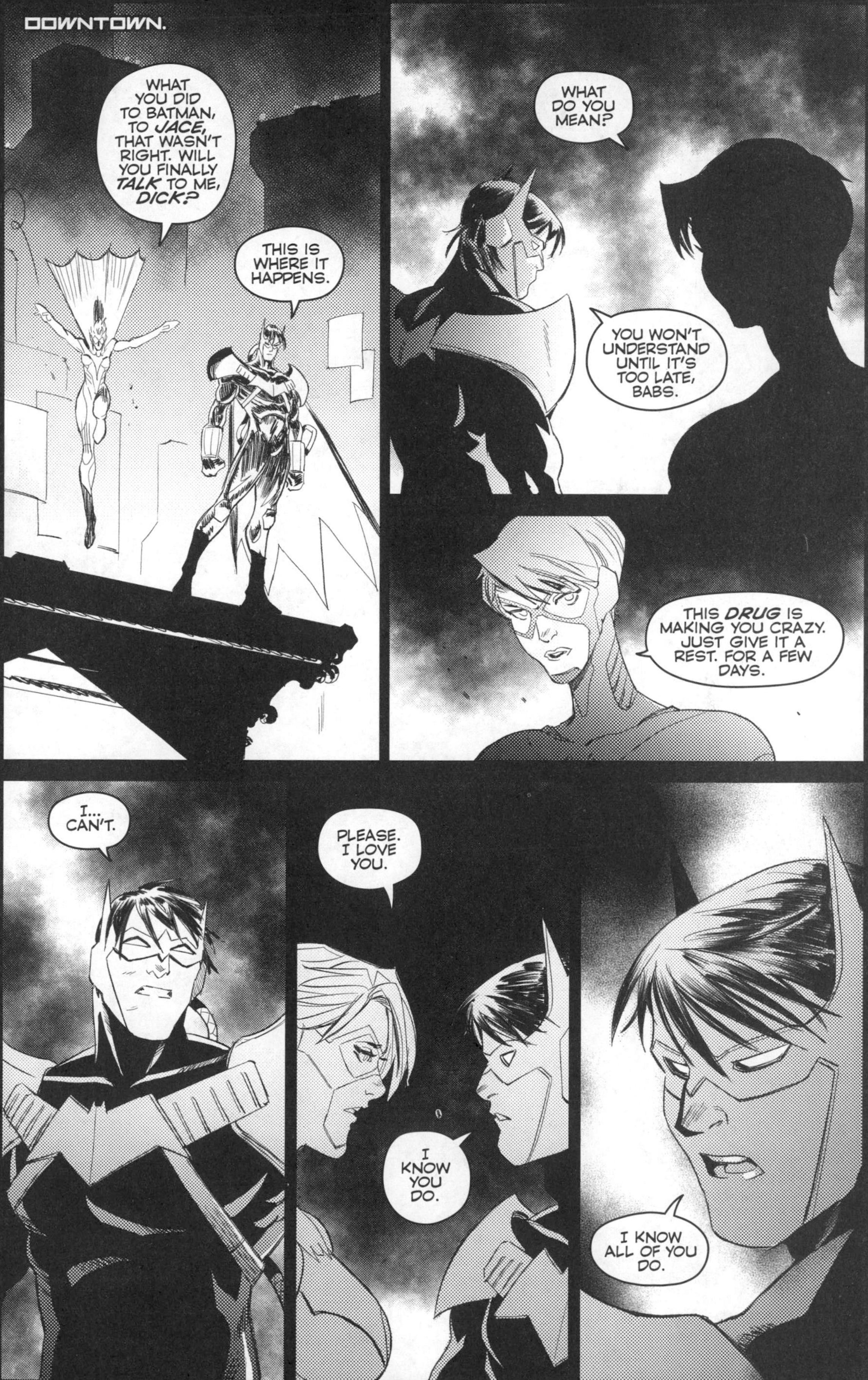
DOWNTOWN.
WHAT YOU DID TO BATMAN, TO JACE, THAT WASN'T RIGHT. WILL YOU FINALLY TALK TO ME, DICK?
THIS IS WHERE IT HAPPENS.
WHAT DO YOU MEAN?
YOU WON'T UNDERSTAND UNTIL IT'S TOO LATE, BABS.
THIS DRUG IS MAKING YOU CRAZY. JUST GIVE IT A REST. FOR A FEW DAYS.
I... CAN'T.
PLEASE. I LOVE YOU.
I KNOW YOU DO.
I KNOW ALL OF YOU DO.

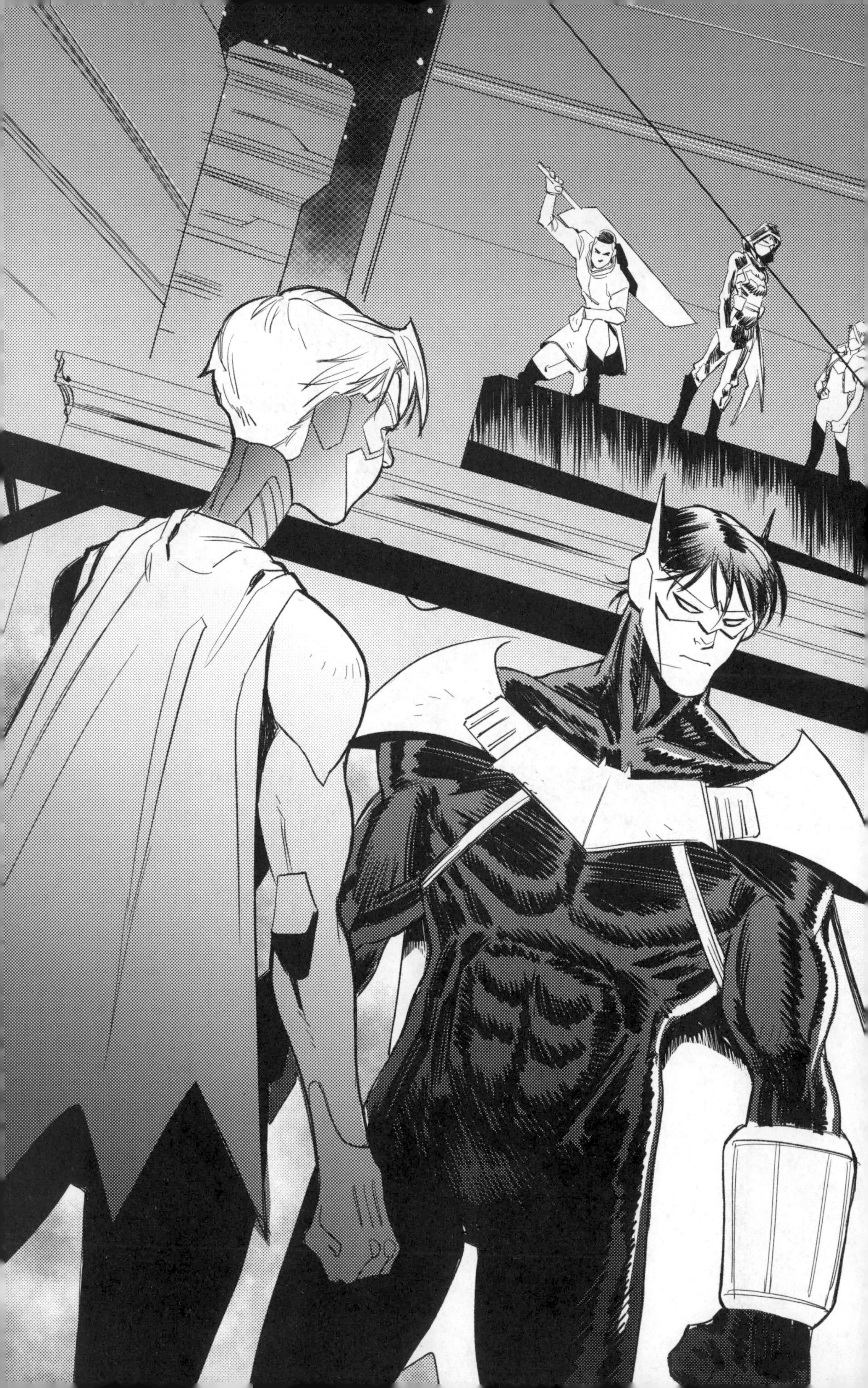

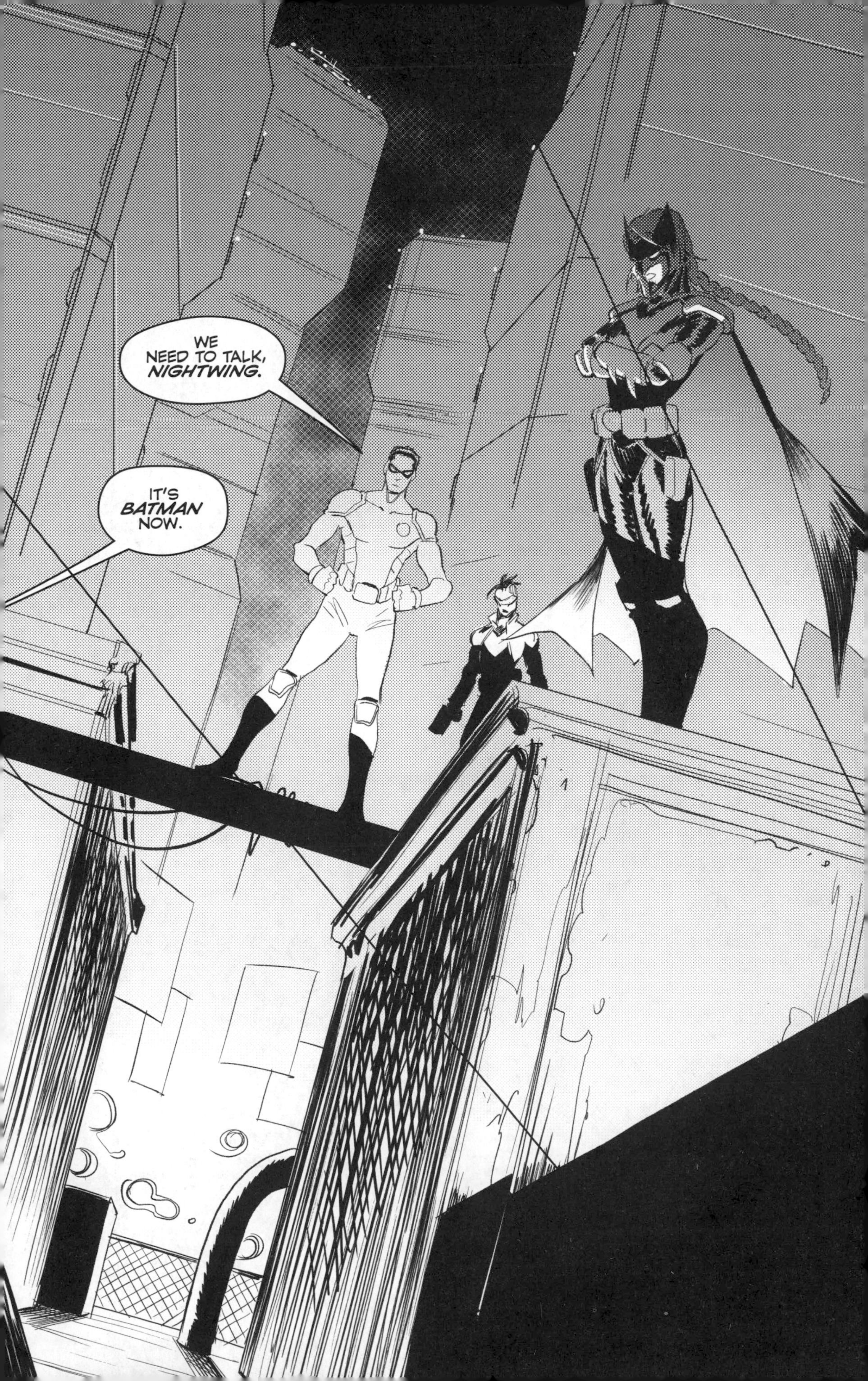
WE NEED TO TALK, *NIGHTWING.*
IT'S *BATMAN* NOW.

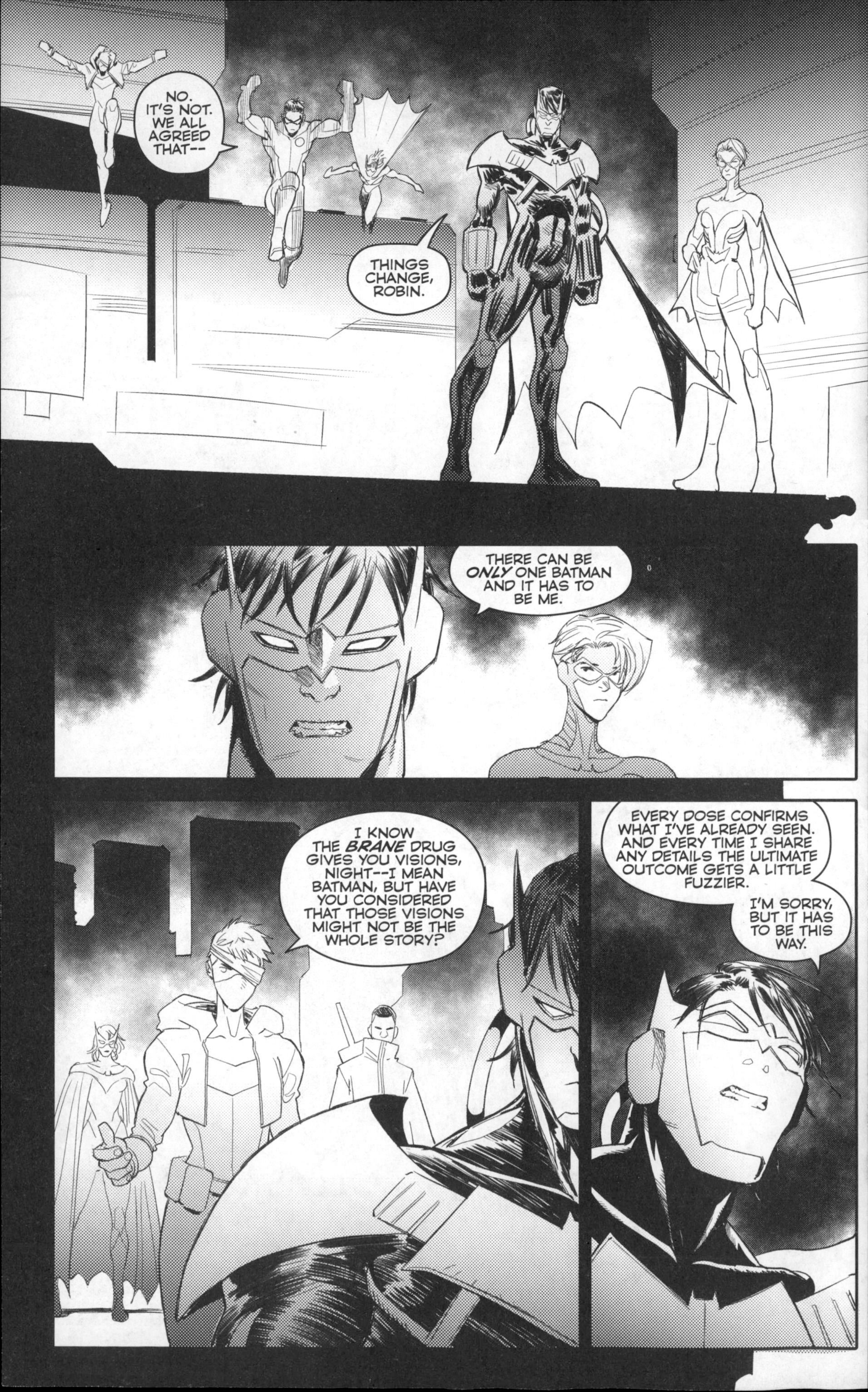
NO. IT'S NOT. WE ALL AGREED THAT--
THINGS CHANGE, ROBIN.
THERE CAN BE ONLY ONE BATMAN AND IT HAS TO BE ME.
I KNOW THE BRANE DRUG GIVES YOU VISIONS, NIGHT--I MEAN BATMAN, BUT HAVE YOU CONSIDERED THAT THOSE VISIONS MIGHT NOT BE THE WHOLE STORY?
EVERY DOSE CONFIRMS WHAT I'VE ALREADY SEEN. AND EVERY TIME I SHARE ANY DETAILS THE ULTIMATE OUTCOME GETS A LITTLE FUZZIER.
I'M SORRY, BUT IT HAS TO BE THIS WAY.

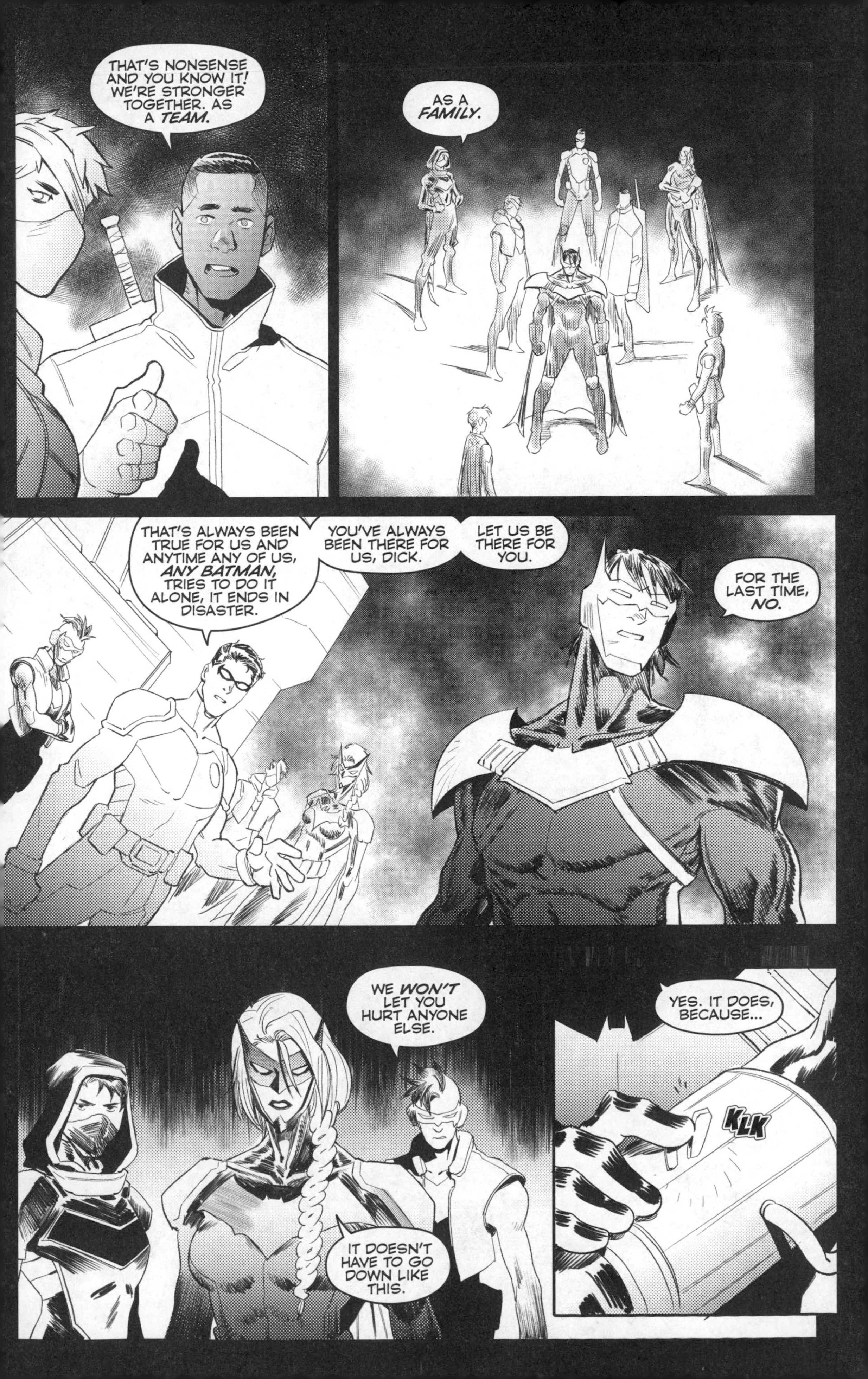
THAT'S NONSENSE AND YOU KNOW IT! WE'RE STRONGER TOGETHER. AS A *TEAM.*
AS A *FAMILY.*
THAT'S ALWAYS BEEN TRUE FOR US AND ANYTIME ANY OF US, *ANY BATMAN,* TRIES TO DO IT ALONE, IT ENDS IN DISASTER.
YOU'VE ALWAYS BEEN THERE FOR US, DICK.
LET US BE THERE FOR YOU.
FOR THE LAST TIME, *NO.*
WE *WON'T* LET YOU HURT ANYONE ELSE.
IT DOESN'T HAVE TO GO DOWN LIKE THIS.
YES. IT DOES, BECAUSE...
KLK

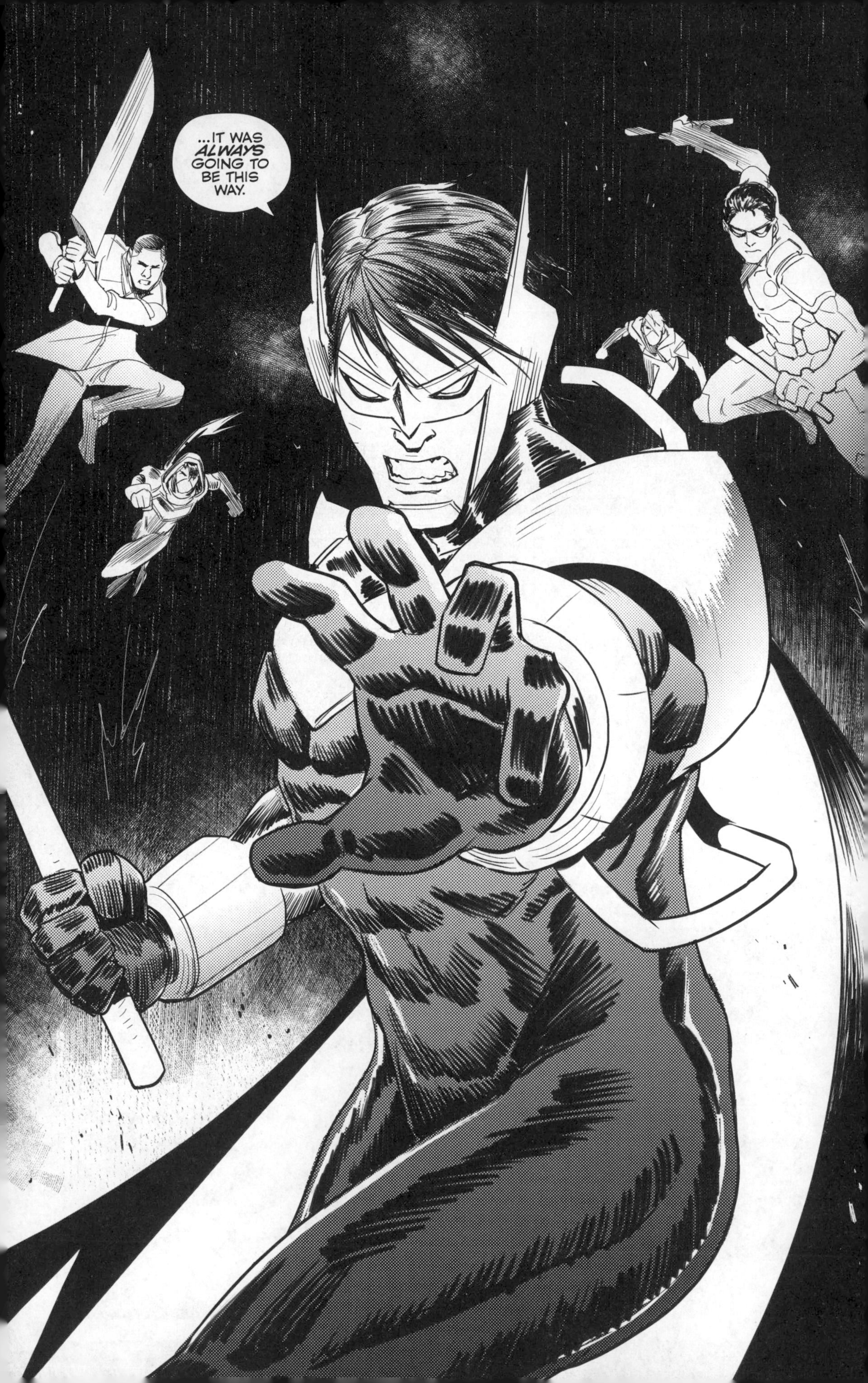
...IT WAS *ALWAYS* GOING TO BE THIS WAY.

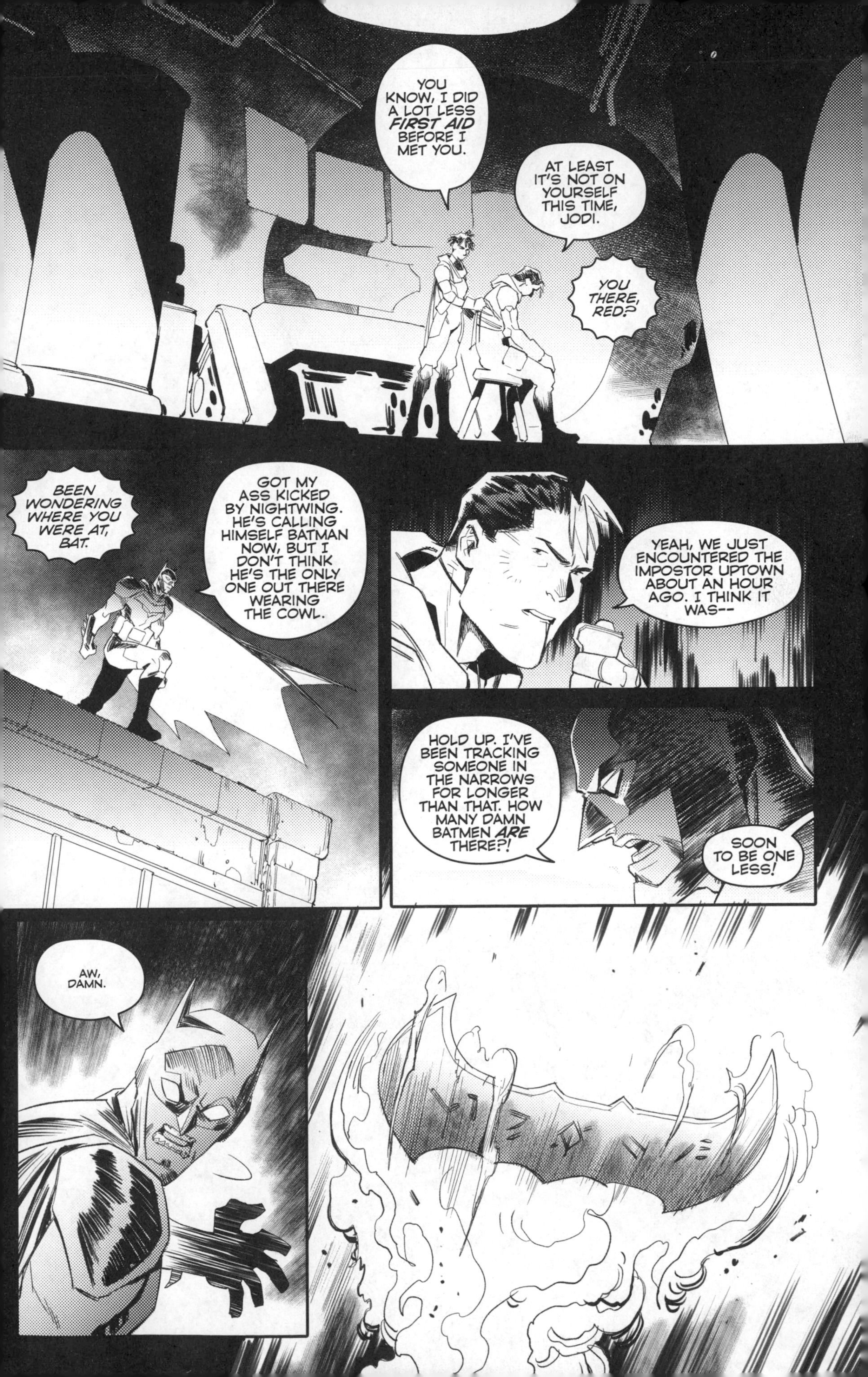

YOU KNOW, I DID A LOT LESS FIRST AID BEFORE I MET YOU.
AT LEAST IT'S NOT ON YOURSELF THIS TIME, JODI.
YOU THERE, RED?
BEEN WONDERING WHERE YOU WERE AT, BAT.
GOT MY ASS KICKED BY NIGHTWING. HE'S CALLING HIMSELF BATMAN NOW, BUT I DON'T THINK HE'S THE ONLY ONE OUT THERE WEARING THE COWL.
YEAH, WE JUST ENCOUNTERED THE IMPOSTOR UPTOWN ABOUT AN HOUR AGO. I THINK IT WAS--
HOLD UP. I'VE BEEN TRACKING SOMEONE IN THE NARROWS FOR LONGER THAN THAT. HOW MANY DAMN BATMEN ARE THERE?!
SOON TO BE ONE LESS!
AW, DAMN.

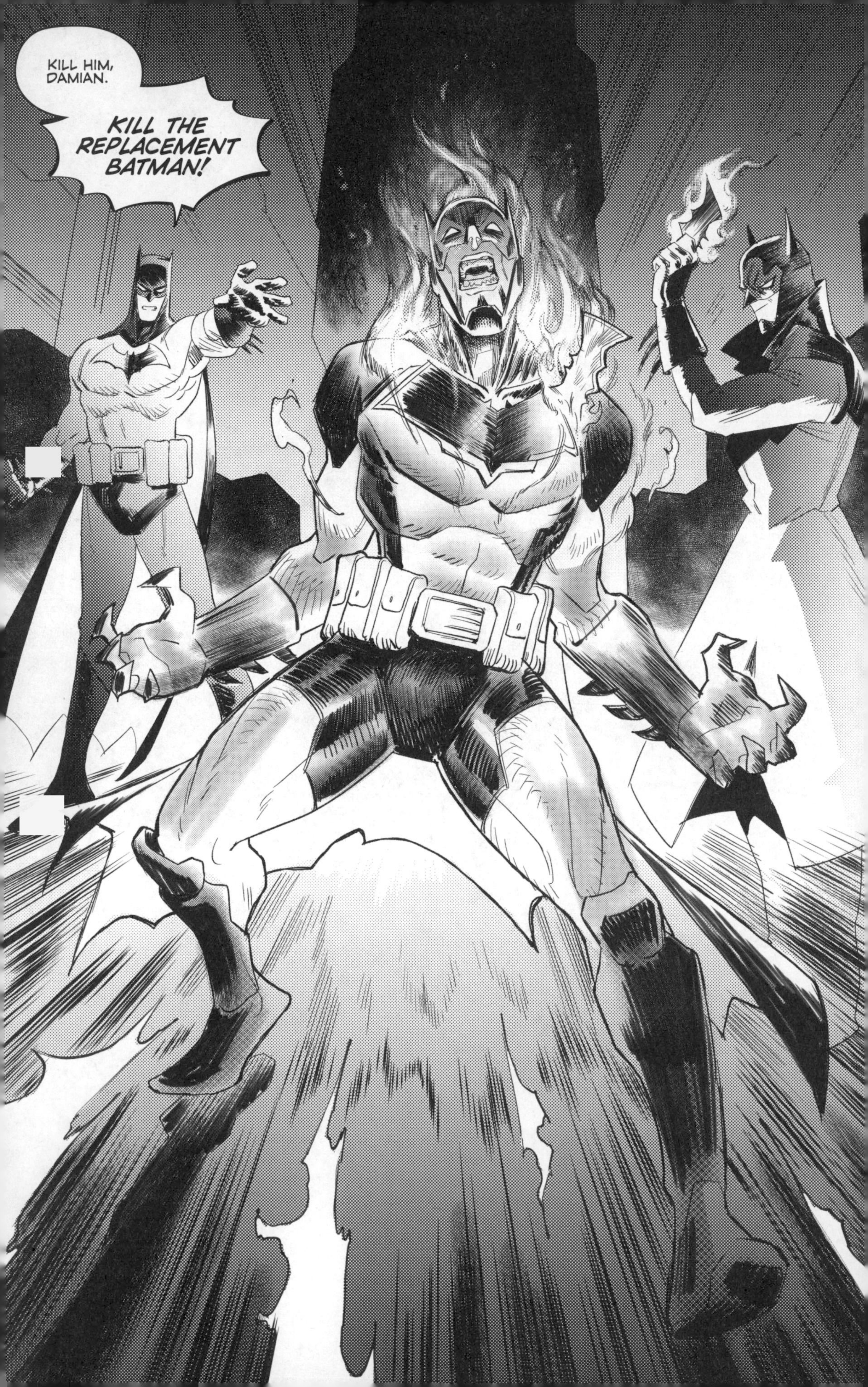
KILL HIM, DAMIAN.
KILL THE REPLACEMENT BATMAN!

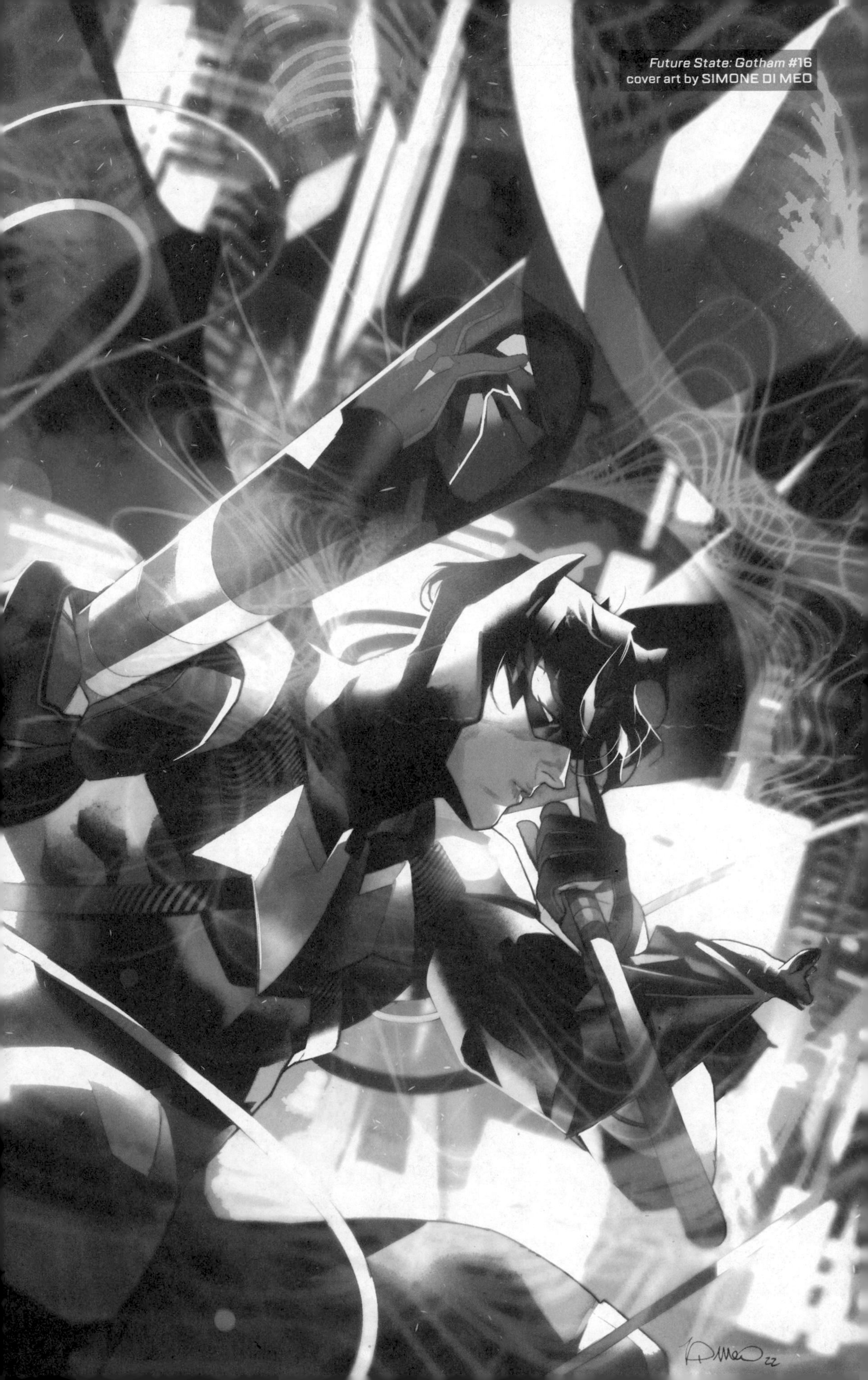

Future State: Gotham #16
cover art by SIMONE DI MEO

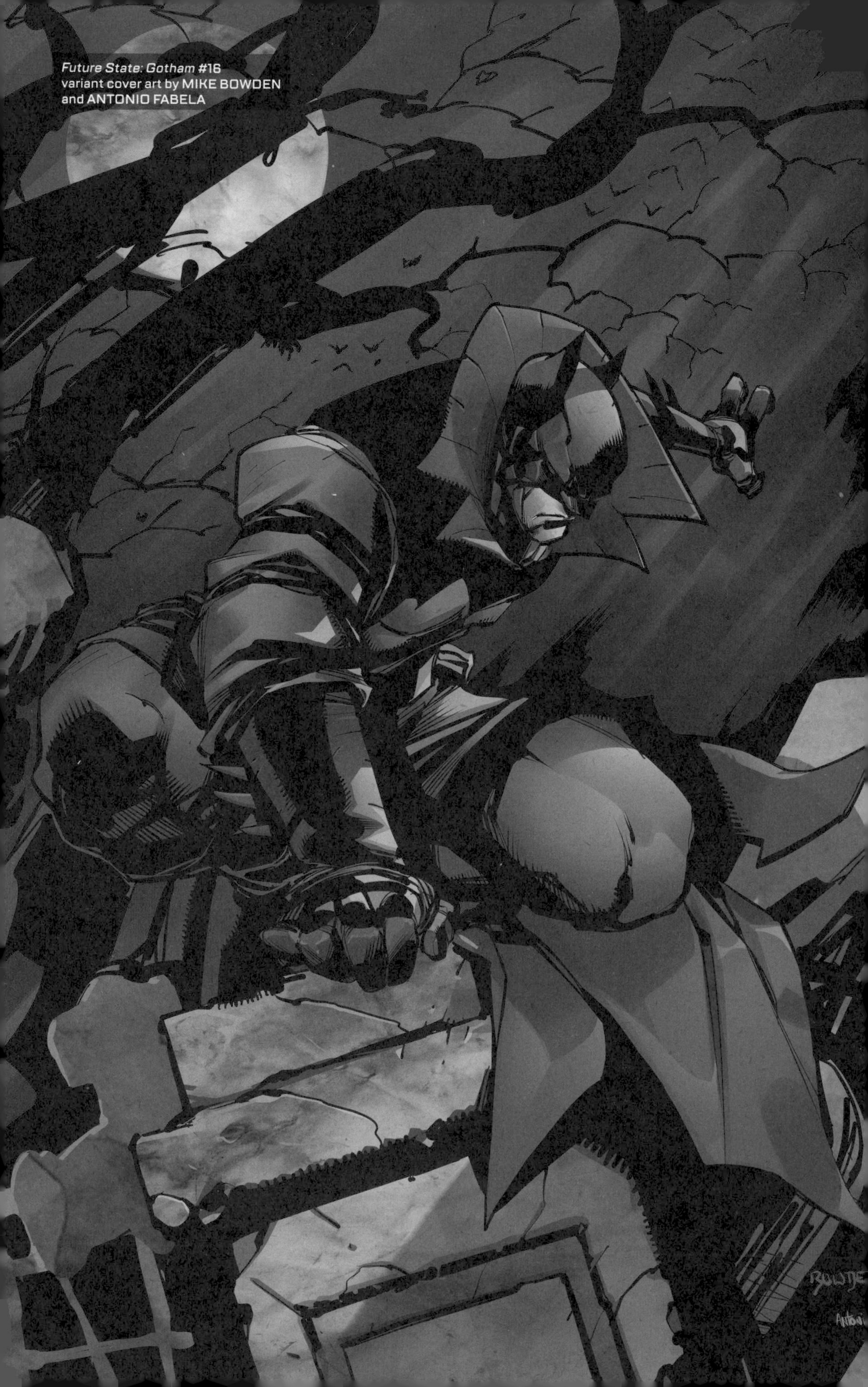

Future State: Gotham #16
variant cover art by MIKE BOWDEN
and ANTONIO FABELA

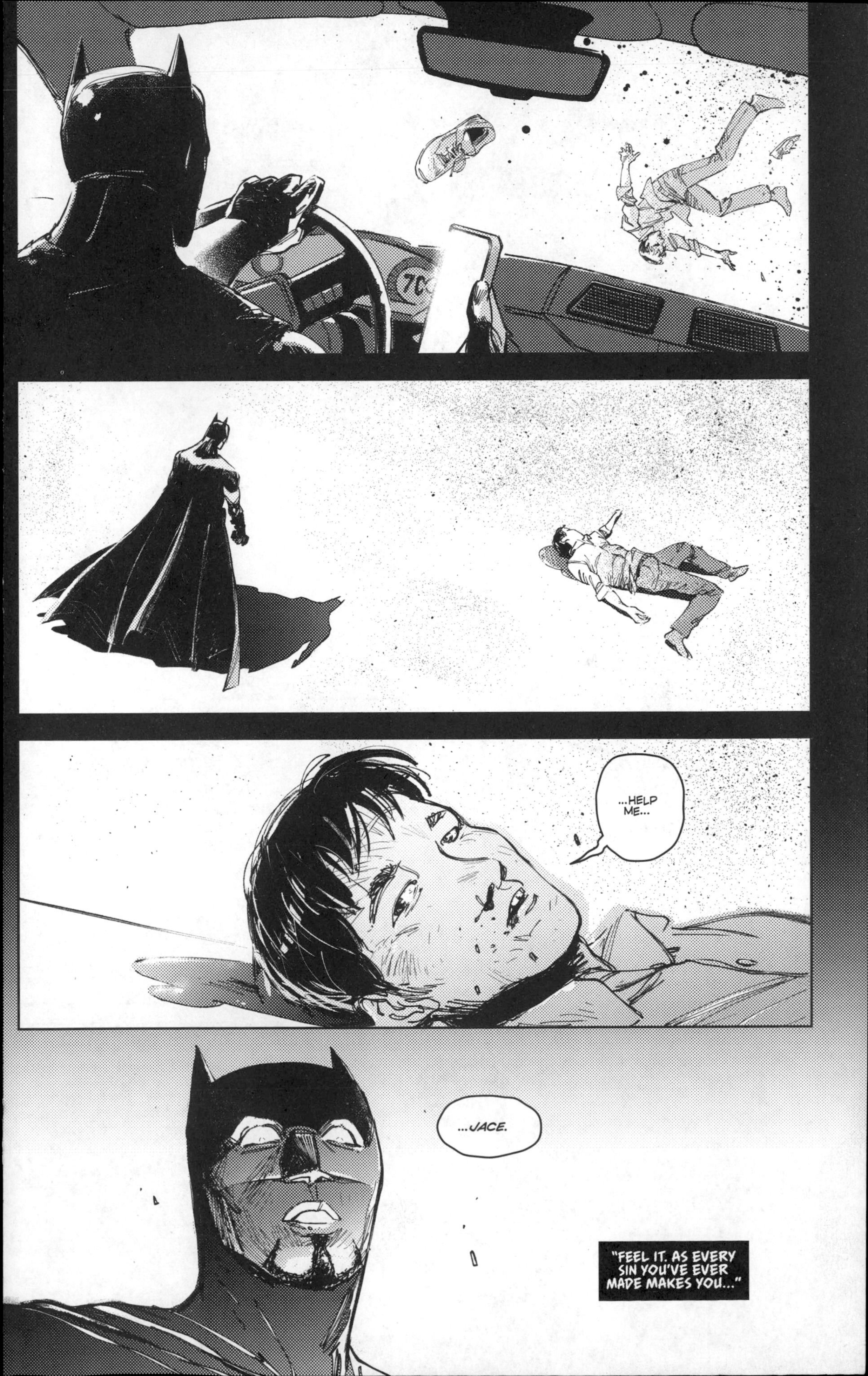
...HELP ME...
...JACE.
"FEEL IT. AS EVERY SIN YOU'VE EVER MADE MAKES YOU..."

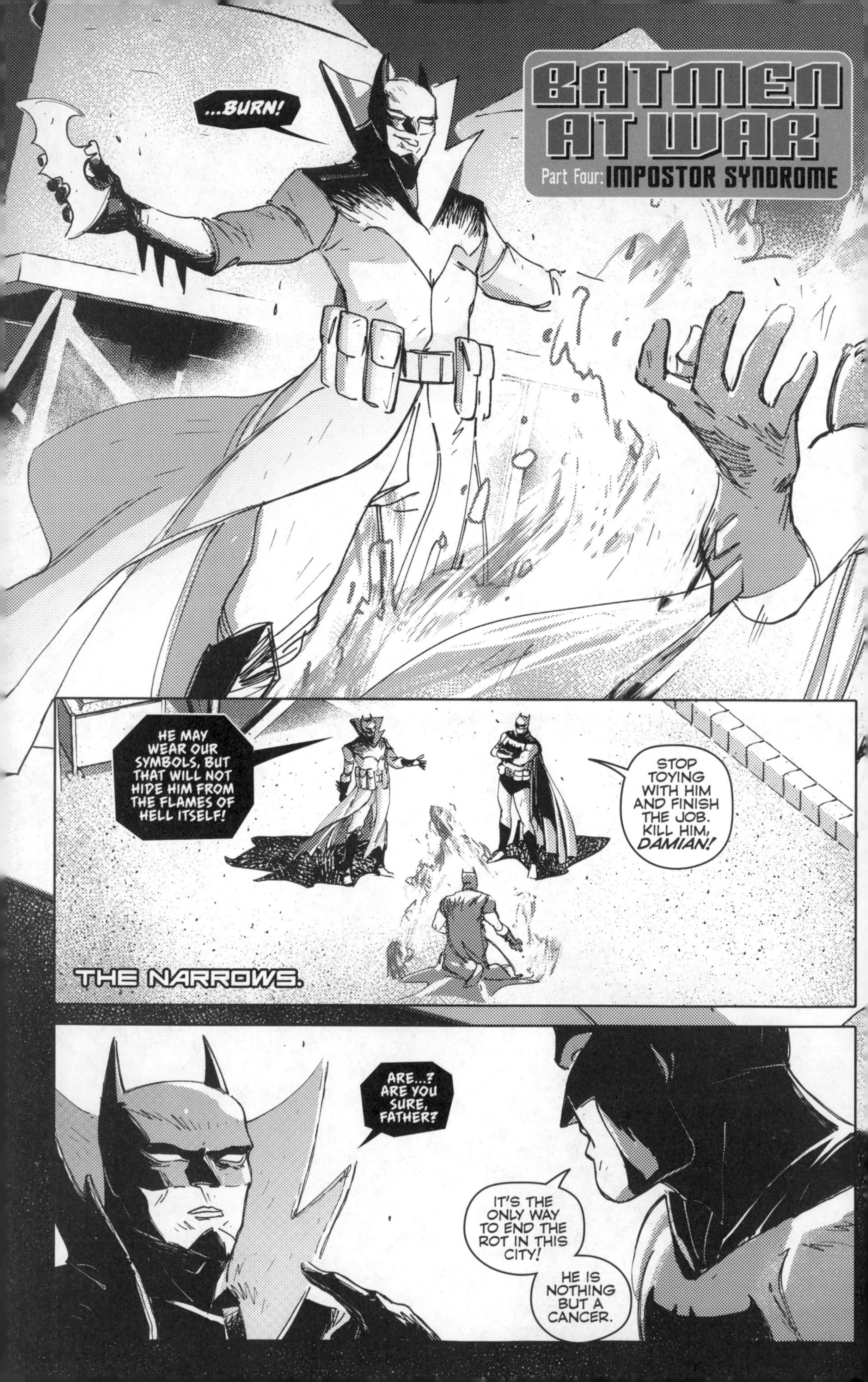
BATMEN AT WAR
Part Four: IMPOSTOR SYNDROME
...BURN!
HE MAY WEAR OUR SYMBOLS, BUT THAT WILL NOT HIDE HIM FROM THE FLAMES OF HELL ITSELF!
STOP TOYING WITH HIM AND FINISH THE JOB. KILL HIM, DAMIAN!
THE NARROWS.
ARE...? ARE YOU SURE, FATHER?
IT'S THE ONLY WAY TO END THE ROT IN THIS CITY!
HE IS NOTHING BUT A CANCER.

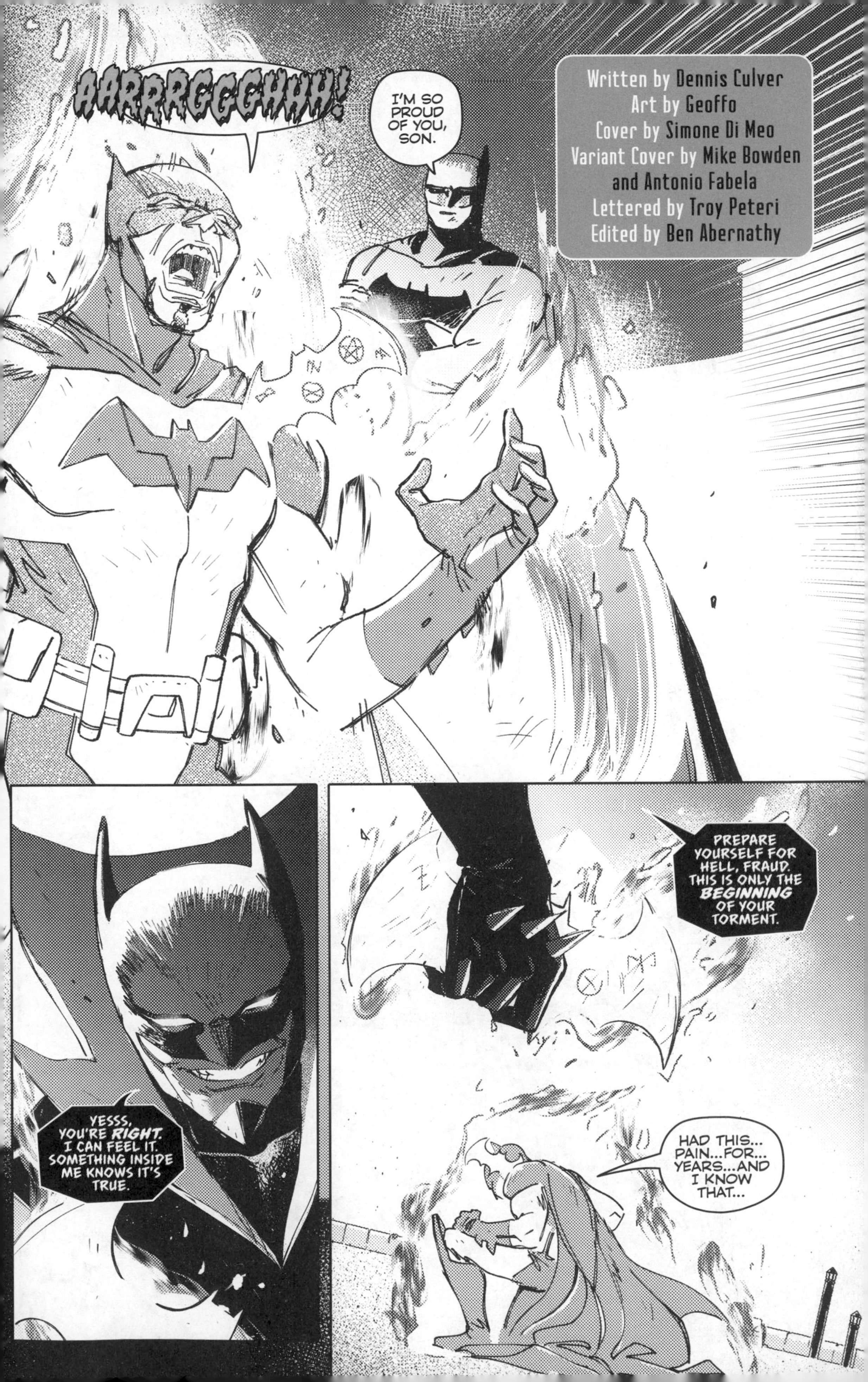
AARRRGGGHHH!
I'M SO PROUD OF YOU, SON.
Written by Dennis Culver
Art by Geoffo
Cover by Simone Di Meo
Variant Cover by Mike Bowden and Antonio Fabela
Lettered by Troy Peteri
Edited by Ben Abernathy
YESSS, YOU'RE RIGHT. I CAN FEEL IT. SOMETHING INSIDE ME KNOWS IT'S TRUE.
PREPARE YOURSELF FOR HELL, FRAUD. THIS IS ONLY THE BEGINNING OF YOUR TORMENT.
HAD THIS... PAIN...FOR... YEARS...AND I KNOW THAT...

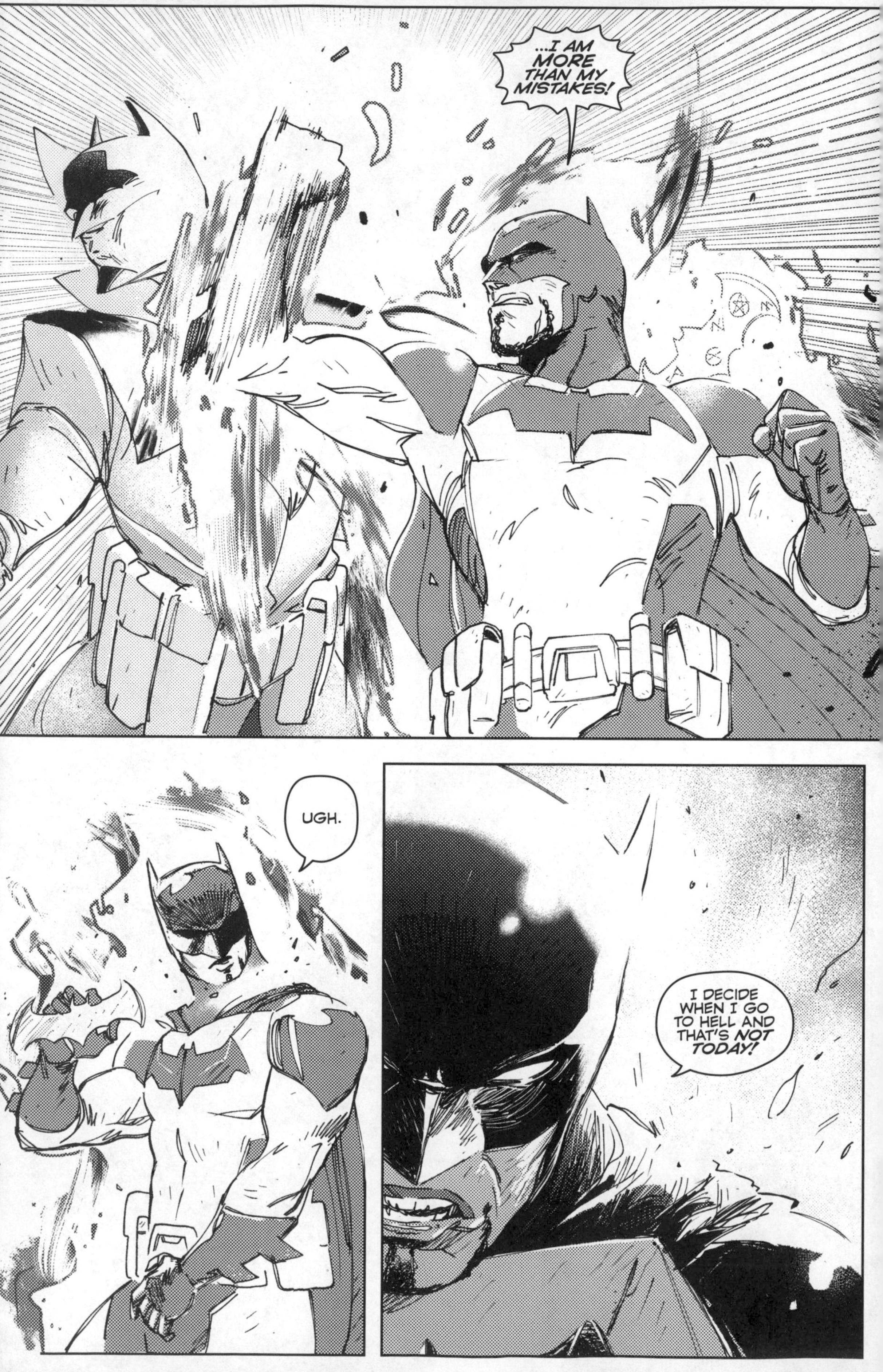
...I AM MORE THAN MY MISTAKES!
UGH.
I DECIDE WHEN I GO TO HELL AND THAT'S NOT TODAY!

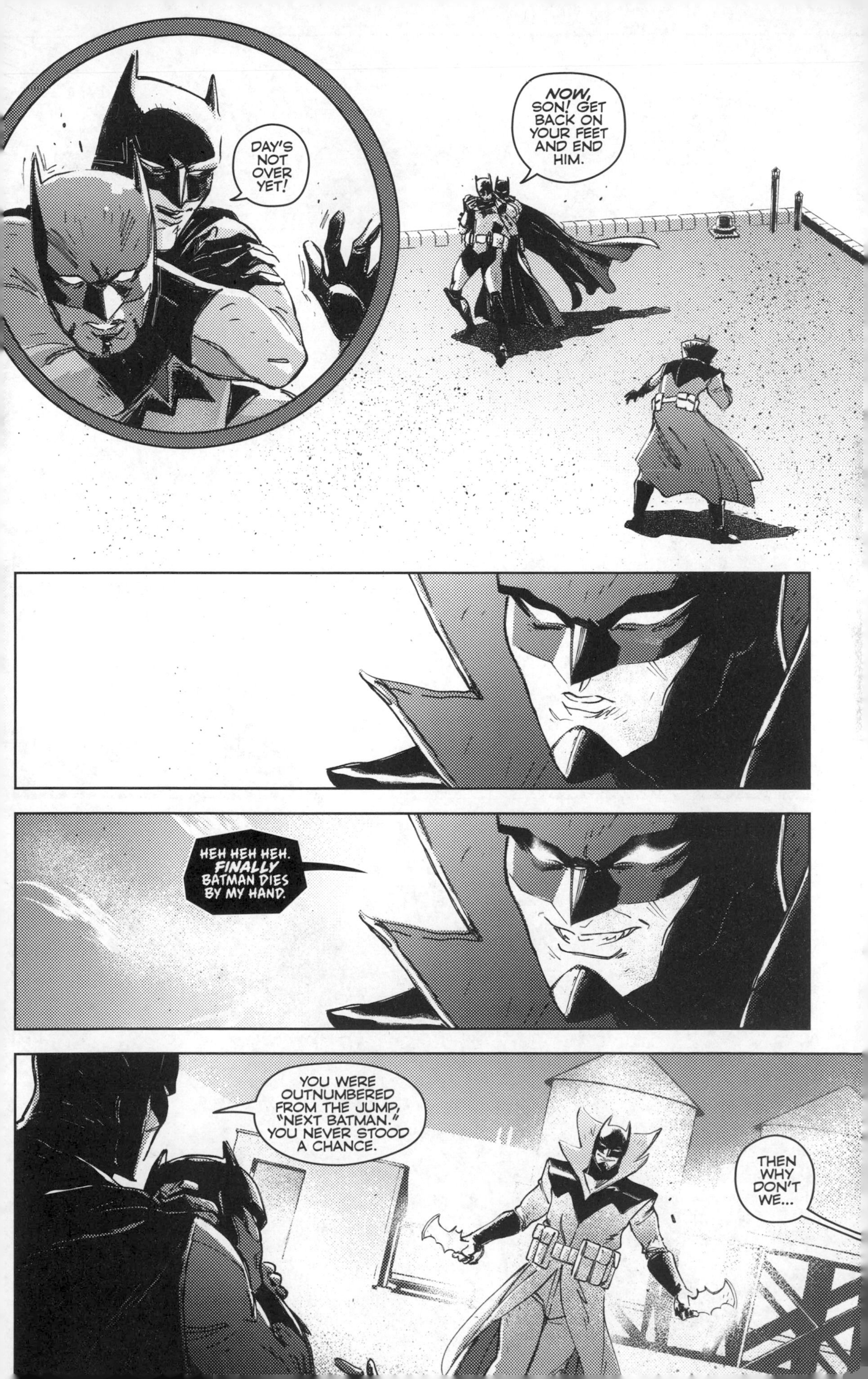
DAY'S NOT OVER YET!
NOW, SON! GET BACK ON YOUR FEET AND END HIM.
HEH HEH HEH. FINALLY BATMAN DIES BY MY HAND.
YOU WERE OUTNUMBERED FROM THE JUMP, "NEXT BATMAN." YOU NEVER STOOD A CHANCE.
THEN WHY DON'T WE...

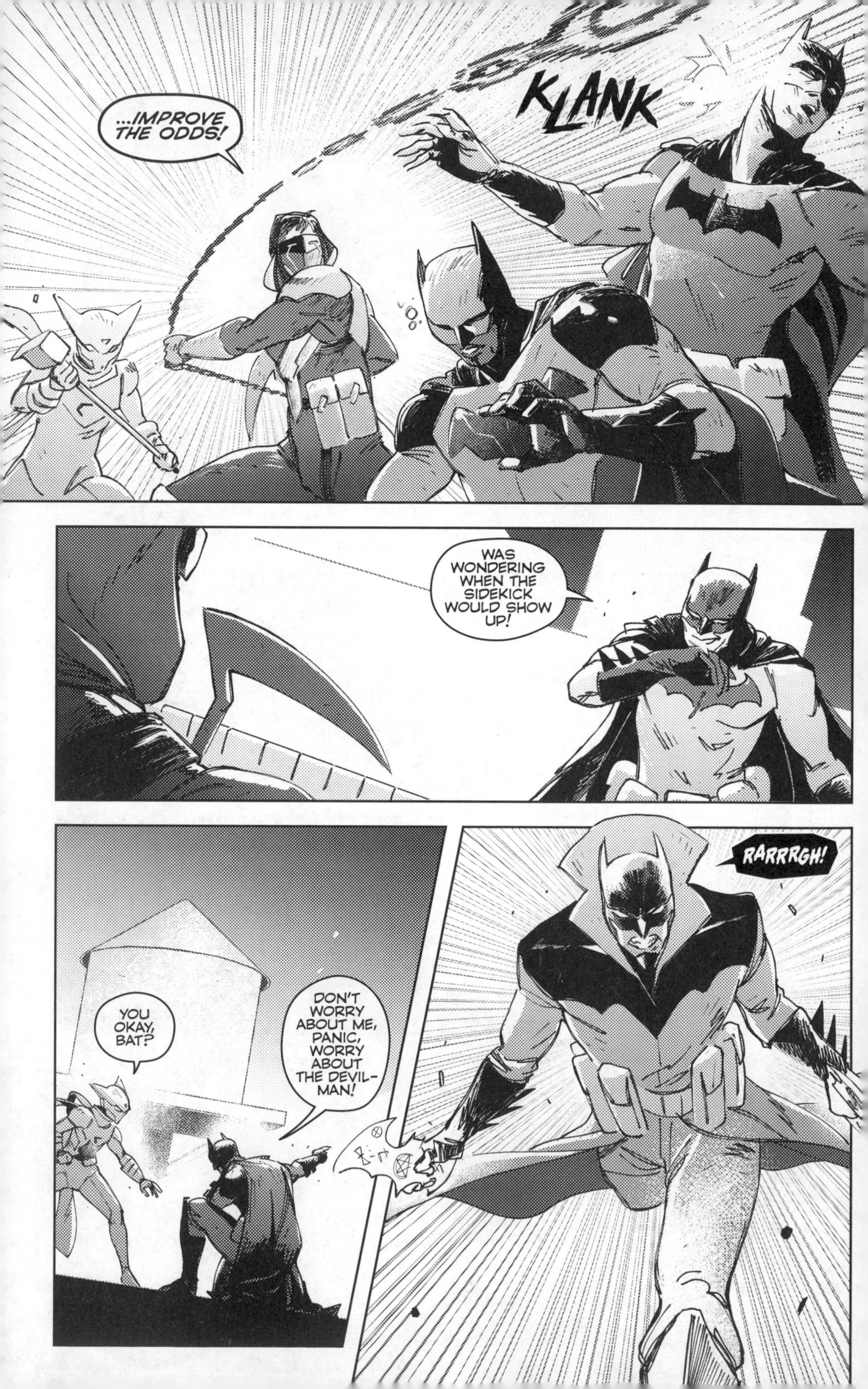
KLANK
...IMPROVE THE ODDS!
WAS WONDERING WHEN THE SIDEKICK WOULD SHOW UP!
YOU OKAY, BAT?
DON'T WORRY ABOUT ME, PANIC, WORRY ABOUT THE DEVIL-MAN!
RARRRGH!

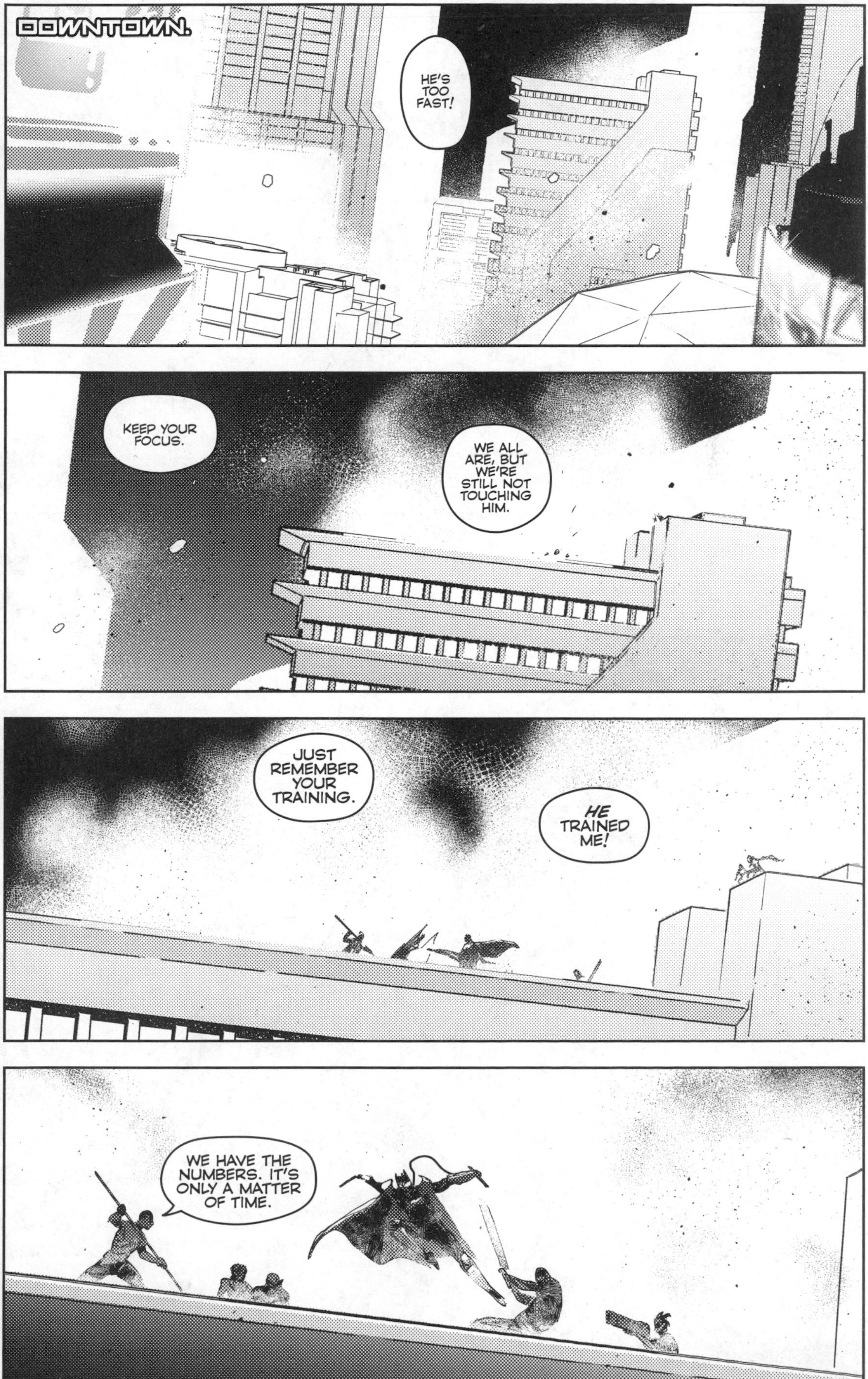
DOWNTOWN.
HE'S TOO FAST!
KEEP YOUR FOCUS.
WE ALL ARE, BUT WE'RE STILL NOT TOUCHING HIM.
JUST REMEMBER YOUR TRAINING.
HE TRAINED ME!
WE HAVE THE NUMBERS. IT'S ONLY A MATTER OF TIME.

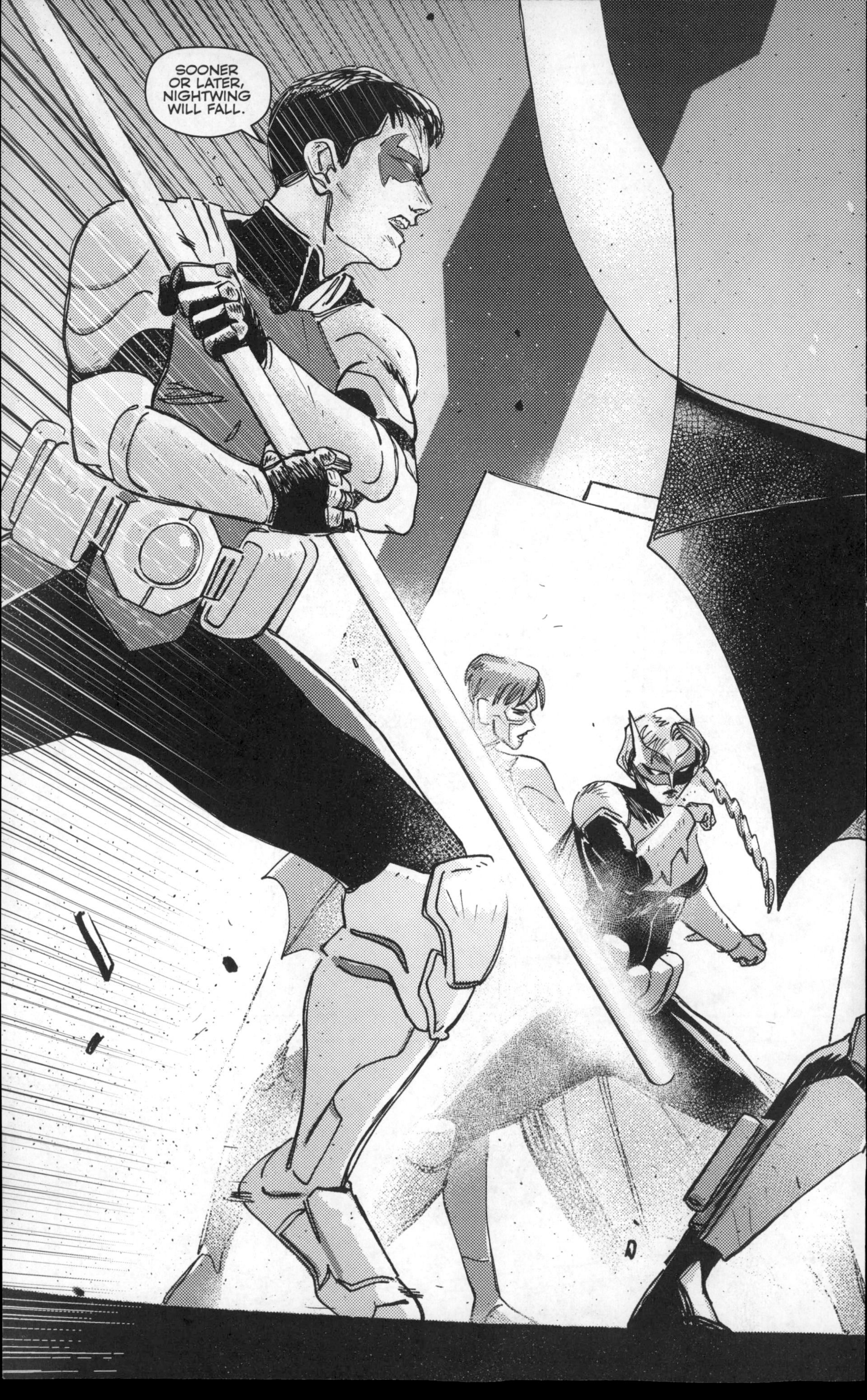
SOONER OR LATER, NIGHTWING WILL FALL.

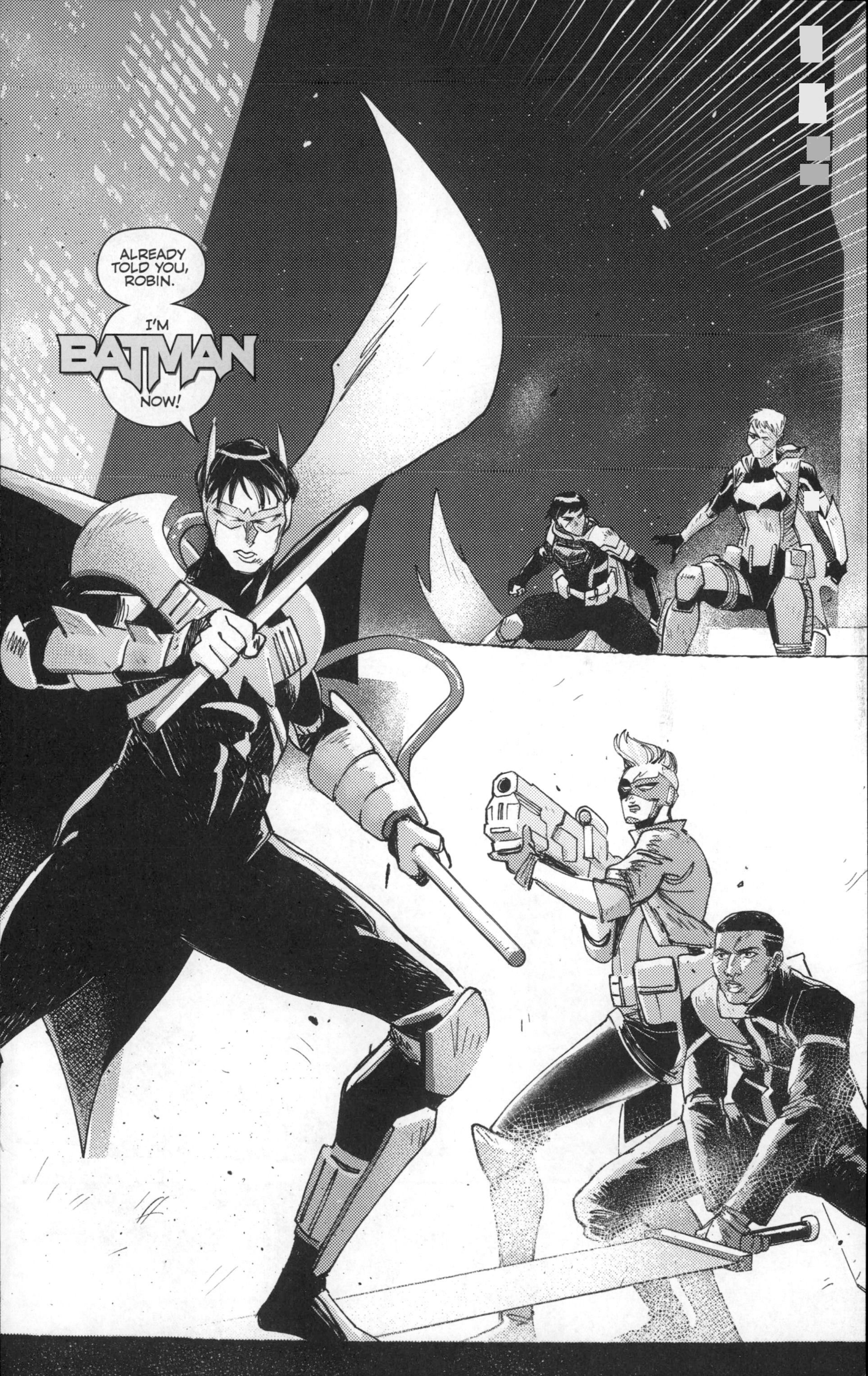
ALREADY TOLD YOU, ROBIN.
I'M BATMAN NOW!

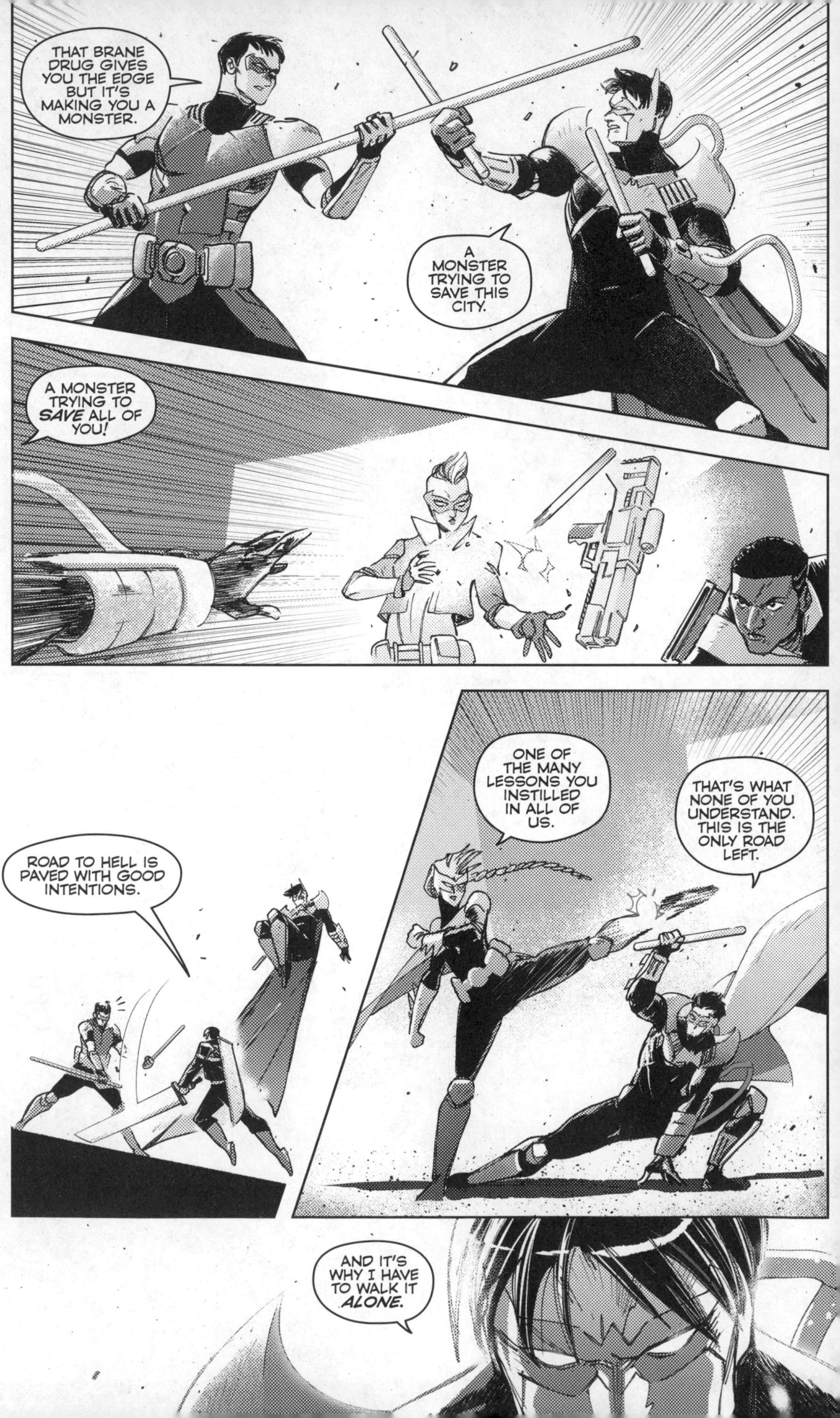

THAT BRANE DRUG GIVES YOU THE EDGE BUT IT'S MAKING YOU A MONSTER.
A MONSTER TRYING TO SAVE THIS CITY.
A MONSTER TRYING TO *SAVE* ALL OF YOU!
ROAD TO HELL IS PAVED WITH GOOD INTENTIONS.
ONE OF THE MANY LESSONS YOU INSTILLED IN ALL OF US.
THAT'S WHAT NONE OF YOU UNDERSTAND. THIS IS THE ONLY ROAD LEFT.
AND IT'S WHY I HAVE TO WALK IT *ALONE*.

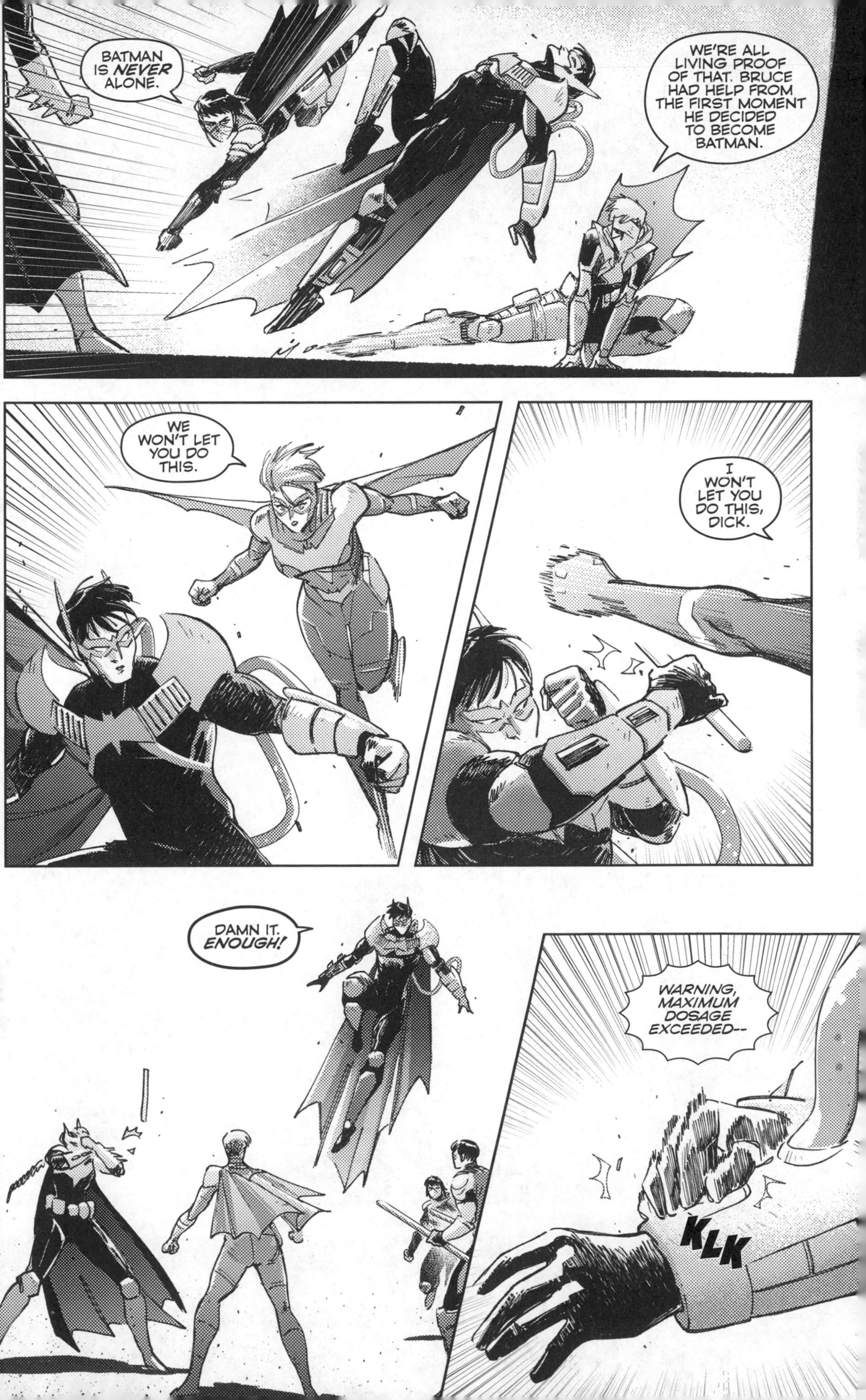
BATMAN IS *NEVER* ALONE.
WE'RE ALL LIVING PROOF OF THAT. BRUCE HAD HELP FROM THE FIRST MOMENT HE DECIDED TO BECOME BATMAN.
WE WON'T LET YOU DO THIS.
I WON'T LET YOU DO THIS, DICK.
DAMN IT. *ENOUGH!*
WARNING, MAXIMUM DOSAGE EXCEEDED--
KLK

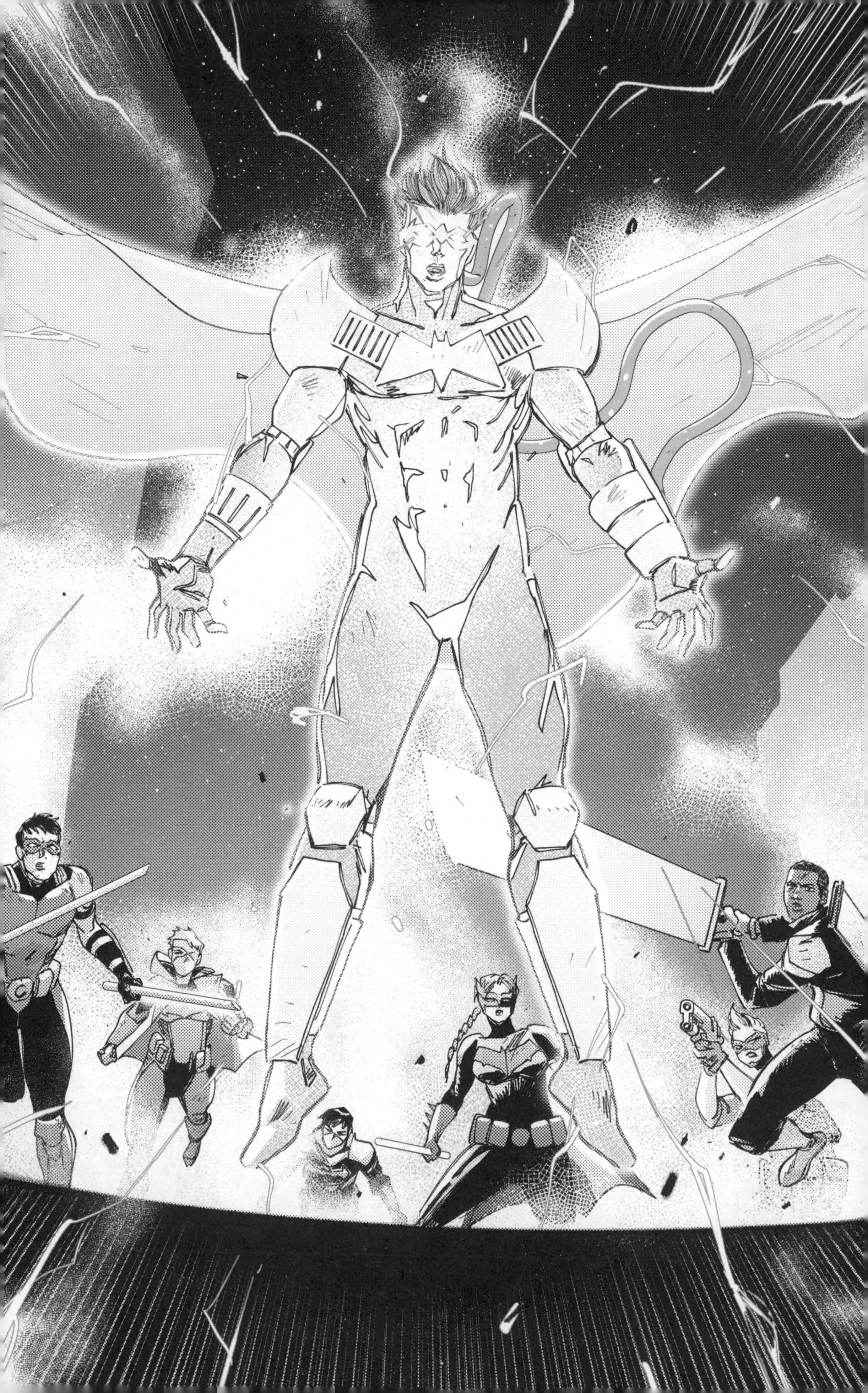

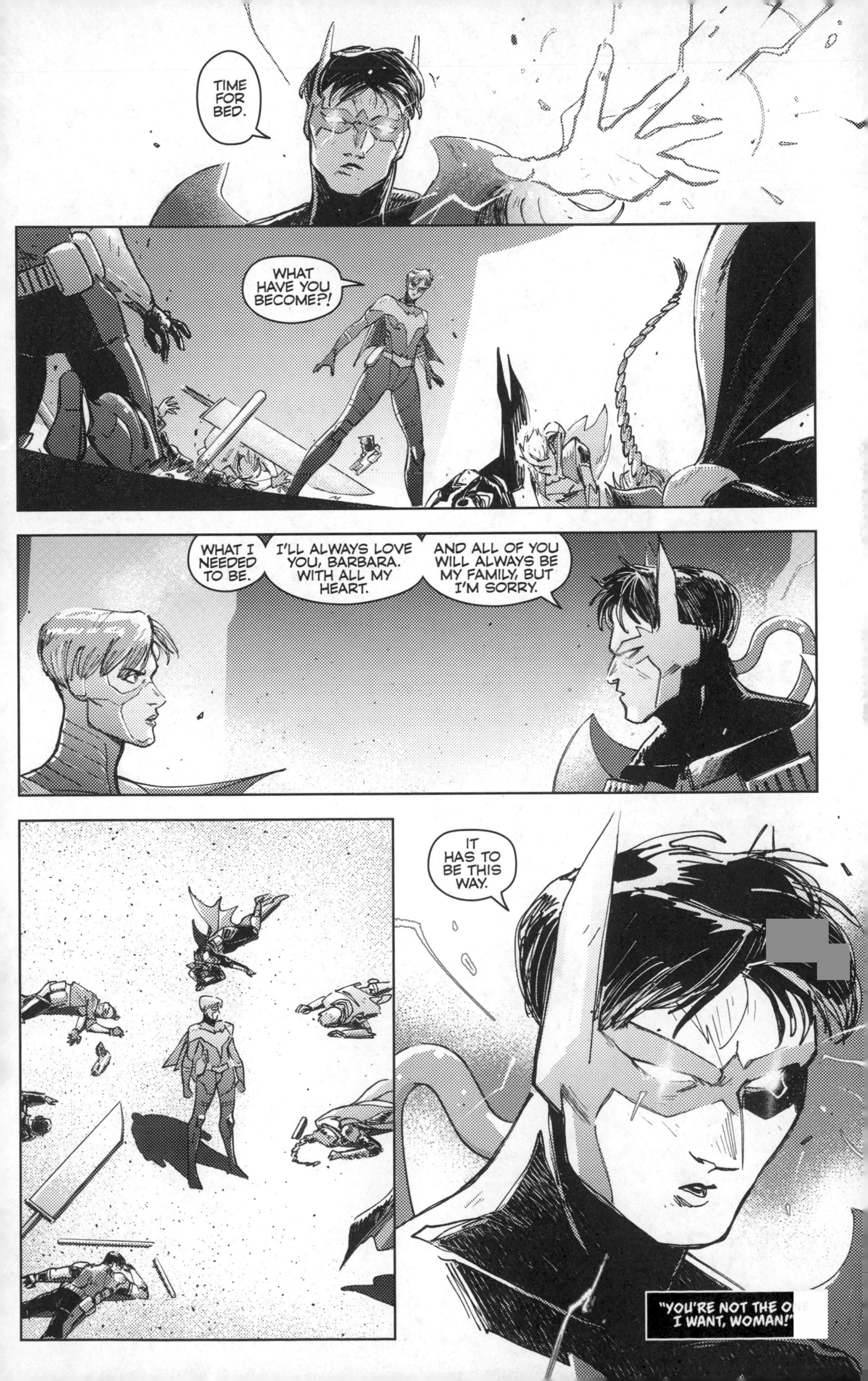
TIME FOR BED.
WHAT HAVE YOU BECOME?!
WHAT I NEEDED TO BE.
I'LL ALWAYS LOVE YOU, BARBARA. WITH ALL MY HEART.
AND ALL OF YOU WILL ALWAYS BE MY FAMILY, BUT I'M SORRY.
IT HAS TO BE THIS WAY.
"YOU'RE NOT THE
I WANT, WOMAN!"

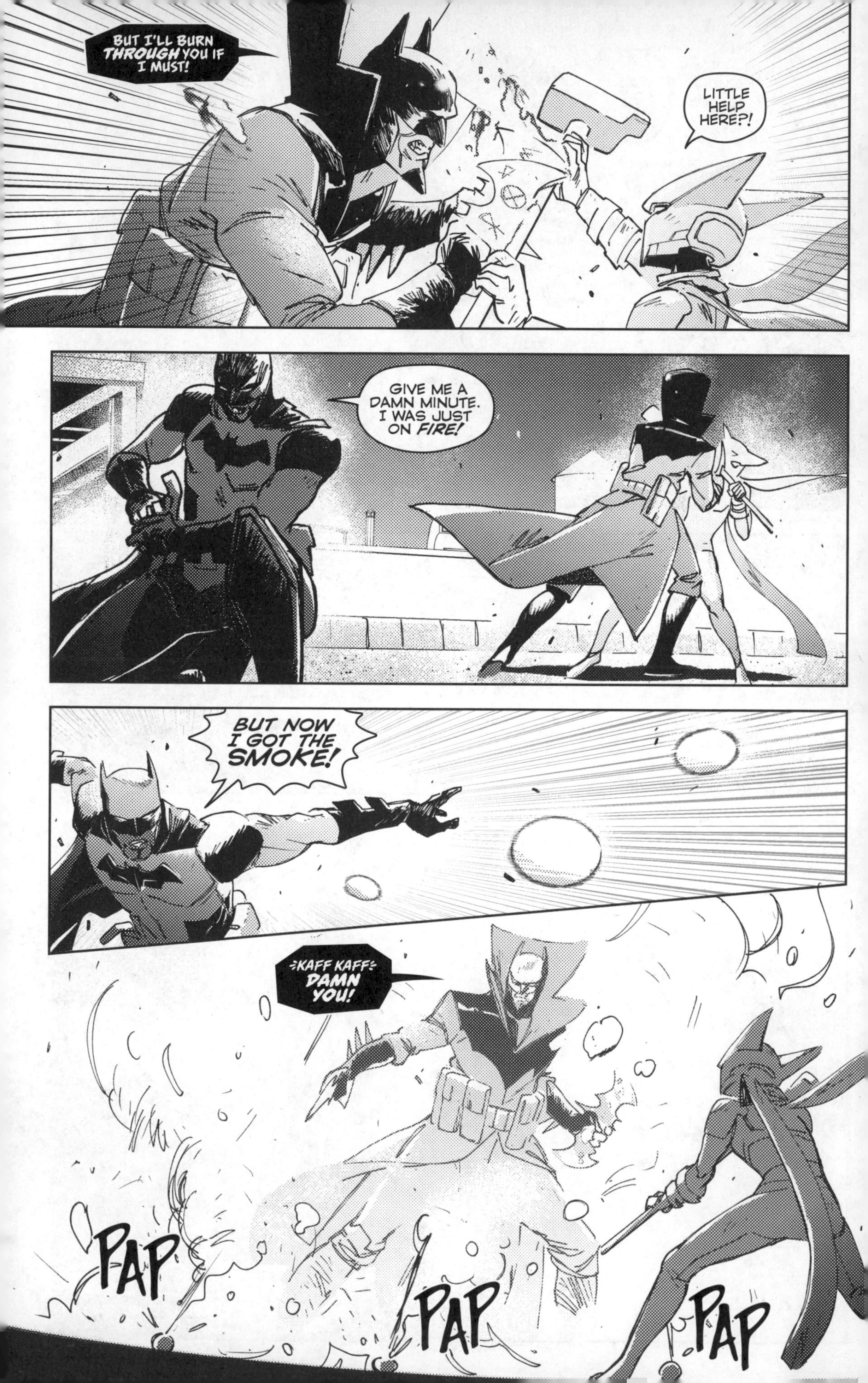
BUT I'LL BURN THROUGH YOU IF I MUST!
LITTLE HELP HERE?!
GIVE ME A DAMN MINUTE. I WAS JUST ON FIRE!
BUT NOW I GOT THE SMOKE!
KAFF KAFF DAMN YOU!
PAP
PAP
PAP

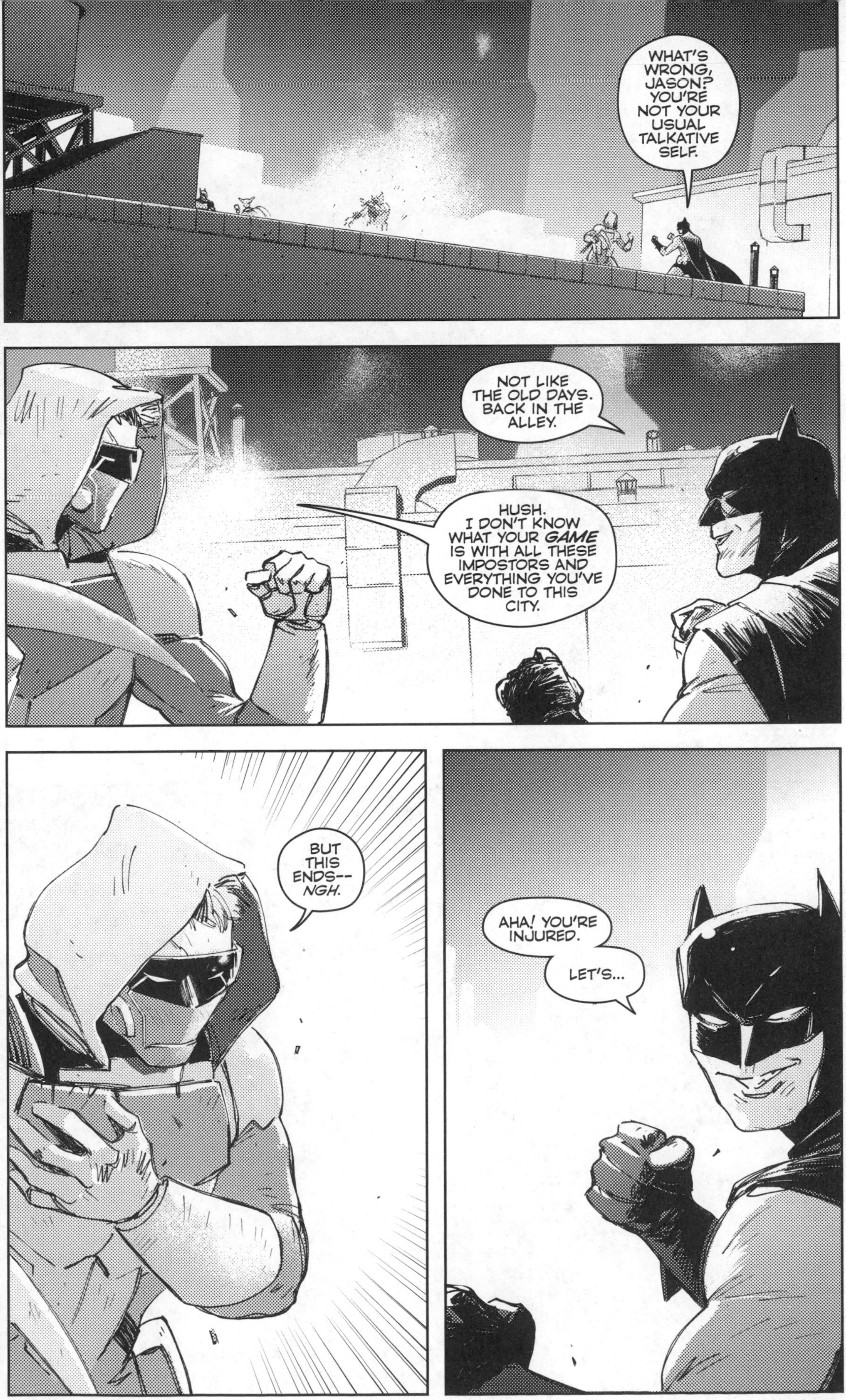
WHAT'S WRONG, JASON? YOU'RE NOT YOUR USUAL TALKATIVE SELF.
NOT LIKE THE OLD DAYS. BACK IN THE ALLEY.
HUSH. I DON'T KNOW WHAT YOUR *GAME* IS WITH ALL THESE IMPOSTORS AND EVERYTHING YOU'VE DONE TO THIS CITY.
BUT THIS ENDS-- *NGH.*
AHA! YOU'RE INJURED.
LET'S...

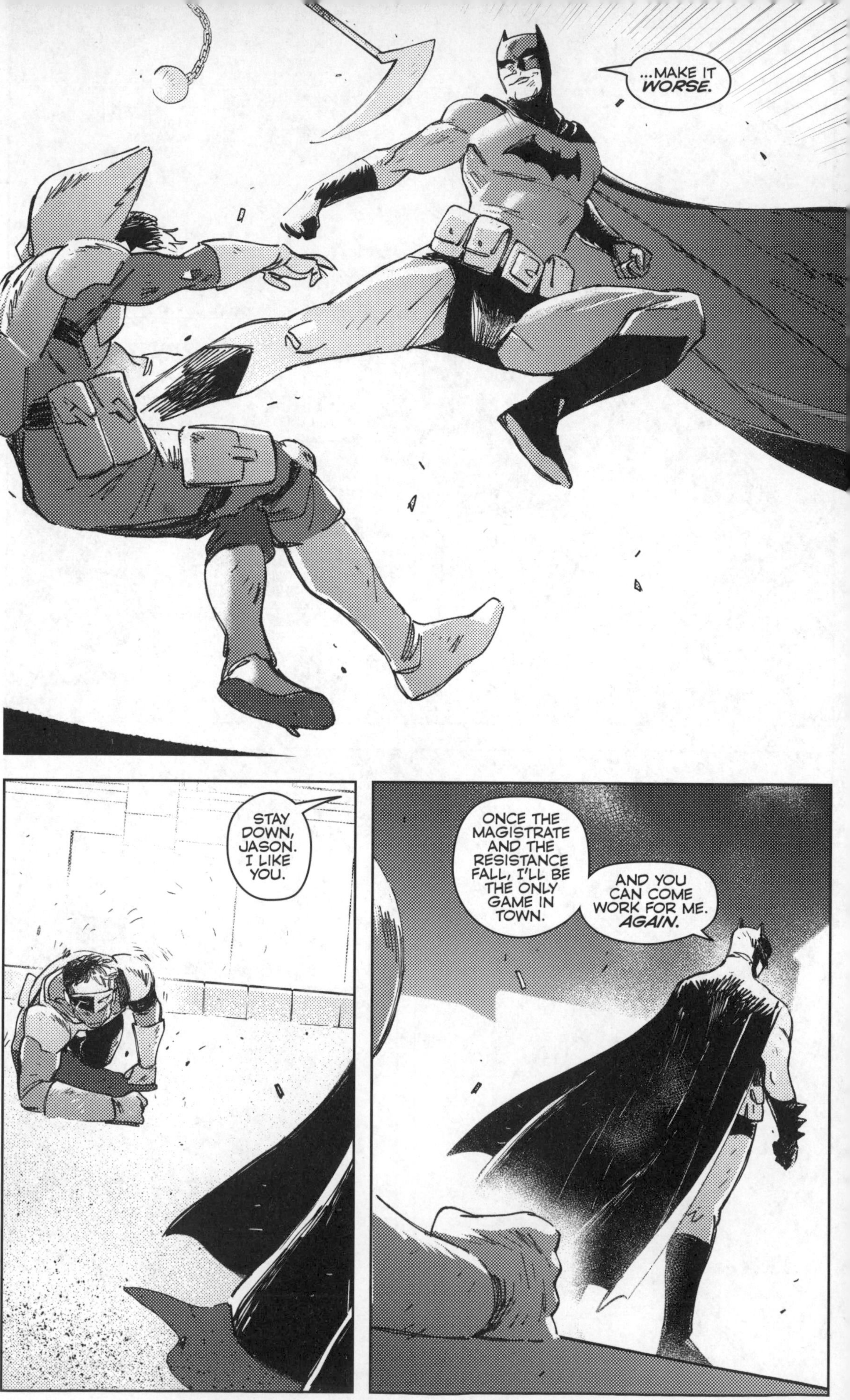
...MAKE IT *WORSE.*
STAY DOWN, JASON. I LIKE YOU.
ONCE THE MAGISTRATE AND THE RESISTANCE FALL, I'LL BE THE ONLY GAME IN TOWN.
AND YOU CAN COME WORK FOR ME. *AGAIN.*

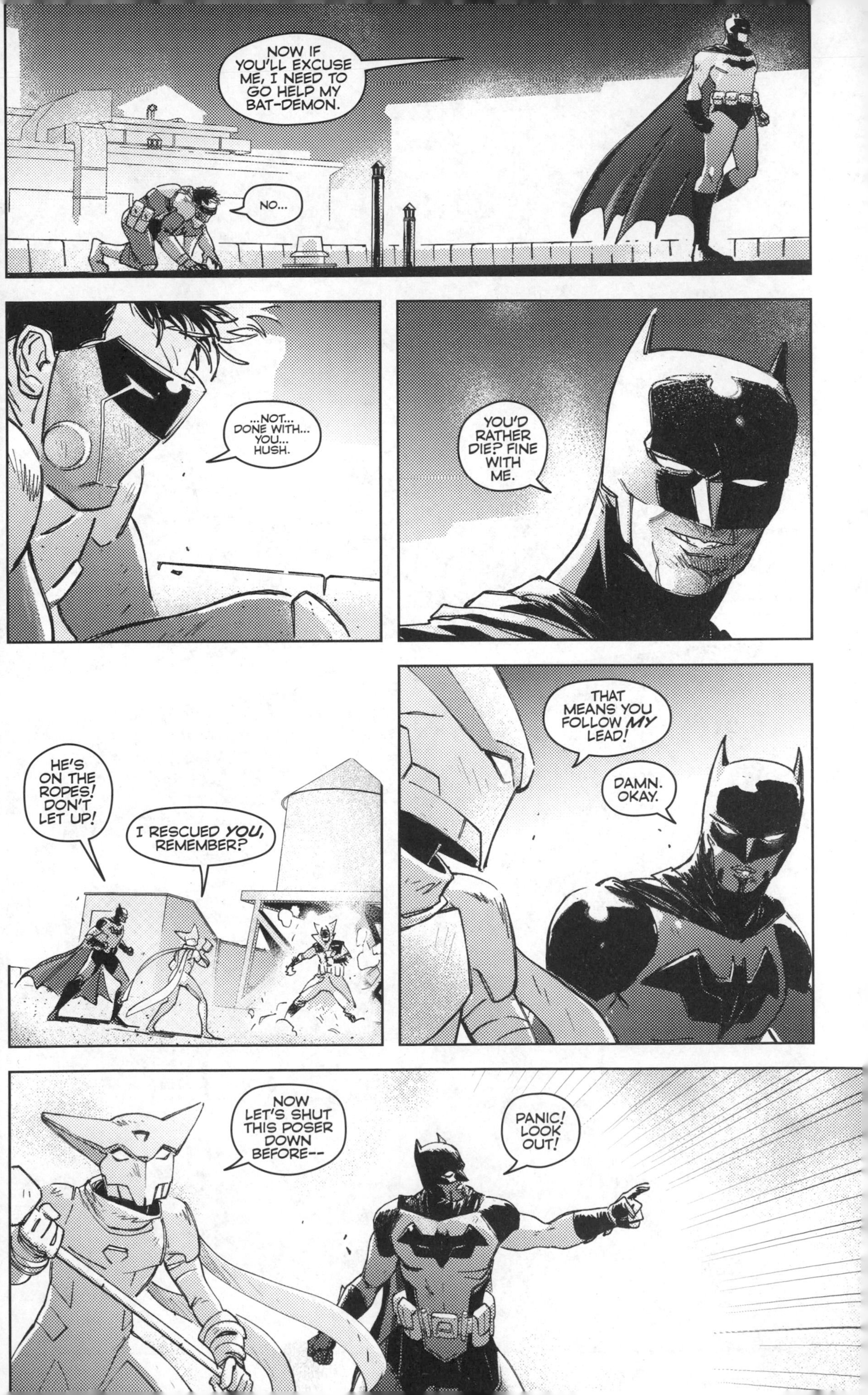
NOW IF YOU'LL EXCUSE ME, I NEED TO GO HELP MY BAT-DEMON.
NO...
...NOT... DONE WITH... YOU... HUSH.
YOU'D RATHER DIE? FINE WITH ME.
HE'S ON THE ROPES! DON'T LET UP!
I RESCUED YOU, REMEMBER?
THAT MEANS YOU FOLLOW MY LEAD!
DAMN. OKAY.
NOW LET'S SHUT THIS POSER DOWN BEFORE--
PANIC! LOOK OUT!

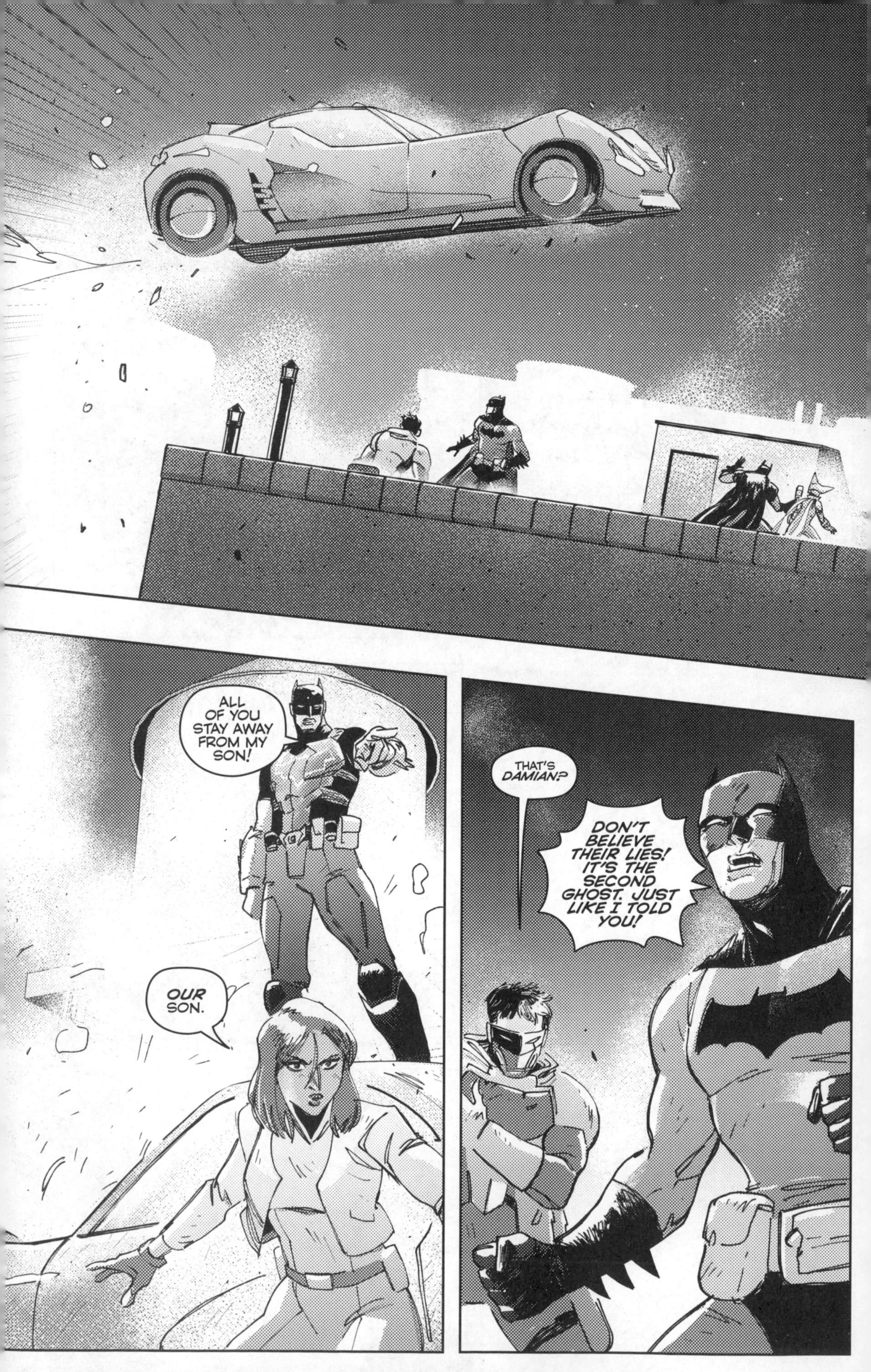
ALL OF YOU STAY AWAY FROM MY SON!
OUR SON.
THAT'S DAMIAN?
DON'T BELIEVE THEIR LIES! IT'S THE SECOND GHOST. JUST LIKE I TOLD YOU!

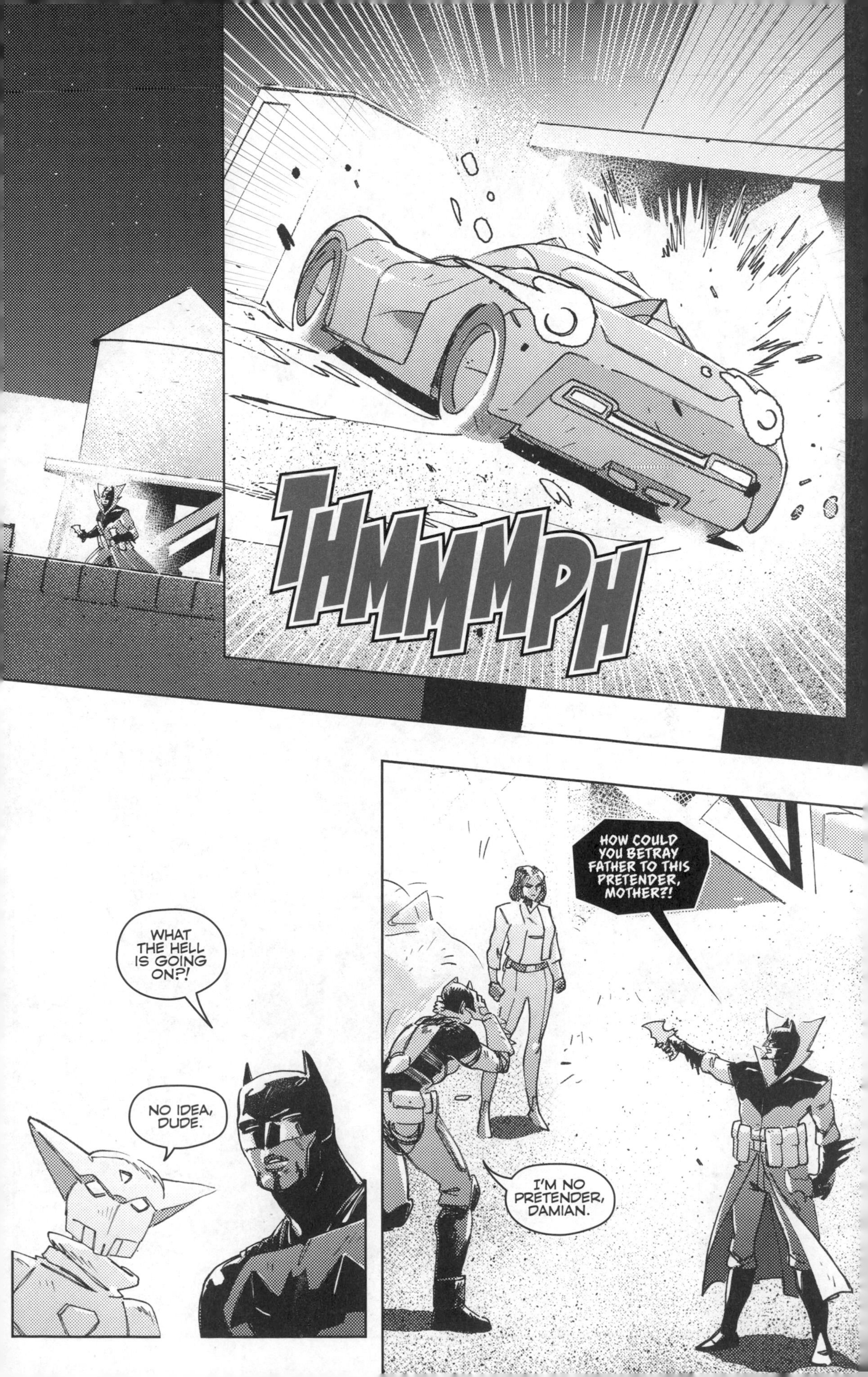
THMMMPH
WHAT THE HELL IS GOING ON?!
NO IDEA, DUDE.
HOW COULD YOU BETRAY FATHER TO THIS PRETENDER, MOTHER?!
I'M NO PRETENDER, DAMIAN.

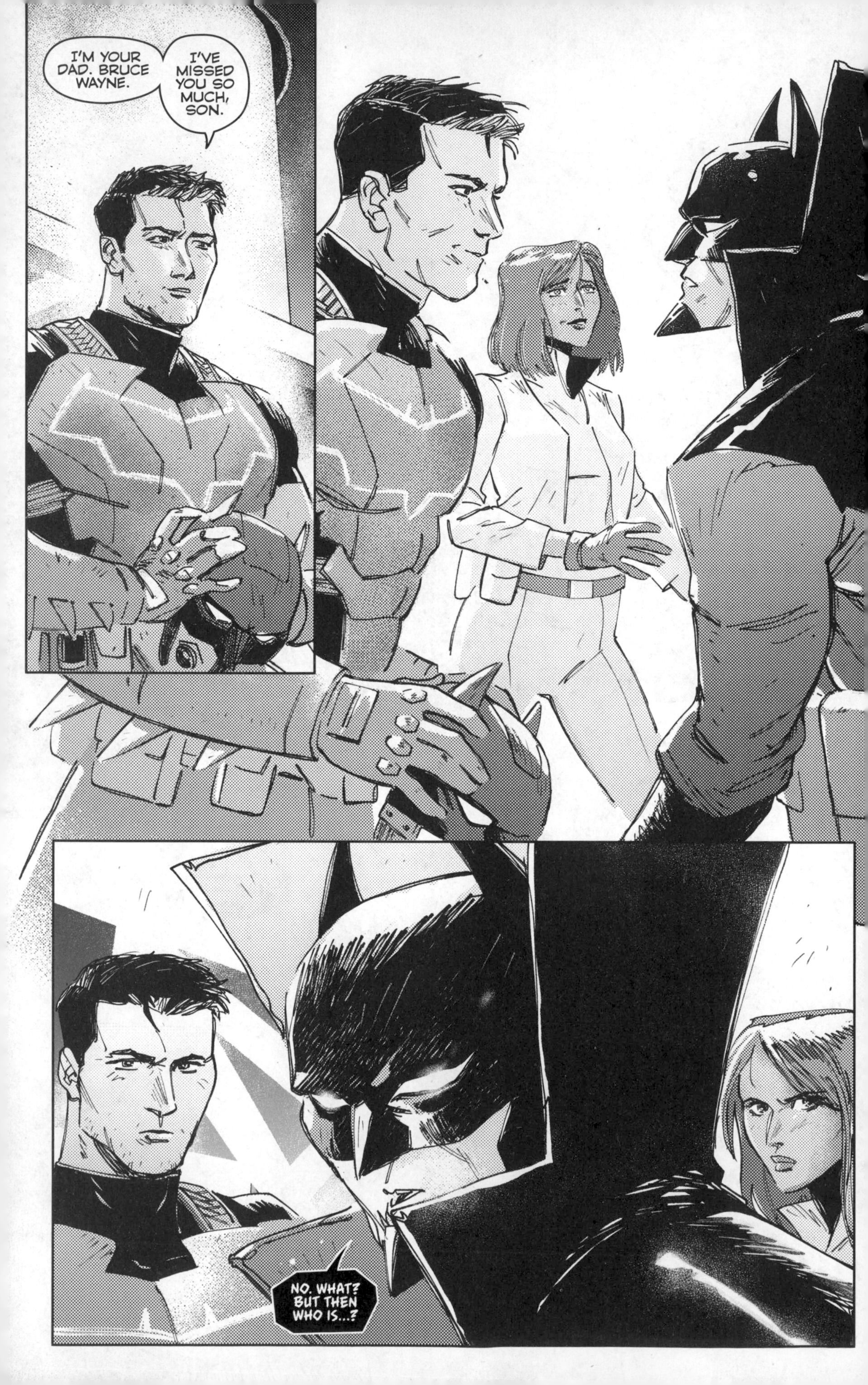

I'M YOUR DAD. BRUCE WAYNE.
I'VE MISSED YOU SO MUCH, SON.
NO. WHAT? BUT THEN WHO IS...?

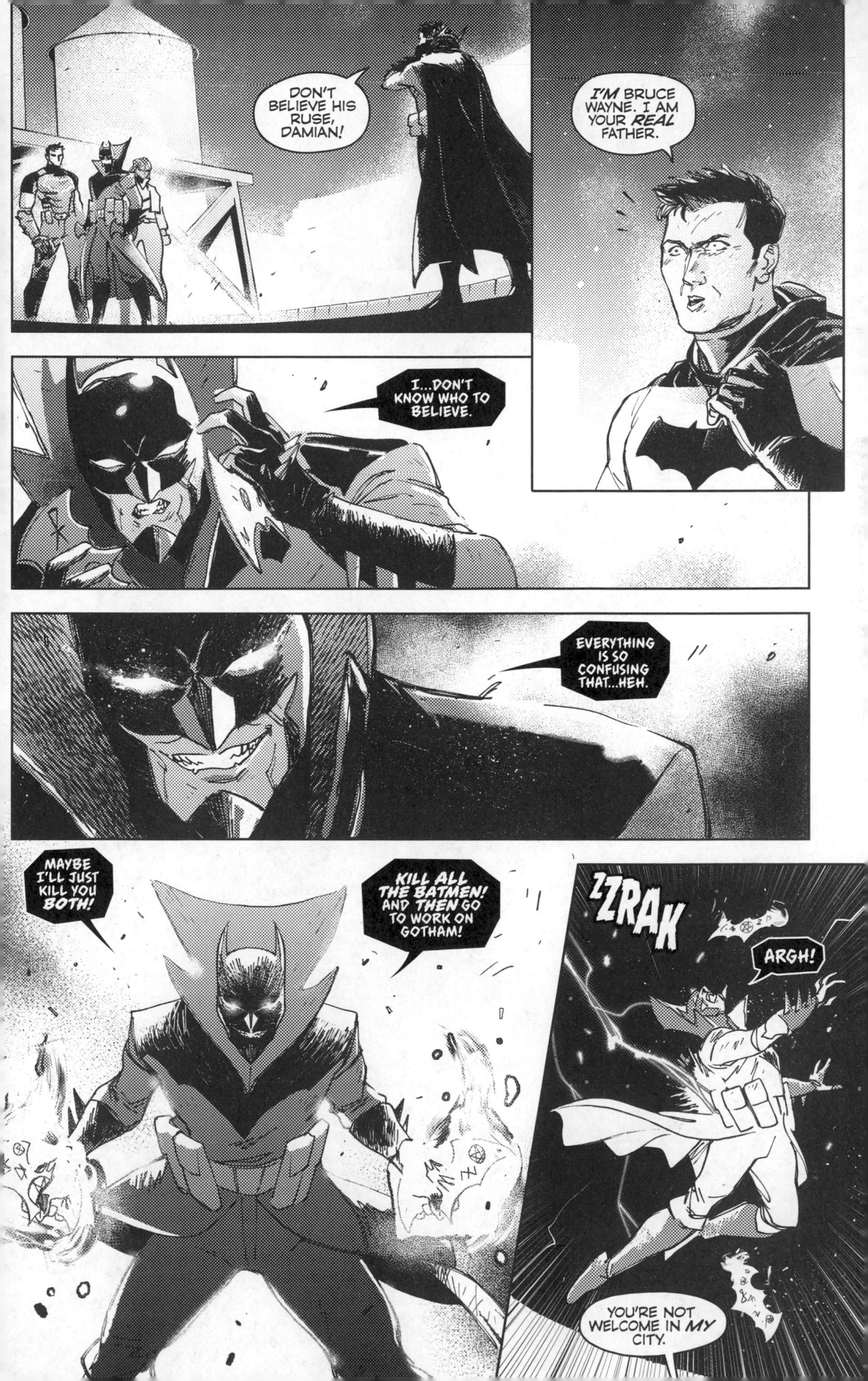
DON'T BELIEVE HIS RUSE, DAMIAN!
I'M BRUCE WAYNE. I AM YOUR REAL FATHER.
I...DON'T KNOW WHO TO BELIEVE.
EVERYTHING IS SO CONFUSING THAT...HEH.
MAYBE I'LL JUST KILL YOU BOTH!
KILL ALL THE BATMEN! AND THEN GO TO WORK ON GOTHAM!
ZZRAK
ARGH!
YOU'RE NOT WELCOME IN MY CITY.

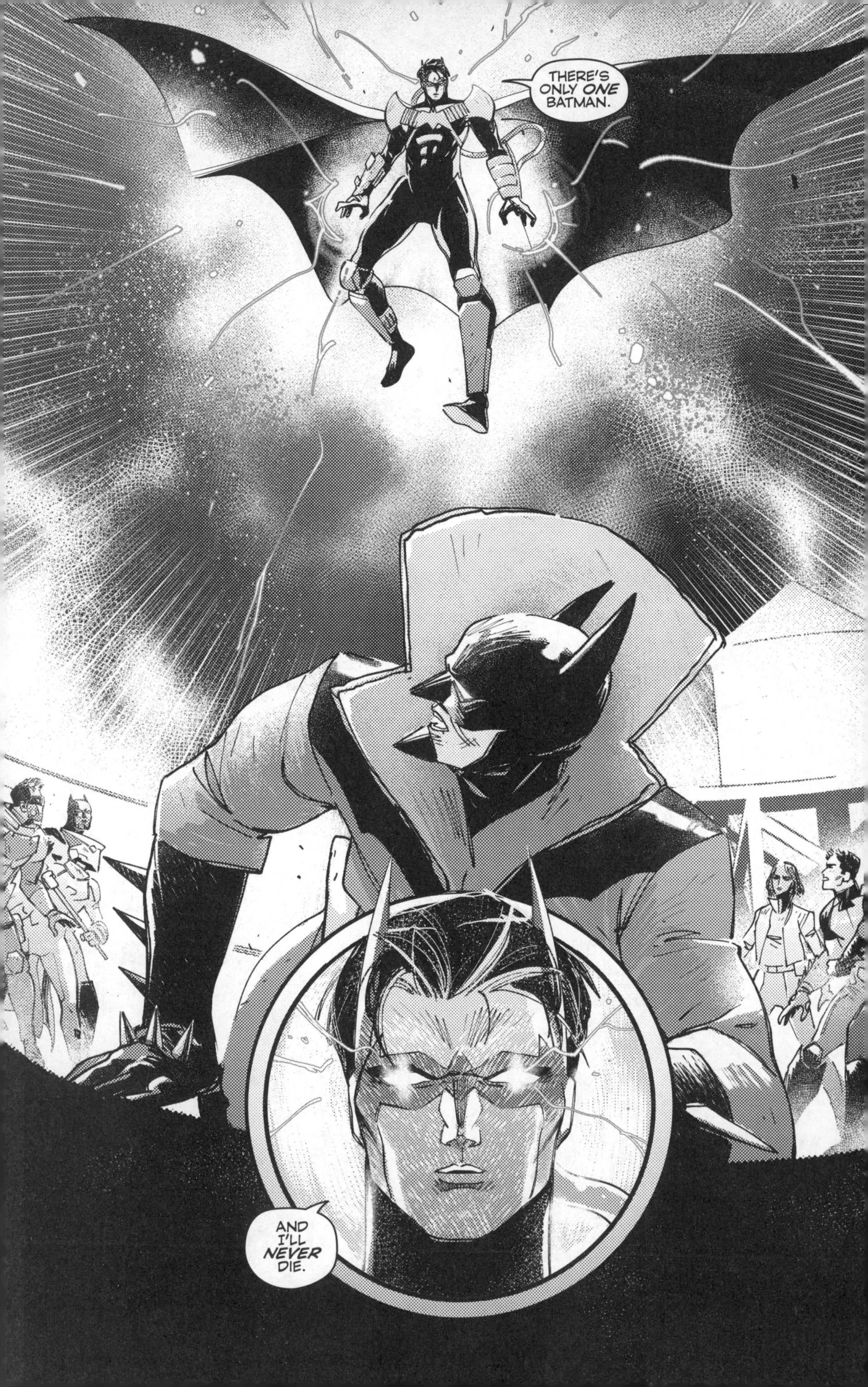
THERE'S ONLY ONE BATMAN.
AND I'LL NEVER DIE.

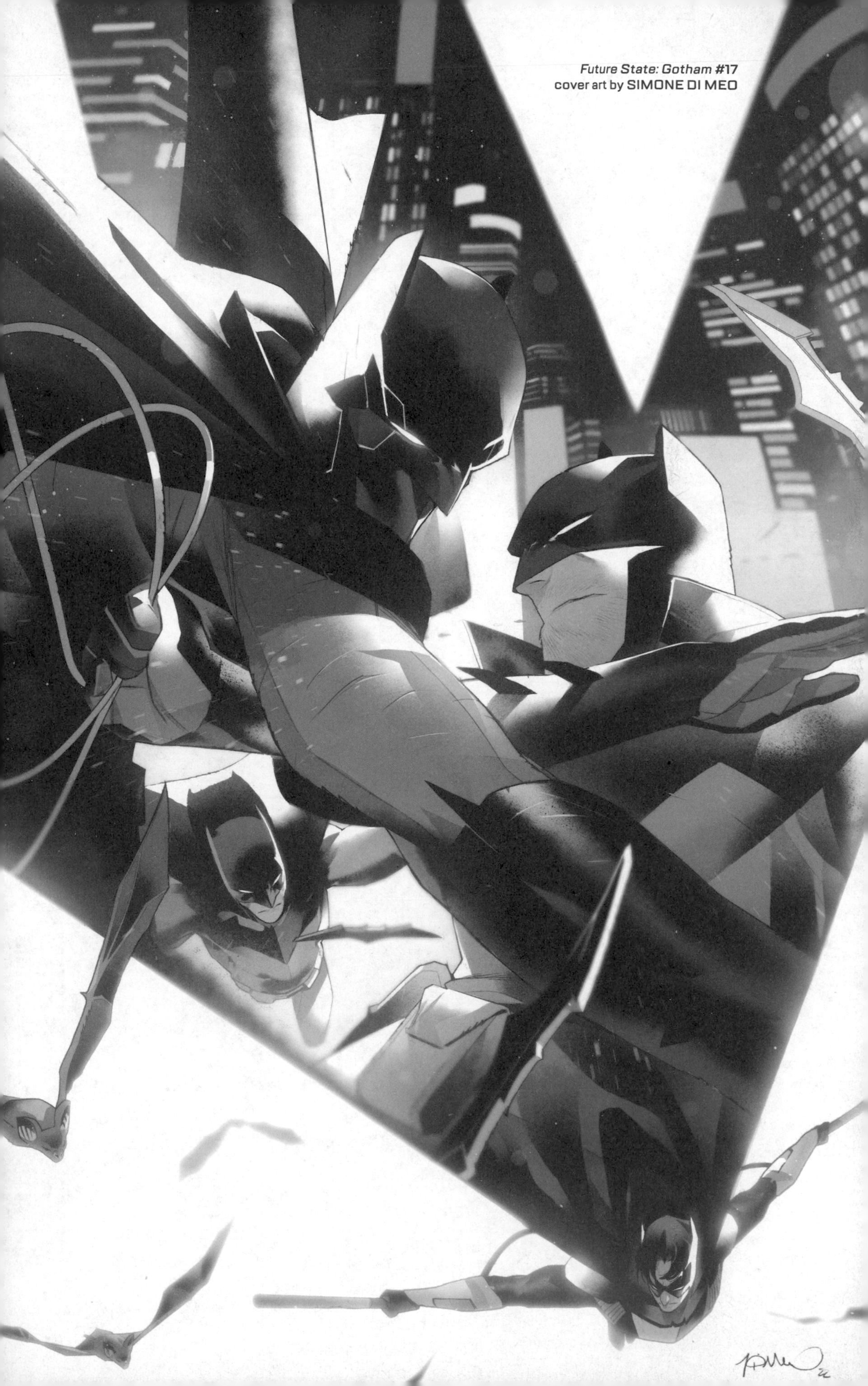

Future State: Gotham #17
cover art by SIMONE DI MEO

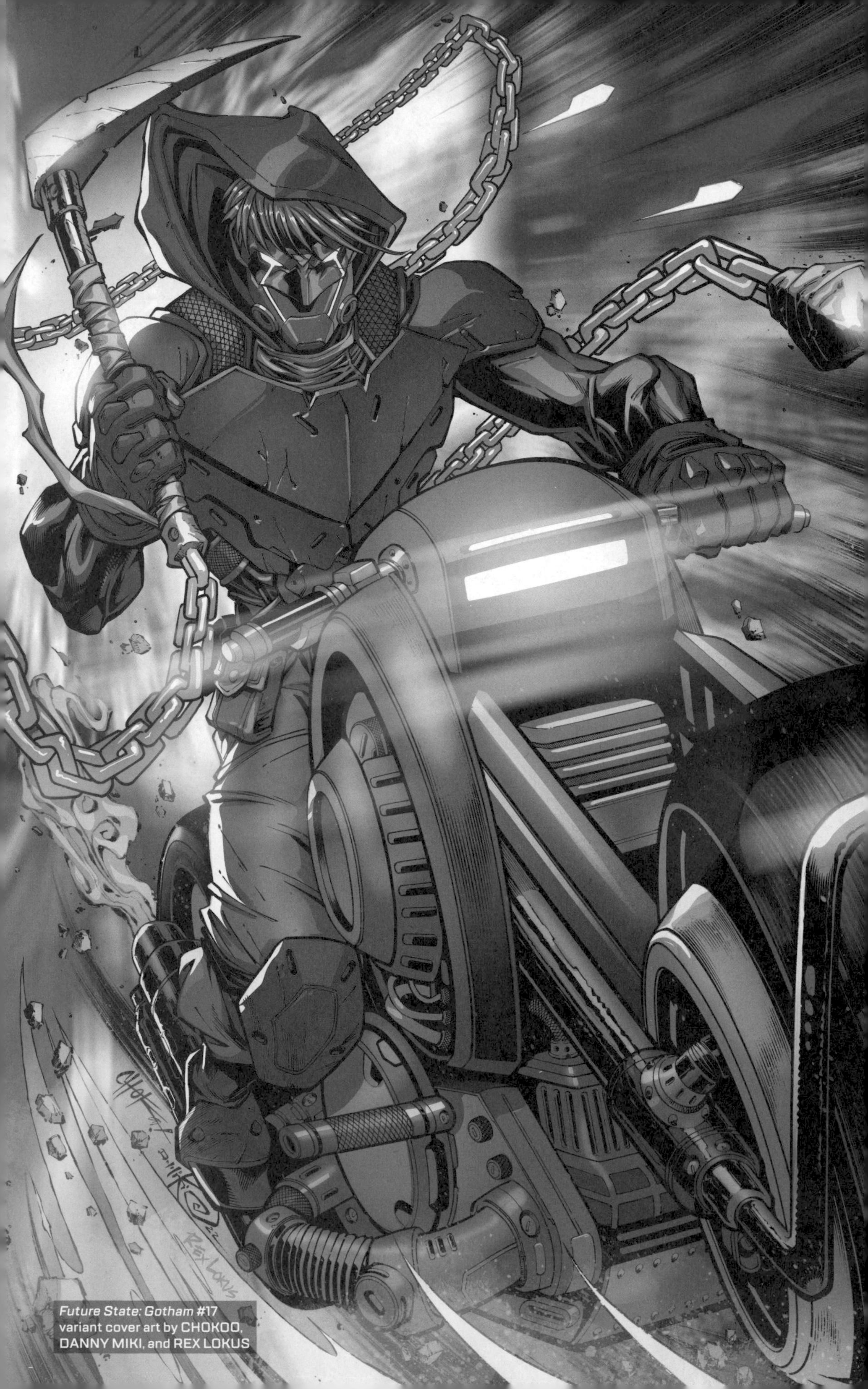

Future State: Gotham #17
variant cover art by CHOKOO,
DANNY MIKI, and REX LOKUS

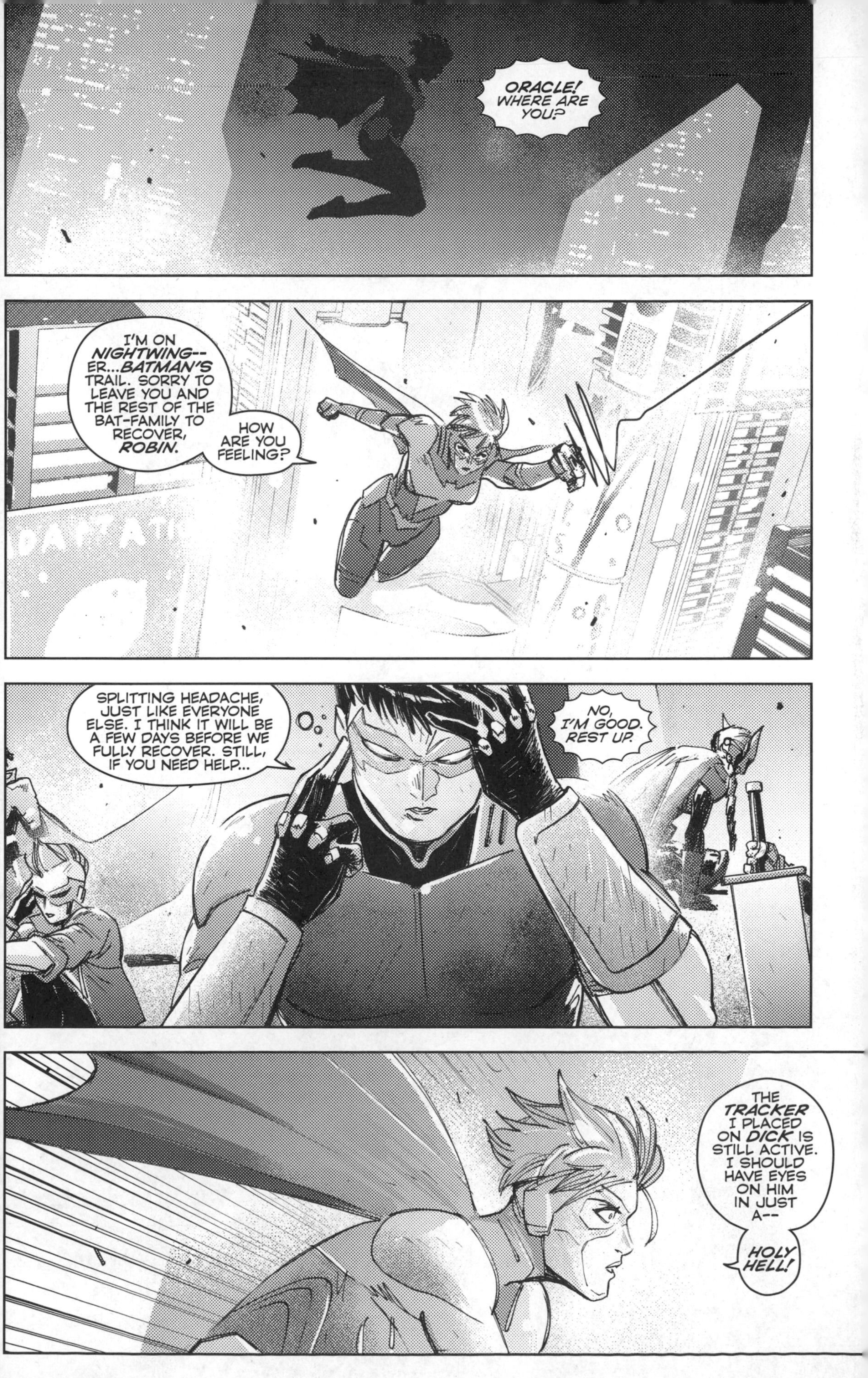
ORACLE! WHERE ARE YOU?
I'M ON NIGHTWING-- ER...BATMAN'S TRAIL. SORRY TO LEAVE YOU AND THE REST OF THE BAT-FAMILY TO RECOVER, ROBIN.
HOW ARE YOU FEELING?
SPLITTING HEADACHE, JUST LIKE EVERYONE ELSE. I THINK IT WILL BE A FEW DAYS BEFORE WE FULLY RECOVER. STILL, IF YOU NEED HELP...
NO, I'M GOOD. REST UP.
THE TRACKER I PLACED ON DICK IS STILL ACTIVE. I SHOULD HAVE EYES ON HIM IN JUST A--
HOLY HELL!

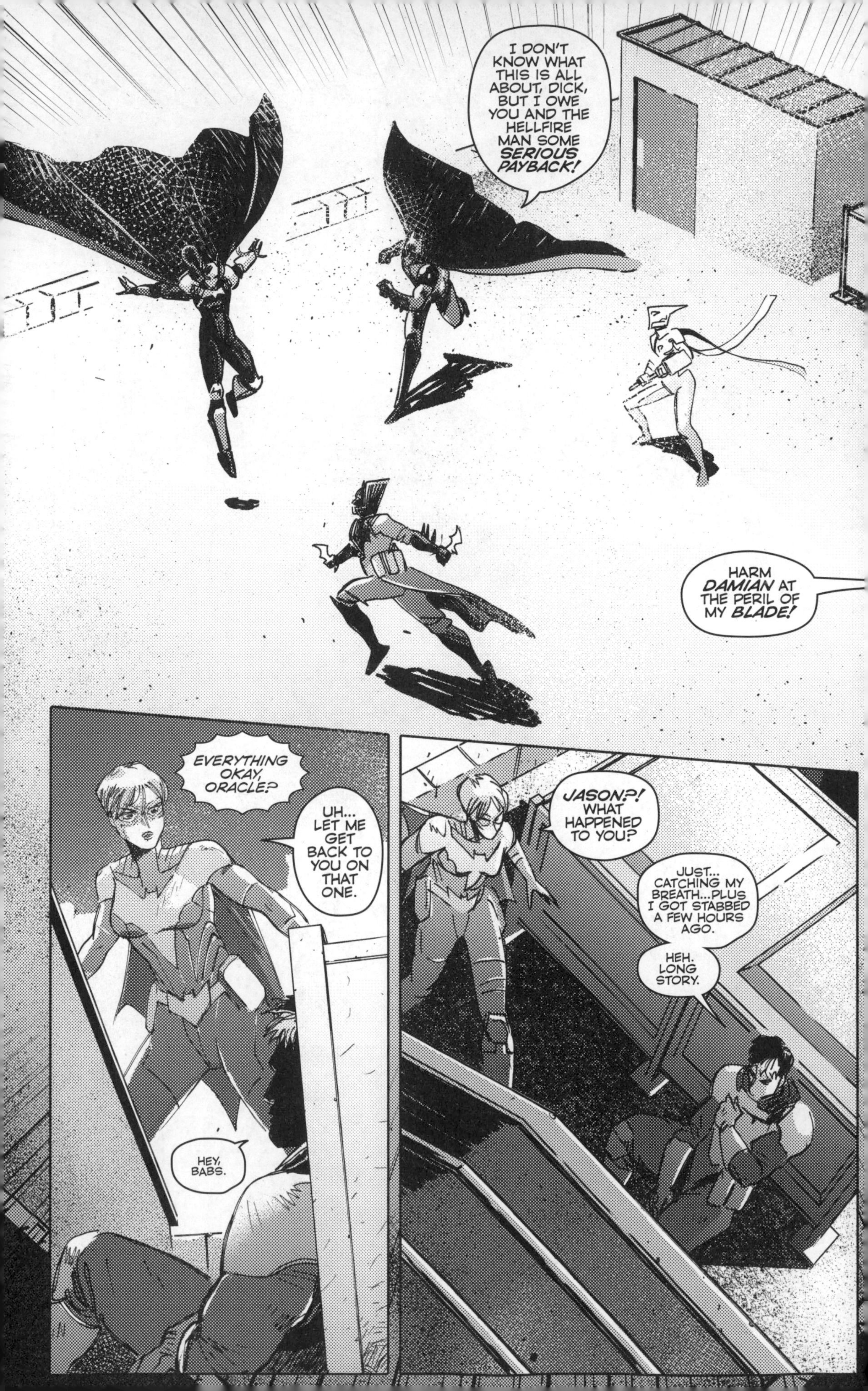
I DON'T KNOW WHAT THIS IS ALL ABOUT, DICK, BUT I OWE YOU AND THE HELLFIRE MAN SOME SERIOUS PAYBACK!
HARM DAMIAN AT THE PERIL OF MY BLADE!
EVERYTHING OKAY, ORACLE?
UH... LET ME GET BACK TO YOU ON THAT ONE.
HEY, BABS.
JASON?! WHAT HAPPENED TO YOU?
JUST... CATCHING MY BREATH...PLUS I GOT STABBED A FEW HOURS AGO.
HEH. LONG STORY.

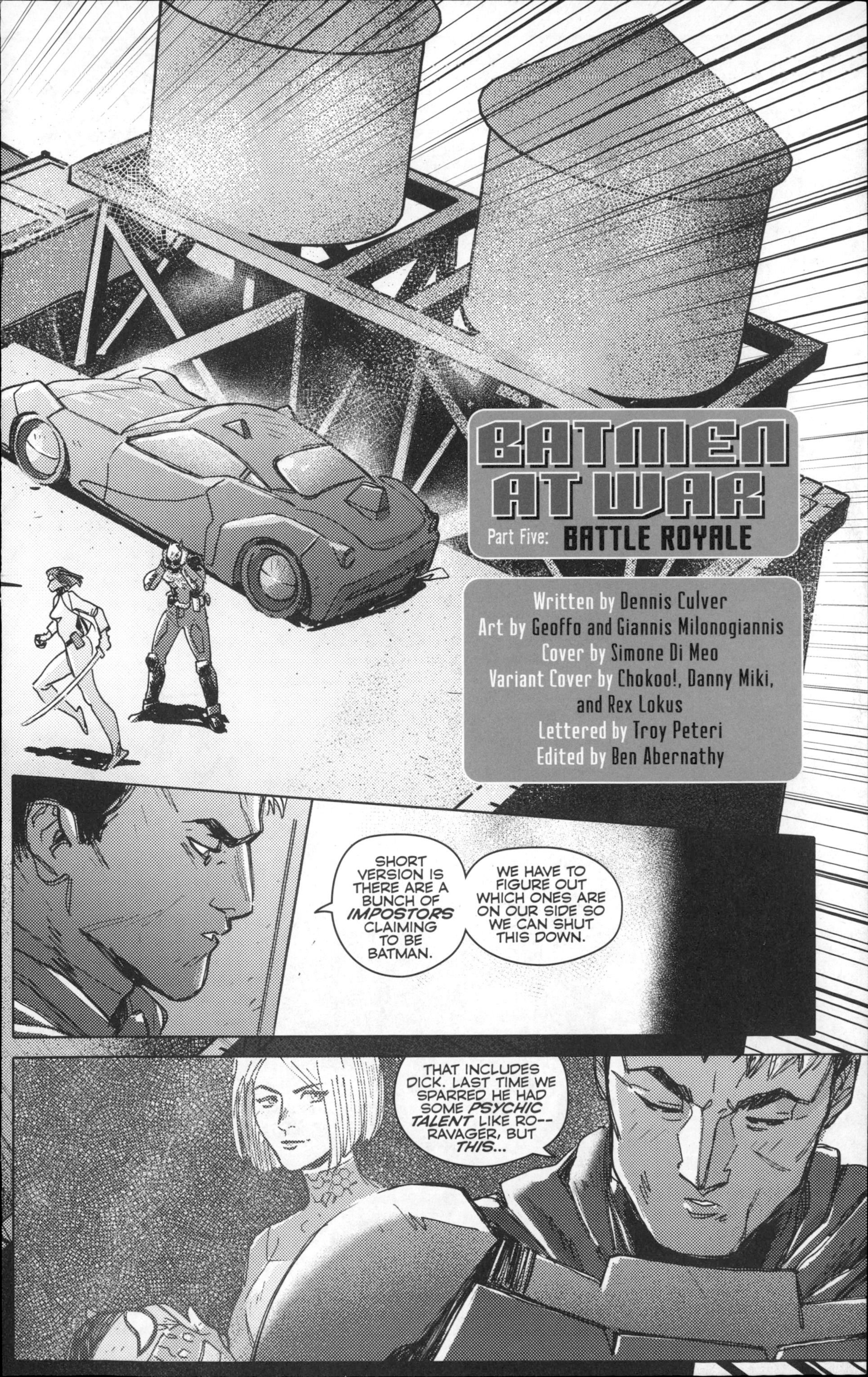
BATMEN AT WAR
Part Five: BATTLE ROYALE
Written by Dennis Culver
Art by Geoffo and Giannis Milonogiannis
Cover by Simone Di Meo
Variant Cover by Chokoo!, Danny Miki, and Rex Lokus
Lettered by Troy Peteri
Edited by Ben Abernathy
SHORT VERSION IS THERE ARE A BUNCH OF *IMPOSTORS* CLAIMING TO BE BATMAN.
WE HAVE TO FIGURE OUT WHICH ONES ARE ON OUR SIDE SO WE CAN SHUT THIS DOWN.
THAT INCLUDES DICK. LAST TIME WE SPARRED HE HAD SOME *PSYCHIC TALENT* LIKE RO-- RAVAGER, BUT *THIS*...

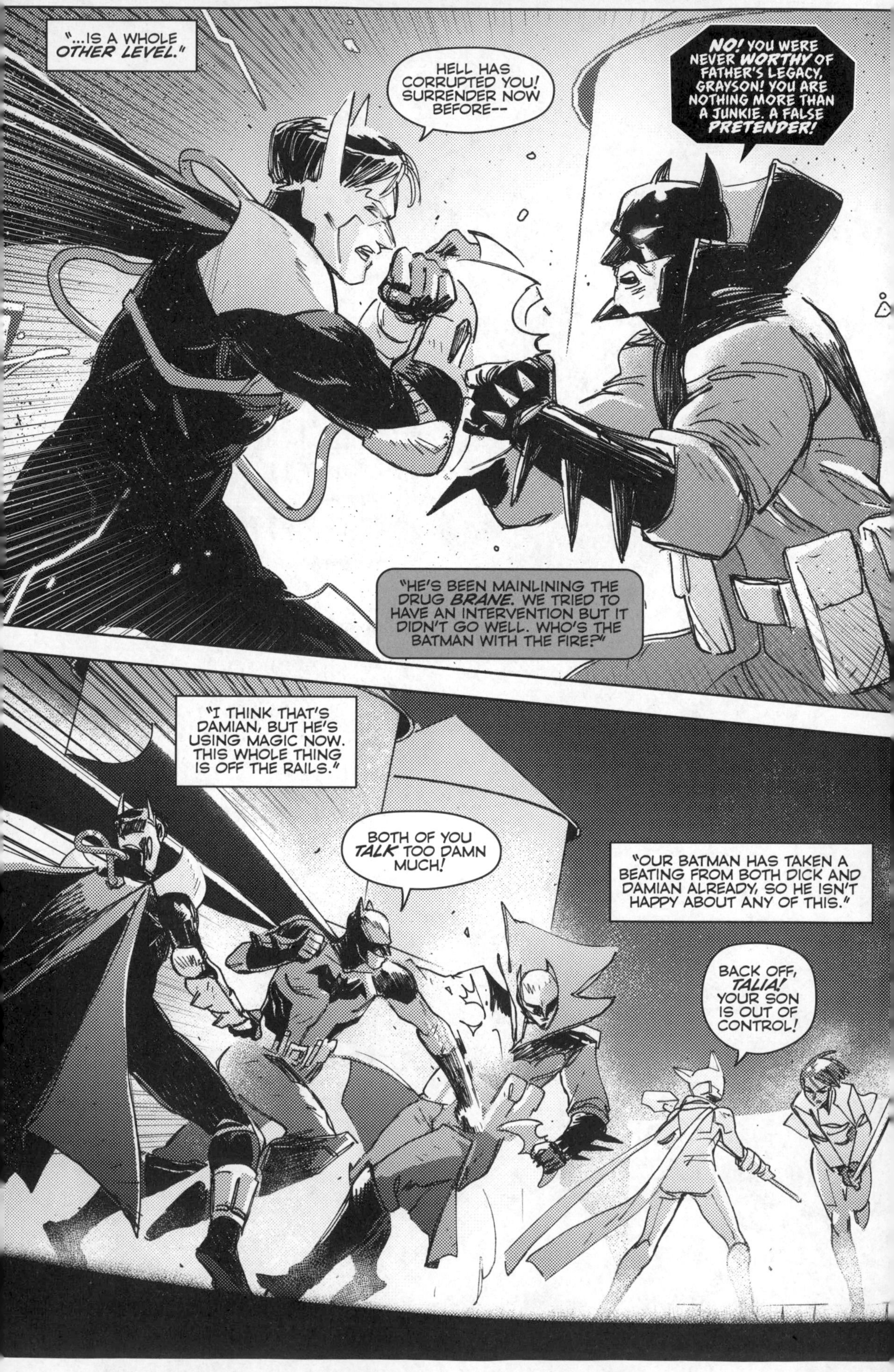
"...IS A WHOLE OTHER LEVEL."
HELL HAS CORRUPTED YOU! SURRENDER NOW BEFORE--
NO! YOU WERE NEVER WORTHY OF FATHER'S LEGACY, GRAYSON! YOU ARE NOTHING MORE THAN A JUNKIE. A FALSE PRETENDER!
"HE'S BEEN MAINLINING THE DRUG BRANE. WE TRIED TO HAVE AN INTERVENTION BUT IT DIDN'T GO WELL. WHO'S THE BATMAN WITH THE FIRE?"
"I THINK THAT'S DAMIAN, BUT HE'S USING MAGIC NOW. THIS WHOLE THING IS OFF THE RAILS."
BOTH OF YOU TALK TOO DAMN MUCH!
"OUR BATMAN HAS TAKEN A BEATING FROM BOTH DICK AND DAMIAN ALREADY, SO HE ISN'T HAPPY ABOUT ANY OF THIS."
BACK OFF, TALIA! YOUR SON IS OUT OF CONTROL!

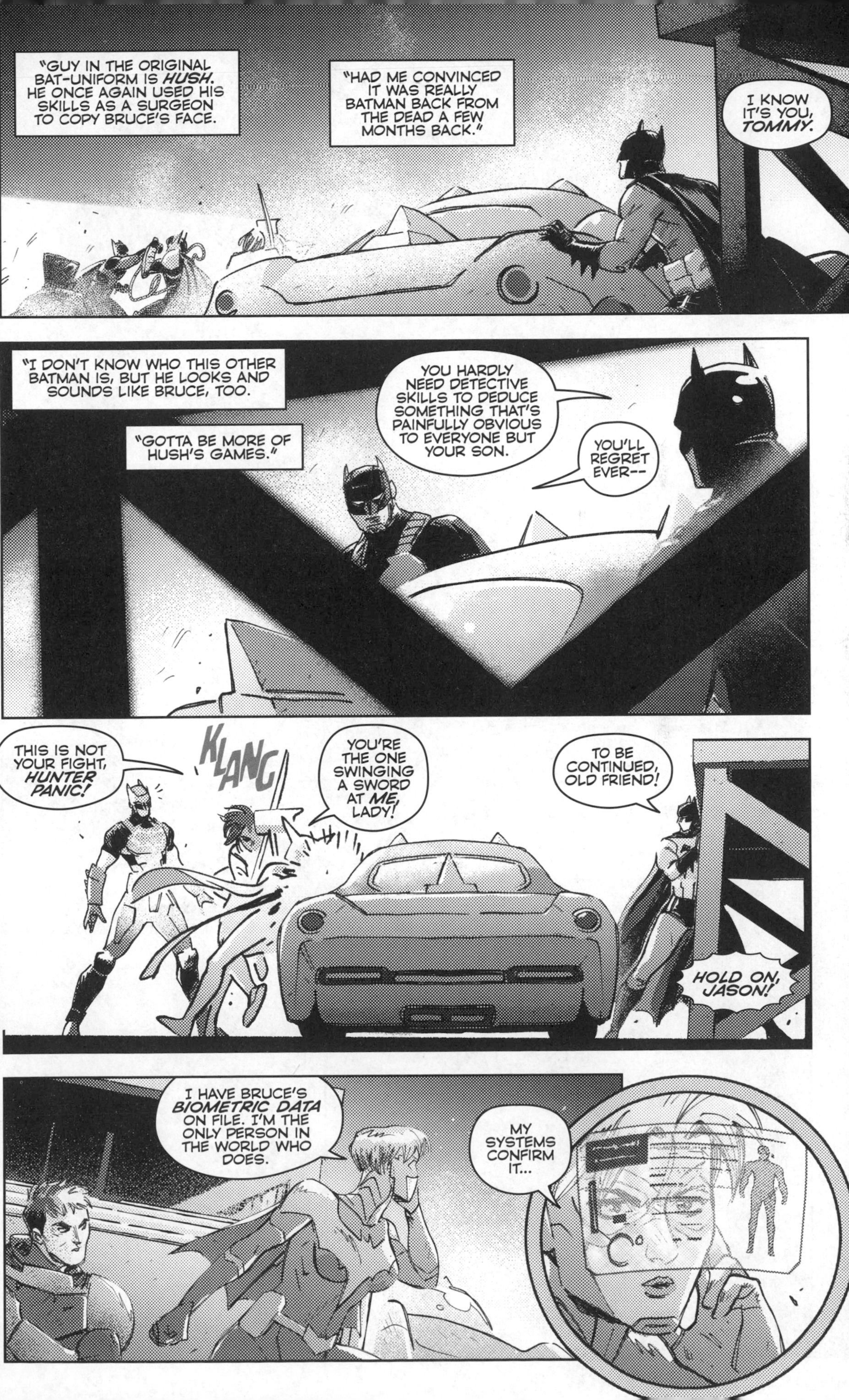
"GUY IN THE ORIGINAL BAT-UNIFORM IS HUSH. HE ONCE AGAIN USED HIS SKILLS AS A SURGEON TO COPY BRUCE'S FACE.
"HAD ME CONVINCED IT WAS REALLY BATMAN BACK FROM THE DEAD A FEW MONTHS BACK."
I KNOW IT'S YOU, TOMMY.
"I DON'T KNOW WHO THIS OTHER BATMAN IS, BUT HE LOOKS AND SOUNDS LIKE BRUCE, TOO.
"GOTTA BE MORE OF HUSH'S GAMES."
YOU HARDLY NEED DETECTIVE SKILLS TO DEDUCE SOMETHING THAT'S PAINFULLY OBVIOUS TO EVERYONE BUT YOUR SON.
YOU'LL REGRET EVER--
THIS IS NOT YOUR FIGHT, HUNTER PANIC!
KLANG
YOU'RE THE ONE SWINGING A SWORD AT ME, LADY!
TO BE CONTINUED, OLD FRIEND!
HOLD ON, JASON!
I HAVE BRUCE'S BIOMETRIC DATA ON FILE. I'M THE ONLY PERSON IN THE WORLD WHO DOES.
MY SYSTEMS CONFIRM IT...

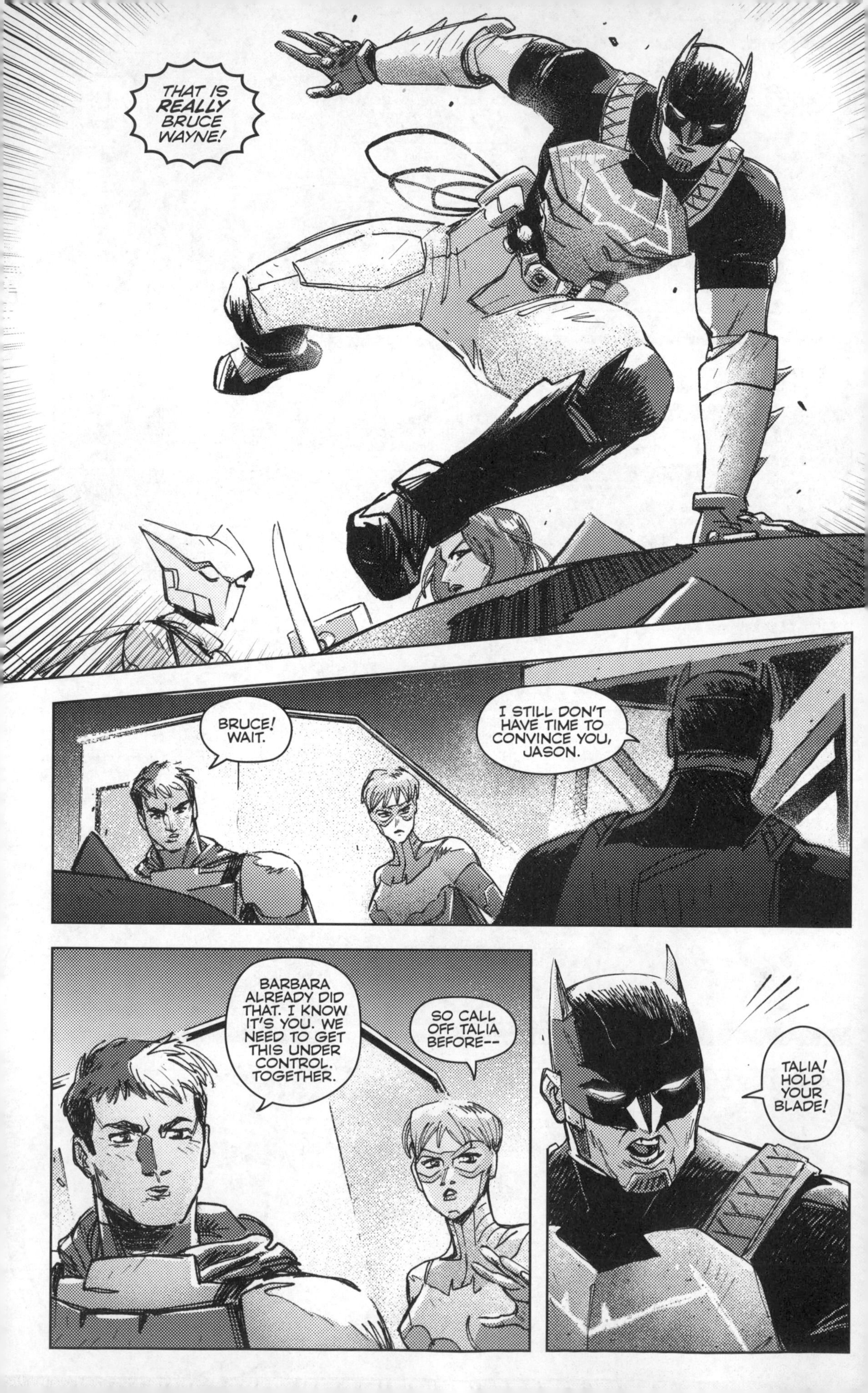
THAT IS *REALLY* BRUCE WAYNE!
BRUCE! WAIT.
I STILL DON'T HAVE TIME TO CONVINCE YOU, JASON.
BARBARA ALREADY DID THAT. I KNOW IT'S YOU. WE NEED TO GET THIS UNDER CONTROL. TOGETHER.
SO CALL OFF TALIA BEFORE--
TALIA! HOLD YOUR BLADE!

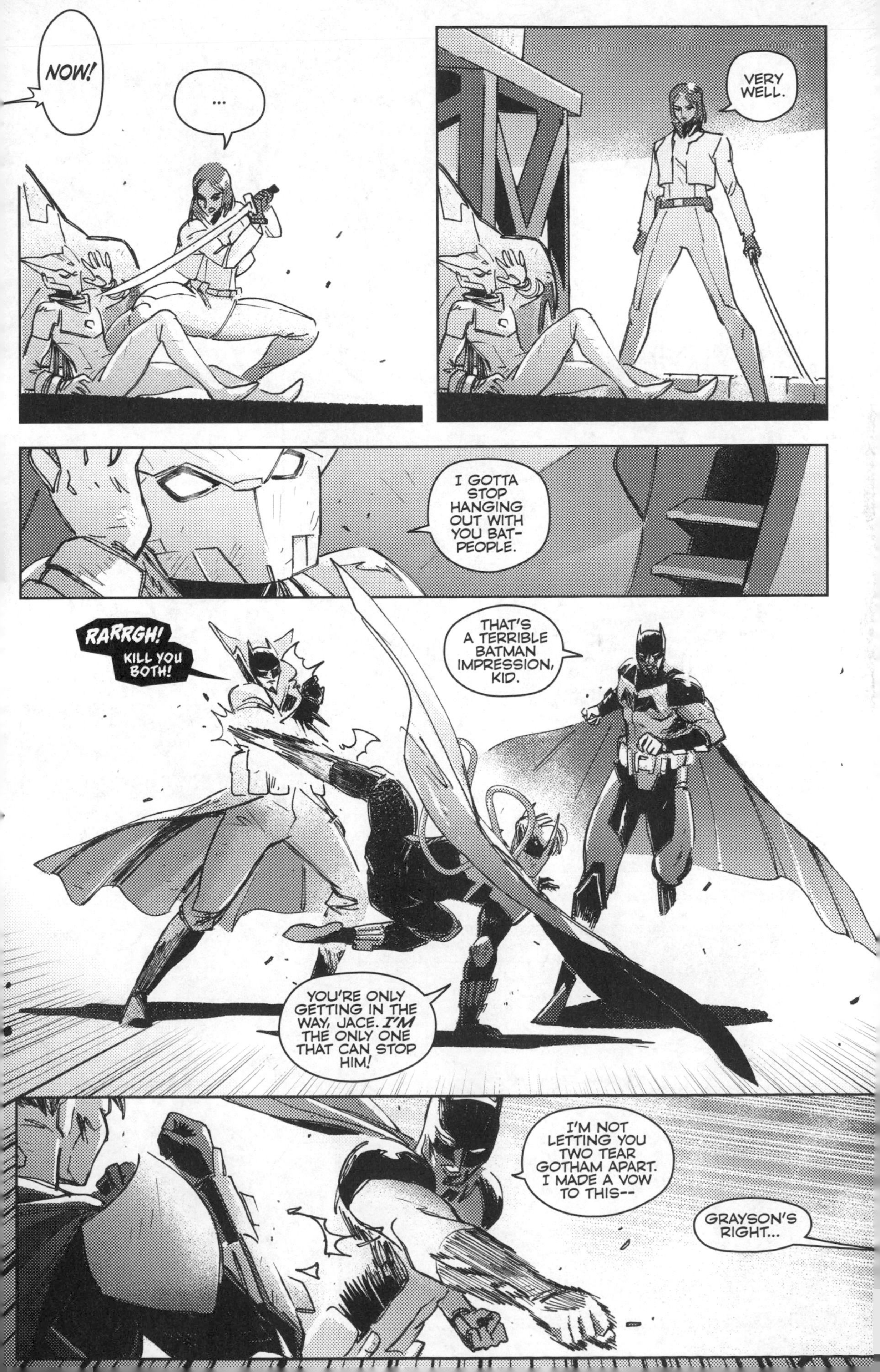
NOW!
...
VERY WELL.
I GOTTA STOP HANGING OUT WITH YOU BAT-PEOPLE.
RARRGH!
KILL YOU BOTH!
THAT'S A TERRIBLE BATMAN IMPRESSION, KID.
YOU'RE ONLY GETTING IN THE WAY, JACE. *I'M* THE ONLY ONE THAT CAN STOP HIM!
I'M NOT LETTING YOU TWO TEAR GOTHAM APART. I MADE A VOW TO THIS--
GRAYSON'S RIGHT...

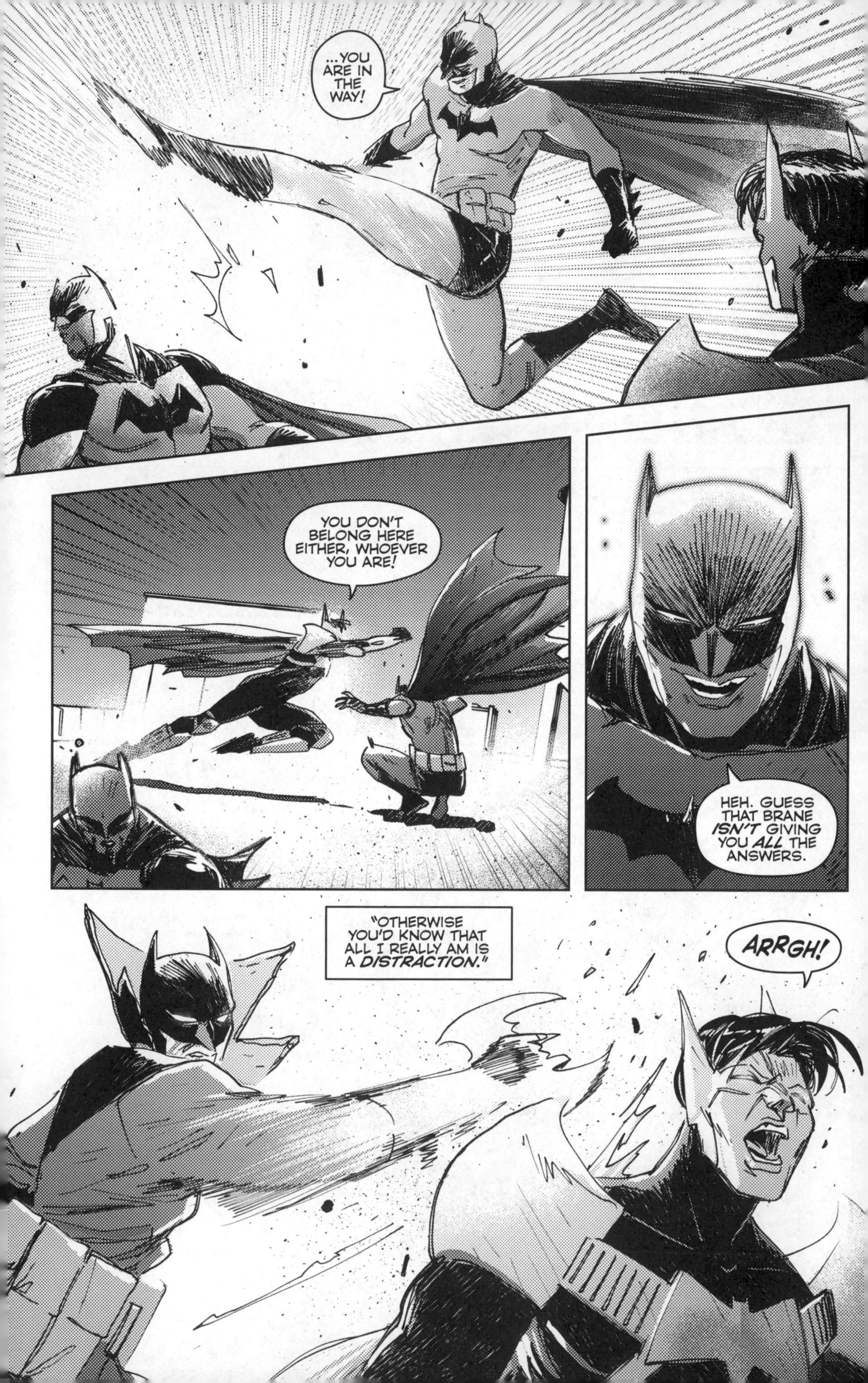
...YOU ARE IN THE WAY!
YOU DON'T BELONG HERE EITHER, WHOEVER YOU ARE!
HEH. GUESS THAT BRANE ISN'T GIVING YOU ALL THE ANSWERS.
"OTHERWISE YOU'D KNOW THAT ALL I REALLY AM IS A DISTRACTION."
ARRGH!

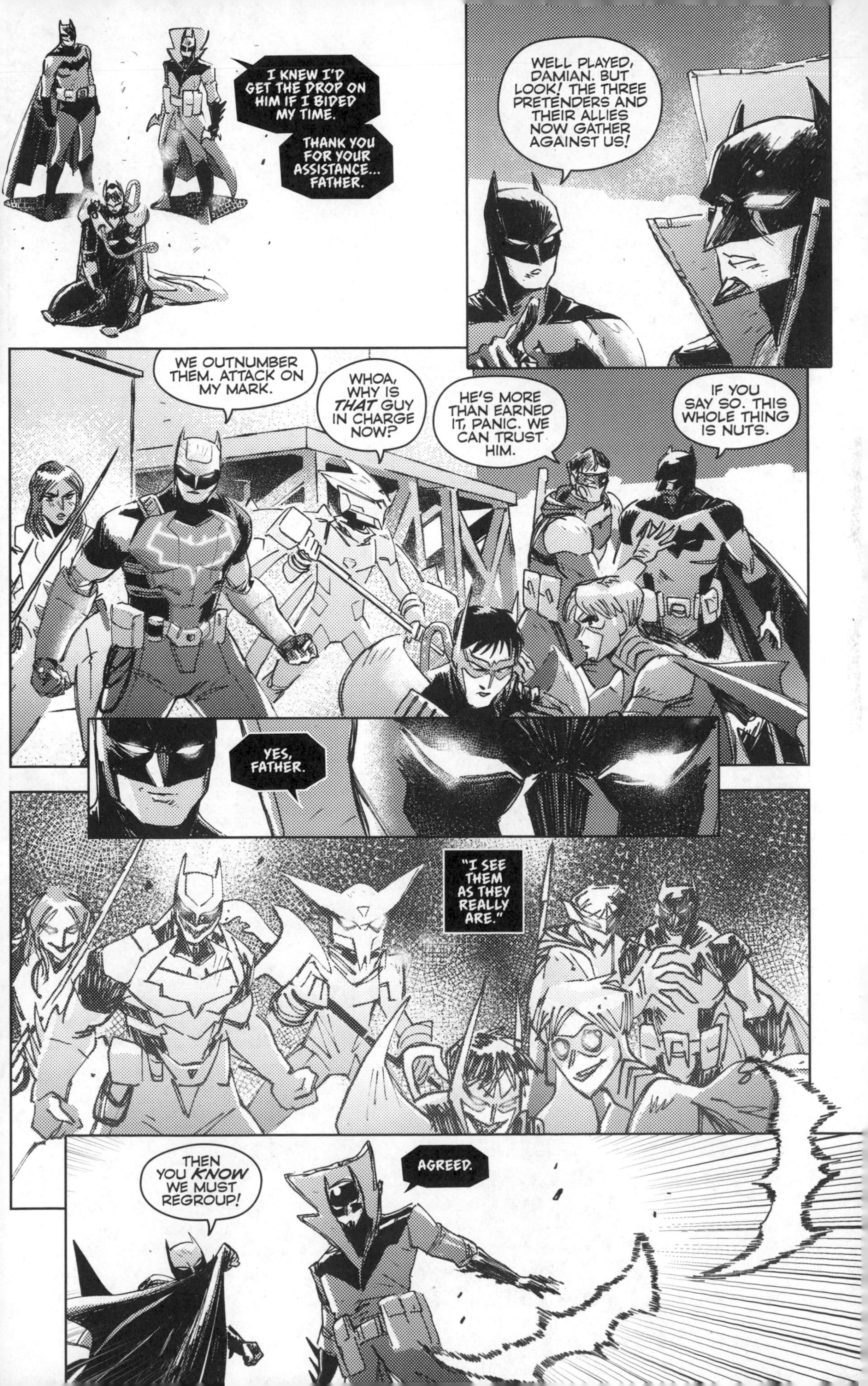
I KNEW I'D GET THE DROP ON HIM IF I BIDED MY TIME.
THANK YOU FOR YOUR ASSISTANCE... FATHER.
WELL PLAYED, DAMIAN. BUT LOOK! THE THREE PRETENDERS AND THEIR ALLIES NOW GATHER AGAINST US!
WE OUTNUMBER THEM. ATTACK ON MY MARK.
WHOA, WHY IS THAT GUY IN CHARGE NOW?
HE'S MORE THAN EARNED IT, PANIC. WE CAN TRUST HIM.
IF YOU SAY SO. THIS WHOLE THING IS NUTS.
YES, FATHER.
"I SEE THEM AS THEY REALLY ARE."
THEN YOU KNOW WE MUST REGROUP!
AGREED.

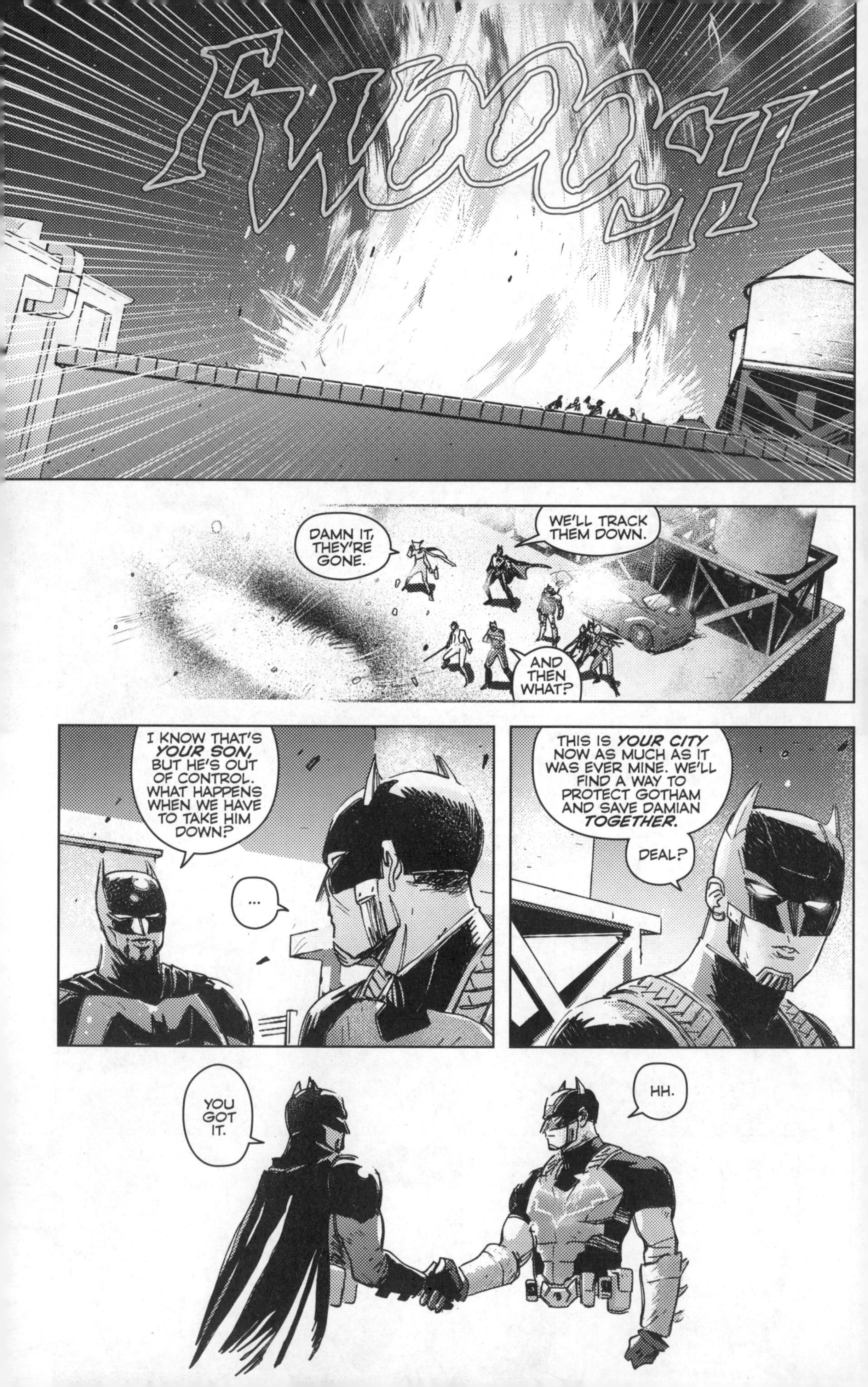
FWOOOSH
DAMN IT, THEY'RE GONE.
WE'LL TRACK THEM DOWN.
AND THEN WHAT?
I KNOW THAT'S YOUR SON, BUT HE'S OUT OF CONTROL. WHAT HAPPENS WHEN WE HAVE TO TAKE HIM DOWN?
...
THIS IS YOUR CITY NOW AS MUCH AS IT WAS EVER MINE. WE'LL FIND A WAY TO PROTECT GOTHAM AND SAVE DAMIAN TOGETHER.
DEAL?
YOU GOT IT.
HH.

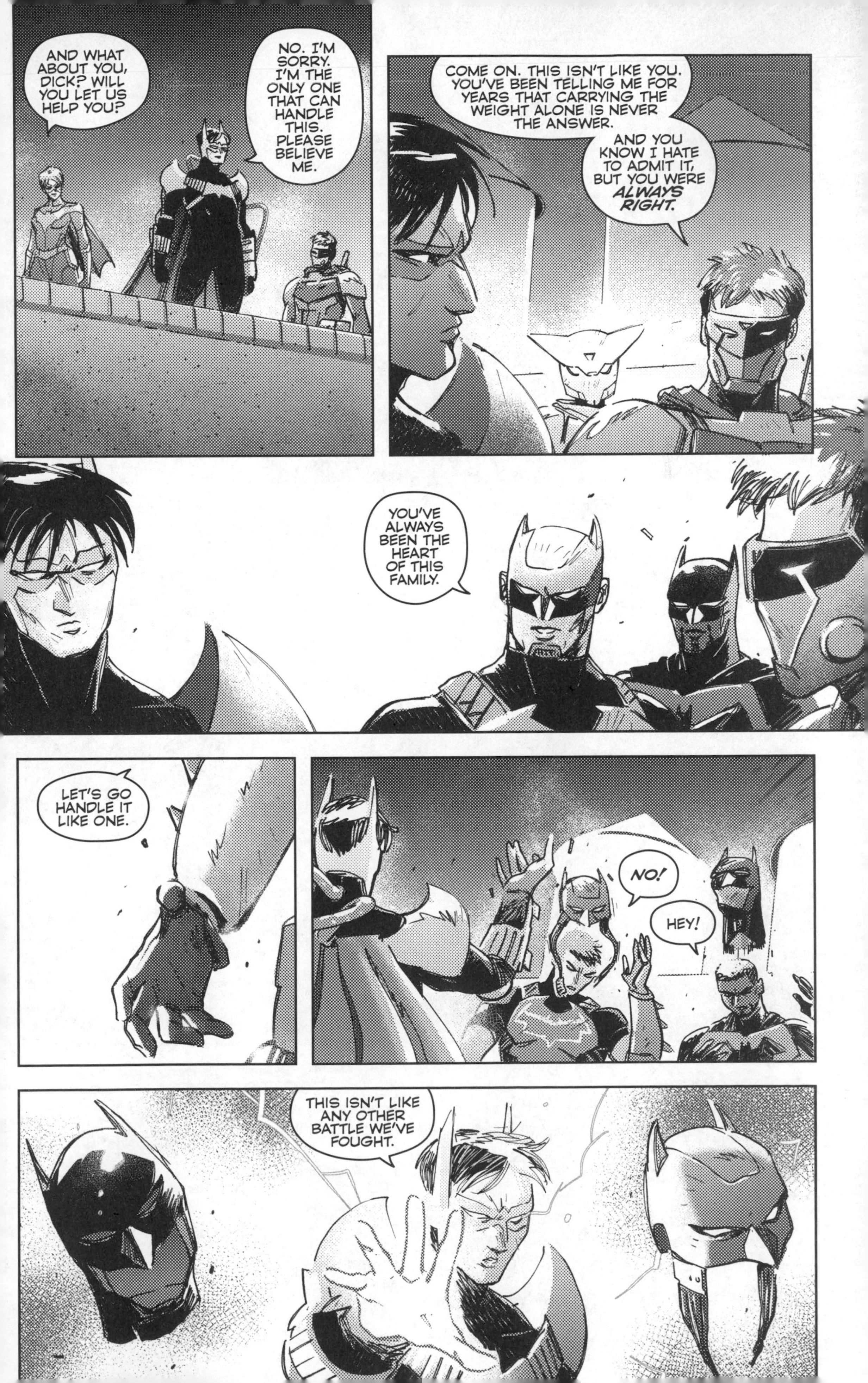
AND WHAT ABOUT YOU, DICK? WILL YOU LET US HELP YOU?
NO. I'M SORRY. I'M THE ONLY ONE THAT CAN HANDLE THIS. PLEASE BELIEVE ME.
COME ON. THIS ISN'T LIKE YOU. YOU'VE BEEN TELLING ME FOR YEARS THAT CARRYING THE WEIGHT ALONE IS NEVER THE ANSWER.
AND YOU KNOW I HATE TO ADMIT IT, BUT YOU WERE ALWAYS RIGHT.
YOU'VE ALWAYS BEEN THE HEART OF THIS FAMILY.
LET'S GO HANDLE IT LIKE ONE.
NO!
HEY!
THIS ISN'T LIKE ANY OTHER BATTLE WE'VE FOUGHT.

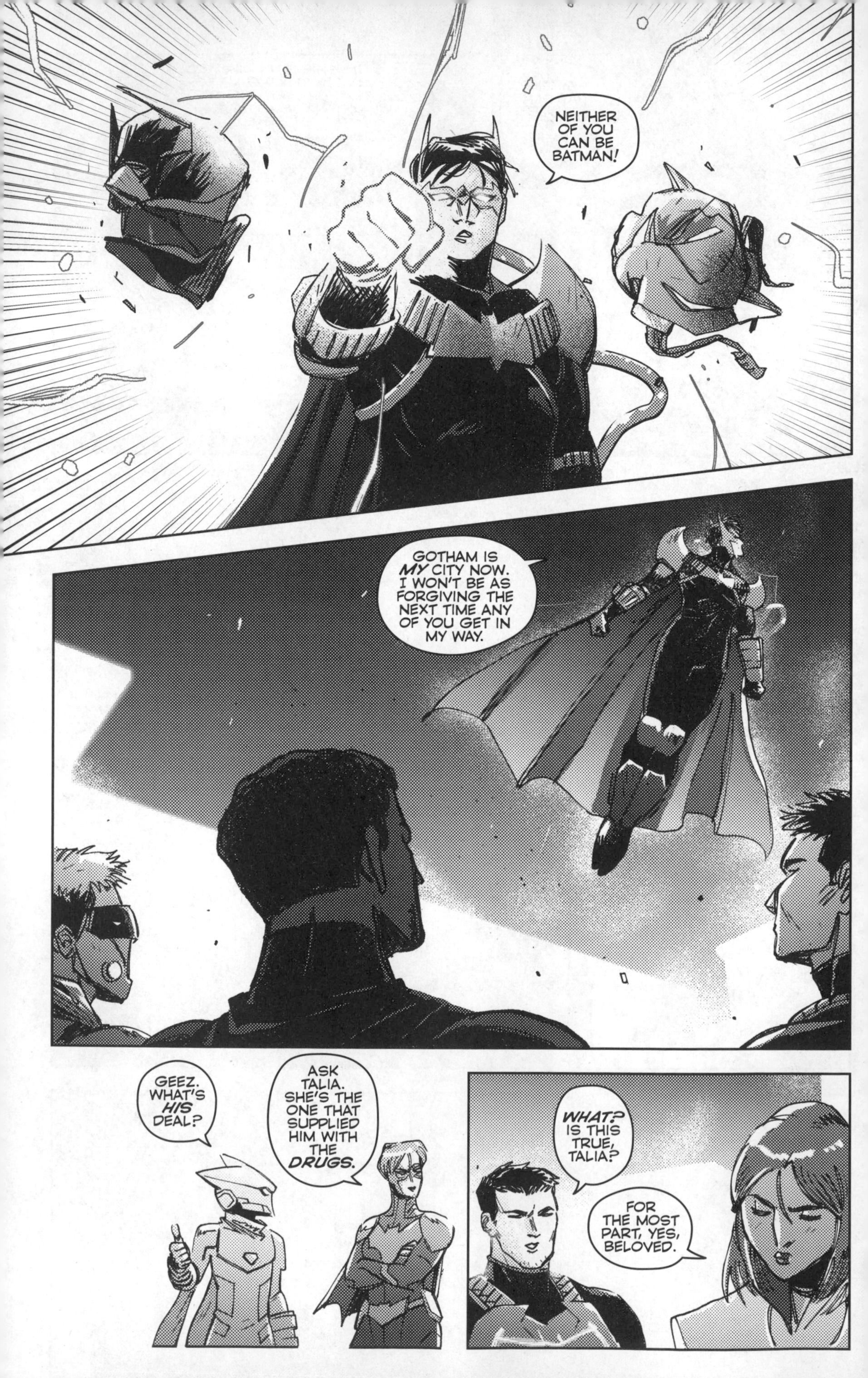
NEITHER OF YOU CAN BE BATMAN!
GOTHAM IS MY CITY NOW. I WON'T BE AS FORGIVING THE NEXT TIME ANY OF YOU GET IN MY WAY.
GEEZ. WHAT'S HIS DEAL?
ASK TALIA. SHE'S THE ONE THAT SUPPLIED HIM WITH THE DRUGS.
WHAT? IS THIS TRUE, TALIA?
FOR THE MOST PART, YES, BELOVED.

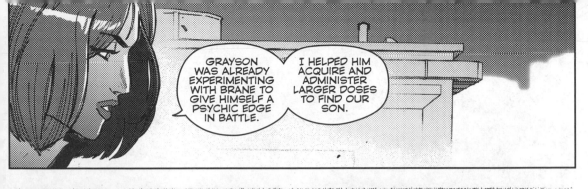

GRAYSON WAS ALREADY EXPERIMENTING WITH BRANE TO GIVE HIMSELF A PSYCHIC EDGE IN BATTLE.

I HELPED HIM ACQUIRE AND ADMINISTER LARGER DOSES TO FIND OUR SON.

"IT WORKED TOO WELL, AND NOT ONLY DID HE LOCATE BOTH YOU AND DAMIAN, HE SAW A *TERRIBLE FATE* FOR GOTHAM THAT HE NOW WORKS TO PREVENT.

"I FEAR THAT DAMIAN IS SOMEHOW THE CAUSE OF THAT. THAT HE HAS GONE TOO FAR DOWN THE PATH TO BECOMING A *DEMON* LIKE HIS *GRANDFATHER*."

THIS ISN'T JUST ON DAMIAN. HUSH HAS BEEN *MANIPULATING* HIM. HE TRIED THE SAME WITH ME EARLIER THIS YEAR. THAT'S THE REAL ENEMY.

WE HAVE TO *SEPARATE* THEM.

WE HAVE TO FIND THEM FIRST, RED.

LEAVE THAT TO ME. THE ONE BENEFIT OF GOING *UNDERCOVER* AND WORKING FOR THE *MAGISTRATE* IS THAT...

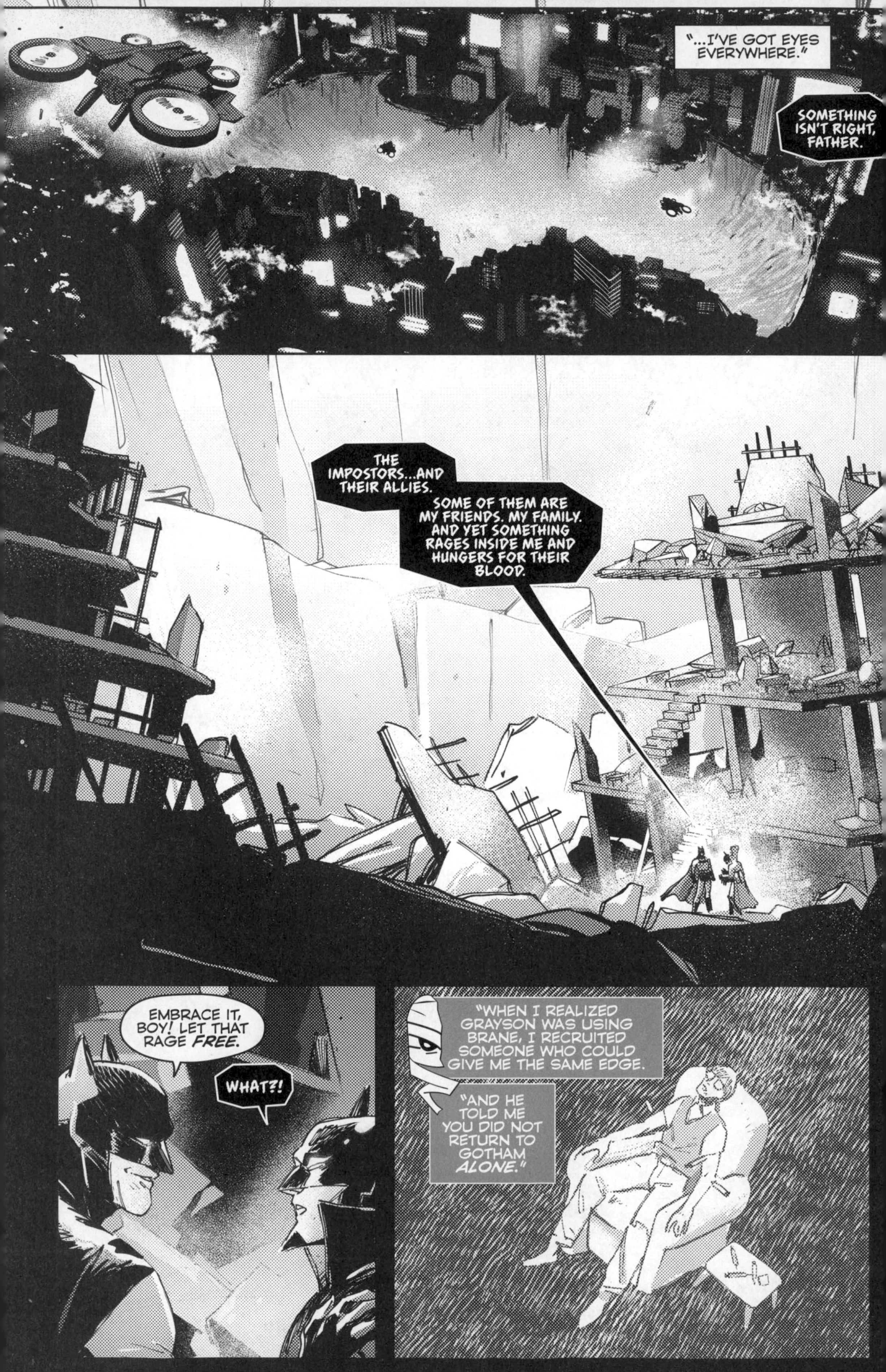
"...I'VE GOT EYES EVERYWHERE."
SOMETHING ISN'T RIGHT, FATHER.
THE IMPOSTORS...AND THEIR ALLIES.
SOME OF THEM ARE MY FRIENDS. MY FAMILY. AND YET SOMETHING RAGES INSIDE ME AND HUNGERS FOR THEIR BLOOD.
EMBRACE IT, BOY! LET THAT RAGE *FREE*.
WHAT?!
"WHEN I REALIZED GRAYSON WAS USING BRANE, I RECRUITED SOMEONE WHO COULD GIVE ME THE SAME EDGE.
"AND HE TOLD ME YOU DID NOT RETURN TO GOTHAM *ALONE*."

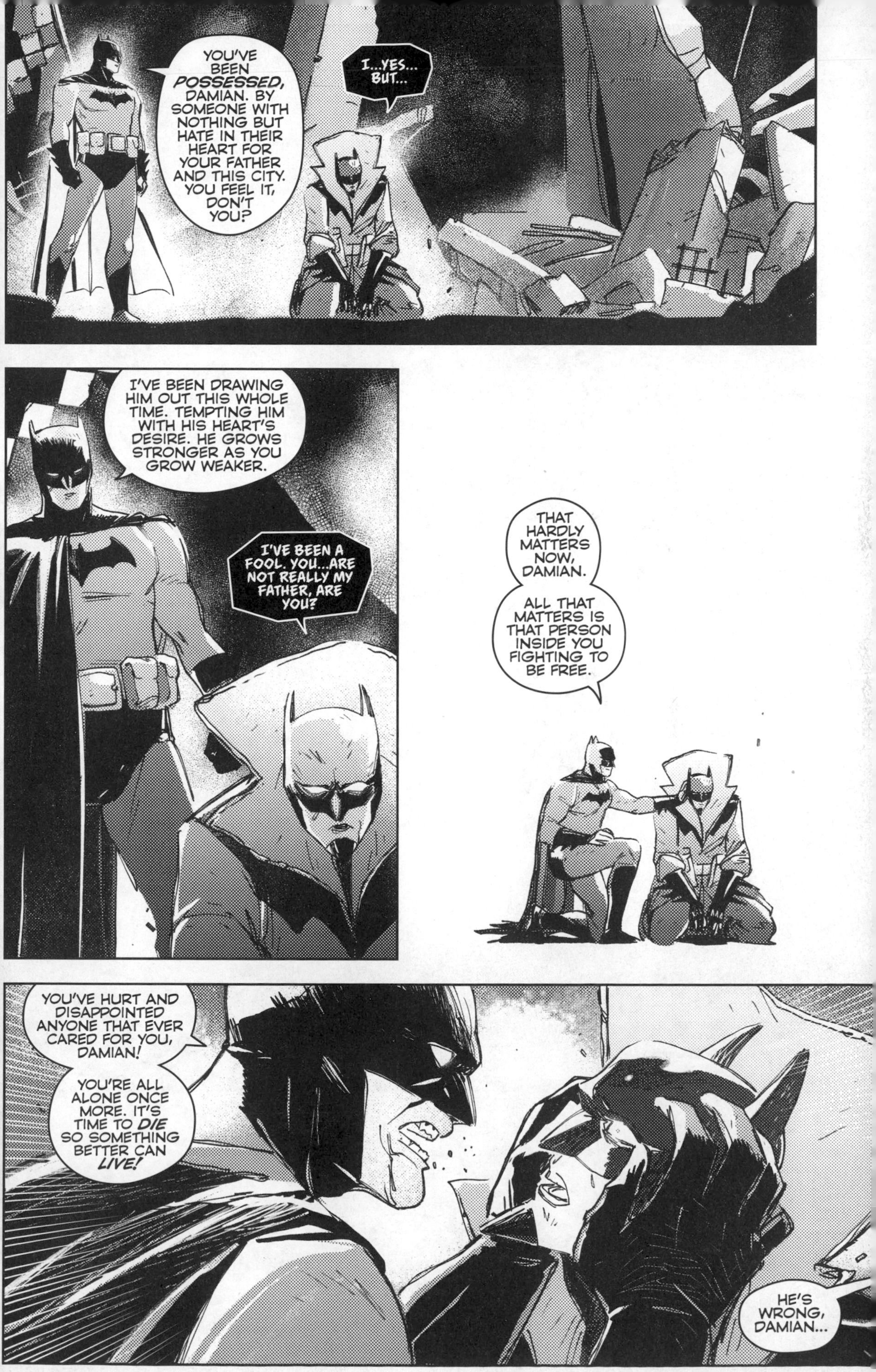
YOU'VE BEEN POSSESSED, DAMIAN. BY SOMEONE WITH NOTHING BUT HATE IN THEIR HEART FOR YOUR FATHER AND THIS CITY. YOU FEEL IT, DON'T YOU?
I...YES... BUT...
I'VE BEEN DRAWING HIM OUT THIS WHOLE TIME. TEMPTING HIM WITH HIS HEART'S DESIRE. HE GROWS STRONGER AS YOU GROW WEAKER.
I'VE BEEN A FOOL. YOU...ARE NOT REALLY MY FATHER, ARE YOU?
THAT HARDLY MATTERS NOW, DAMIAN.
ALL THAT MATTERS IS THAT PERSON INSIDE YOU FIGHTING TO BE FREE.
YOU'VE HURT AND DISAPPOINTED ANYONE THAT EVER CARED FOR YOU, DAMIAN!
YOU'RE ALL ALONE ONCE MORE. IT'S TIME TO DIE SO SOMETHING BETTER CAN LIVE!
HE'S WRONG, DAMIAN...

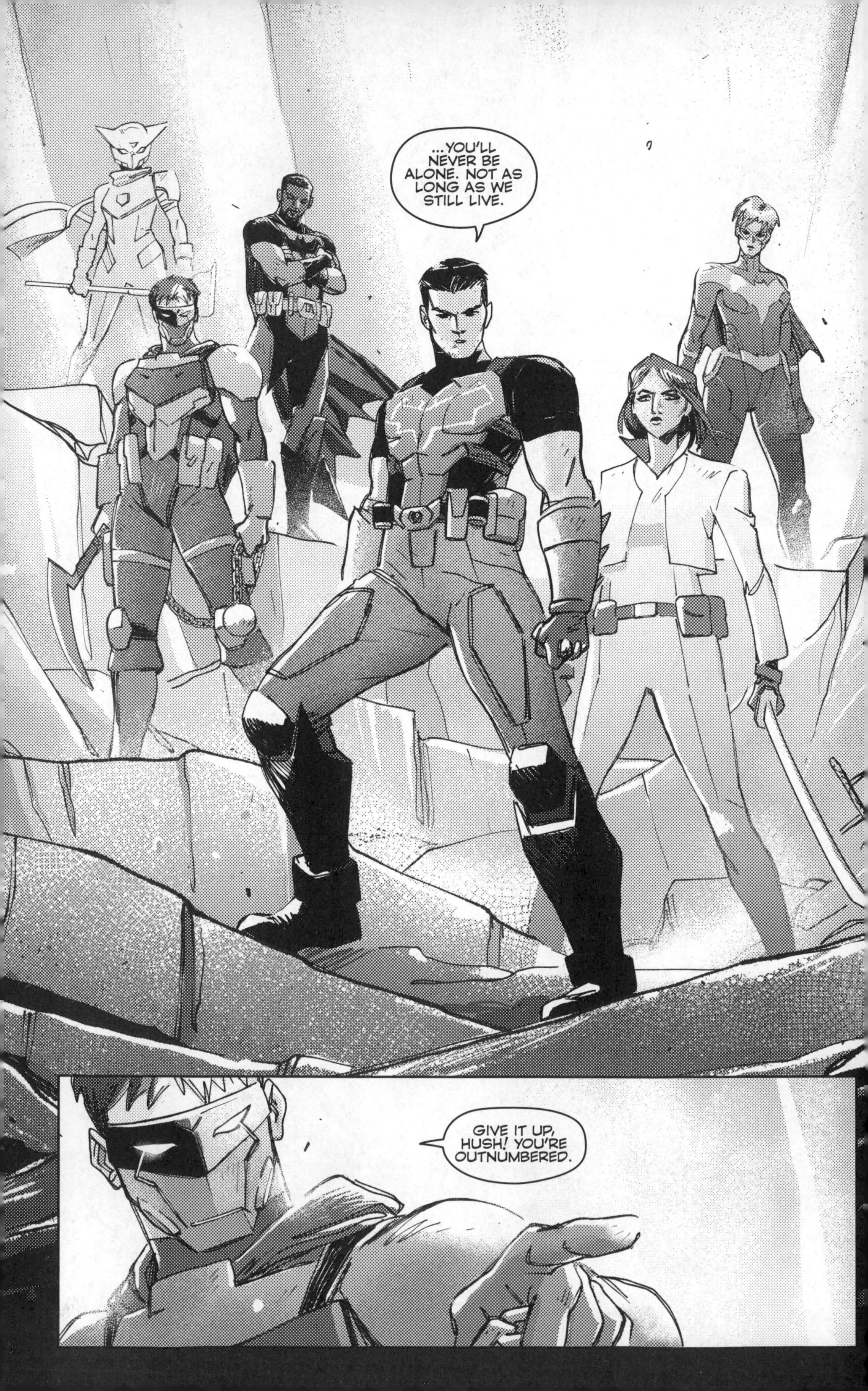
...YOU'LL NEVER BE ALONE. NOT AS LONG AS WE STILL LIVE.
GIVE IT UP, HUSH! YOU'RE OUTNUMBERED.

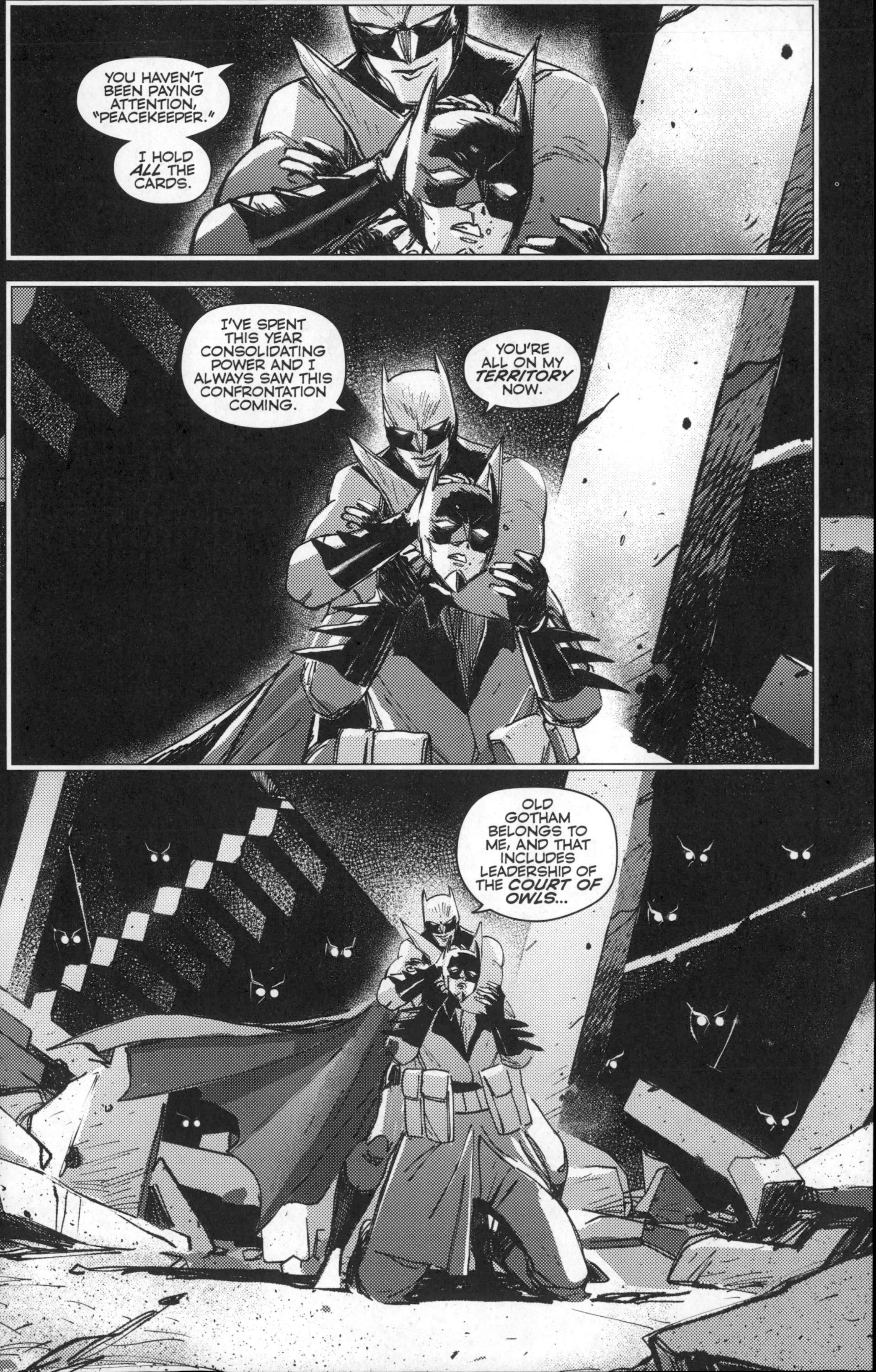
YOU HAVEN'T BEEN PAYING ATTENTION, "PEACEKEEPER."
I HOLD *ALL* THE CARDS.
I'VE SPENT THIS YEAR CONSOLIDATING POWER AND I ALWAYS SAW THIS CONFRONTATION COMING.
YOU'RE ALL ON MY *TERRITORY* NOW.
OLD GOTHAM BELONGS TO ME, AND THAT INCLUDES LEADERSHIP OF THE *COURT OF OWLS*...

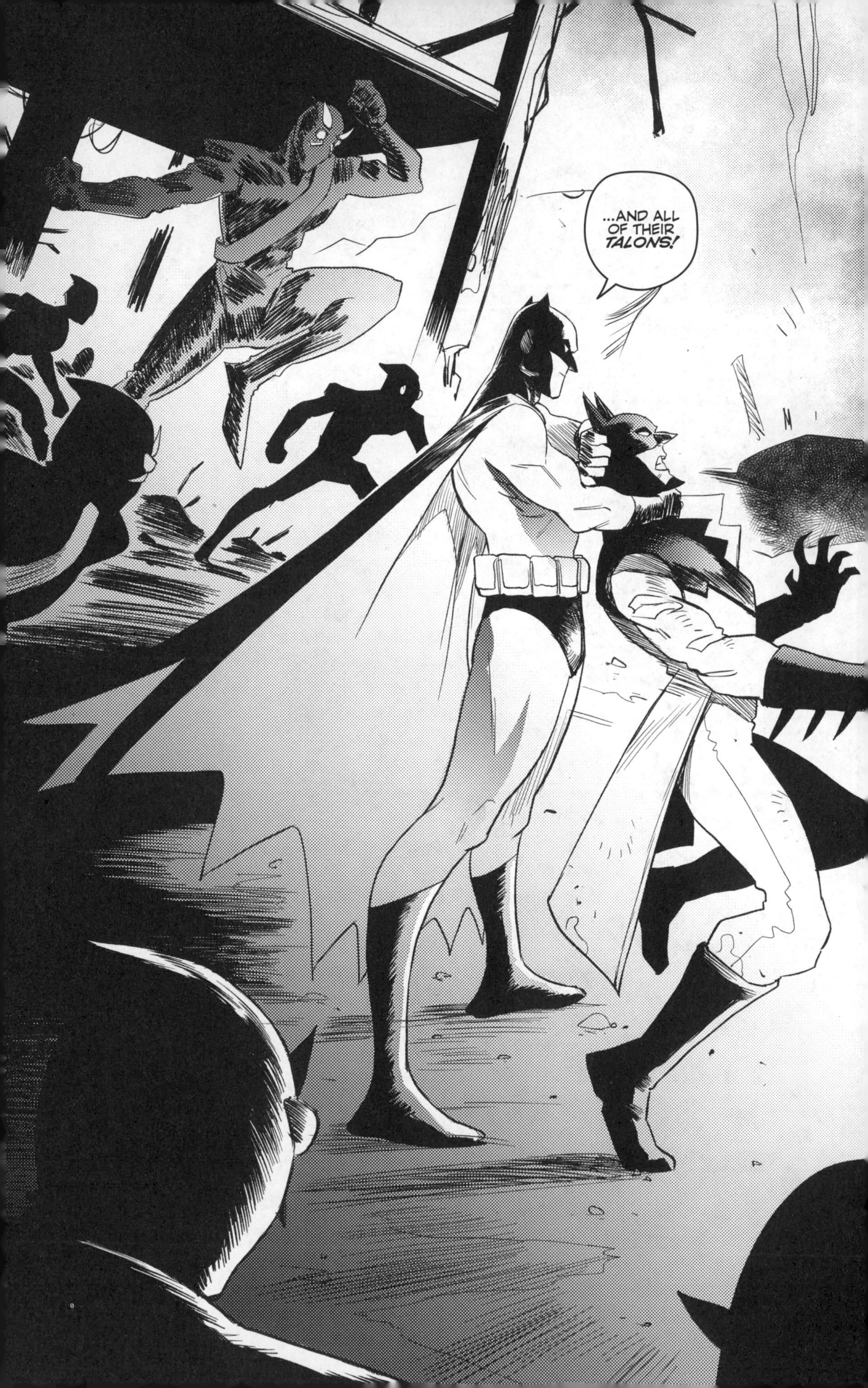
...AND ALL OF THEIR TALONS!

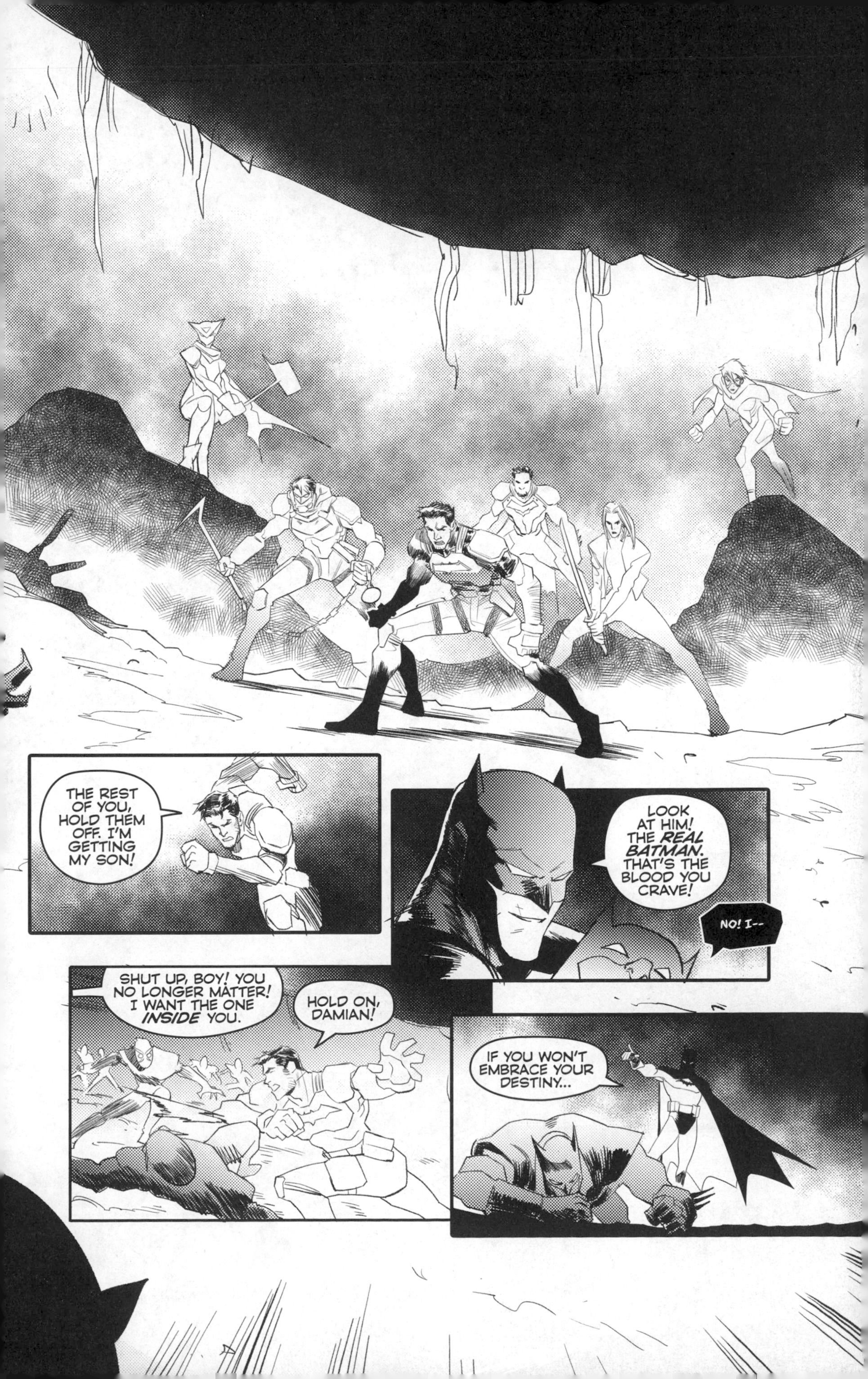
THE REST OF YOU, HOLD THEM OFF. I'M GETTING MY SON!
LOOK AT HIM! THE *REAL BATMAN.* THAT'S THE BLOOD YOU CRAVE!
NO! I--
SHUT UP, BOY! YOU NO LONGER MATTER! I WANT THE ONE *INSIDE* YOU.
HOLD ON, DAMIAN!
IF YOU WON'T EMBRACE YOUR DESTINY...

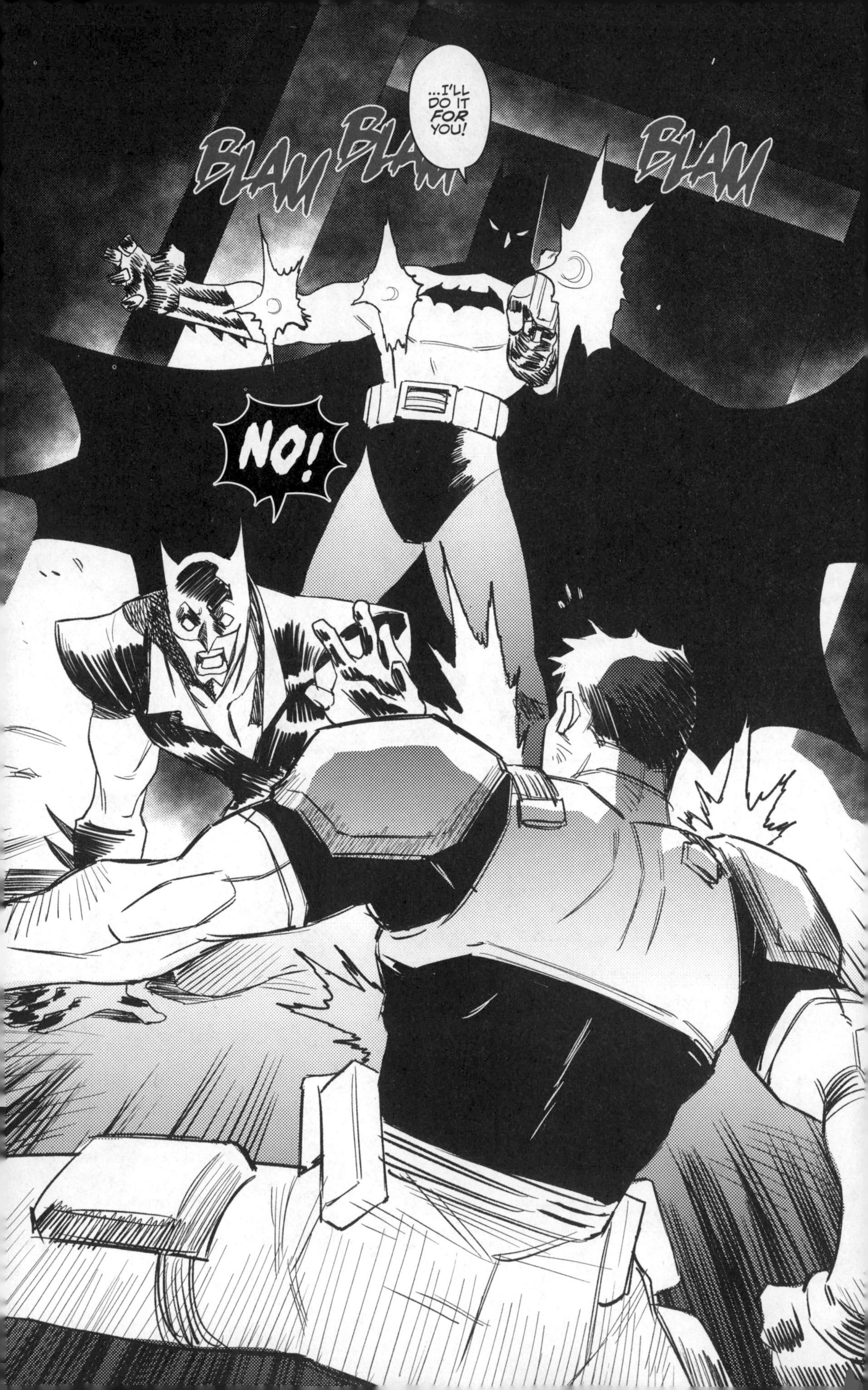
BLAM BLAM
...I'LL DO IT FOR YOU!
BLAM
NO!

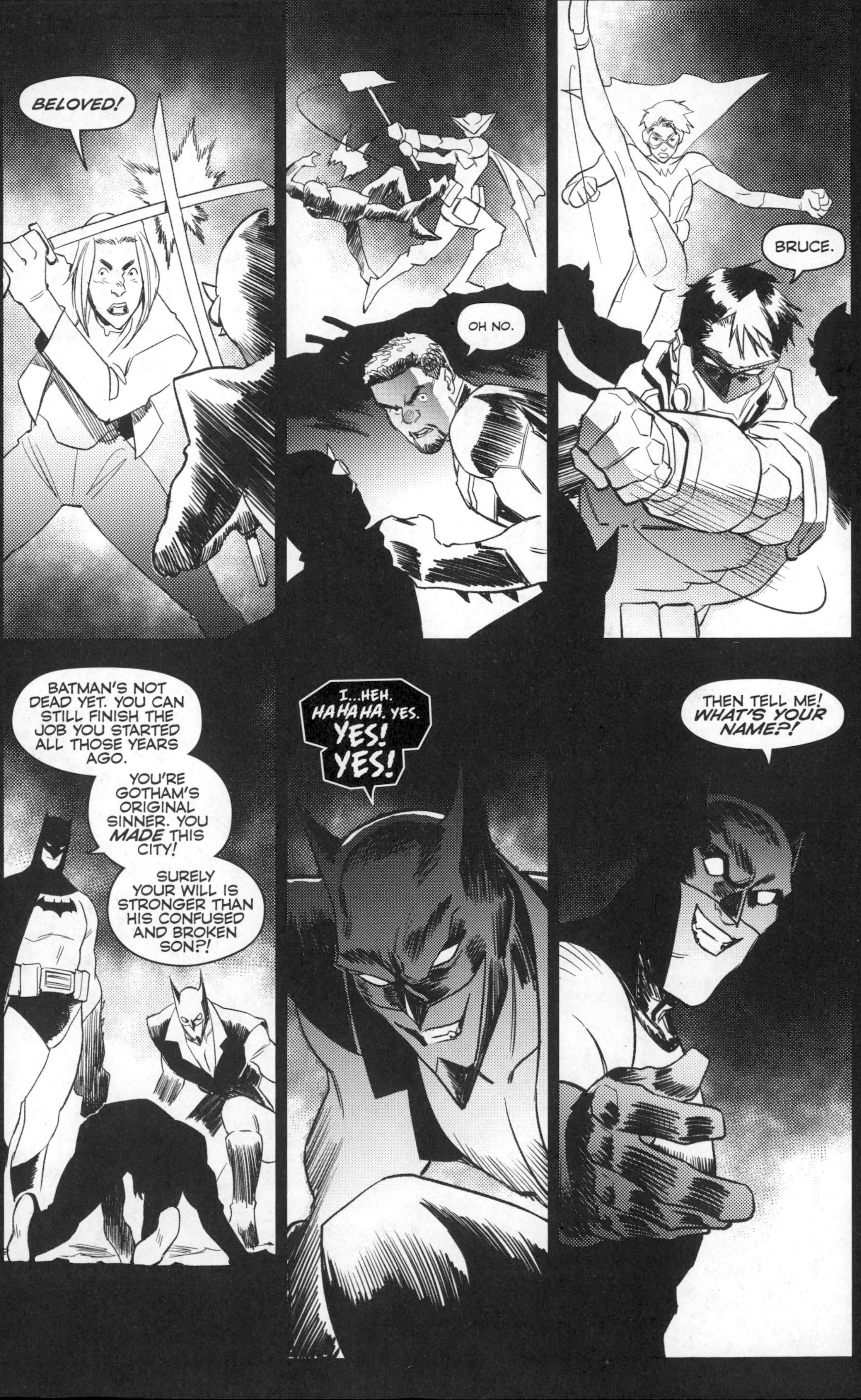
BELOVED!
OH NO.
BRUCE.
BATMAN'S NOT DEAD YET. YOU CAN STILL FINISH THE JOB YOU STARTED ALL THOSE YEARS AGO.
YOU'RE GOTHAM'S ORIGINAL SINNER. YOU *MADE* THIS CITY!
SURELY YOUR WILL IS STRONGER THAN HIS CONFUSED AND BROKEN SON?!
I...HEH. HAHAHA. YES. YES! YES!
THEN TELL ME! WHAT'S YOUR NAME?!

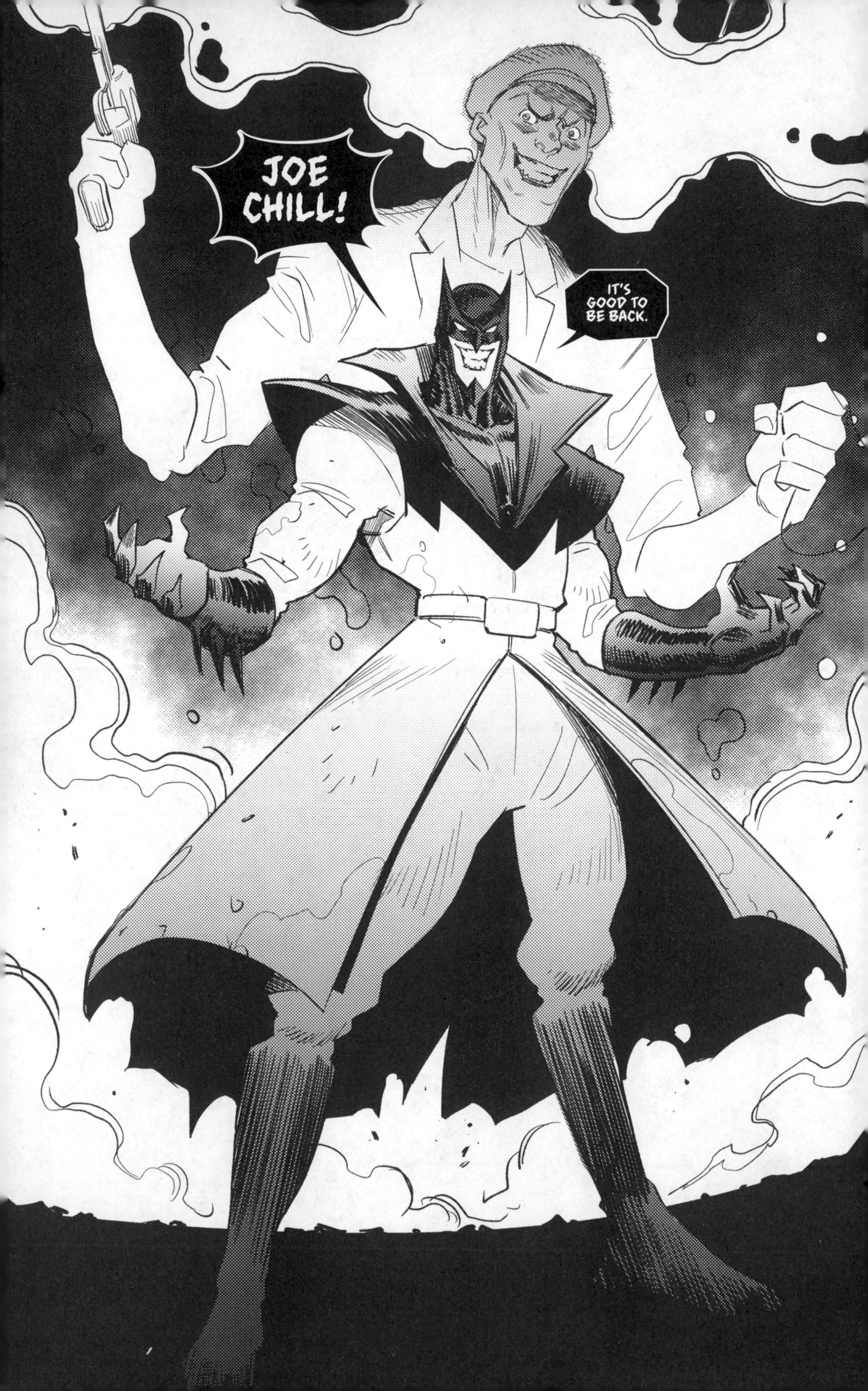
JOE CHILL!
IT'S GOOD TO BE BACK.

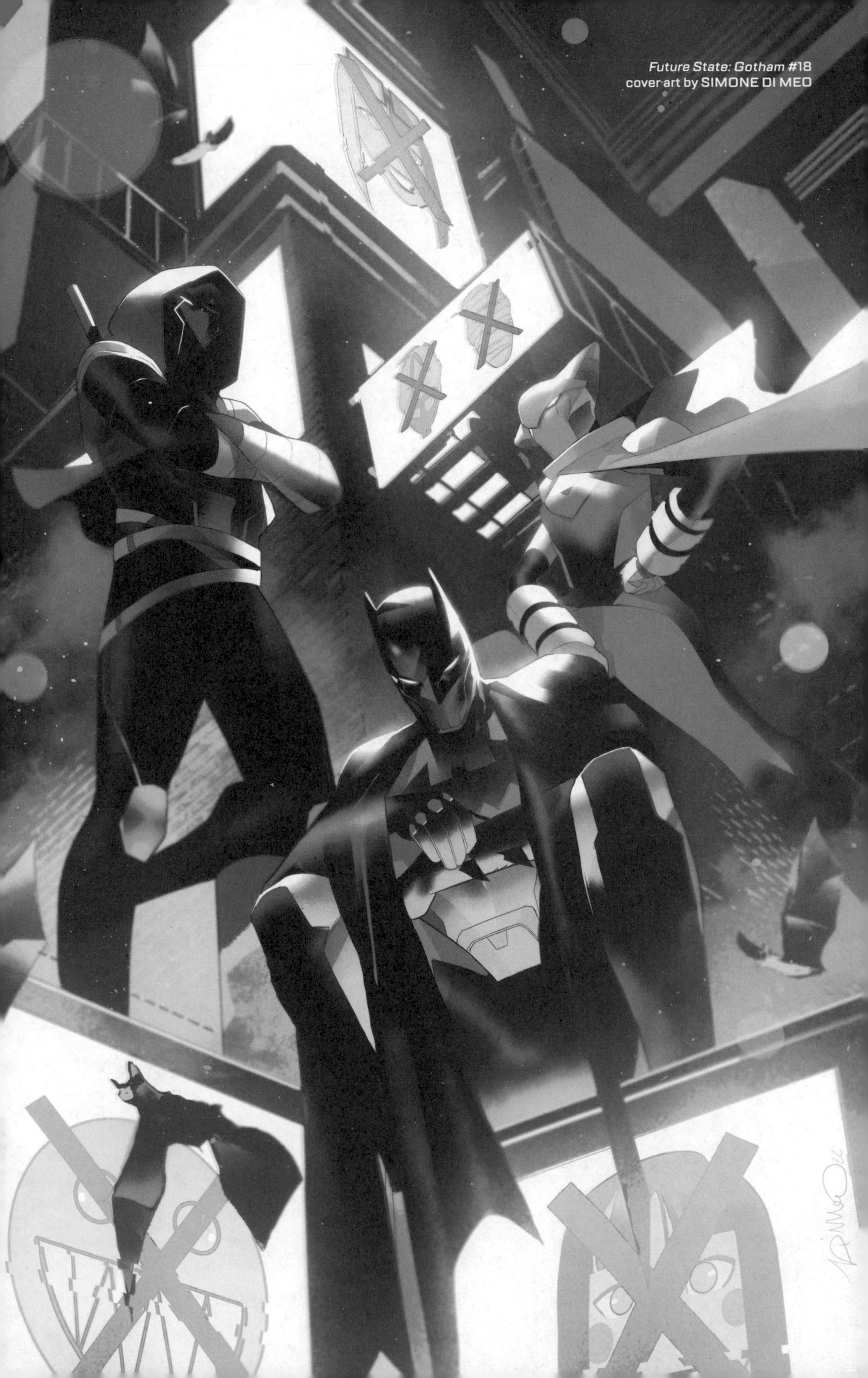

Future State: Gotham #18
cover art by SIMONE DI MEO

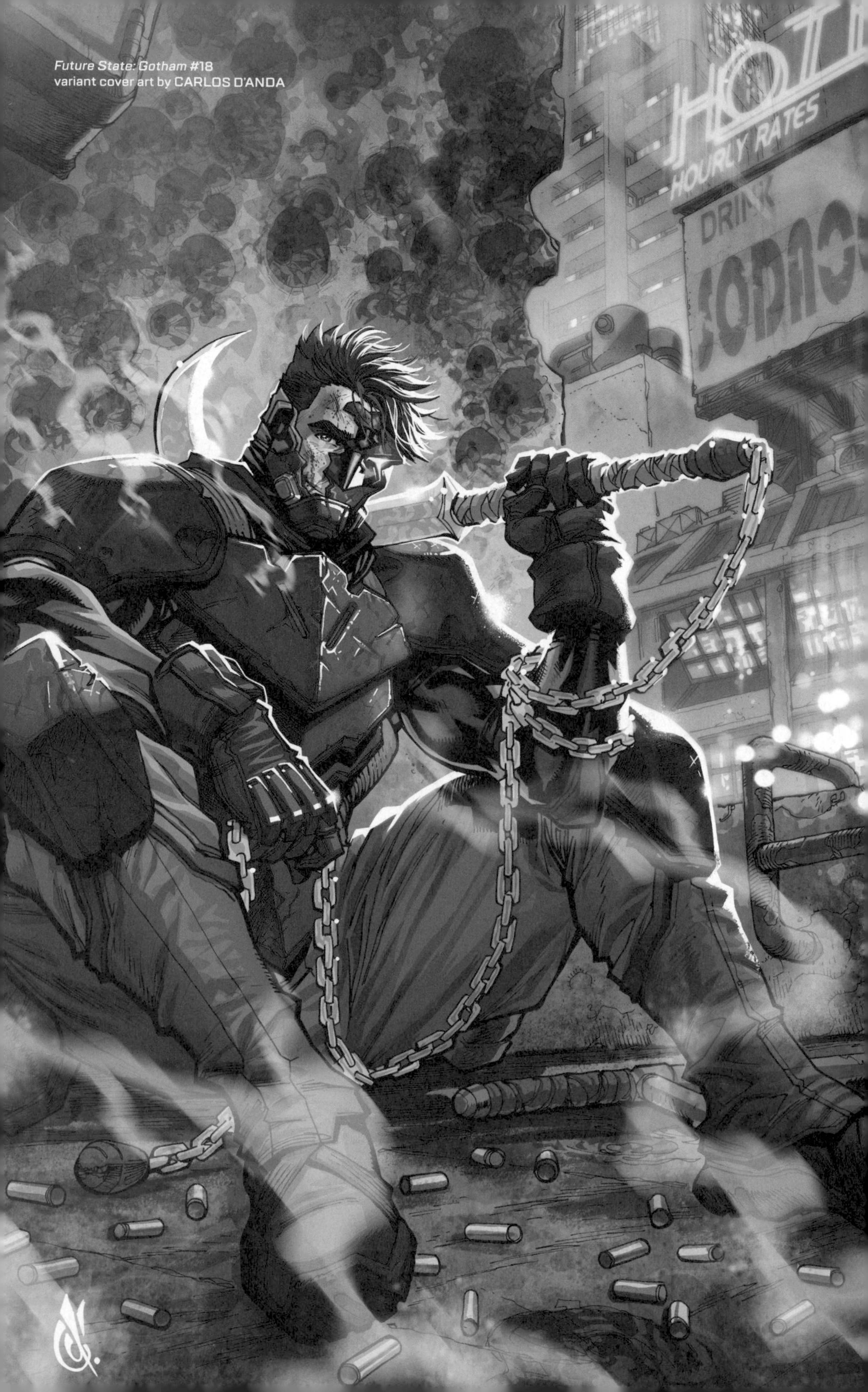
HOURLY RATES

Future State: Gotham #18
variant cover art by CARLOS D'ANDA

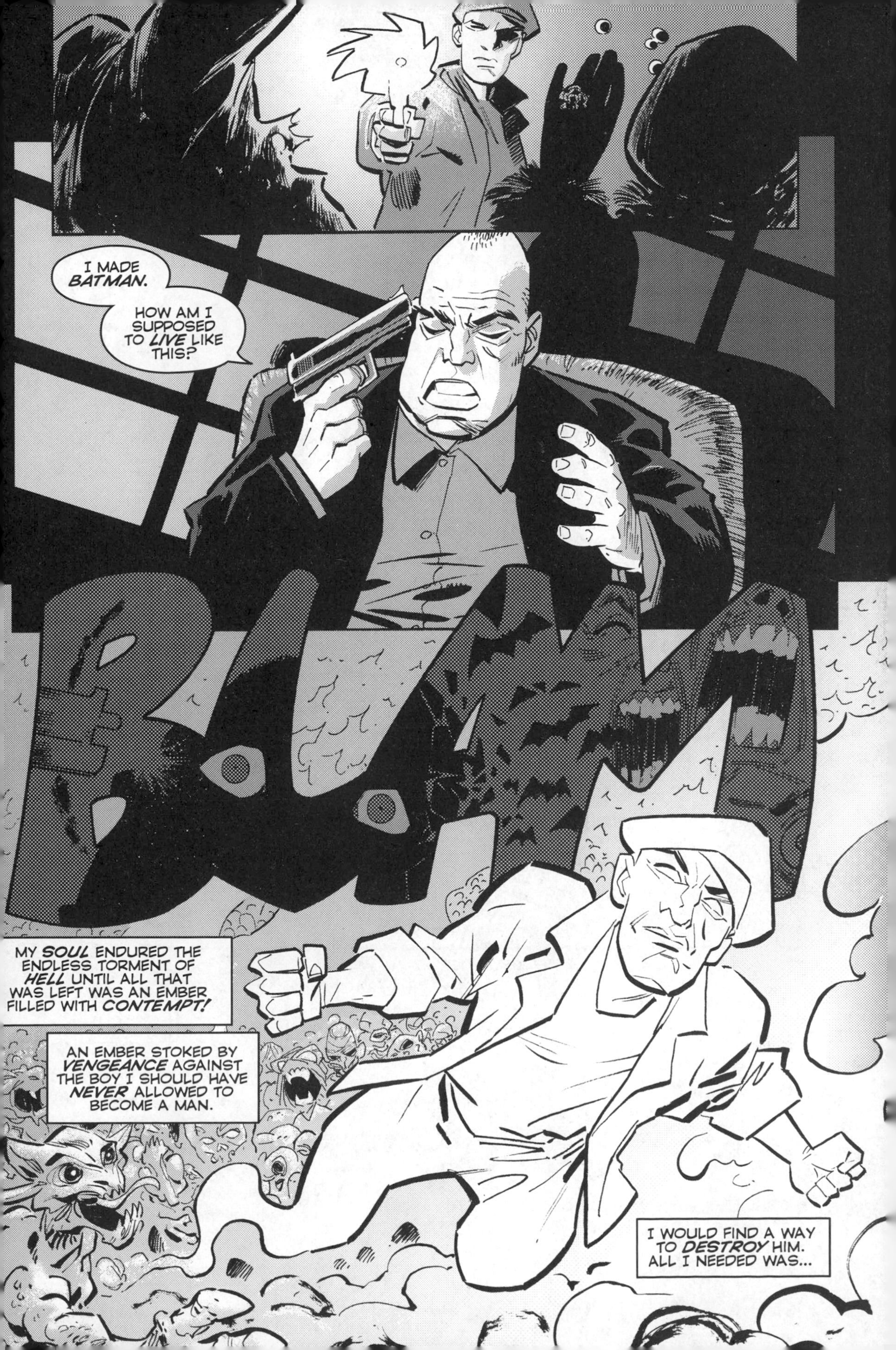
I MADE BATMAN.
HOW AM I SUPPOSED TO LIVE LIKE THIS?
BLAM
MY SOUL ENDURED THE ENDLESS TORMENT OF HELL UNTIL ALL THAT WAS LEFT WAS AN EMBER FILLED WITH CONTEMPT!
AN EMBER STOKED BY VENGEANCE AGAINST THE BOY I SHOULD HAVE NEVER ALLOWED TO BECOME A MAN.
I WOULD FIND A WAY TO DESTROY HIM. ALL I NEEDED WAS...

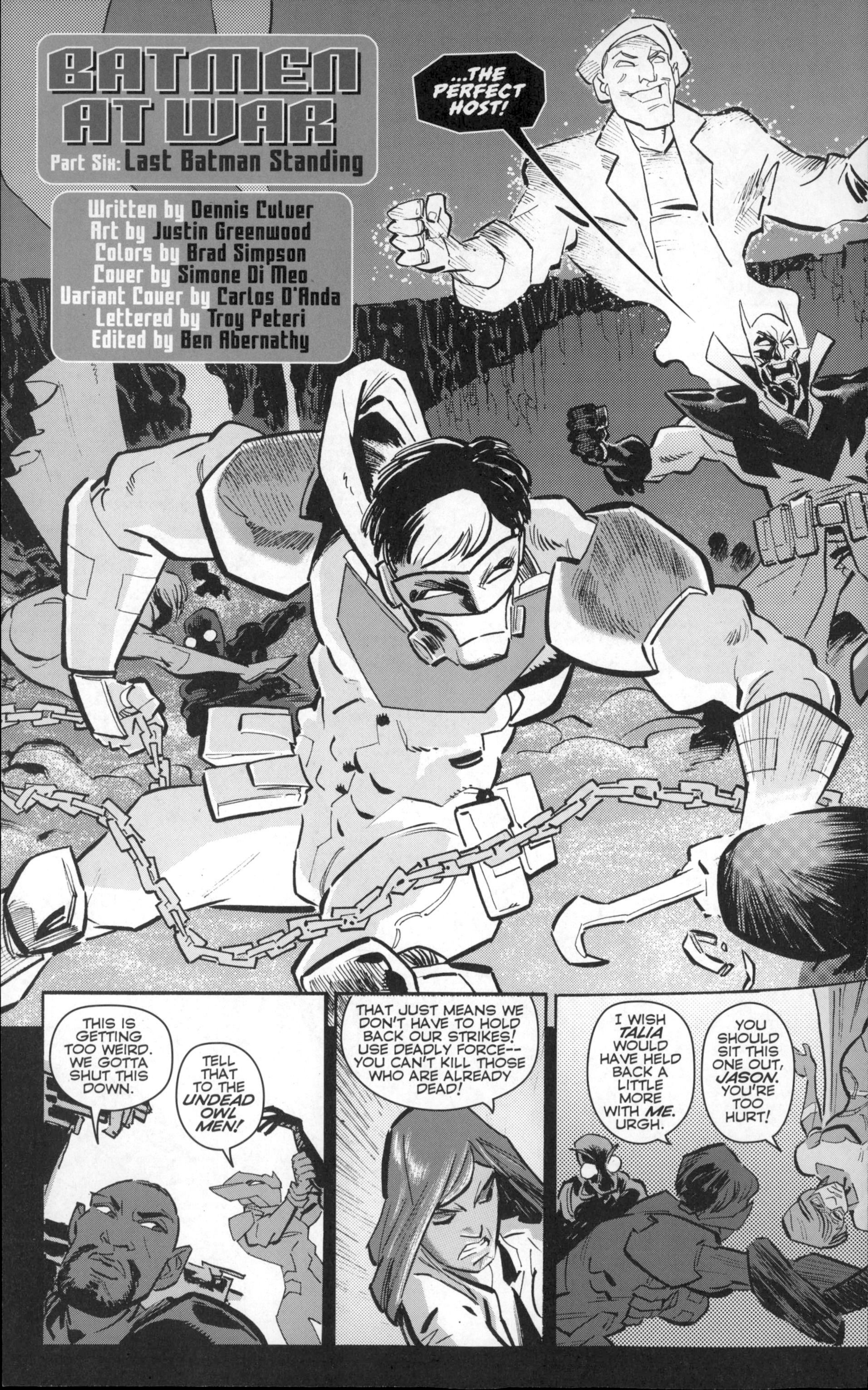
BATMEN AT WAR
Part Six: Last Batman Standing
Written by Dennis Culver
Art by Justin Greenwood
Colors by Brad Simpson
Cover by Simone Di Meo
Variant Cover by Carlos D'Anda
Lettered by Troy Peteri
Edited by Ben Abernathy
...THE PERFECT HOST!
THIS IS GETTING TOO WEIRD. WE GOTTA SHUT THIS DOWN.
TELL THAT TO THE *UNDEAD OWL MEN!*
THAT JUST MEANS WE DON'T HAVE TO HOLD BACK OUR STRIKES! USE DEADLY FORCE-- YOU CAN'T KILL THOSE WHO ARE ALREADY DEAD!
I WISH *TALIA* WOULD HAVE HELD BACK A LITTLE MORE WITH *ME.* URGH.
YOU SHOULD SIT THIS ONE OUT, *JASON.* YOU'RE TOO HURT!

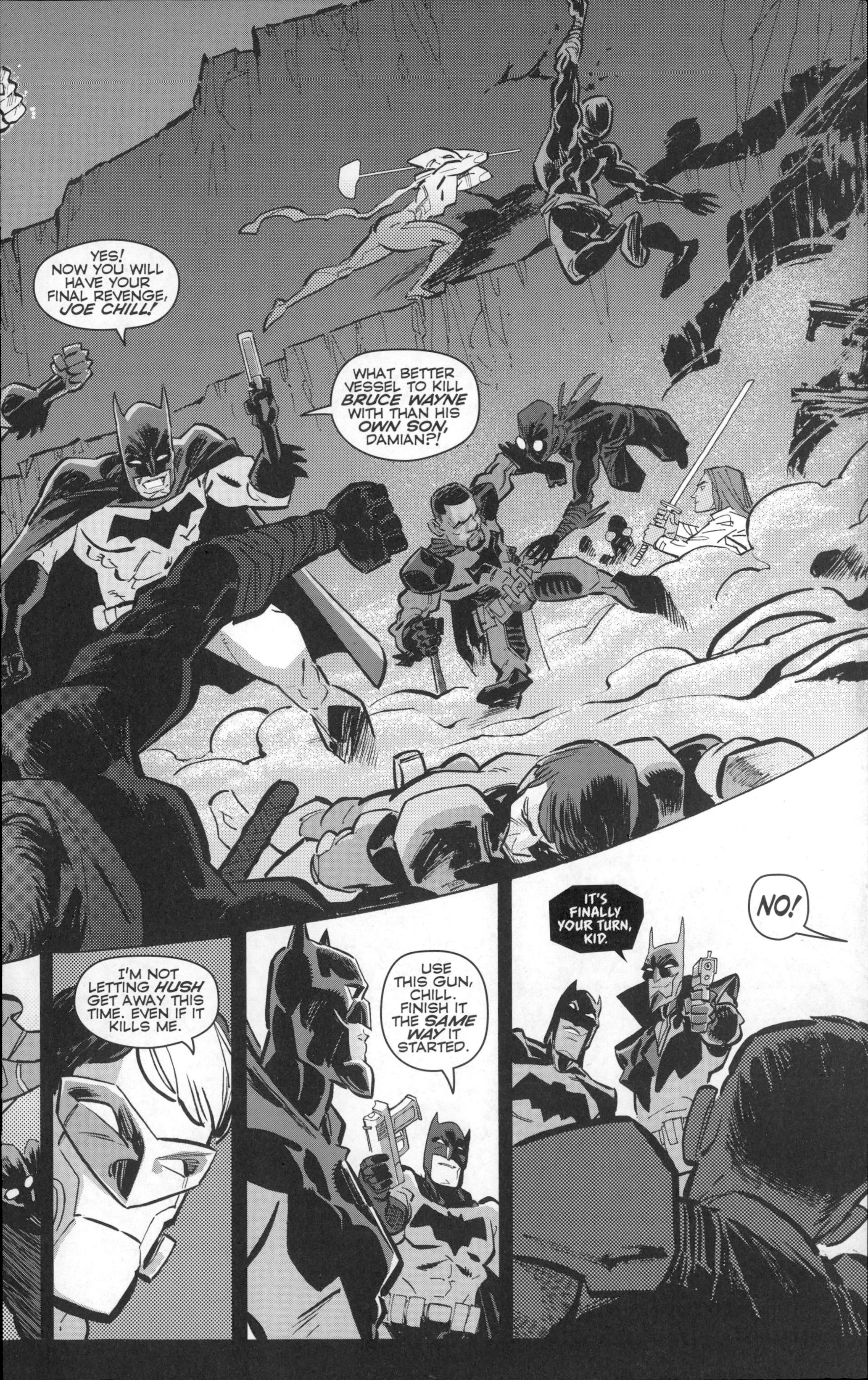
YES! NOW YOU WILL HAVE YOUR FINAL REVENGE, JOE CHILL!
WHAT BETTER VESSEL TO KILL BRUCE WAYNE WITH THAN HIS OWN SON, DAMIAN?!
I'M NOT LETTING HUSH GET AWAY THIS TIME. EVEN IF IT KILLS ME.
USE THIS GUN, CHILL. FINISH IT THE SAME WAY IT STARTED.
IT'S FINALLY YOUR TURN, KID.
NO!

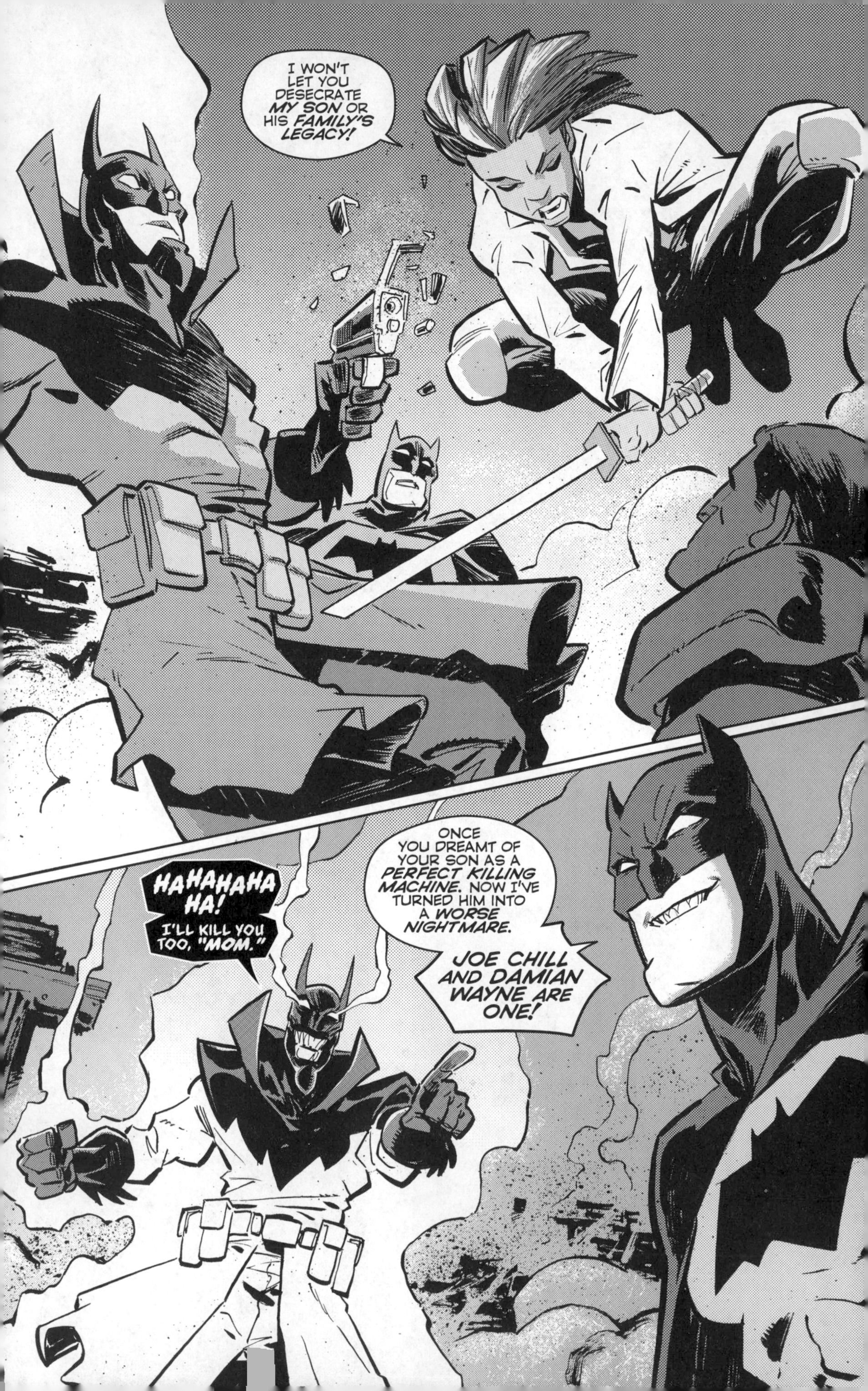
I WON'T LET YOU DESECRATE MY SON OR HIS FAMILY'S LEGACY!
HAHAHAHA HA!
I'LL KILL YOU TOO, "MOM."
ONCE YOU DREAMT OF YOUR SON AS A PERFECT KILLING MACHINE. NOW I'VE TURNED HIM INTO A WORSE NIGHTMARE.
JOE CHILL AND DAMIAN WAYNE ARE ONE!

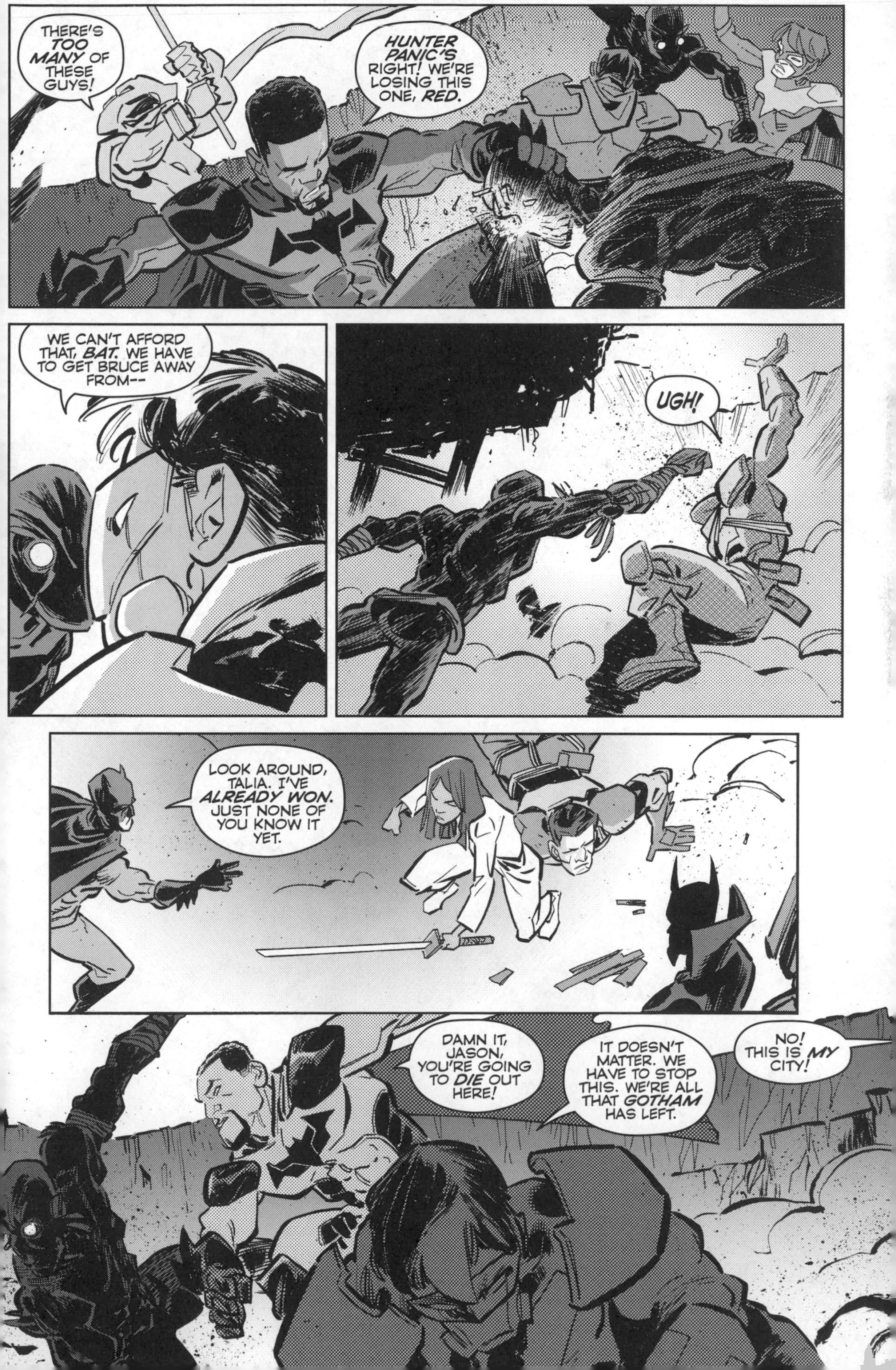
THERE'S TOO MANY OF THESE GUYS!
HUNTER PANIC'S RIGHT! WE'RE LOSING THIS ONE, RED.
WE CAN'T AFFORD THAT, BAT. WE HAVE TO GET BRUCE AWAY FROM--
UGH!
LOOK AROUND, TALIA. I'VE ALREADY WON. JUST NONE OF YOU KNOW IT YET.
DAMN IT, JASON, YOU'RE GOING TO DIE OUT HERE!
IT DOESN'T MATTER. WE HAVE TO STOP THIS. WE'RE ALL THAT GOTHAM HAS LEFT.
NO! THIS IS MY CITY!

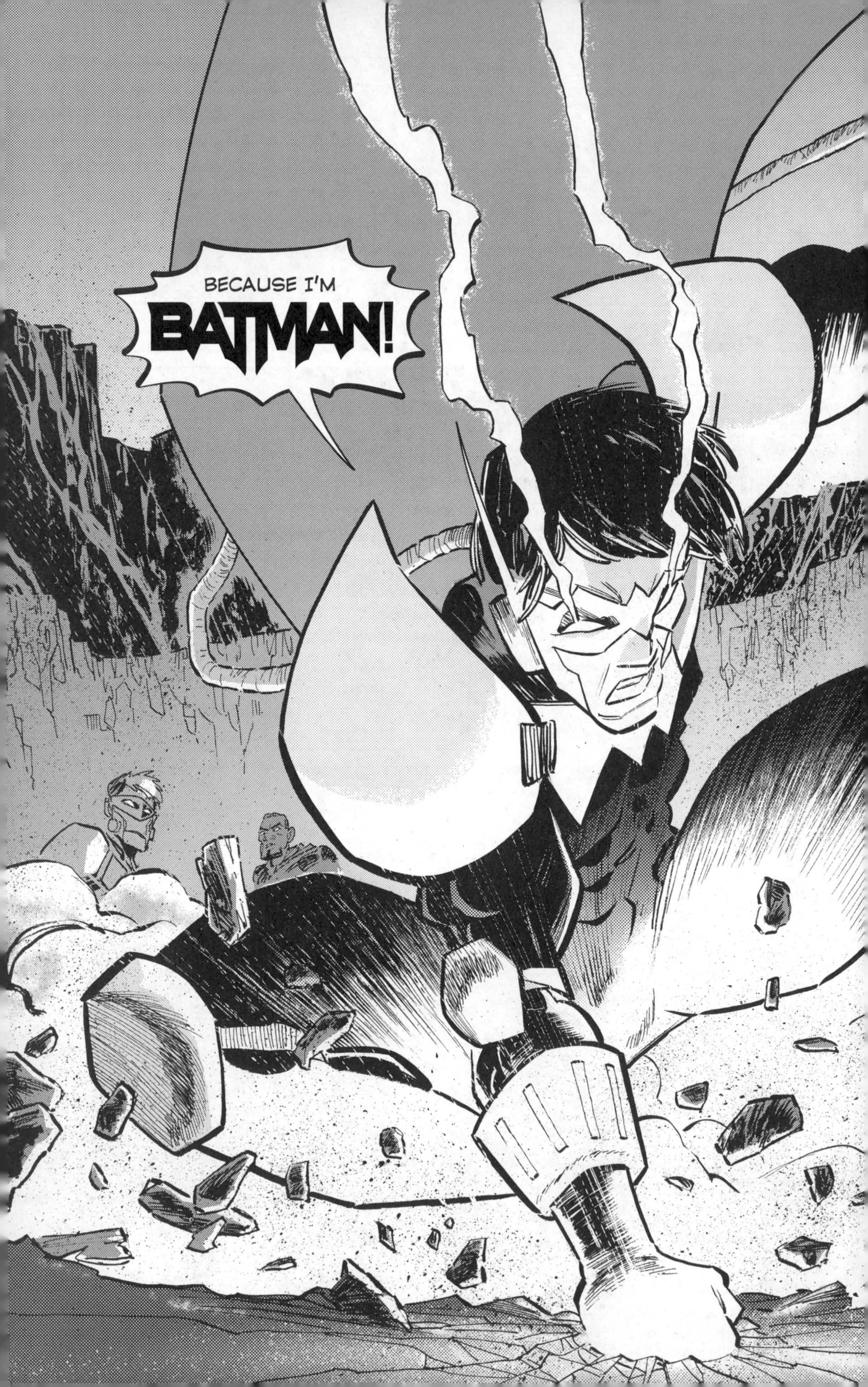
BECAUSE I'M BATMAN!

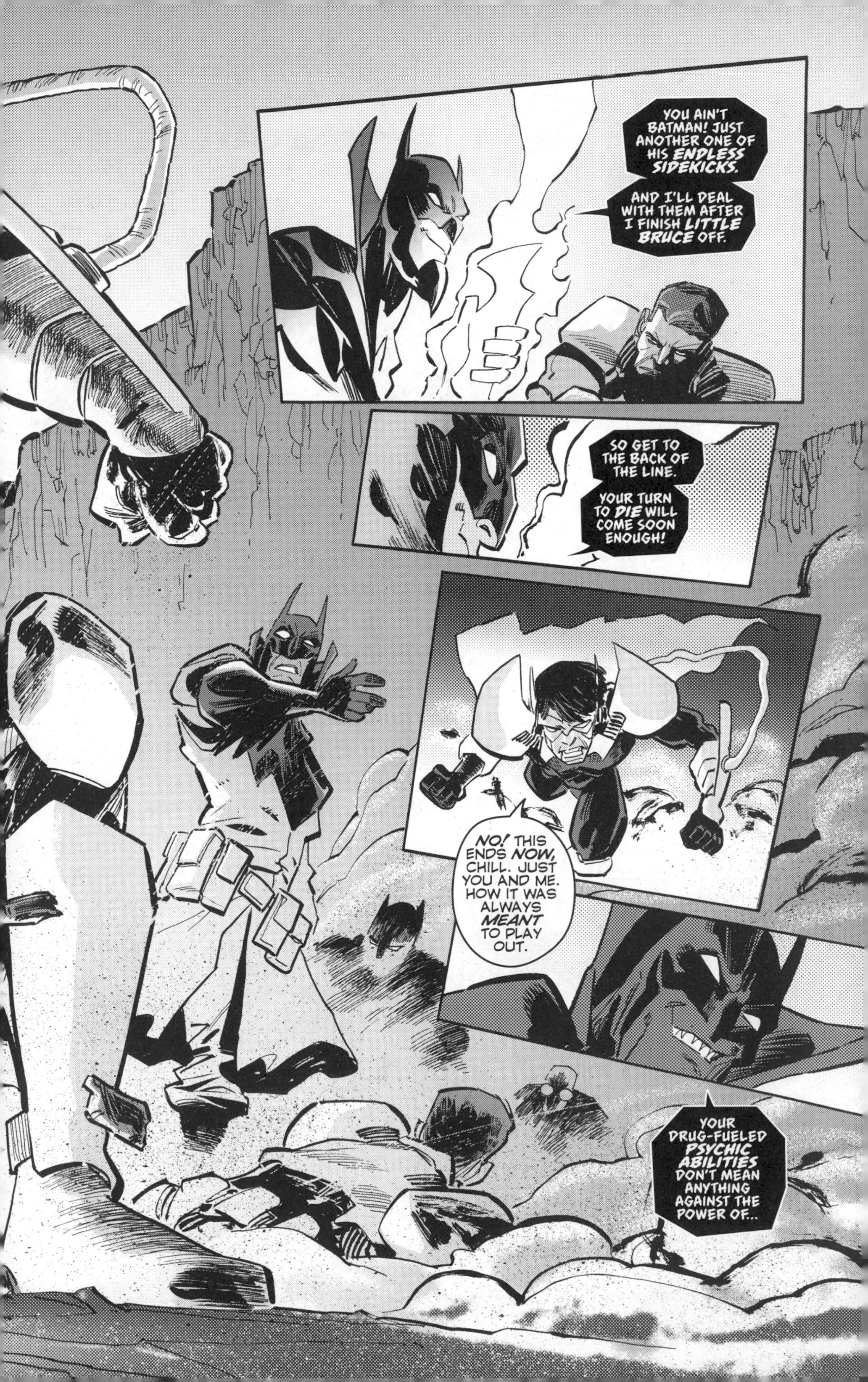
YOU AIN'T BATMAN! JUST ANOTHER ONE OF HIS ENDLESS SIDEKICKS.
AND I'LL DEAL WITH THEM AFTER I FINISH LITTLE BRUCE OFF.
SO GET TO THE BACK OF THE LINE.
YOUR TURN TO DIE WILL COME SOON ENOUGH!
NO! THIS ENDS NOW, CHILL. JUST YOU AND ME. HOW IT WAS ALWAYS MEANT TO PLAY OUT.
YOUR DRUG-FUELED PSYCHIC ABILITIES DON'T MEAN ANYTHING AGAINST THE POWER OF...

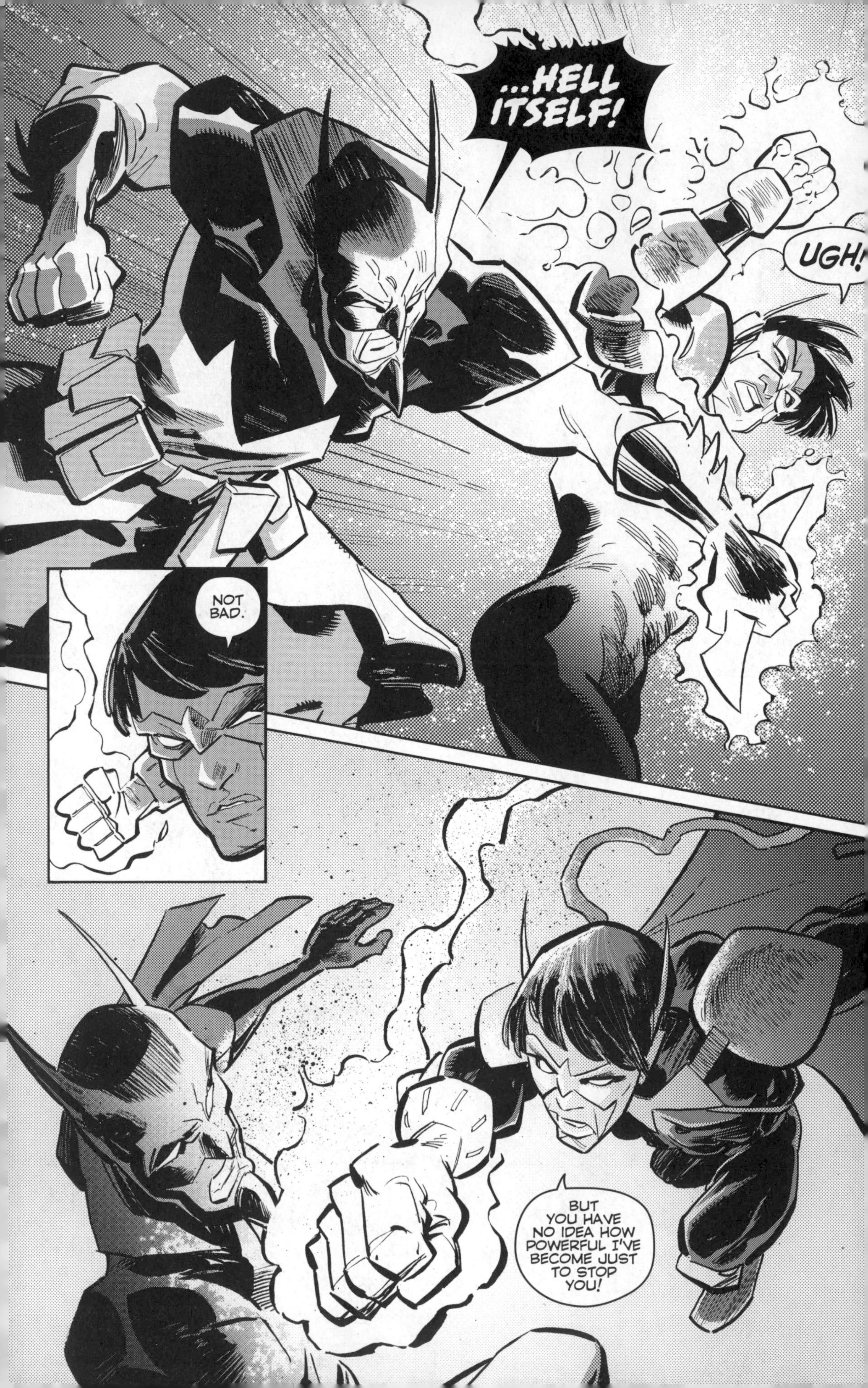
...HELL ITSELF!
UGH!
NOT BAD.
BUT YOU HAVE NO IDEA HOW POWERFUL I'VE BECOME JUST TO STOP YOU!

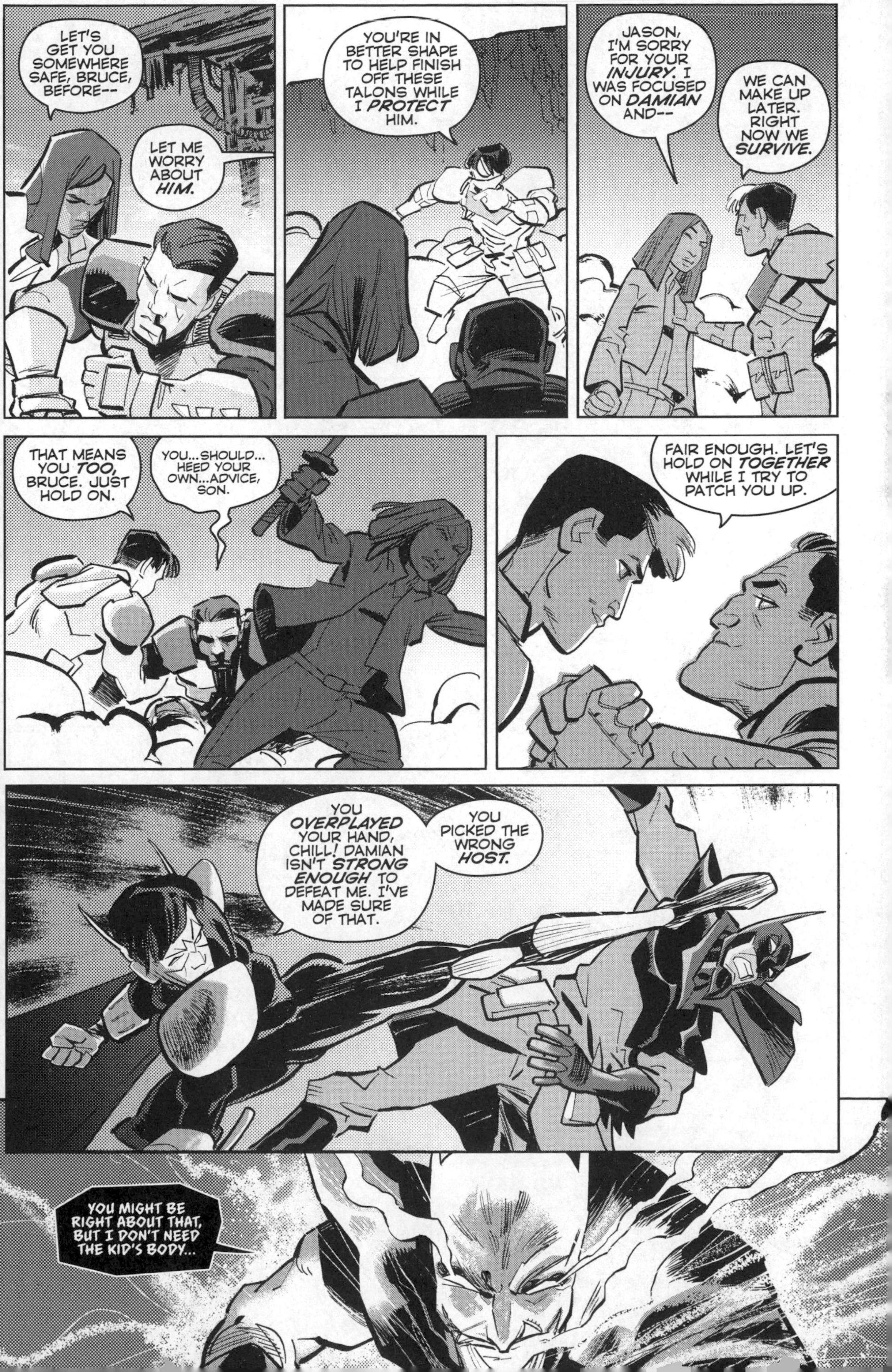
LET'S GET YOU SOMEWHERE SAFE, BRUCE, BEFORE--
LET ME WORRY ABOUT HIM.
YOU'RE IN BETTER SHAPE TO HELP FINISH OFF THESE TALONS WHILE I PROTECT HIM.
JASON, I'M SORRY FOR YOUR INJURY. I WAS FOCUSED ON DAMIAN AND--
WE CAN MAKE UP LATER. RIGHT NOW WE SURVIVE.
THAT MEANS YOU TOO, BRUCE. JUST HOLD ON.
YOU...SHOULD... HEED YOUR OWN...ADVICE, SON.
FAIR ENOUGH. LET'S HOLD ON TOGETHER WHILE I TRY TO PATCH YOU UP.
YOU OVERPLAYED YOUR HAND, CHILL! DAMIAN ISN'T STRONG ENOUGH TO DEFEAT ME. I'VE MADE SURE OF THAT.
YOU PICKED THE WRONG HOST.
YOU MIGHT BE RIGHT ABOUT THAT, BUT I DON'T NEED THE KID'S BODY...

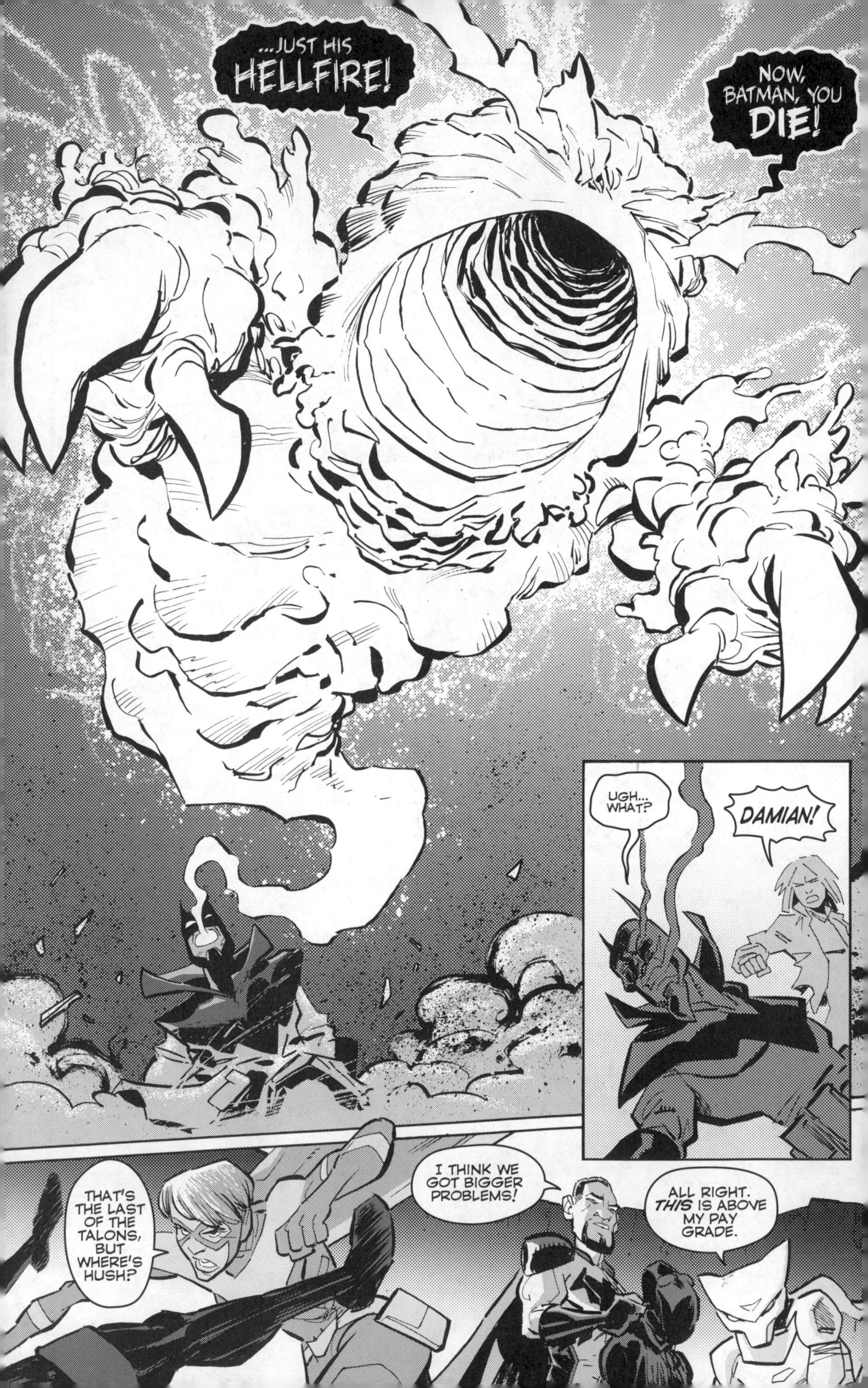
...JUST HIS HELLFIRE!
NOW, BATMAN, YOU DIE!
UGH... WHAT?
DAMIAN!
THAT'S THE LAST OF THE TALONS, BUT WHERE'S HUSH?
I THINK WE GOT BIGGER PROBLEMS!
ALL RIGHT. THIS IS ABOVE MY PAY GRADE.

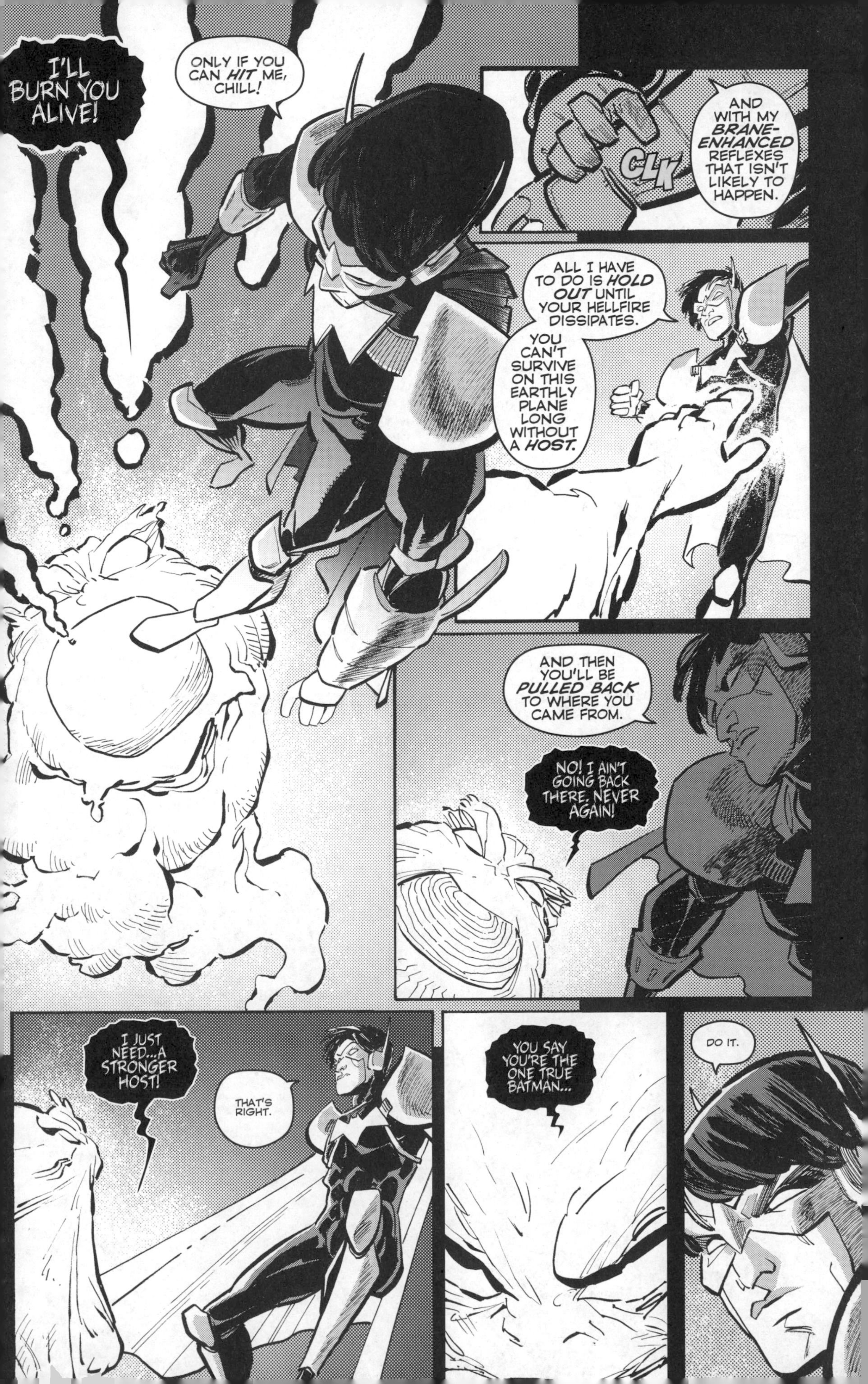
I'LL BURN YOU ALIVE!
ONLY IF YOU CAN HIT ME, CHILL!
AND WITH MY BRANE-ENHANCED REFLEXES THAT ISN'T LIKELY TO HAPPEN.
CLK
ALL I HAVE TO DO IS HOLD OUT UNTIL YOUR HELLFIRE DISSIPATES.
YOU CAN'T SURVIVE ON THIS EARTHLY PLANE LONG WITHOUT A HOST.
AND THEN YOU'LL BE PULLED BACK TO WHERE YOU CAME FROM.
NO! I AIN'T GOING BACK THERE. NEVER AGAIN!
I JUST NEED...A STRONGER HOST!
THAT'S RIGHT.
YOU SAY YOU'RE THE ONE TRUE BATMAN...
DO IT.

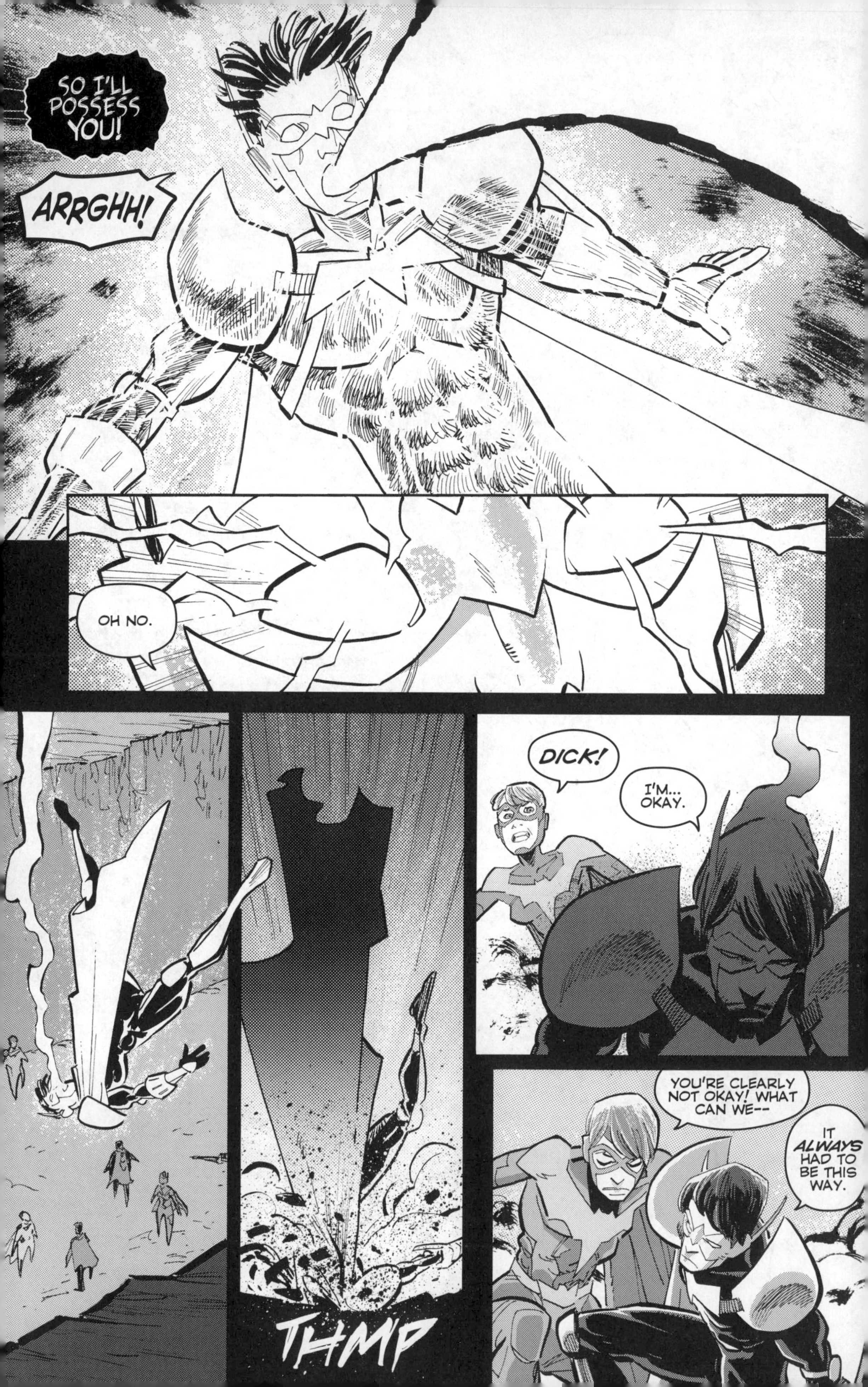
SO I'LL POSSESS YOU!
ARRGHH!
OH NO.
THMP
DICK!
I'M... OKAY.
YOU'RE CLEARLY NOT OKAY! WHAT CAN WE--
IT ALWAYS HAD TO BE THIS WAY.

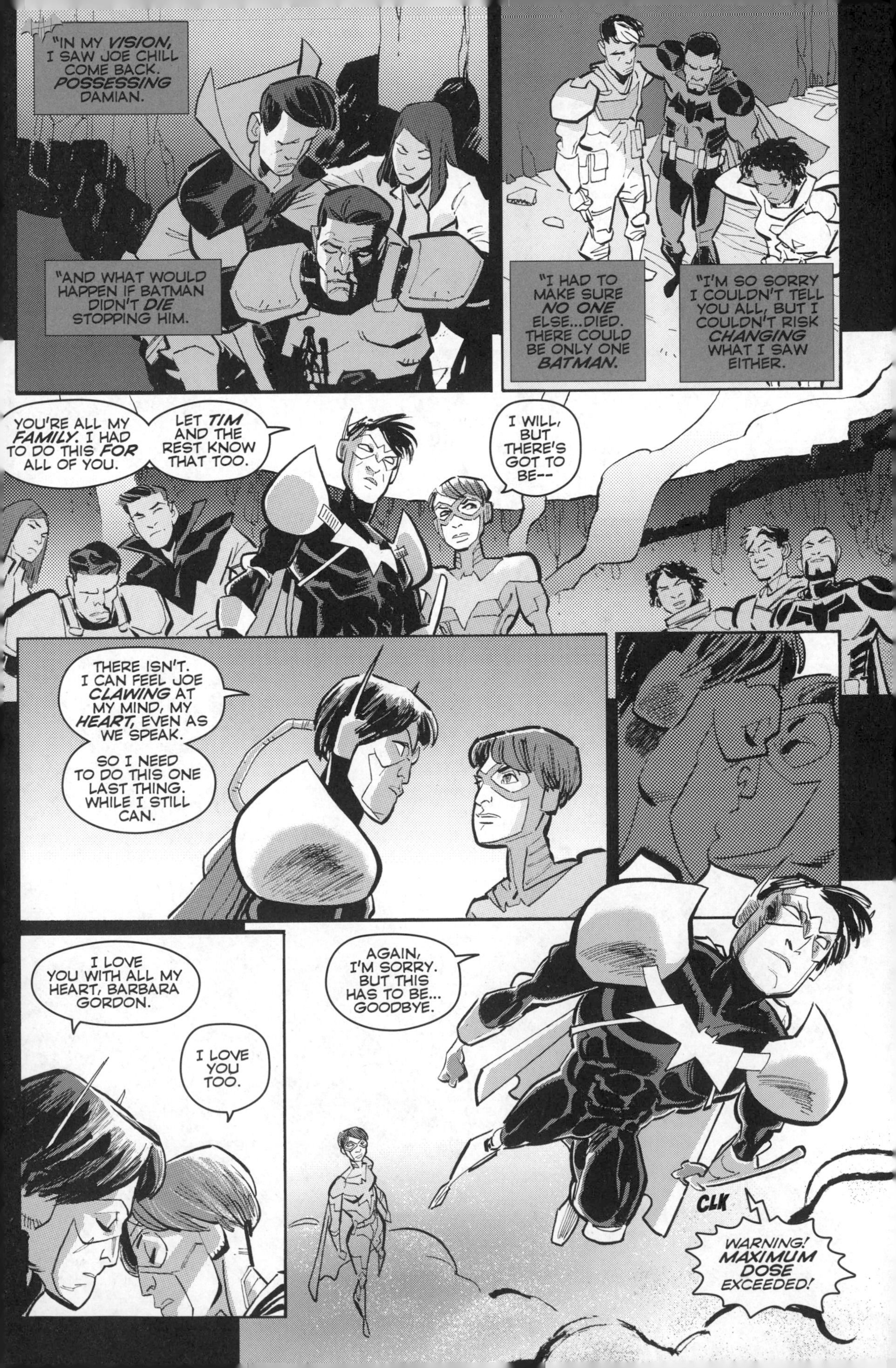
"IN MY *VISION,* I SAW JOE CHILL COME BACK. *POSSESSING* DAMIAN.
"AND WHAT WOULD HAPPEN IF BATMAN DIDN'T *DIE* STOPPING HIM.
"I HAD TO MAKE SURE *NO ONE* ELSE...DIED. THERE COULD BE ONLY ONE *BATMAN.*
"I'M SO SORRY I COULDN'T TELL YOU ALL, BUT I COULDN'T RISK *CHANGING* WHAT I SAW EITHER.
YOU'RE ALL MY *FAMILY.* I HAD TO DO THIS *FOR* ALL OF YOU.
LET *TIM* AND THE REST KNOW THAT TOO.
I WILL, BUT THERE'S GOT TO BE--
THERE ISN'T. I CAN FEEL JOE *CLAWING* AT MY MIND, MY *HEART,* EVEN AS WE SPEAK.
SO I NEED TO DO THIS ONE LAST THING. WHILE I STILL CAN.
I LOVE YOU WITH ALL MY HEART, BARBARA GORDON.
I LOVE YOU TOO.
AGAIN, I'M SORRY. BUT THIS HAS TO BE... GOODBYE.
CLK
WARNING! *MAXIMUM DOSE* EXCEEDED!

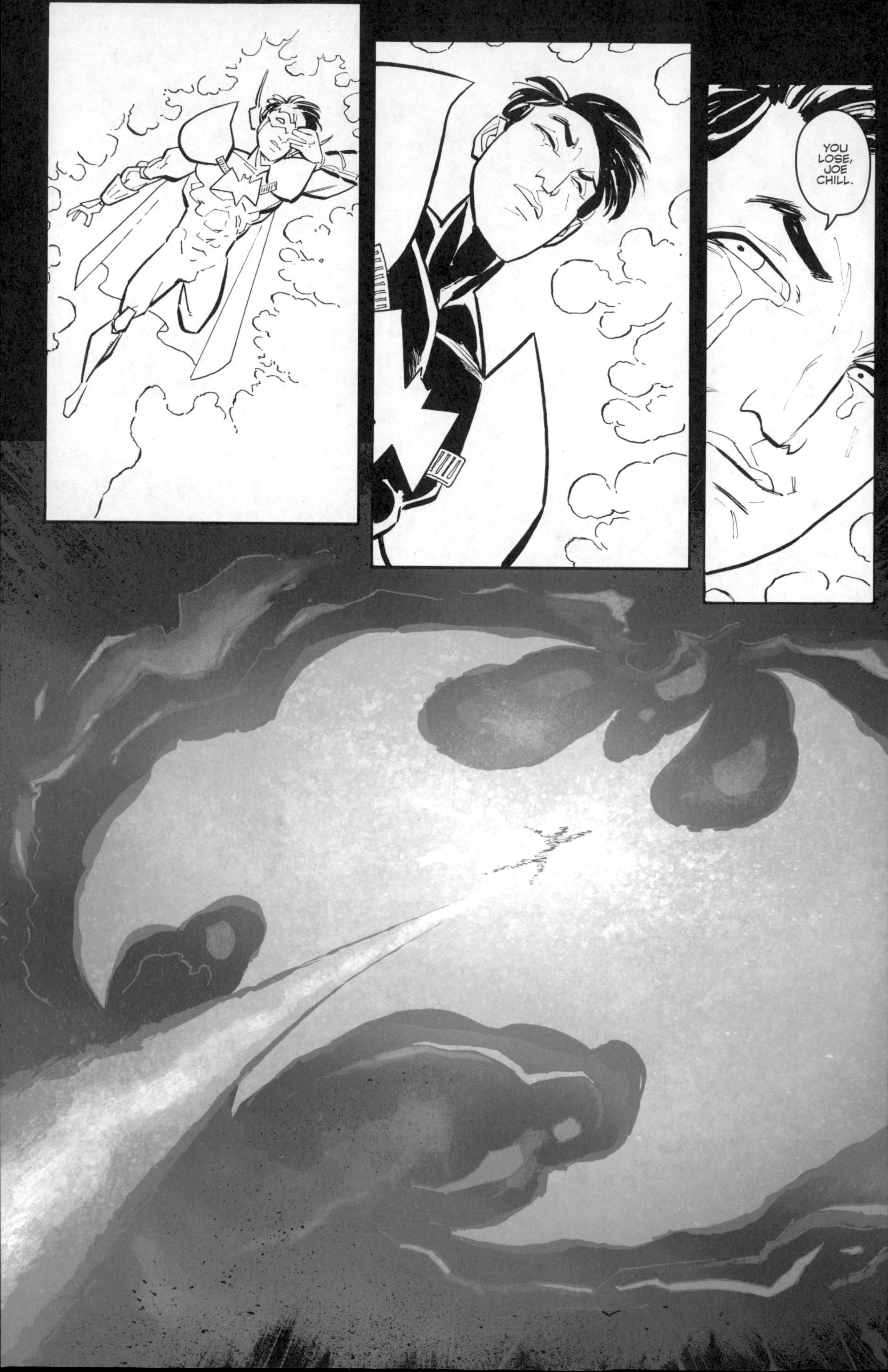
YOU LOSE, JOE CHILL.

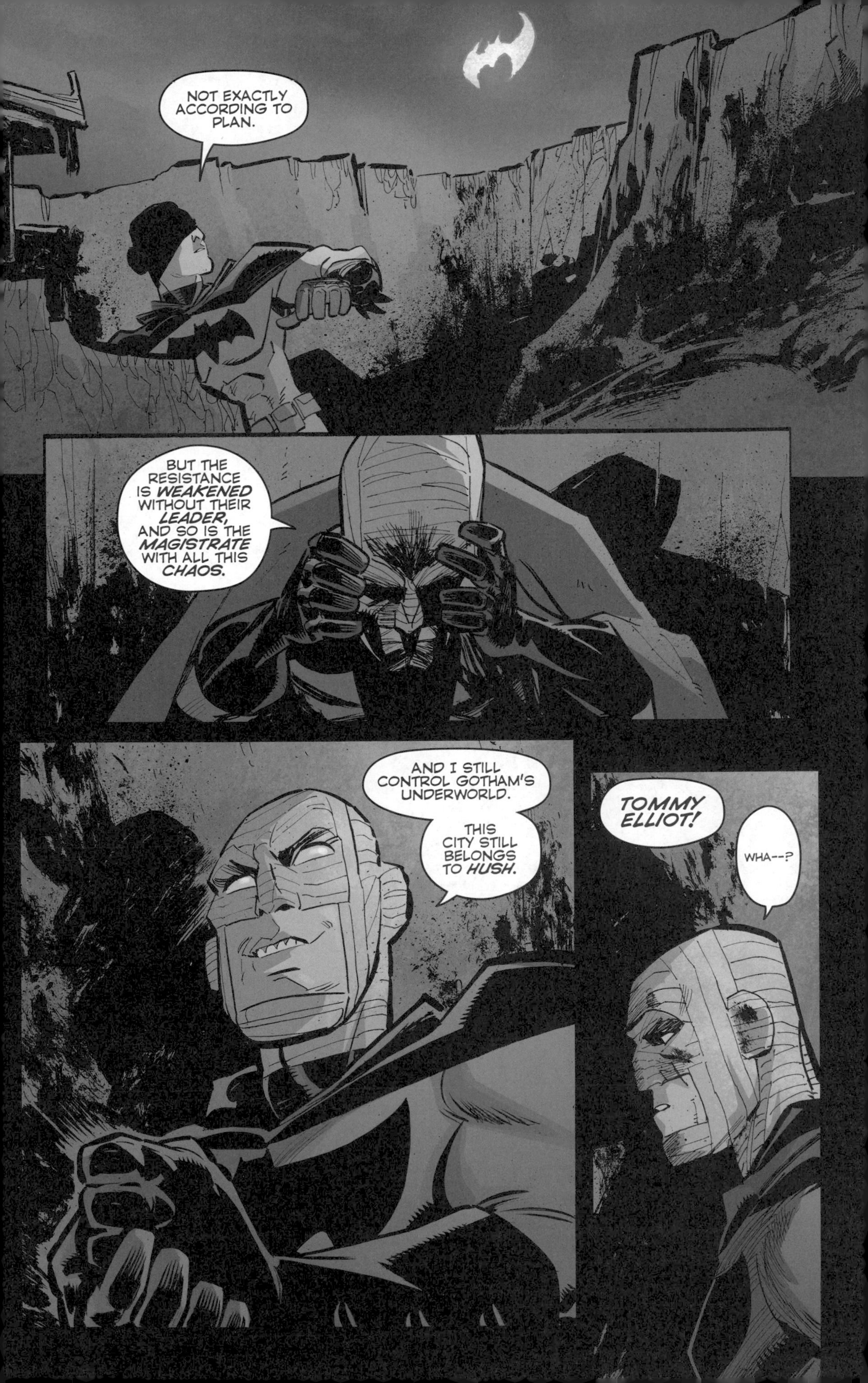
NOT EXACTLY ACCORDING TO PLAN.
BUT THE RESISTANCE IS WEAKENED WITHOUT THEIR LEADER, AND SO IS THE MAGISTRATE WITH ALL THIS CHAOS.
AND I STILL CONTROL GOTHAM'S UNDERWORLD.
THIS CITY STILL BELONGS TO HUSH.
TOMMY ELLIOT!
WHA--?

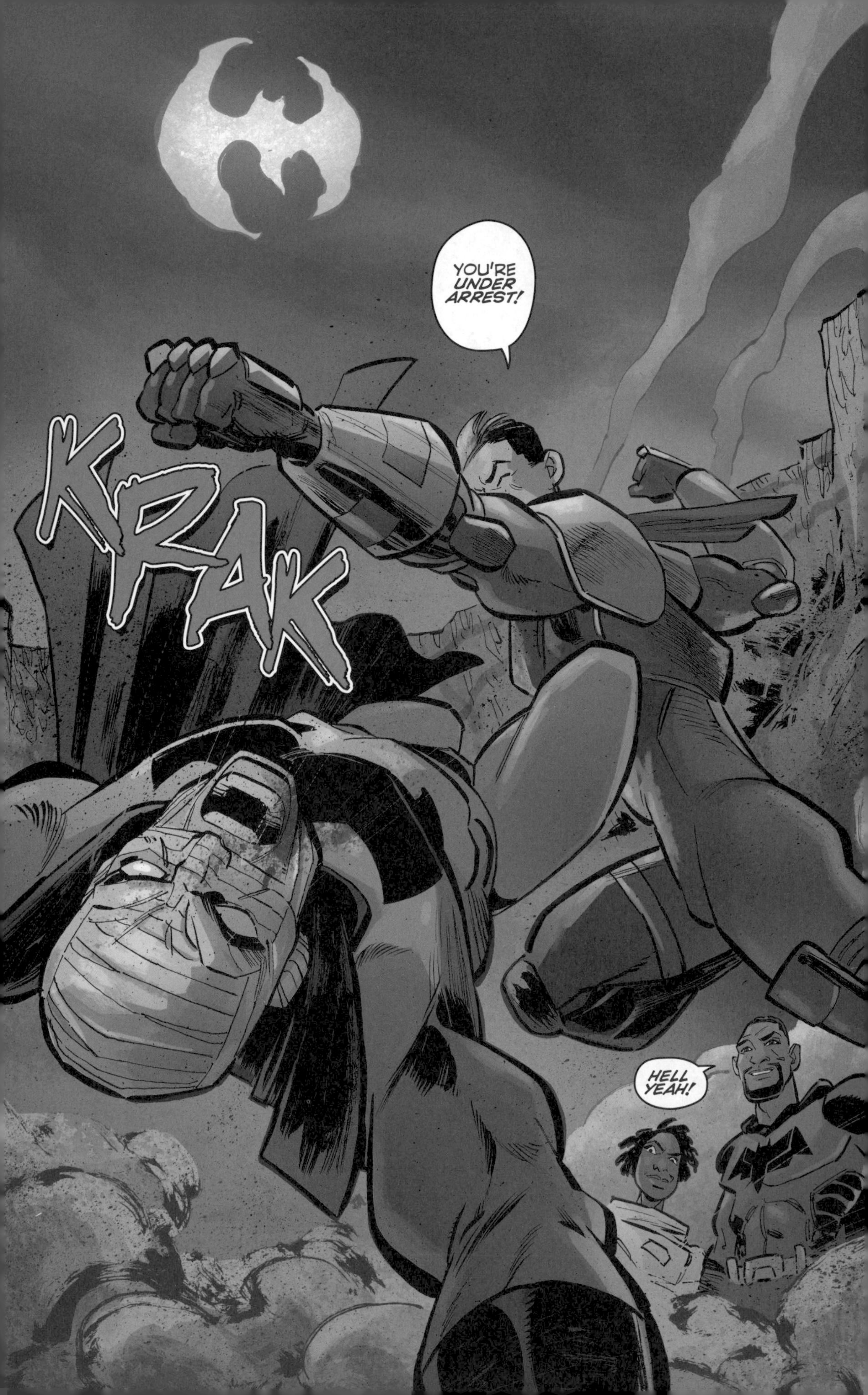
YOU'RE UNDER ARREST!
KRAK
HELL YEAH!

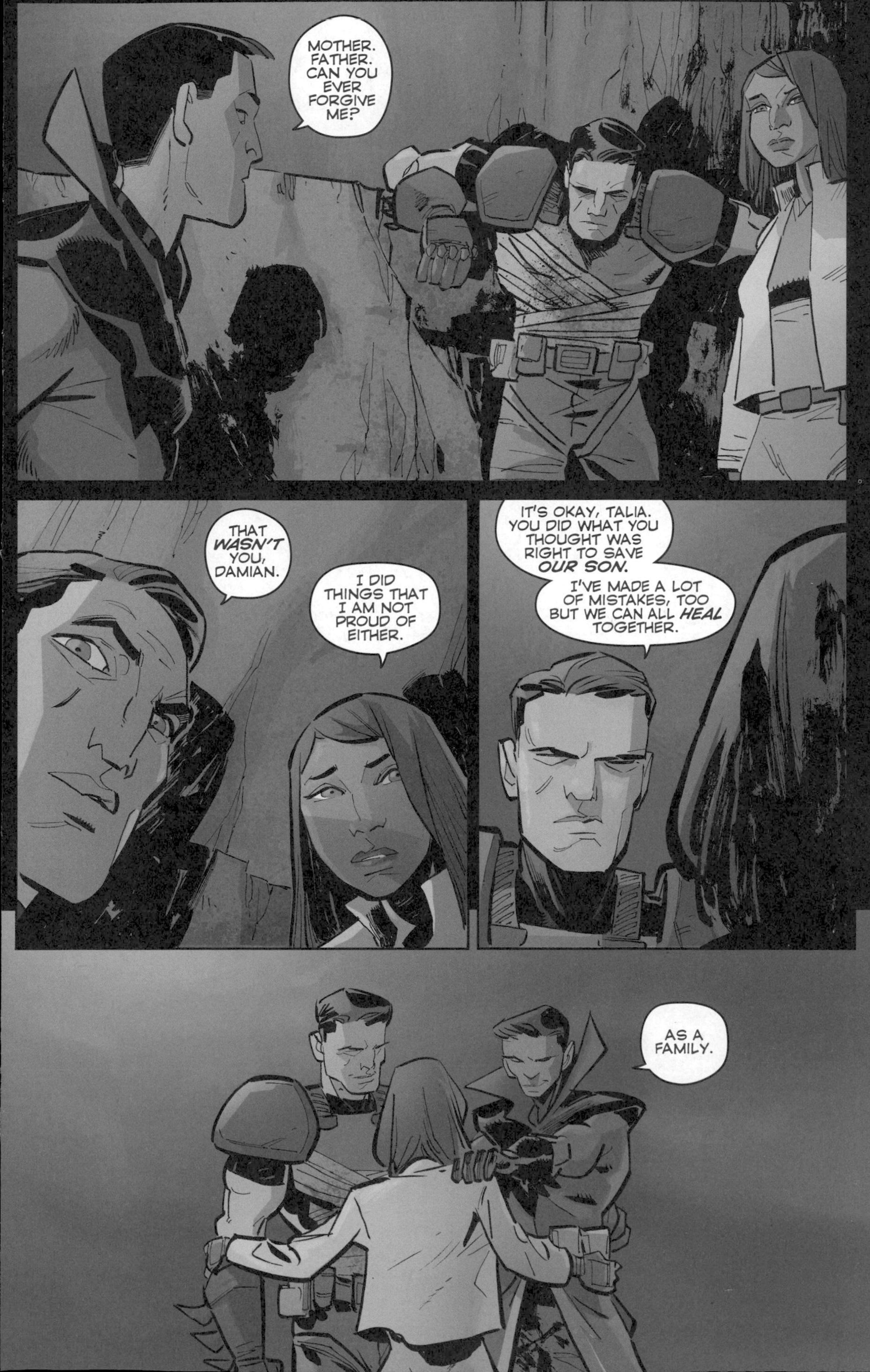
MOTHER. FATHER. CAN YOU EVER FORGIVE ME?
THAT *WASN'T* YOU, DAMIAN.
I DID THINGS THAT I AM NOT PROUD OF EITHER.
IT'S OKAY, TALIA. YOU DID WHAT YOU THOUGHT WAS RIGHT TO SAVE ***OUR SON.***
I'VE MADE A LOT OF MISTAKES, TOO BUT WE CAN ALL ***HEAL*** TOGETHER.
AS A FAMILY.

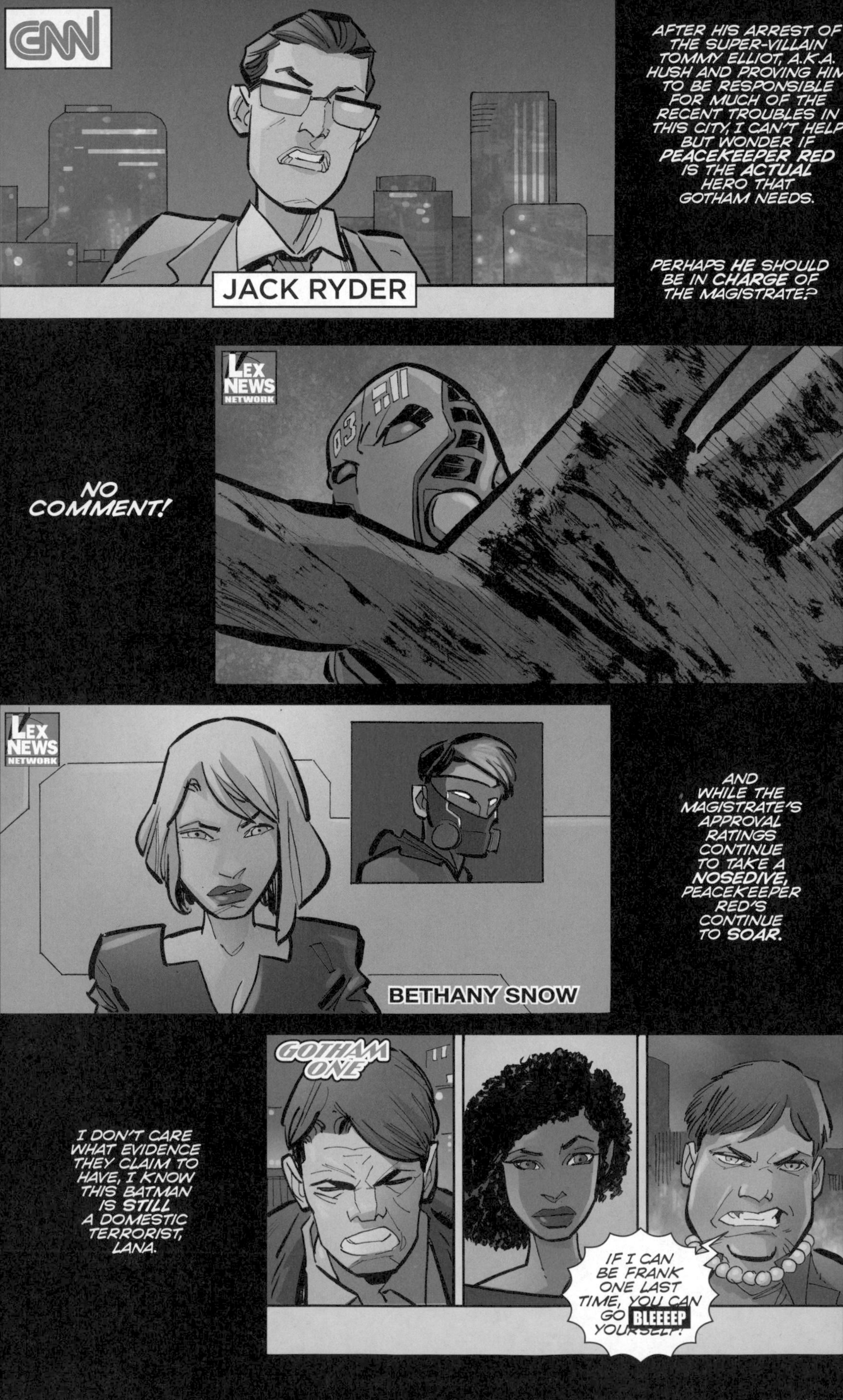
CNN
JACK RYDER
AFTER HIS ARREST OF THE SUPER-VILLAIN TOMMY ELLIOT, A.K.A. HUSH AND PROVING HIM TO BE RESPONSIBLE FOR MUCH OF THE RECENT TROUBLES IN THIS CITY, I CAN'T HELP BUT WONDER IF PEACEKEEPER RED IS THE ACTUAL HERO THAT GOTHAM NEEDS.
PERHAPS HE SHOULD BE IN CHARGE OF THE MAGISTRATE?
LEX NEWS NETWORK
NO COMMENT!
LEX NEWS NETWORK
BETHANY SNOW
AND WHILE THE MAGISTRATE'S APPROVAL RATINGS CONTINUE TO TAKE A NOSEDIVE, PEACEKEEPER RED'S CONTINUE TO SOAR.
GOTHAM ONE
I DON'T CARE WHAT EVIDENCE THEY CLAIM TO HAVE, I KNOW THIS BATMAN IS STILL A DOMESTIC TERRORIST, LANA.
IF I CAN BE FRANK ONE LAST TIME, YOU CAN GO BLEEEEP YOURSELF!

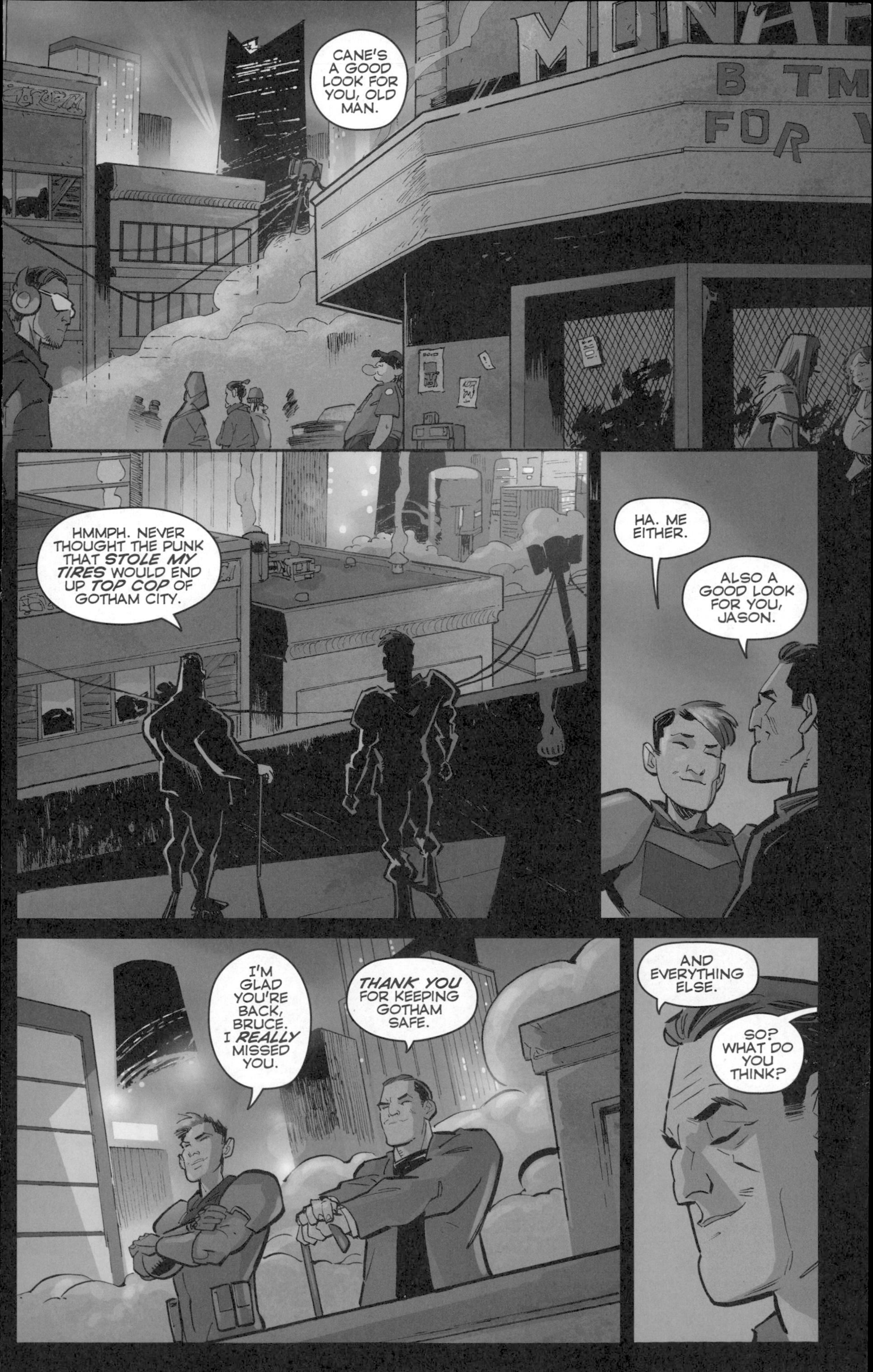
CANE'S A GOOD LOOK FOR YOU, OLD MAN.
HMMPH. NEVER THOUGHT THE PUNK THAT **STOLE MY TIRES** WOULD END UP **TOP COP** OF GOTHAM CITY.
HA. ME EITHER.
ALSO A GOOD LOOK FOR YOU, JASON.
I'M GLAD YOU'RE BACK, BRUCE. I **REALLY** MISSED YOU.
THANK YOU FOR KEEPING GOTHAM SAFE.
AND EVERYTHING ELSE.
SO? WHAT DO YOU THINK?

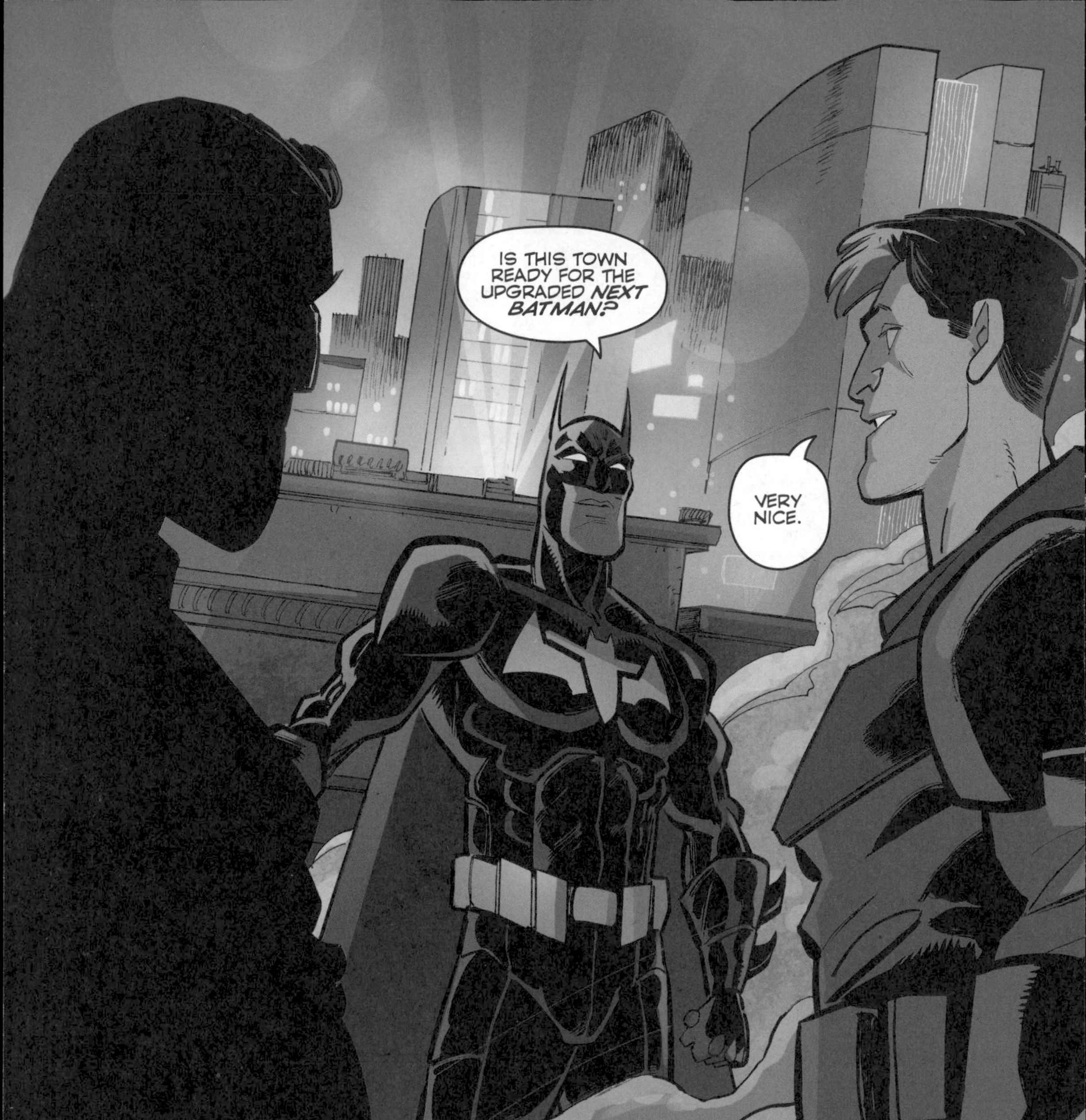
IS THIS TOWN READY FOR THE UPGRADED NEXT BATMAN?
VERY NICE.
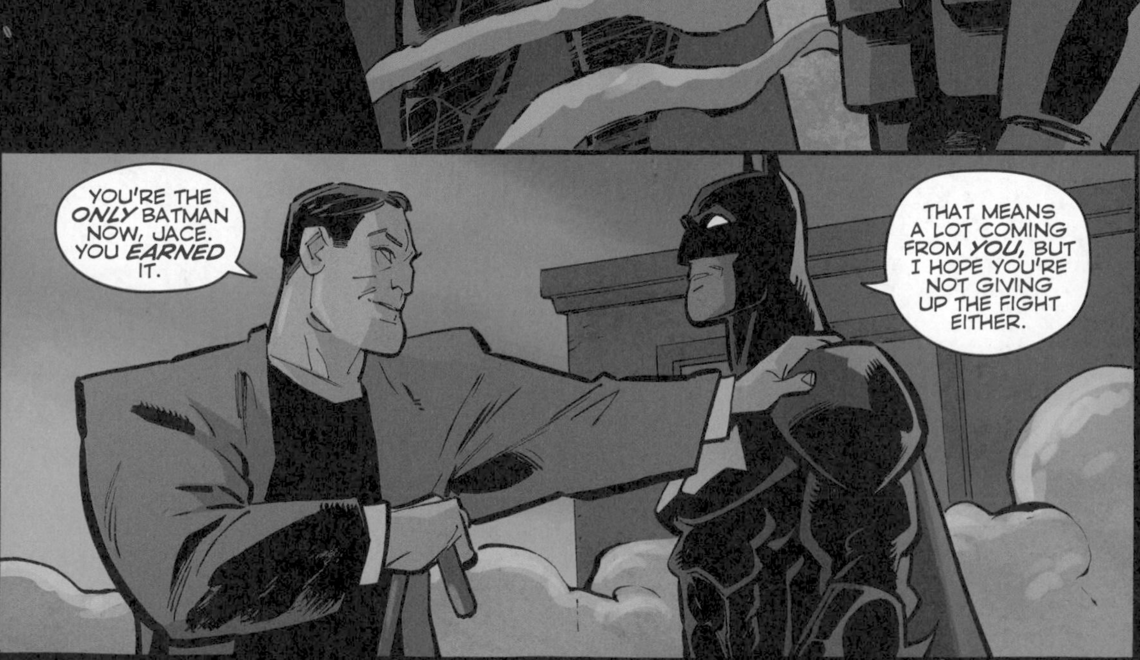
YOU'RE THE ONLY BATMAN NOW, JACE. YOU EARNED IT.
THAT MEANS A LOT COMING FROM YOU, BUT I HOPE YOU'RE NOT GIVING UP THE FIGHT EITHER.

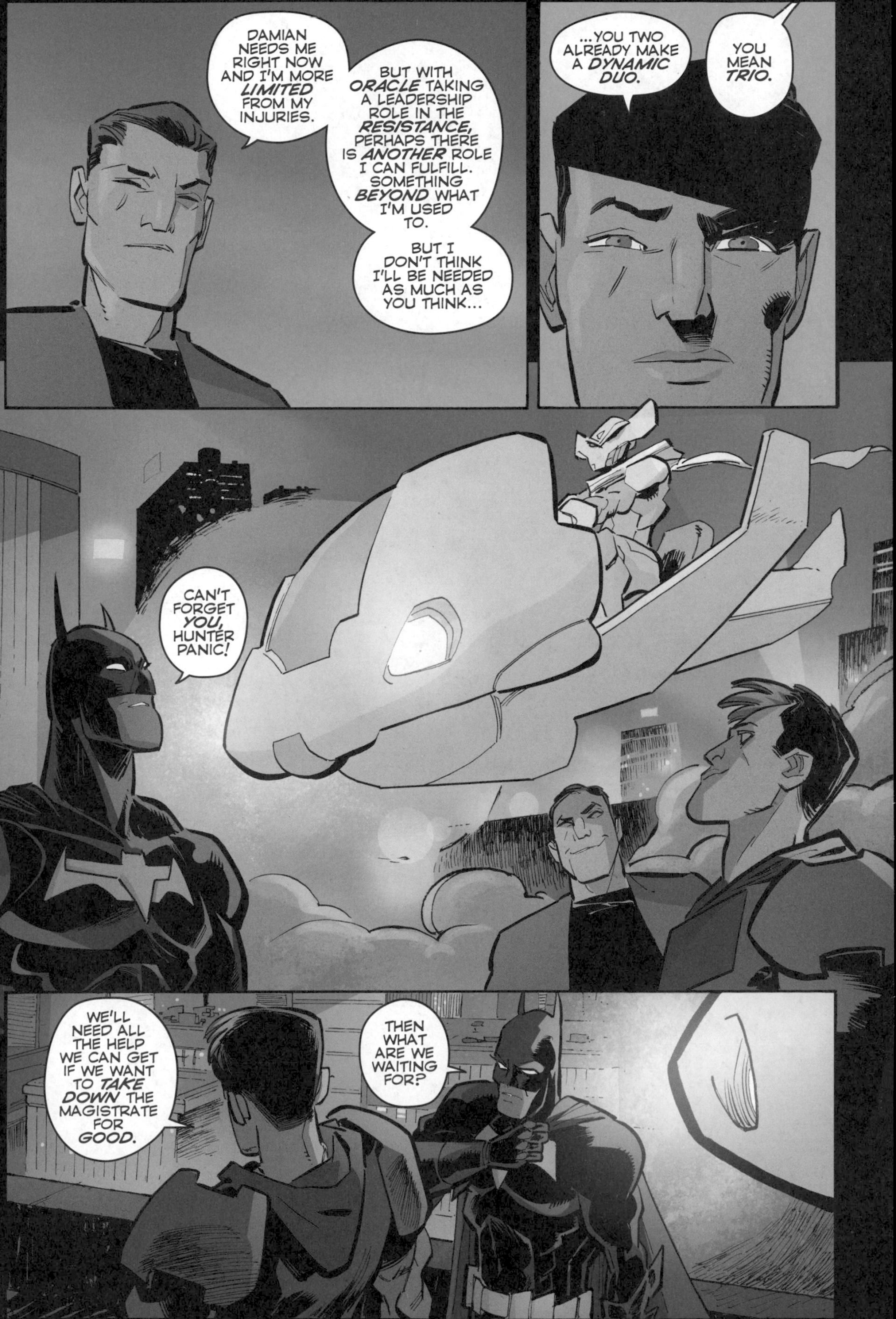
DAMIAN NEEDS ME RIGHT NOW AND I'M MORE *LIMITED* FROM MY INJURIES.
BUT WITH *ORACLE* TAKING A LEADERSHIP ROLE IN THE *RESISTANCE,* PERHAPS THERE IS *ANOTHER* ROLE I CAN FULFILL. SOMETHING *BEYOND* WHAT I'M USED TO.
BUT I DON'T THINK I'LL BE NEEDED AS MUCH AS YOU THINK...
...YOU TWO ALREADY MAKE A *DYNAMIC DUO.*
YOU MEAN *TRIO.*
CAN'T FORGET *YOU,* HUNTER PANIC!
WE'LL NEED ALL THE HELP WE CAN GET IF WE WANT TO *TAKE DOWN* THE MAGISTRATE FOR *GOOD.*
THEN WHAT ARE WE WAITING FOR?

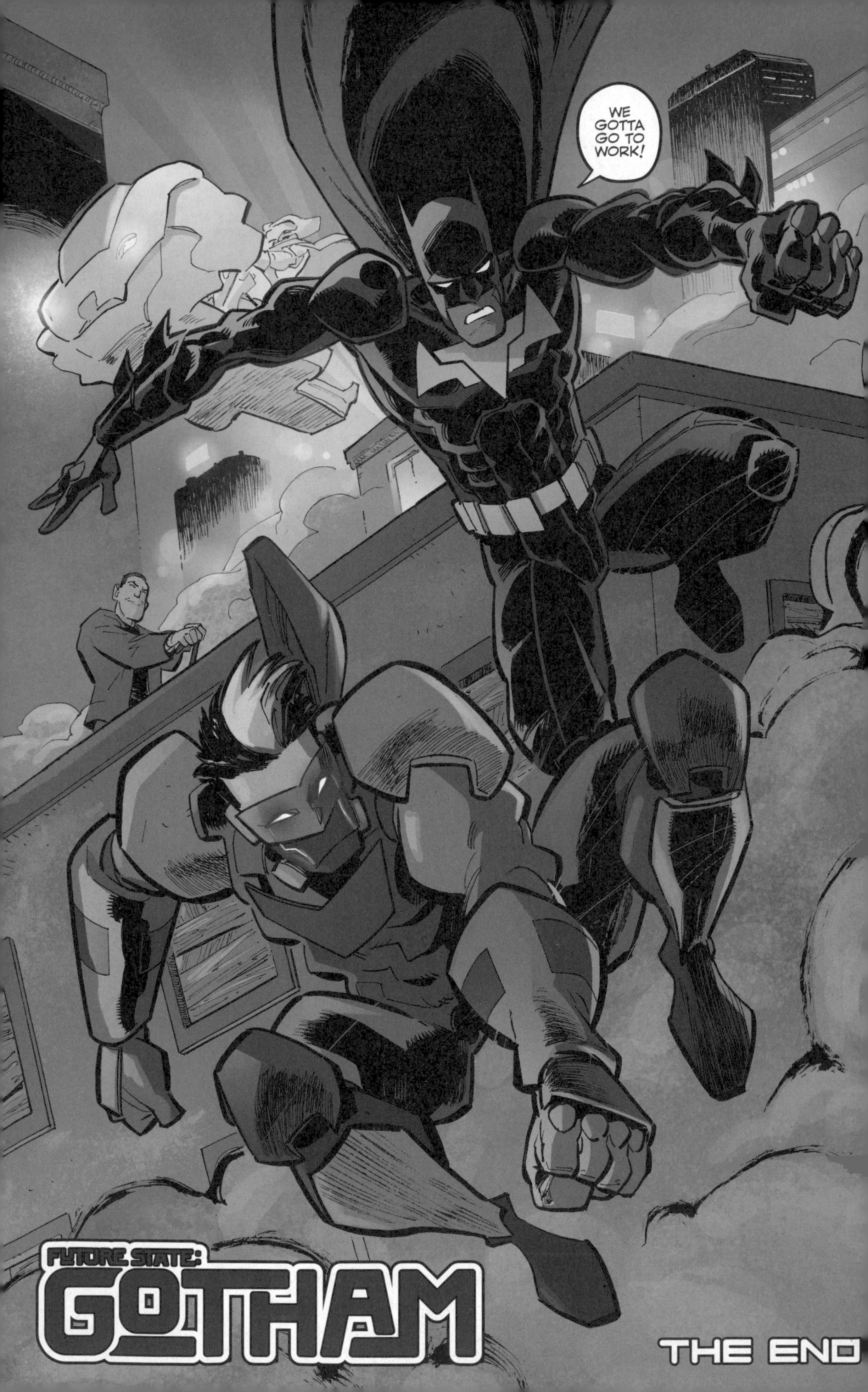
WE GOTTA GO TO WORK!
FUTURE STATE: GOTHAM
THE END

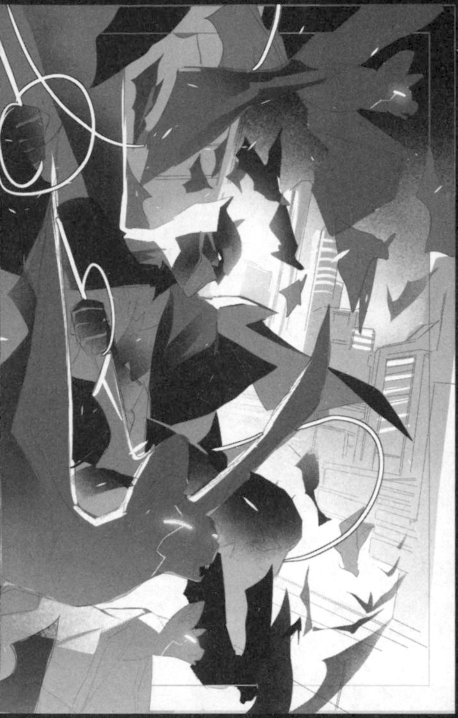

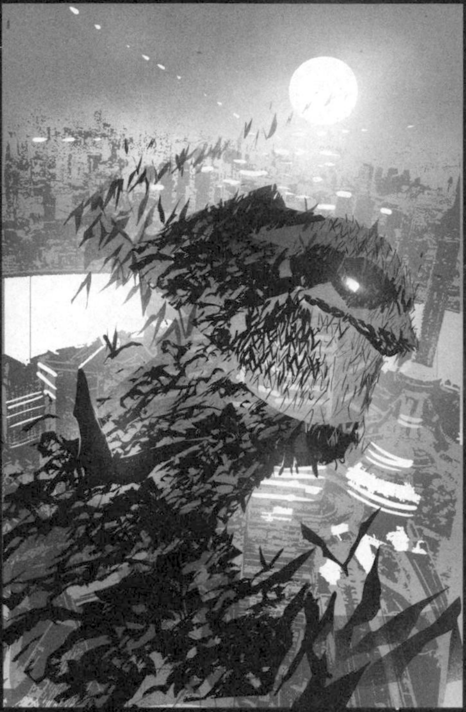

COVER SKETCHES AND INKS BY SIMONE DI MEO

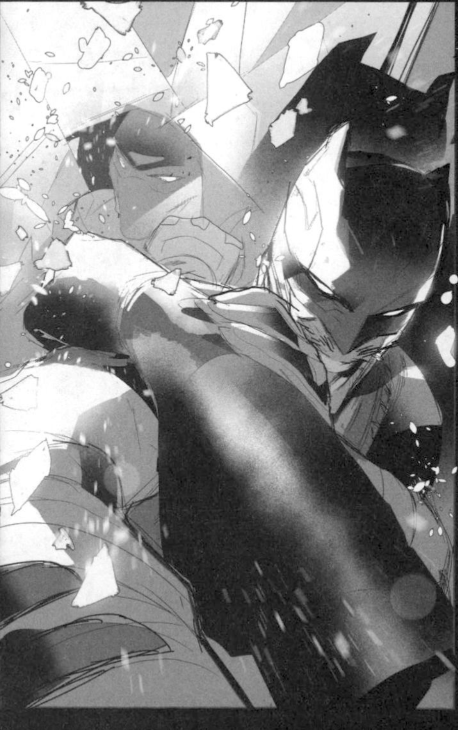

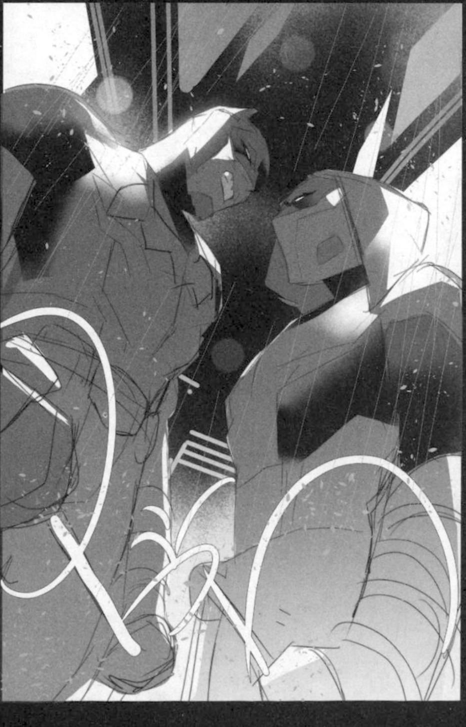